THE
CUBAN
THREAT

THE CUBAN THREAT

Carla Anne Robbins

McGRAW-HILL BOOK COMPANY
New York   St. Louis   San Francisco   Hamburg   Mexico   Toronto

1 2 3 4 5 6 7 8 9 D O C D O C 8 7 6 5 4 3

ISBN 0-07-053080-7

Library of Congress Cataloging in Publication Data

Robbins, Carla Anne.
The Cuban threat.
1. United States—Foreign relations—Cuba.
2. Cuba—Foreign relations—United States.
3. Cuba—Foreign relations—1959–   . I. Title.
E183.8.C9R618 1983   327.7291073   82–9950
ISBN 0-07-053080-7   AACR2

Book design by Nancy Dale Muldoon

FOR MY PARENTS

Contents

Foreword by Wayne S. Smith xi

1. The Cuban Threat 1
2. Revolution for Export: The Early Years 7
3. Containing the Threat: The Origins of U.S.–Cuban
   Hostilities 72
4. Uneasy Allies: Cuba and the Soviet Union 135
5. The Great Retreat: Castro's Harsh Realities 169
6. A Global Threat: Angola to Central America 207
7. Debunking the Cuban Myth: First Steps Toward a
   New American Policy 266
   Notes 312
   Index 339

Acknowledgments

Many friends and colleagues have played an important role in this book. I'd like to thank my editors Jane Freundel Levey, Alfred E. Prettyman, and Elsa Dixler for their support and enthusiastic direction. I'd like to thank my advisers at the University of California, Berkeley, David Collier, Kenneth Jowitt, and Robert M. Price for giving me solid training in political science and then supporting my decision to turn my research into a popular book.

I'd like to thank William M. LeoGrande of The American University for his advice and criticism and for tolerating my many odd-hour calls to discuss some newly discovered nugget or wrestle with some tough concept. I'd like to thank Abraham F. Lowenthal of the Woodrow Wilson International Center for Scholars for his criticism and many years of direction and for introducing me to the intricacies of Washington. I'd also like to thank Wayne Smith for his advice on the manuscript and for his own writing and commentaries on U.S. foreign policy. We are all richer for his experience and courage.

I have been blessed with wonderful friends, many of them writers, all of them critics. Warmest thanks and love to Catherine Clinton, who has been my role model both as a writer and as a woman, to George Hager for the champagne and the good humor, to Holly Hyans for her cool eye and her fierce support, to Catherine O'Neill for her elegance and acerbic wit and for always knowing what I'm thinking, and to Diane Snelling for her consistent love and support, though she rarely agrees with what I'm writing. A special thank you to David E. Pitt, who is not only a dear friend but also a great pinch-hitting editor. And George A. Krimsky deserves extra mention for giving me a much-needed push at a critical moment and for his faith in me.

Above all, I send my thanks to my parents, Selma Sinert Robbins and Joseph E. Robbins, and to my sister, Rochelle Lee Robbins, who taught me that to question is both a right and a duty of citizenship. It is to them, and to all people who defend that right around the world, that this book is dedicated.

C. A. R.
New York
December 1982

Foreword by
Wayne S. Smith

For over two decades, the Cuba policies of one American administration after another have failed. In large part, this is because our
policy makers have not dealt with the problem as it is; rather,
they have taken it out of context and blown it out of all rational
proportion. This is not to say there is no element of truth behind
the myth. There is. Export of revolution was indeed a Cuban policy
during the 1960s, and Cuba has acknowledged that it gave material
assistance to Latin American guerrilla groups during that period.
Even today, Cuba insists on a doctrine of revolutionary solidarity
and continues to provide support to a few guerrilla groups in the
area, though on a far more selective basis than previously. Recently,
too, the expression of revolutionary solidarity has taken the form
of a Cuban expeditionary force in Africa of at least 35,000 men.

No American administration should be oblivious to these foreign
policy lines on Cuba's part. They must be of concern to us, especially
as Cuba is the military ally of the Soviet Union, our principal adver-
sary on the global stage. But it is precisely because of that, because

the issue is such an important one, that we should proceed from the most accurate and dispassionate analysis possible. Our policy should be informed by a realistic appraisal of Cuban intentions and capabilities and should address substance rather than shadows. Unfortunately, this has not often been the case. Cuba is a peculiarly emotional issue in the United States; clear analysis is at a premium. From my own experience, I can say, sadly, that this is especially true within the U.S. Government.

In implementing its foreign policy intelligently in a given situation, a state normally utilizes the best available approach to advance its interests and achieve its objectives. Even in dealing with adversaries, confrontation is rarely considered the most effective approach; rather, it is a last resort to be brought to bear only after diplomacy fails. Not so with American policy toward Cuba. Having begun with confrontation, we have stuck with it year after year. With all the tremendous resources and wide options available to us, we seem not to have the wit and imagination to bring them into play. It is distressing to see a great nation so limit itself to a unidimensional approach. In the Cuban context, diplomacy rather than confrontation is seen as the last resort. The position taken by the Reagan Administration is illustrative. It has suggested that only should Cuba change its policies could a diplomatic process begin. This rather puts the cart before the horse, for in the absence of a diplomatic process, no change is likely to take place. It is the former that must produce the latter, not the other way around.

Often, having for one reason or another exaggerated the magnitude of the so-called Cuban problem, American policy makers have then fashioned a response equally out of proportion. They have been so carried away by their own rhetoric that they have addressed the skewed projections of the problem rather than its reality. Cuba's export-of-revolution policies in the 1960s, for example, did represent a challenge to U.S. policy makers, but our reaction was counterproductive. By blowing the problem out of proportion, by giving the impression that there was a Cuban under every bush, we unintentionally made Castro look larger than life, omnipresent if not omniscient. In discussing this period with me a short time ago in Havana, a

Cuban official expressed puzzlement over this very point. He noted: "During the 1960s and even up to the present, the United States has frequently discussed Cuba in such terms as to suggest it is a superpower. The tone is hostile, but you always give us credit for far more capabilities than we in fact have. You flatter us. We often wonder why?"

Jimmy Carter's handling of the Soviet brigade issue was another case in point. Though the Soviet troops in question had been in Cuba for years and posed no conceivable threat to us, the Carter Administration, for domestic political reasons, decided to portray their presence as a new and threatening development. The Soviets were testing us, the argument ran; if we did not respond energetically, they might draw dangerous conclusions. Hence we glowered ominously and said the status quo was unacceptable. This was silly, for there was not the slightest chance the Soviets and Cubans would accede to demands that the brigade be withdrawn. The Carter Administration itself, too late, realized that it had painted itself into a corner. The status quo turned out to be acceptable after all, but only after the Administration had done tremendous damage to its own credibility and prestige.

The Reagan people, unfortunately, learned nothing from Carter's mistakes. Shortly after the inauguration, UN Ambassador Jeane Kirkpatrick assured a Washington audience that we now had the reality of Soviet nuclear submarines operating out of Cuba. This was sheer poppycock. No Soviet nuclear or missile submarine had called in a Cuban port since 1974. Ambassador Kirkpatrick was simply posturing for a domestic audience. She should have considered her words more carefully, however; insouciance is out of place in making such allegations, for they imply a violation of the 1962 U.S.–Soviet understanding and carry with them nothing less than the possibility of a full-scale confrontation between the superpowers. Had Kirkpatrick's assertions been true, the Reagan Administration's duty would have been clear. But they were not true, and, fortunately, on this occasion she was simply not taken seriously. The principal harm, then, was to the Administration's, and to her own, credibility.

The Reagan Administration's position in Central America could not be so easily ignored. A realistic appraisal would have been that the conflict there was essentially internal in nature. With the old order collapsing, there is a struggle to see who fills the vacuum. Cuba of course sympathizes with the more radical elements seeking to take power. It gave limited support and advice, first to the Sandinistas in Nicaragua, then to the guerrillas in El Salvador. With the failure of the latter's offensive in January of 1981, however, both Cuba and Nicaragua cut back their support to the guerrillas and emphasized the need for a political solution in El Salvador and a wish for better relations with the United States.

The moment seemed ripe for imaginative diplomacy. Unfortunately, the Reagan Administration was not the least interested in diplomacy. Rather, it was intent on striking the most macho posture possible and in demonstrating that it knew how to stop communism in its tracks. Its objective was nothing less than forcing a complete military and political triumph in Central America: The guerrillas would be wiped out in El Salvador, the Nicaraguans and Cubans brought to their knees. And to dramatize and inflate the magnitude of the victory it was thus to win, the Administration portrayed the situation in Central America as a major East-West test of wills. This was not an internal conflict; rather, Secretary Haig assured us, it was a matter of Soviet–Cuban aggression. We were drawing a line against Soviet expansionism. Talk about blowing things out of proportion!

Again, we were dealing with shadows rather than substance. To be sure, the Cubans were giving some assistance to the guerrillas, and at least part of our effort should have been directed to that aspect of the problem. But the problem as a whole was far more complex and required subtleties of approach beyond the simplistic "good guys versus Moscow and Havana" context put forward by the Administration. For one thing, such a context virtually ruled out the possibility of appealing to and dealing with the many non-Communist components of the opposition. After all, if we were dealing with a case of Soviet–Cuban aggression, then all those in opposition to the Junta had to be considered Soviet–Cuban allies.

It also militated strongly against negotiations. As this was defined as a case of external aggression, that aggression had to end before any talks could begin. Meanwhile, according to the Administration's rosy predictions, adumbrated elections would start the country on the road to a solution, leaving the opposition in its dust.

Predictably, however, as the elections were unbalanced and did not include the opposition, they resulted in a right-wing government that, on the one hand, was even more opposed to contacts with the opposition than had been the Duarte Government and, on the other, seemed intent on taking measures, such as undermining the agrarian reform, deliberately designed to lose popular support.

Rather than the full political and military victory it had expected, the Reagan Administration has found itself involved in an open-ended situation of continuing violence and escalating tensions to which we simply have no response and no solution. Having eschewed diplomacy, but also having realized that a military option might indeed create more problems than it would solve, the Administration is left with no policy at all. Once again, as at the Bay of Pigs, as in dealing with the issue of the Soviet brigade, and, as in so many other past episodes, our tendency to take out of context and proportion any problem related to Cuba has had painful consequences. Some day, American policy makers really must begin to base themselves on accurate and objective assessments of Cuban reality rather than the exaggerations and politically expedient panderings of the past two decades.

Carla Anne Robbins's excellent book is just such a carefully balanced study. Should American policy makers ever decide to analyze the Cuban problem objectively, this should be recommended reading for them. Other observers of the Cuban scene need not wait for that day. Objective, nonpolemical, and solidly researched, this work examines various aspects of Cuba's foreign policies and relationships as they are rather than as they have been depicted by others. It deals with substance rather than shadow. One may not agree with each and every one of Ms. Robbins's conclusions, and there may be arguments over nuances of interpretation, but one cannot but be impressed by the scholarship and intellectual honesty behind this book. It is an important contribution to the field that even long-time observers will read with much profit.

W.S.S.

Wayne S. Smith was Chief of the United States Interest Section in Havana from July 1979 until he left the Foreign Service in August 1982 because of serious disagreements with the Reagan Administration. He is now a Senior Associate of the Carnegie Endowment for International Peace.

THE
CUBAN
THREAT

1

The Cuban Threat

O N the afternoon of April 28, 1965, President Lyndon B. Johnson ordered the landing of 500 United States Marines near
Santo Domingo in the Dominican Republic. Within a week nearly
23,000 troops had arrived. They would remain on the island for
the next seventeen months. It was the United States' first military
intervention in Latin America in almost forty years.[1]

Initially Washington said the intervention was necessary to prevent the loss of American lives in the Dominican Republic's increasingly bloody civil war. But as the American military presence rapidly
escalated, it became clear that the Johnson Administration had a
different and much broader agenda. The marines were really sent
to stop the Dominican Republic from being taken over by Cuban-
backed Communist forces, or what the Administration called "Castro Communists." The U.S. was not about to see the Dominican
Republic become a second Cuba.

Speaking on national television the night of May 2, 1965, President

Johnson described the extent of the Communist threat to the Dominican Republic. Although the previous week's uprising had begun as "a popular democratic revolution," it had been "seized and placed into the hands of a band of Communist conspirators. . . . many of them trained in Cuba," who were using the political disorder to install a Communist dictatorship. This, said Johnson, the United States would not allow:

> The American nations cannot, must not, and will not permit the establishment of another Communist government in the Western hemisphere. . . . This is what our beloved President John F. Kennedy meant when, less than a week before his death, he told us: "We in this hemisphere must also use every resource at our command to prevent the establishment of another Cuba in this hemisphere."[2]

In the six years since Fidel Castro had seized power just ninety miles from American shores, the fear of a "second Cuba" had come to dominate Washington's policy toward Latin America. This concern with the Cuban threat had escalated to the point of near hysteria in the days preceding the Dominican intervention as embassy and intelligence officials in Santo Domingo deluged Washington with reports of widespread Communist subversion throughout the country. Rebel leaders were said to be receiving political instructions directly by telephone from Cuba; rebel arms were said to be pouring in from several Communist countries, including Red China, delivered by a Cuban "minisubmarine," and Che Guevara—the infamous architect of Castro's guerrilla victory—was said to have infiltrated the country to direct the rebel forces.[3]

Washington's charges of a Communist takeover met with public skepticism in the United States. Demands from the press that evidence of Communist subversion be made public were repeatedly refused on security grounds. With pressure for disclosure mounting, the Administration released a list of fifty-eight Communists said to be leading the uprising. The list did not stand up well to public scrutiny. Of the fifty-eight alleged Communist leaders, five had been listed twice, and another twelve were found to be out of the country, ill, or in jail.[4]

Almost every official charge of Communist subversion failed to be verified. Despite the best efforts of the CIA and the FBI—both dispatched to the Dominican Republic with orders from Johnson to bring back proof of Communist subversion—no conclusive evidence was ever produced. With time, most observers have come to agree that, aside from twenty or thirty Cuban-trained rebels and some propaganda support broadcast from Cuba to Santo Domingo, there never was a significant Communist threat in the Dominican Republic.[5]

The Dominican intervention was a costly mistake. It did untold damage to the Alliance for Progress in Latin America, alienating many of our natural allies in the struggle for development by resurrecting fears of the "Big Stick," while convincing the Latin American oligarchy that there was really no need to change the status quo. For Latin America, the lesson of the Dominican intervention was that the United States, despite its stated commitment to equality and progress, would take the side of reaction when the chips were down. All the right wing had to do was to claim a Communist threat. In the United States the Dominican intervention became a symbol of Washington's pathologic duplicitousness. The "credibility gap" and the "Vietnam syndrome" both have their roots in the Dominican intervention.

The events of April 1965 were not an anomaly. Every President since Dwight D. Eisenhower has charged the Castro Government with international subversion and sought similar hard-line policies to contain the Cuban threat. During the 1960s, Cuban agents were believed to be fomenting revolution in almost every Latin American country, leading guerrilla operations in Argentina, plotting political assassinations in Colombia, shipping arms to Venezuela, and inciting student riots in Puerto Rico. Cuban-based guerrilla training schools were said to be graduating thousands of Latin American subversives each year who were then sent back to their homelands to lead Cuban-style revolutions. One Senate report charged the Castro regime with smuggling Red Chinese heroin into the United States to finance its guerrilla activities.[6]

Since it took office in January 1981, the Reagan Administration has issued several reports outlining in detail the alleged Cuban threat to American security.[7] The Administration has charged Havana with providing arms, training, and vital political direction to the revolutionaries in Nicaragua and El Salvador. The Castro Government is also said to be giving guerrilla training and asylum to insurgents and terrorists from countries throughout Central and South America, such as Colombia's M-19 guerrillas, Uruguay's Tupamaros, Argentina's Montoneros, and Chile's MIR. A recent State Department report has even charged the Cubans with establishing a drug smuggling ring—this time from Colombia—to help finance guerrilla activities throughout the hemisphere.[8]

The familiar ring of these charges may be more of a testament to Washington's consistently dogmatic perception of Cuba than to an actual consistent or long-lived Cuban threat. In fact, most of the allegations raised against Cuba during the 1960s proved to be either spurious or vastly exaggerated. While the Castro Government was ideologically committed to the export of revolution, it never had the military means or the support of its allies necessary to mount a major campaign. Despite Washington's alarums, there were never more than a few hundred Cuban guerrillas fighting in Latin America during the 1960s. As for the reports of arming and training revolutionaries, by the early 1970s American intelligence analysts had come to admit that these too were exaggerated. Between 1961 and 1969 no more than 1,500 Latin American guerrillas were trained in Cuba, a far cry from the original estimates of 1,500 to 2,500 a year.[9]

The Reagan Administration's recent charges have been received with a great deal of skepticism from both the public and the media. The Administration's White Paper on El Salvador has been roundly debunked for both misrepresenting and exaggerating the facts of the Cuban involvement there, and for its overall conclusion that the current instability is the result of Cuban-sponsored insurgency rather than genuine popular resistance to El Salvador's military-dominated regime.[10]

More recently, the Administration was twice embarrassed after two alleged Nicaraguan guerrillas captured in El Salvador failed to confirm the link between Havana, the Sandinista Government, and the Salvadoran opposition. One of the guerrillas turned out to be a Nicaraguan student passing through El Salvador on his way home for vacation from classes in Mexico.[11] The other, when brought to Washington for a much publicized press briefing, admitted to being a guerrilla, but insisted that he was acting completely on his own and that he had only claimed to have been trained in Cuba and Ethiopia to avoid further torture.[12]

This blindness appears all the more tragic when our perception of Cuba is compared with Washington's other foreign policies. Over the past decade—and particularly since the Vietnam debacle—the United States has been developing a more open-minded perception of both the Communist bloc and the Third World. Today, we are negotiating arms limitations with the Russians and have made peace with the once-hated Chinese. Washington has shown itself capable of tolerating a degree of diversity in the Third World, and even in Latin America. The Reagan Administration claims it is keeping lines of communication open with Nicaragua and is quietly exploring areas of negotiation with the Angolan regime. Yet its perception of Cuba is as rigid and dogmatic as ever.

It is time for us to take a more critical look at both Cuba and our perceptions and misperceptions of the Cuban threat. Specifically, we must ask: What are the Cubans *really* doing in Nicaragua, El Salvador, Angola, Ethiopia, and elsewhere? Why are they doing it? What effect do Cuban policies have on American interests?

While these questions are simple, the answers are not. First, information is scarce. Cuba is a closed society without a free press or public access to the policy-making process. At the same time, misinformation—stemming both from conscious distortion and unconscious dogmatism—abounds in the United States.

The costs of such misrepresentations and errors are high. Washington's persistent and vocal charges of Cuban subversion have been met with skepticism and considerable derision by even our traditional allies in Latin America and Western Europe. The Reagan Administration's threats of unilateral action against Cuba or Nicaragua—"going to the source" of regional subversion—as well as its commitment to a military solution in El Salvador have resurrected fears of a return to "Big Stick" policies. At the same time, the Administration's obsession with Cuban subversion has blinded it to the genuine need for social change in Central America. Once again, the United States is allying itself with reaction rather than progress in the hemisphere.

The record of the last twenty years is clear: Not only are these policies costly, but they also do not work. After two decades of containing the Cuban threat, the Castro Government is still in power and today has an international reach greater than many European governments. Currently, there are more than 35,000 Cuban combat troops and another 10,000 Cuban civilian advisers stationed overseas.[13] Cuba now has working relations with most of our allies, and in 1976 was elected chairman of the Movement of Nonaligned Nations. Clearly, all is not idyllic for Cuba's diplomatic relations, but only the most repressive regimes—such as Pinochet's Chile— still subscribe to Washington's perception of the Cuban threat.

It also is difficult for Americans to understand Cuban policies. We are bound by prejudices born of more than two decades of isolation and hostility. To understand the Cuban threat, we must readjust some of our basic beliefs about international politics and American interests. We must discard certain traditional assumptions, including the notion that Cuba is inevitably a pawn of the Soviet Union, and that American security requires the complete agreement of our hemispheric neighbors. And we must consider the historical record from a Cuban perspective, looking back over twenty-two years of unremitting American hostility.

This book assembles the best information available to illuminate Cuban policies, their roots, and their effects. It also examines many of the assumptions and myths that have guided—and misguided— American policy toward Cuba. These twin aims will meet to answer two basic questions that have plagued American policy makers for the last two decades: How real is the Cuban threat? And how must the United States respond?

2
Revolution for Export: The Early Years

IN late November 1956, Fidel Castro and eighty-one armed compatriots set sail from Tuxpan, Mexico, in a small yacht, the *Granma*.[1] Their destination: Cuba. Their goal: the overthrow of the dictator Fulgencio Batista. Due to poor navigation, bad weather, and dangerous overcrowding on the *Granma*, the crossing took longer than planned. Castro's band arrived in Cuba two days after an uprising that was supposed to have coincided with the landing.

To make matters worse, the *Granma* did not land in the planned safe harbor at Niquero, where it was to be met by members of the Cuban revolutionary underground. Instead, the yacht was beached at the swampy Playa de los Colorados. It took the guerrillas three hours just to get to solid ground. Much of their ammunition had to be left behind. As they scrambled onto the beach, the men were spotted and strafed by a Cuban fighter plane.

For two days Castro's group pressed inland toward the Sierra Maestra, where they planned to set up a guerrilla base. On the third day they could walk no further. Their boots were new, and they had had little to eat since arriving in Cuba. As they rested in a cane field, around four o'clock in the afternoon of December 5, the rebels were surprised by a unit of Batista's army. Their whereabouts had been revealed by a peasant guide.

Twenty-four of Castro's band were killed almost immediately. Others were captured, some to be tried later and shot. Most of those who escaped into the hills chose to abandon. the mission. Of the eighty-two men who left Mexico on the *Granma,* only twelve—*los doce* as they were later known—finally reassembled in the Sierra Maestra. It was from this base of twelve men that Castro built the rebel army that two years later triumphantly took Havana.

What is memorable about the *Granma* invaders is the miracle of their survival, rather than the near-disaster of the landing. Indeed, the entire story of the Cuban revolution is one of survival against terrible odds. Not only did Castro build a Rebel Army of 1,500 from a base of twelve men; he then took that army of 1,500 and defeated Batista's army of 50,000.

That incredible victory convinced Castro and his followers of both their right to rule Cuba and the invincibility of their strategy. In January 1959, Che Guevara wrote:

> The example of our revolution for Latin America and the lessons it implies have destroyed all cafe theories: we have shown that a small group of resolute men supported by the people and not afraid to die if necessary can take on a disciplined army and defeat it. This is a basic lesson.[2]

Their strategy and its applicability to revolutions throughout Latin America and the Third World became an article of faith in the new Cuban ideology and a basic premise for Cuban foreign policy during the 1960s. Cuba's commitment to the export of revolution also became a primary concern in American security policy in the hemisphere, and a major issue of contention in the increasingly important Cuban–Soviet alliance. By 1967 Castro had publicly seceded from the international Communist movement and established his own International so as to maintain his commitment to the export of revolution.

LIBERATION: THE FIRST ATTEMPTS

On July, 26, 1960, in a speech commemorating the opening battle of the Cuban revolution, Fidel Castro declared the Cuban commitment to liberating all of Latin America. Turning toward the Sierra Maestra, the mountains where his own revolution had been fought and won, Castro declared:

> Here facing the unconquered mountain range, facing the Sierra Maestra, let us promise one another that we shall continue to make our fatherland an example that will make the Andes mountain range into the Sierra Maestra of all America.[3]

Two months later, Castro reaffirmed that commitment in the "Declaration of Havana":

> It is the duty of oppressed and exploited nations to fight for their liberation. . . . It is the duty of each nation to make common cause with all the oppressed, colonized, [and] exploited peoples. . . .[4]

Much has been made of the Castro regime's early attempts to export revolution to the Caribbean. The threat of Cuban-backed revolutions was the justification for Washington's efforts to overthrow the Castro regime and spend millions of dollars arming the rest of the hemisphere. In fact, however, there were only three offensives launched from Cuba in 1959. Each was small and poorly armed, and all failed. Moreover, the degree of official Cuban support for these attacks has never been clearly established. Of the forays launched against Panama, Haiti, and the Dominican Republic in 1959, Cuba claimed credit only for the Dominican invasion. Although the other offensives did take place, it is unclear whether they were organized by the Government or by revolutionary exiles living in Cuba. Nonetheless, the little evidence there is shows that in its early years the Cubans provided Caribbean revolutionaries with asylum, some military training, and a very limited number of arms.

A Bad Start: Panama

The first exile attack was launched in late April 1959, four months after Castro took power, when an estimated eighty-four Cubans and Panamanians set sail from Cuba to liberate Panama. Within hours of landing, the invasion was crushed. Although most observers agreed that the Castro government was behind the attack,[5] Havana denied the charge. Clearly, the Panama expedition put the new Castro regime in a difficult position. Since the government of Panama was not a dictatorship, the attack had no ideological justification. And to make matters worse, at the time of the attack, Castro was visiting Washington trying to allay American fears and woo foreign aid.

Both Castro and Guevara subsequently condemned the entire affair as the work of "a group of adventurers headed by a cafe *barbudo* who had never been in the Sierra Maestra . . . [who] managed to fire the enthusiasm of a group of boys to carry out the adventure." Guevara even claimed that the Cuban leadership had "worked with the Panamanian Government to destroy it."[6] It is true that on landing in Panama the invaders surrendered to an Organization of American States investigating team after, they claimed, having received an appeal from Havana to call off the expedition. In any case, the Panamanian Government never charged the Castro regime with responsibility for the invasion.[7]

Nicaragua

A month later an attack was launched against the despotic regime of Luís Somoza in Nicaragua, a traditional favorite of Caribbean revolutionaries and a sworn enemy of Castro. On the first of June, two planes of revolutionaries left Costa Rica for Nicaragua. A day later Somoza protested to the OAS that yachts filled with armed revolutionaries were preparing to land. The implication was that the yachts had sailed from Cuba, but no evidence was offered. Once again, Havana denied all involvement in the attack. In fact, the June 1st invasion was carried out not by Cubans, but by a group of Nicaraguan exiles living in Costa Rica. A competing group of Cuban-based exiles had also been preparing an invasion of Nicaragua, but when the Costa Rican expedition failed they abandoned their plans.[8]

10

The Dominican Republic

Less than two weeks later, an attack designed to overthrow the dictator Rafael Trujillo of the Dominican Republic was launched from Cuba. Castro's hostility to Trujillo dates back to his college days, when he joined an abortive expedition of several hundred Latin American revolutionaries trying to overthrow the Dominican despot.[9] Since Castro's victory in Cuba, Trujillo had given asylum to Fulgencio Batista and a large number of Cuban exiles.

On June 14, some 200 Dominican exiles and ten Cubans commanded by a Rebel Army officer left Cuba in a plane and two launches for the northern coast of the Dominican Republic. The plan was similar to the landing of the *Granma*. The guerrillas were to establish a *foco*—a small, armed, mobile guerrilla band—in the mountains while revolutionaries in the cities would rally mass demonstrations and strikes. Like the abortive landing of the *Granma,* the invasion was a total failure. Within hours of their arrival, the guerrillas were either taken prisoner or tracked down and shot by Trujillo's army. The planned urban uprisings never materialized— thirty years of Trujillo's dictatorship had left the people too terrorized to rebel. Unlike the landing of the *Granma,* there were no survivors to establish a *foco* in the mountains. Trujillo was more thorough than Batista.[10]

The Castro Government's involvement in this expedition is undeniable. On June 16, two days after the attack was launched, Castro appealed publicly for support for the Dominican invaders. But when the Trujillo Government protested to the OAS, Castro felt compelled to recant his role in the Dominican invasion. "Our strategy," he said, "is to repel aggression, not to attack, but to defend ourselves and our own territory."[11]

Haiti

In mid-August 1959, an expeditionary force moved against the dictatorship of François "Papa Doc" Duvalier in Haiti. According to the Duvalier regime, the invading force of some thirty revolutionaries was composed entirely of Cubans, was led by an Algerian who had served with Castro in the Sierra Maestra, and was financed by a former Haitian senator and avowed enemy of Duvalier, Louis Déjoie. Che Guevara was said to have organized the whole affair. Like its predecessors, the expedition was a complete failure, and Havana never responded to the Duvalier regime's charges of complicity.[12]

It is clear that Castro was ambivalent about exporting revolution from Cuba. From the start of his regime, Castro was torn by the conflicting demands of his roles as revolutionary and statesman. As revolutionary, he was committed to the overthrow of dictators. Speaking in Caracas in January 1959, he had vilified the dictators of the Dominican Republic, Nicaragua, and Paraguay—two of the three regimes that claimed to have been attacked by the Cubans that year. He was also committed to aiding revolutionary exiles, as he had been aided during his years of Mexican exile. And as revolutionary nationalist, he was committed to promoting the model of the Cuban revolution throughout Latin America and the Third World.

It must also be noted that plotting the overthrow of dictators is a well-respected tradition among Latin America's democratic left. During the late 1940s, a group of social democratic exiles known as the Caribbean Legion launched military attacks on dictatorships in the Dominican Republic (several times), Costa Rica, and Nicaragua, though only the 1948 attack on Costa Rica was successful. During its brief lifetime the Caribbean Legion boasted the participation of such Latin American luminaries as Romulo Betancourt of Venezuela, José Figueres of Costa Rica, Juan Arévalo and Jacobo Arbenz of Guatemala, Juan Bosch of the Dominican Republic, and Fidel Castro—all of whom later became presidents of their countries. None, except Castro, was ever a Communist.[13]

Selflessness, tradition, pride, self-interest—all led Castro in the early years to lend support to other Caribbean revolutionaries.

THE DIPLOMATIC IMPERATIVE

By 1959 Castro had become more than a *barbudo,* or bearded guerrilla leader. He was also a head of state, facing numerous pragmatic concerns about his country's survival. Geopolitics and economics both dictated that Cuba forge conventional diplomatic relations with its Latin American neighbors. Moreover, in the early years, Castro had faith in the possibility of social democratic change in Latin America.

In January 1959, three weeks after taking power, Castro flew to Caracas to meet with Venezuela's President, Romulo Betancourt. In a private meeting Castro proposed to Betancourt that their two nations form a progressive bloc within the OAS, committed to social change and united against dictatorship and imperialism in the hemisphere. Castro pointed out that Cuba and Venezuela had much in common. Both had been recently liberated from repressive dictators. Both were facing major social and development problems. Both had strong reasons to resent U.S. meddling and paternalism. Finally, Castro and Betancourt were old comrades in arms from the days of the Caribbean Legion.

According to Betancourt, Castro's specific policy suggestions, though antiimperialist in tone, were in substance liberal and very much in keeping with the New Frontier politics then taking hold in the United States. Among his proposals was a Latin American common market. As for the United States, Castro said that the time had finally come for Washington to begin adapting to the realities of Latin American politics and addressing the needs of Latin American development. The United States, he said, "will not always be defending the interests of monopolies" in the hemisphere.[14]

Castro then broached what must have been one of the major reasons for the visit. He told Betancourt he was "thinking of having a game with the gringos." Would the Venezuelans back Cuba with a loan of $30 million and oil? Betancourt's response to these overtures was cordial but firmly negative. As much as he respected Castro and the Cuban people, Venezuela was going to take a different route.[15]

In April 1959, Castro visited the United States as a guest of the American Society of Newspaper Editors. The trip was a public relations triumph. He was met everywhere by cheering crowds that seemed captivated by the image of a romantic revolutionary hero still clad in the green fatigues and unkempt beard of his days in the Sierra Maestra. In New York thirty thousand people turned out to hear the Cuban leader speak at a rally in Central Park. Castro also addressed students at Harvard, Princeton, and Columbia and met with Henry R. Luce of *Time,* Arthur Ochs Sulzberger, publisher of the *New York Times,* Frank Bartholomew, then head of UPI, and the Foreign Affairs Committee of the Senate. He met twice with top Eisenhower Administration officials: Acting Secretary of State Christian A. Herter and Vice President Richard M. Nixon, though these meetings were distinctly cool. It is clear, however, that both sides were cautiously willing to form some type of relationship, of which this visit was the first step.[16]

Why Castro visited the United States was not as clear as the reason for his Venezuelan trip two months earlier. At a press conference in Washington, Castro was asked whether he had come to ask for U.S. aid. "We didn't come here to get money," he replied. "Many have come here to sell their souls. We want only sympathy and understanding."[17] Castro's pride and his revolutionary credentials would not allow him to say anything else. Yet despite the disclaimers, it appears that the Cubans *did* intend to ask for American aid—but in private, after Castro had returned to Cuba.[18]

Later, in the recriminations about who "lost Cuba," many American liberals (including then-Senator John F. Kennedy) suggested that had Castro asked for help during his visit, or had the United States offered it, Castro might never have gone over to the socialist bloc. But all this is speculation. What is clear is that the Cubans were interested enough to make overtures to the United States, but cautious enough to plan for rejection. Castro's request for Venezuelan back-up aid revealed as much.

From the United States, Castro went to Canada, where he was greeted with the same warmth. After Canada, instead of returning to Cuba as he had originally planned, Castro and his entourage flew south for his first Latin American goodwill tour, which included stops in Buenos Aires, Rio de Janeiro, and Montevideo.[19] In Buenos Aires, Castro startled a meeting of OAS ministers by proposing that the United States underwrite the Latin American economies with a grant of $30 billion in public aid over the next ten years. Castro assured his audience that his proposal was sincere and plausible. With the Marshall Plan, Washington had already underwritten Europe's economic recovery on a comparably grand scale. A similar plan for Latin America would provide rich markets for U.S. goods, and so have long-term benefits for the United States.[20] Although Castro's proposal was rejected by Washington as too expensive and too ambitious, less than two years later the Kennedy Administration offered a similar scheme to the OAS ministers under the rubric of the Alliance for Progress.

Once again, it is not clear whether Castro seriously expected the United States to accept his proposal or was just twisting the lion's tail. According to Javier Pazos, whose father, Felipe Pazos, was director of the Cuban National Bank at the time:

> Castro was very enthusiastic about his private Alliance for Progress scheme. . . . My impression was that he was contemplating the possibility of staying on the American side of the fence as the sponsor of this and as the leader of a Nasser-type revolution.[21]

Over the next two years Havana continued to make overtures to bourgeois regimes in Latin America. Che Guevara attended the 1961 Punta del Este meetings of the OAS at which the Alliance for Progress was established, and met with presidents Arturo Frondízi of Argentina and Jânio Quadros of Brazil.[22] The Cubans invited several moderate, but left-of-center, Latin American leaders to Havana to view the progress of their revolution. The trip was made by Salvador Allende of Chile, Lázaro Cárdenas of Mexico, Jacobo Arbenz of Guatemala, Quadros, and Cheddi Jagan of Guyana, all of whom were progressive statesman committed to the electoral route to social change and to doing business with the United States. All had held, or come close to holding, power, and so were potential allies of Cuba, should Castro decide to take the Nasser route. Conversations with Allende and Quadros in the early 1960s made social democracy look possible for Latin America. Today, only after military coups in Brazil, Argentina, Chile, and Uruguay, has it become clear that such hopes were naïve.

The Break with the United States

The breakdown in U.S.–Cuban relations that occurred in January 1961 was not inevitable. In the first months after the Cuban revolution, both parties had made a number of cautious overtures. But these overtures did not mask strong mutual distrust and suspicion.

The U.S. hostility toward the new Castro regime grew out of the volatile combination of the Monroe Doctrine and the Cold War. Cuba's hostility to the United States was born in 1898, when the United States intervened in the Cuban War of Independence, commonly known as the Spanish–American War. American troops were supposedly sent to help Cuban patriots expel their colonial masters. But once the Americans landed, it was almost impossible to get them to go home. The troops were finally withdrawn in 1901, but only after the new Cuban legislature agreed to amend their constitution, giving the United States the right to intervene in Cuba whenever the U.S. deemed it necessary, for "the preservation of Cuban independence and the maintenance of stable government. . . . protecting life, property and individual liberty."[23] Over the next thirty-three years, until the Platt Amendment was rescinded as part of Franklin Delano Roosevelt's Good Neighbor Policy, Cuba suffered a full eight years of American military occupation. The 1954 U.S.-backed overthrow of the Arbenz regime in Guatemala did little to quiet Cuba's long-standing fear of U.S. intervention.[24]

The year 1959 was at best one of armed truce between Cuba and the United States. While Castro's economic ministers quietly planned on U.S. aid, Castro openly ridiculed the United States for everything from the 1898 intervention to its military support for the Batista dictatorship. Although publicly the Eisenhower Administration maintained open relations with the new regime—Nixon had received Castro in Washington—in private it was drawing up plans for the Bay of Pigs invasion as early as March 1960. But Castro, with visions of Guatemala and Arbenz before him, was one step ahead of the Americans. He placed the Cuban National Militia on full alert in November 1959, warning of an impending U.S. invasion. This was four months before the CIA plans were begun.

The following year, recriminations and fear escalated, moving Cuba and the United States even farther apart. Each cabinet shakeup in Havana was greeted in Washington with new alarums that Cuba was going Communist. The thousands of Cuban exiles who streamed into Miami, bearing stories of torture, privation, and Communist infiltration, fanned the flames. The numerous attacks on Cuban shores by exiles stationed in Miami had almost no effect on the Cuban economy or Castro's power, but they did serve to reinforce his suspicions. Washington's failure to stop the exile attacks was interpreted as U.S. hostility. And Cuba's establishment of trade relations with the Soviet Union, Yugoslavia, China, and Poland in the spring of 1960 was seen in Washington as proof that Cuba was indeed going Communist.

In this grim atmosphere, events seemed to overtake the actors. In January 1961, Washington and Havana officially broke relations. Three months later, Castro's worst fears were realized when the United States backed an invasion by Cuban exiles at the Bay of Pigs.

Enter Moscow

The Soviet Union played only a small role in the breakdown of U.S.–Cuban relations. There has been a tendency to forget that the Soviet Union was hesitant to commit its support to the Castro regime in the early years. Moscow did not wish to jeopardize its newborn détente with Washington, and feared that any strong commitment on its part would provoke a U.S. attack against Cuba. The Soviets also feared a replay of the 1954 U.S.-supported overthrow of the Arbenz regime in Guatemala. Finally, Castro appeared to be something of a dark horse to the Soviet leadership. He was not even a Communist.[25]

The Cuban–Soviet alliance grew gradually. The first Cuban–Soviet economic agreement was signed in April 1959. The Russians agreed to buy 170,000 tons of sugar, 30,000 tons less than they had bought from Batista in 1958. In February 1960, the Soviet deputy premier, Anastas Mikoyan, on his way home from Mexico, led a trade fair to Cuba and offered Havana its first Soviet aid, a $100 million credit to purchase industrial equipment. But not until May 1960 did Cuba and the Soviet Union establish diplomatic relations.

The pace began to pick up in the summer of 1960, as U.S.–Cuban relations rapidly deteriorated. In the first week of July, when Washington slashed Cuba's sugar import quota, the Soviet Union stepped in to take up the slack, saving Cuba from economic ruin. At the same time, Soviet Premier Nikita S. Khrushchev made his first military commitment to Cuba, warning the United States that, "figuratively speaking," any intervention in Cuba could be met by Soviet missile fire.

Limited arms shipments from Eastern Europe began soon after. That same month, Raúl Castro, Fidel's brother and head of the Cuban armed forces, traveled to Moscow, where he was assured that the socialist block would defend Cuba against the economic ruin of a U.S. embargo. Yet although these commitments were intended to reassure the Cuban leadership, they were still only qualified commitments. Khrushchev's phrase, "figuratively speaking," haunted the Cuban leadership and left it feeling insecure and unprotected in the face of mounting U.S. hostility. After Khrushchev's capitulation in the October 1962 missile crisis these fears seemed more than justified.

And so the split with Washington did not diminish Castro's interest in his hemispheric neighbors. If anything, Castro needed them more. Even though the Communist bloc had agreed to replace the United States as the major client for Cuba's sugar and had offered some commitments to Cuba's defense, there was still not enough support. Isolation in the hemisphere would mean total dependence on the Soviet Union. And Cuba had long known the frustrations and the dangers of trading with only one partner. There also was hope that hemispheric opinion would restrain the United States from attacking Cuba directly, a hope soon dashed by the Bay of Pigs invasion.

ISOLATION

Starting in late 1961, Cuba's relations with its Latin American neighbors began to deteriorate. In November, Venezuela severed ties with Cuba for alleged subversive activities; Peru and Colombia soon followed suit. In Punta del Este on January 31, 1962, Cuba's membership in the OAS was formally suspended on the grounds that its Marxist–Leninist ideology was "incompatible with the interests of the hemisphere."[26]

There are many reasons for the breakdown in Cuba's relations with the Latin American states. Cuba has blamed the United States, claiming that Washington had applied all sorts of diplomatic and economic pressure in an effort to isolate Cuba from the hemisphere. The United States, on the other hand, has argued that the Cubans have only themselves to blame: Their reckless adventurism and complete disregard for the norms of conventional diplomacy alienated their Latin American neighbors. There is more than a grain of truth in both explanations, but neither tells the whole story.

There is little doubt that the United States *tried* to play a major role in isolating Cuba from the hemisphere. Washington first moved against Cuba in August 1960, when, at a special meeting of the OAS in San José, Costa Rica, Secretary of State Christian A. Herter tried to persuade Latin American foreign ministers to condemn Cuba for endangering the peace of the hemisphere. But the U.S. motion was voted down by the conference, which chose instead to condemn all extrahemispheric intervention and declared totalitarianism to be inconsistent with the continental commitment to democracy. Neither Castro nor Cuba was mentioned by name.[27]

Washington scored a major success with the August 1962 ratification of the Alliance for Progress in Punta del Este. It would be simplistic to suggest that the Alliance was created solely to undercut Castro's influence in the hemisphere, but there is little doubt that the program, by holding out the possibility of social reform without violent revolution, both increased U.S. influence among Latin America's leaders and reduced the attractiveness of the Cuban model. The success of Washington's efforts was reflected five months later in the Punta del Este decision to suspend Cuba from the OAS. Washington played a major role in all of the subsequent votes against Cuba.

Nevertheless, despite U.S. perseverance and persuasion, it was more than four years after the first U.S. motion in 1960 that sanctions were formally levied against Cuba in July 1964.[28] The delay suggests that the sanctions were not solely the result of U.S. pressures. Cuba must also take some responsibility for the collapse of its relations with its Latin American neighbors—failures due not to lack of interest on the part of Havana, but rather to a mixture of diplomatic bumbling, rash and unconsidered actions, and Cuba's basic ambivalence about its role in Latin American politics.

First, the *barbudos* proved to be better guerrillas than diplomats. Between December 1959 and March 1961, Cuban ambassadors managed to alienate no less than nine different governments by using their embassies to meddle in the internal affairs of their host states. In most of these cases, the acts of interference were really more violations of the diplomatic norms than the result of any organized plot to subvert regimes. The embassies distributed literature, set up pro-Cuban lobbies, and contacted opposition political groups. One by one, Venezuela, Guatemala, Nicaragua, Peru, El Salvador, Bolivia, Panama, Uruguay, and Honduras declared the Cuban ambassadors *personae non grata,* expelled embassy personnel, and closed embassies and consulates.[29]

A second cause of the breakdown in Cuban–Latin American relations was the general immoderation of Cuban propaganda, and Castro's simple inability to leave well enough alone. Castro's defiance had made him a hero at home and to many young revolutionaries abroad, but to fellow statesmen in Latin America, his hyperbole was immature, if not actually threatening. And Castro even managed to bungle support when it was his.

The OAS decision taken in Costa Rica in August 1960 had been a defeat for the United States, not for Cuba. Although the OAS ministers condemned totalitarianism and extrahemispheric intervention, they had not followed the U.S. suggestion to name either Castro or Cuba in the resolution. Instead of trying to calm his neighbors' fears, an angry Castro responded to the OAS's "Declaration of San José" with his own "Declaration of Havana," in which he defiantly called on all the oppressed peoples of Latin America to follow the Cuban example and break free of U.S. imperialism. He then announced that Cuba was establishing diplomatic relations with the People's Republic of China (a pariah state in the hemisphere). And finally, in direct defiance of the OAS condemnation of extrahemispheric interference, he "accepted and thanked the Soviet Union for its missile aid."[30] The fact that the Soviet Union had never actually offered missiles to Cuba—Khrushchev had been very careful to speak only in "figurative" terms—did not deter Castro.

Castro repeated this performance a year and a half later in response to the 1962 OAS decision to suspend Cuba's membership. While there is no denying that the suspension was a hostile act, the OAS had been careful not also to levy sanctions against Cuba. It merely stated that Cuba, by declaring its commitment to Marxism–Leninism, had voluntarily removed itself from the hemispheric organization.[31] Moreover, most of the large and influential Latin American states had voted against the suspension. Nonetheless, Castro's "Second Declaration of Havana," issued on February 4, 1962, was the most vitriolic of his speeches of that period. Speaking to the "hungry Indian masses, the peasants without land, the exploited workers" of Latin America, Castro called on them to rise up:

> Already they can be seen armed with stones, sticks, machetes, in one direction and another each day occupying lands, sinking hooks into the land which belongs to them and defending it with their lives. They can be seen carrying signs, slogans, flags; letting them flap in the mountain or prairie winds. And the wave of anger, of demands for justice, of claims for rights, which is beginning to sweep the lands of Latin America will not stop. That wave will swell with each passing day. For that wave is composed of the greatest number, the majorities in every respect, those whose labor amasses the wealth and turns the wheels of history. Now they are awakening from the long, brutalizing sleep to which they had been subjected.[32]

This speech must have alarmed even Cuba's most sympathetic neighbors. At the time, leaders all over Latin America were desperately trying to implement controlled reforms and in the process were walking a tightrope between right-wing oligarchs and left-wing revolutionaries. Such pronouncements from Castro, whether or not they were backed with material support, could only have been inflammatory.

This diplomatic bumbling and hyperbole were more than just the result of Cuban inexperience or Castro's own immaturity as a head of state (although both factors were significant). They were symptomatic of a basic ambivalence the Cubans were feeling about their role in Latin America. Since the days in the Sierra Maestra, the *barbudos* had spoken of continental revolution—it was the dream of Castro as a young man, Che as a young man, indeed, of all the Cuban revolutionaries dating back to José Martí and the 1898 revolution against Spain. But as Castro soon learned, the requirements of staging a revolution are very different from those of maintaining one. Standard diplomacy, open trade and participation in international forums were all necessary for Cuba's survival. In contrast to their leaders' early expectations, the Cuban revolution had not sparked a continental revolution, and their early efforts to foment revolution had failed miserably.

To understand fully the reasons for the breakdown in Cuban–Latin American relations, one must look beyond both Cuba and the United States to the political conditions in Latin America. From the beginning, Castro's revolution posed a problem for the Latin American states. Castro was an obvious, explicit threat to the rightist dictatorships of the Caribbean and Central America. But the Cuban revolution was a challenge even to left-of-center regimes, such as those of Betancourt in Venezuela, Frondízi in Argentina, and Quadros in Brazil. These leaders all shared Castro's strong commitment to social change—land reform, social welfare, improvements in education and health care, and a more equal distribution of wealth. All had begun to question U.S. political and economic domination. But all were proceeding slowly. Their own internal political instabilities, as well as real material constraints, mandated caution, or so each claimed. By contrast, Castro's sweeping reforms and overt challenges to Washington inevitably raised questions among the democratic left about the credentials of their leaders as reformers and nationalists.

The Cuban leader's popularity with the Latin American masses was undeniable. During Castro's 1959 visit to Venezuela, Betancourt rather uneasily acknowledged that popularity when he said that if elections were held that day in Venezuela, there was no doubt in his mind "that Castro would win."[33] But Castro's status was a double-edged sword. At first, his popularity with the Latin American masses bound the Latin American states to support Castro. But as Castro moved farther left and called on the other states to do likewise, that popularity became more of a threat. When the Jorge Alessandri Government in Chile broke relations with Cuba on the eve of the 1964 presidential elections, and it had no noticeable effect on the fortunes of his Christian Democratic Party (Christian Democrat Eduardo Frei defeated Castro's ally, Salvador Allende, handily), the Cubans lost a major bargaining chip in their relations with the Latin American democracies.

Above all else, the collapse of Cuba's relations with its Latin American neighbors was a casualty of a hemispheric move to the right. Military coups in Argentina and Peru in 1962 and in Brazil and Bolivia in 1964 installed regimes that were overtly hostile to Castro. Indeed, the fear of Castroism was a major factor in these and subsequent military coups in Latin America.[34]

By 1964 Havana had apparently abandoned its bid for diplomatic influence in Latin America. The OAS sanctions adopted that year isolated Cuba both politically and economically from all its neighbors except Mexico. Yet even without the sanctions, 1964 would have been a discouraging year for anyone committed to progressive change in Latin America. That year the left-leaning Brazilian regime led by João Goulart was overthrown in a military coup, and Chile's socialist Salvador Allende was defeated in his presidential bid. Castro had gone to great lengths to cultivate both of these social democrats.

The Cubans fluctuated between the demands of their role as guerrillas and their role as statesmen for as long as the Latin American states would allow. Finally, after their expulsion from the OAS, the levying of sanctions and the severing of diplomatic relations by all the Latin American states except Mexico, the Cubans were forced to choose one role: They would be revolutionaries.

FULL-TIME GUERRILLAS: THE CASE
OF VENEZUELA

At this point, Cuba turned its full attention to guerrilla warfare. What had earlier been a temperamental and ideological commitment

23

to the export of revolution became essential to the republic's survival. Only ninety miles from the United States, cordoned off by a trade embargo, surrounded by increasingly hostile Latin American regimes, the Cubans must have felt as isolated in Latin America as the Russians did in Europe after their 1917 revolution. Like the Russians, the Cubans tried to overcome their isolation by overthrowing the hostile governments surrounding them, and installing more sympathetic regimes.

Cuba was, of course, not completely without allies. Beginning in 1960, the Soviet Union committed itself to meeting Cuba's economic as well as military needs. But complete isolation from the hemisphere meant complete dependence on the Soviet Union.

Cuba's 1963 commitment to guerrilla warfare was substantially different from earlier efforts to export revolution. In 1959 the Cuban strategy had been merely to take advantage of already existing revolutionary conditions. Havana had directed its attacks toward those Caribbean despots who appeared to be on the verge of collapse or violent ouster. In 1959 Cuba's declared enemies were the dictatorships of Trujillo and Somoza—traditional targets of the Latin American democratic left that lacked both domestic and international support. All that was needed to overthrow them, according to the Cubans, was a symbolic push, like the *Granma* landing. The Cuban strategy in these early years was no more sophisticated than providing that push.

By 1963, the Castro regime was no longer interested in overthrowing petty despots. The newly Marxist–Leninist Cuba was now committed to fomenting revolutions in the most well-developed political systems in Latin America, such as Venezuela, Colombia, Argentina, and Brazil. These were neither despotisms nor pariah states. Staging a revolution in any of these states would require much more than a symbolic push. The Cubans were in for a much longer haul, of which the first step was the creation of revolutionary conditions.[35]

The change in Cuba's policy toward Venezuela is the best example of the shift in Cuba's attitudes and strategy toward Latin America. From the beginning of the revolution, Havana had expressed a strong interest in Venezuela. Castro, as mentioned earlier, flew to Caracas in January 1959 to discuss with Betancourt a possible Cuban–Venezuelan front against dictatorships and imperialism. Castro found Venezuela attractive for several reasons—not the least of which were its oil and ports. Moreover, Betancourt's credentials as a left-of-center progressive and alumnus of the Caribbean Legion were impeccable. And as Castro pointed out during his visit to Caracas, Cuba and Venezuela shared a common resentment of U.S. paternalism. In 1959, when Castro's goals were the defeat of dictatorships, the implementation of democratic social change, and an improved bargaining position *vis-à-vis* the United States, Venezuela was Castro's first choice as an ally.

But Betancourt did not share Castro's vision. As he told the Cuban leader at their 1959 meeting, his plans for Venezuela entailed evolution, not revolution. These plans coincided with the goals of the Alliance for Progress, and Venezuela became a major recipient of U.S. largesse and a showcase for the strategy of democratic reform.

Castro's goals also changed significantly. As a recent convert to Marxist–Leninist philosophy, Castro wanted revolution, not moderate social change. Social democrats like Betancourt—whether at home or abroad—were now condemned as spoilers and apologists for the status quo. By late 1963 Castro was also losing hope of ever finding an accommodation with the United States. The sides between Washington and Havana were drawn, and Betancourt and the Venezuelans had chosen the enemy camp. By 1963 Venezuela had gone from being Castro's first-choice ally against dictatorships to being number one on the Cuban hit list for the export of revolution.

It has been argued that Castro's enmity toward Venezuela began with Betancourt's rejection in 1959.[36] There is, however, a less personal and one-sided explanation. In the early 1960s, both Cuba and Venezuela were conscious of their symbolic roles in the hemisphere, and how they conflicted. Both were aware of the responsibilities and perquisites of serving as a showcase: Venezuela for the U.S.-funded strategy of democratic reform, Cuba for the Soviet strategy of social revolution. Given these roles, a clash was inevitable. To prove the success of his chosen route, each leader was virtually required to demonstrate the failure of the other.

25

The combatants were not evenly matched. Venezuela's resources, size, and historic dominance in the hemisphere far overshadowed Cuba's. Moreover, the Venezuelans could count on the backing of the U.S. and the entire mechanism of the OAS. Venezuela's attacks on Cuba were limited to an early break in diplomatic relations and a leading role in the motions to have Cuba suspended from the OAS and isolated from the hemisphere.

Despite their obvious weakness, the Cubans were quite determined to give the Venezuelans a run for their money. It is true that Castro's concern with Venezuela was almost obsessive. But the concern was not with Betancourt or any personal humiliation; rather, it was with Venezuela, which he saw as the linchpin of Latin America. Venezuela was to Castro what Germany had been to Lenin: If the revolution was to succeed anywhere in the hemisphere, it would *have* to succeed in Venezuela.

Cuba's strategy for Venezuela was similar to that adopted by the urban-based Cuban underground during the struggle against Batista: to create revolutionary conditions by provoking government repression through a concerted program of urban terrorism and armed insurrection. The immediate goal was the disruption of the 1963 presidential elections. As the Cubans and the Venezuelan guerrillas saw it, if these elections were disrupted and the military provoked into seizing power, the democratic reform route would be completely discredited in Venezuela. Betancourt and the democratic reformers were equally committed to holding the elections. If the elections were held successfully, it would be the first time in sixteen years that a civilian government in Venezuela had handed power over to another civilian government through legitimate political channels. Both sides saw the fate of Venezuela's democratic system hanging in the balance of the 1963 elections. This was the situation in spring 1963, when the Cubans began to implement their new strategy of revolution for Latin America by shipping several tons of weapons and ammunition to the Venezuelan revolutionary underground.[37]

Despite Cuban aid, the strategy failed. The Venezuelan elections were held, as 94 percent of the electorate went to the polls, refusing to be cowed by terrorism. But even after this crushing defeat, the

Cubans did not abandon their hopes for revolution in Venezuela— or elsewhere in the hemisphere.

A DANGEROUS CONFLICT

Castro's new commitment to armed struggle was not shared by his reform-minded Communist brethren in Latin America. In the early years after the revolution, both sides tried to find a compromise. But with time, historical circumstances made such a compromise insupportable. By the mid-1960s, Castro had split with the reform parties—calling them traitors and defeatists—and transferred his support to splinter groups actively engaged in armed struggle on the continent. By 1967 the split had grown so wide that it threatened Cuba's alliance with the Soviet Union.

Even during his own revolution, Castro had differed with the Cuban Communist Party, the Partido Socialista Popular (PSP). He was suspicious of all Comintern-dominated Latin American parties. In his opinion, their roots were not in Latin America, but far away in Moscow, and so they couldn't be expected to wage the sort of struggle required by the particular conditions of Latin America. A 1959 editorial in *Revolución,* the official newspaper of Fidel's 26th of July movement, rejected Cuba's Soviet-controlled Communist Party, the PSP, saying there was nothing wrong with being a Communist "pure and simple,"

> but to be a Communist in a party that belongs to the [Communist International] is something else again, for it undoubtedly means adopting a type of Marxism compromised by the interests of a metropolis that one blindly believes will bring about the establishment of socialism in the entire world.[38]

The Cuban Communist Party had been equally suspicious of Castro. From the beginning they had opposed Castro's struggle, calling it putschist and adventurist. By Comintern standards, Cuba under Batista was not ripe for revolution. The PSP only cast its lot with Castro's July 26th movement less than six months before Castro came to power.

After Castro took control in Havana and declared his commitment to Marxism–Leninism, relations with the "old Communists" still remained uneasy. His lack of a trained party bureaucracy led Castro in the early years to depend on the PSP organization. But once he had developed his own group of trained cadres, Castro purged most of the old Communists from his party. Castro never really came to trust the allegiances of the old PSP.

As for the other Latin American Communist parties, Castro knew he needed their support if his plans for a continental socialist revolution were ever to succeed. On the other hand, he was not sure they had the right attitudes, loyalties, or even the courage to take the steps necessary for revolution.

The Latin American parties viewed Castro with an equal measure of ambivalence and anxiety. On the one hand, Castro *had* staged the first socialist revolution in the Western hemisphere, and for that reason alone deserved their admiration and total support. On the other hand, Castro had been successful where all the rest had failed. The success of his revolution was a constant reminder of their failure, and a direct challenge to their claims to lead the Communist movement on the continent. To make matters worse for these experienced, organizational infighters, not only had Castro made his revolution without the help of the Communist party, he had made it without the help of *any* party, and instead of apologizing for that fact, his ideology actually celebrated it. In a speech to the Cuban trade unions in March 1966, Castro declared:

> Who will make the revolution in Latin America? The people, the revolutionaries, with a party or without it![39]

Moreover, despite his success, the Latin American party leaders still refused to accept the fact that Castro's strategy of armed struggle could be applied in *their* own countries. These men were not soldiers, but politicians who believed that if communism was ever to succeed in Latin America it would come through political action. Whatever paeans they might make to Castro's revolution for the sake of international solidarity, in their hearts they believed the revolution was a fluke.[40]

Given these basic differences, conflict between Castro and the

Latin American parties seemed inevitable. The Soviet Union recognized this danger early on, and in 1964 convened the Havana Conference of Communist Parties to head off an irrevocable split. An additional benefit for Moscow would be the chance to isolate Peking from the Latin American movements. Not one of the region's pro-Chinese parties was invited to the Havana Conference.[41]

The compromise that was worked out in Havana in December 1964 appeared to be the best possible solution. Both sides recognized the legitimacy of the other's chosen strategy and pledged to aid in each other's struggle. In concrete terms, this meant that the traditionally cautious Latin American Communist parties chose— or were forced—to overcome their resistance to armed struggle and endorsed the guerrilla movements in Venezuela, Colombia, Guatemala, Honduras, Paraguay, and Haiti. In return Havana agreed to support the remaining Latin American parties in their efforts to achieve change through peaceful means. Specifically, the Cubans had to abandon their pronouncements on the inevitability of armed struggle and their support for the many pro-Castroite splinter groups that had sprung up independent of, and at times in opposition to, the official Communist parties.[42]

The Havana Compromise should not be dismissed cynically, though it certainly had all the markings of a marriage of convenience. For despite the obvious differences between the parties, there was at the time significant room for compromise. After all, the Latin American leaders were Communists, and the Cuban success must have raised their hopes, even if it challenged their political security. Certainly there were some who were willing to try a new strategy. And Castro himself had a long history as a social democrat and had been something of an accomplished political infighter in the days before he took to the hills. In fact, his first anti-Batista act, the 1953 attack on the Moncada Barracks, had been prompted by the cancellation of the elections in which Castro had planned to run for the Cuban senate.

Indeed, for some time after the conference, it seemed that this new commitment would have an impact beyond mere words. The Venezuelan party stepped up its support for its guerrilla wing in

1965. The Colombian Communists announced support for their previously ignored guerrilla *focos*. The Guatemalan party established a new organization committed to guerrilla struggle.

The Russians also kept to their part of the bargain and increased support for armed struggle in Latin America. *Pravda,* in an editorial issued in January 1965, endorsed the efforts of guerrillas fighting in "Venezuela, Guatemala, and various other countries [who], weapons in hand, continue a just battle to defend their national interests."[43] Nor was this Soviet support merely symbolic. In March 1965, two messengers carrying $330,000 in cash for the Venezuelan guerrillas were arrested by Venezuelan police. The couriers were Italian, yet all observers agree that the money originated in the Soviet Union.[44]

For a brief time, Havana also seemed to be keeping its part of the bargain. In early 1965 the Cubans transferred support from an independent Castroite group in Guatemala to the guerrilla movement endorsed by the Communist party in Guatemala.[45]

AN END TO COMPROMISE

Events, however, conspired against the compromise. The American bombing of North Vietnam in February 1965 and the landing of 23,000 U.S. troops in the Dominican Republic that April shocked the Cubans. To Havana, these acts signaled a new, more aggressive U.S. attitude toward communism in the Third World, and an attack on Cuba could not be far behind.

These events also shook Cuba's faith in the Soviet Union. Moscow had stood by complacently while U.S. bombs rained on Vietnam, and the Russians had made no attempts to block the U.S. intervention in the Dominican Republic. All the doubts raised by the Cuban missile crisis came rushing back. Could the Cubans really depend on the Russians to defend them against an American attack?

By mid-1965 the Cubans began to argue that a new strategy toward American imperialism was necessary. The only way to repel the new American offensive, they felt, was for the socialist bloc to take the offensive as well. In Vietnam, this meant the socialist bloc would have to take a harder stand against the United States, regardless of the danger to world peace. In the rest of the Third World, and particularly in Latin America, this meant creating even more guerrilla struggles to halt American imperialism. In the words of Che Guevara, it meant creating "two, three, many Vietnams."

The Latin American Communist parties and their Soviet counterpart did not agree. Like the Cubans, they also believed that the events of 1965 spelled a new American backlash in the Third World. But unlike the Cubans, they did not believe that a more aggressive policy toward American imperialism was the best response. Instead, they advocated retrenchment and conservation of forces, a return to the united front strategy.

The Cubans might have tolerated this new approach had it remained merely theoretical. Similar shifts between united front and revolutionary strategies had dominated the Communist writings in both the Soviet Union and Latin America for nearly forty years. But it soon became clear that this position was not merely another theoretical tack. In October 1965 Havana was informed that the Venezuelan Communist Party (PCV) had reevaluated its strategy and was planning to pull out of the armed struggle.[46] This Havana would not tolerate. To its enemies list of Latin American oligarchies and social democrats was now added the reform-minded Latin American Communist parties. Whatever doubts the Cubans had about the Soviet Union were as yet unspoken.

THE TRICONTINENTAL CONFERENCE

On January 3, 1966, the Tricontinental Conference opened in Havana in the Hall of the Ambassadors of the once-luxurious Havana Hilton, now the Habana Libre Hotel. Many of its over 500 delegates were mainstream diplomats—little different from the men and women who represented their countries at meetings of the Nonaligned Movement, the Organization of African Unity, and the United Nations. Some, however, were genuine revolutionaries, members of the Vietcong, Guatemala's Rebel Armed Forces, and the Palestine Liberation Organization. Under Castro's careful direction, the interests of these revolutionaries were dramatically showcased.

At one meeting a North Vietnamese militiawoman presented Cas-

31

tro with a ring fashioned from the wreckage of a U.S. plane she said she had personally shot down over North Vietnam. At another meeting, a member of the Vietcong presented representatives of Venezuela's revolutionary National Liberation Front with the helmet of a dead American pilot downed in Vietnam. It was these displays that drew Washington's attention and led a Senate staff report in 1966 to describe the conference ominously as "the most powerful gathering of pro-Communist, anti-American forces in the history of the Western hemisphere."[47]

What was remarkable about the conference, however, was not its anti-American rhetoric, but its anti-Soviet tone—a fact lost on most Americans at the time. Castro used the Tricontinental to make explicit his new commitment to armed struggle, and to bring into the open his growing disagreements with his Soviet-bloc allies. At the conference Castro spoke forcefully of the need to create a truly continental revolution. Although the Latin American movements might be weak individually, and the conditions not yet ripe, when united, said Castro, these movements would be able to overcome all material constraints and defeat imperialism.

Castro was no doubt aware that such a broad commitment to armed struggle in Latin America directly violated the compromise reached at the 1964 Havana Conference, which had agreed on the appropriateness of armed struggle in only a limited number of states. For Castro, however, the time for compromise and qualification was long past:

> If revolutionaries would devote less time and energy to theoretical speculation and a bit more to practical work, and if we would finally understand that, sooner or later, all peoples or nearly all, will be obliged to take up arms and emancipate themselves, then the hour of freedom on this continent will be close at hand.[48]

The Tricontinental Conference was a watershed both for Cuba's commitment to armed struggle and for Cuba's relationship with the Soviet Union. For this reason, it is useful to include a brief history of the conference. The origins of the Tricontinental are similar to those of the 1964 Havana Conference. Like the 1964 conference, it was conceived by Moscow to further the international standing of both Moscow and Havana, while undercutting Peking's influence in the Third World. Once again, Moscow was trying to use Castro to isolate the Chinese. This time, however, Castro managed to use these Soviet concerns to promote his own commitment to Proletarian Internationalism, and his position as an independent Third World leader.

The Afro Asian People's Solidarity Organization (AAPSO) took its ideological inspiration from the 1955 Bandung Conference of Afro-Asian leaders, although its first meeting was held in Cairo in 1957.[49] Its three major backers were Egypt, the Soviet Union, and China. The AAPSO was established at a particularly critical point in Moscow's relations with the Third World. The Soviet Union, under the new leadership of Nikita Khrushchev, was just breaking out of the isolation of the Stalin years, and looked particularly on the emerging states of Africa and Asia as the site of progressive change, and as natural allies in its struggle against the West.

The Afro-Asian movement's interests were much more in harmony with Cuban concerns than were those of Bandung's other child, the Movement of Nonaligned Nations. The AAPSO's original charter was consciously antiimperialist and explicitly committed to alleviating the economic exploitation of the Third World. But the movement never really took off. Its political energies were soon sapped by the incessant bickering and maneuvering for control by the Russians and Chinese. As early as 1964, many of the moderate and politically significant African and Asian groups had abandoned AAPSO. Those that remained did so merely for what little aid and publicity the organization could bring them.[50]

Moscow's and Peking's interest in AAPSO lay in its utility as a weapon in the continuing Sino–Soviet rivalry. To the Soviet Union, membership in AAPSO was particularly important. It legitimated their claims as an Asian—via Siberia—and, therefore, Third World state. Were they to be ousted from AAPSO, as the Chinese insisted, the Soviets would then be grouped in the camp of Western developed states—enemies of the Third World. Moscow's ouster would leave Peking as the only other Communist nation that could claim a leadership role in the Third World.

The question of Latin American participation in AAPSO was

raised by the Cubans as early as 1961. But no steps were taken to include the Latin Americans, because the Chinese and Soviets could not agree on a formula for choosing delegates from the welter of pro-Soviet and pro-Chinese factions in Latin America. The success of the 1964 Havana Conference opened new doors for the Soviets—or so they thought. The Soviets came to the 1965 AAPSO conference with a plan: AAPSO would be expanded to include Latin America. The delegates would be chosen by Cuba, the vanguard of the Latin American revolution. Moscow was sure that Peking would not dare to oppose the plan, or question Castro's credentials as a revolutionary. At the same time, the success of the 1964 Havana Compromise left leaders in Moscow feeling reasonably sure that the Cubans would make the right choices—inviting pro-Soviet Communist parties to participate.

One other development convinced Moscow that the time was right to include Latin America. During the 1964 AAPSO meeting, the Chinese won the conference's endorsement of Peking as the site of the upcoming Fifth Summit Conference. The Soviets wanted to deprive the Chinese of that honor. Moscow knew that if the members agreed to change the site, the movement would be polarized still further. The only alternative would be to change the very makeup of the organization. If a new organization were created by adding the Latin Americans, then the Peking conference would be canceled automatically and a new vote taken. With the addition of more than twenty pro-Soviet Latin American delegations—over a quarter of the conference's anticipated eighty—Moscow was sure to win.

The Soviet plan was only a partial success. Havana's invitation to a Tricontinental Conference in January 1966 was accepted, but it would not be an official AAPSO meeting, and the Peking conference would be held as planned. Despite this setback, the Soviets pressed on with their plan. Their hope was that in the euphoria of the Havana Conference the delegates would solidify the new alliance by forming a new organization then and there, dissolving the outdated AAPSO, and abandoning the Peking conference as well.

For a while it looked like Moscow might actually get its way.

34

At the preparatory meetings of the Tricontinental Conference, the Cubans proposed a slate of delegates composed solely of the pro-Soviet Communist parties (in accordance with the 1964 Havana Compromise). When the Chinese challenged this obviously stacked deck, the Cubans compromised by proposing that each country send a committee representing a broad range of left, antiimperialist, and national liberation groups. The official makeup of these groups would be decided in the Havana preparatory meetings several months before the conference. The Chinese accepted this compromise, and the Soviets remained hopeful that they would still prevail.

But this was not to be. The events of 1965—Johnson's Dominican intervention, the bombing of Vietnam, the retreat of the Venezuelan Communists from their commitment to armed struggle—propelled the Cubans from the Havana Compromise and toward more radical solutions. The Tricontinental Conference became the forum for the articulation of Cuba's shift to the revolutionary left.

The Latin American delegates were chosen between September and December 1965, the same time that the Cubans were abandoning their side of the Havana Compromise. When the invitations were issued, the full extent of Havana's shift became clear. Of the twenty-two pro-Moscow Communist parties invited to the 1964 Havana Conference, only three headed delegations to the Tricontinental Conference. The remaining committees were composed of both traditional Communists and splinter groups committed to armed struggle, often in opposition to the traditional Communist parties.[51]

Cuba's behavior at the conference diverged even more explicitly from Soviet designs. As the conference's host and chairman, Castro was able to exercise an enormous amount of power: giving the showcased welcoming and concluding speeches, and orchestrating the debates and the voting. It was at the Tricontinental that the Soviets and the Third World got their first taste of Castro's formidable political skills and his plans for global influence.

Castro used his power to promote Havana's interests over Moscow's.[52] It became apparent that Castro's endorsement of the Soviet plan for dissolving AAPSO was only perfunctory. If a new organization was to be formed, the Cubans wanted the headquarters to be in Havana, and not in Cairo, as the Soviets suggested. The

Soviets assumed that, if the meeting were held in Cairo, the site of the first AAPSO conference, they could maneuver the absorption of the old Afro Asian People's Solidarity Organization into the new Afro–Asian–Latin American organization with little difficulty. This, the Russians believed, was the only way to deprive the Chinese of their Peking summit.

As the debate raged, Castro became increasingly adamant about wanting the secretariat in Havana. He personally visited several delegations to lobby for his position and even closed the Havana airport to make sure that no delegate would leave the conference before an agreement was reached. In the end the Soviets were forced to abandon their plans for merger and accept the continuation of AAPSO and the parallel organization of a Latin American Solidarity Organization (OLAS) and a permanent Tricontinental directorate headquartered in Havana. The directorate would coordinate AAPSO's and OLAS's activities, but the summits would be convened separately. The Peking conference would be held as planned.

For the Soviets, this was a major and public defeat. Not only had they lost all hope of denying the Chinese their conference, but they had been outmaneuvered by Castro, who used the formation of a new Latin American organization as a springboard to establish his own position as an independent and competitive leader of the socialist bloc and the Third World.

Havana's growing radicalism and its attendant challenges to Moscow's interests were apparent at the Tricontinental Conference in more than these organizational maneuverings. The Cubans made the conference a platform for their most explicit endorsements of armed struggle to date. Under Havana's careful direction, the conference endorsed and pledged to support armed struggle throughout the world, with specific emphasis on Cuba's major interests in Vietnam and Venezuela. The conference's final resolutions included a demand that:

> . . . the revolutionary forces represented in the Tricontinental Conference [intensify] their efforts so that the authentic representatives of the countries that are fighting, weapons in hand, may receive

economic, financial, and material aid, including weapons and ammunition.[53]

The Cubans scored one further organizational victory for armed struggle and their role as revolutionary leaders. When the executive secretariat of the new joint Afro–Asian and Latin American directorate was chosen in Havana, only three socialist countries were represented—Cuba, North Vietnam, and North Korea. The Soviet Union and China were then invited to join the Committee for Aid and Assistance to National Liberation Movements. The message was clear: The Soviets and Chinese were expected to pay for the liberation struggles, but the real leadership now lay in the hands of those who struggled.

A Cuban Concession

Havana did make one concession to Moscow at the Tricontinental Conference—or so it seemed at the time. On the eve of the conference, Castro publicly broke with Peking, attacking China for allegedly cutting its rice shipments to Cuba. Castro also accused the Chinese of trying to impose their ideology on the Cuban people, of using their embassy in Havana to distribute pro-Chinese propaganda to members of the Cuban military, and of even trying to establish "direct contact with Cuban officers."[54] Two months later, Castro went even further, openly attacking the Chinese leadership, calling Mao's ideology "lightweight," and suggesting that the Chinese leader was senile.[55] At this onslaught, Peking recalled its ambassador from Havana.

It has generally been assumed that, after years of espousing neutrality in the Sino–Soviet dispute, Castro, the ideologue, finally took sides for the most crass and calculating of reasons: The Soviets, and not the Chinese, could afford to pay Cuba's bills. There is no doubt that this fact played a major part in the eventual alignments. But there is more to the story of the Sino–Cuban split than simple greed. Castro's rejection of Peking was intimately tied to basic disagreements over the issue of armed struggle in Latin America—specifically, who would lead it and how it would be fought. These

37

disagreements have been obscured by the funding issue and the fact that the Cubans and Chinese appeared to have an enormous amount in common ideologically—certainly more in common than either had with the Soviets.

True, Peking shared Havana's fundamental commitment to Third World revolution. Yet, when it came down to actually fighting the revolution in Latin America, the Cubans and Chinese often ended up on opposite sides. The problem may well have been that the two countries were too close ideologically—so close that they found themselves competing for the hearts and minds of the same revolutionary groups in Latin America, those termed the Latin American "Jacobin Left."[56] The Chinese saw the Cubans as upstarts in this competition, newcomers to socialism and to the strategy of people's war, which they claimed to have invented. The Cubans, on the other hand, saw the Chinese as foreigners, and kept asking what Maoist thought could possibly have to do with the particular conditions of Latin American revolution.

Although jingoism may have been the root cause of their disagreement, neither side had trouble justifying its position in the most academic and apparently objective terms. Specifically, the Chinese regarded the Cuban theories of guerrilla warfare as adventurist and dangerously revisionist. In their view, the Cubans were too willing to ignore material constraints. Peking sympathized with Havana's desire to have the revolution as soon as possible (Mao had, after all, refused to be discouraged by Stalin's assertions that conditions in China were not ripe for armed struggle); but its own revolution had taken several decades to win. The Cubans were too impatient.

Castro rejected these criticisms, informing the Chinese that Cuba had no need for "lessons in [revolutionary] conduct." But what he found more distasteful was the actual conduct of the Maoist groups in Latin America. These groups, in Castro's estimation, were overly doctrinal and very ineffective. Although they talked a better line on armed struggle than the pro-Moscow groups, they ended up doing much less. The pro-Peking factions spent almost all their time and propaganda attacking Moscow for its revisionism, rather than actually waging war on the Latin American oligarchies. In Bolivia, for example, members of the pro-Chinese wing of the Bolivian Communist Party had refused to support Guevara, claiming that conditions in Bolivia were not ripe. One of Che's followers even accused the pro-Chinese faction of having expelled one of their members for giving aid to Che in the hills. When Guevara died, the Chinese did not send condolences to Havana. Later they criticized Guevara openly, accusing him of having failed because of insufficient knowledge of the conditions in Bolivia, for allowing the army to predominate over the party, and for generally following "an adventurist line."[57]

The Sino–Cuban split in early 1966 undoubtedly pleased Cuba's Soviet allies because it strengthened their position in the Sino–Soviet competition. It may very well have taken some of the sting out of Castro's subsequent behavior at the Tricontinental Conference. But without the Sino–Cuban split, Havana would have been unable to eliminate one of the major competitors in its own bid for leadership of the Latin American and Third World revolution.

GOING PUBLIC

Havana's commitment to armed struggle and rejection of the reform-minded Communist parties and their Moscow supporters became increasingly strident during 1966 and 1967. In July 1966, Castro directly attacked what he called the "defeatist" elements in Latin America, or those who still refused to adopt the strategy of armed struggle, saying they were not only misinformed but actually dangerous to the cause of revolution:

> Defeatist elements always emerge and when the revolutionaries suffer a loss the former say, "You see we are right, this road was a dead end." And the imperialists say, "You see we are right, the revolutionaries have failed." And this strange coincidence occurs between what imperialism and the oligarchies are preaching and what certain gentlemen who call themselves revolutionary are preaching.[58]

The Cuban commitment to armed struggle reached new heights in January 1967 with the publication in Havana of Régis Debray's handbook of guerrilla warfare, *Revolution in the Revolution?* Régis Debray was a young French intellectual and radical who had come to Cuba in the mid-1960s to study the revolution. He wrote *Revolution in the Revolution?* after extensive interviews with top Cuban leaders, including Castro and Guevara. The book was first published in Havana by the government press, which distributed it widely both in Cuba and internationally.

In *Revolution in the Revolution?* Debray codified the principles of armed struggle that Castro had developed in the course of his growing split with the Latin American Communists.[59] The "revolution in the revolution" was the challenge Castro posed to Latin America's outmoded commitment to political strategies, and the explicit transfer of revolutionary credentials from the traditional Latin American Communist parties to the guerrilla groups espousing the Cuban theory of armed struggle.

Revolution in the Revolution? assembles polemic, exhortation, and concrete, tactical information for anyone seeking to stage a revolution in Latin America. The book immediately became essential reading for radicals throughout Latin America, Europe, and the United States. According to Debray, the Cuban revolution offered four basic lessons for the would-be revolutionary. First, the strategy of armed struggle is appropriate almost anywhere in Latin America. Second, even in states that do not appear to be fully ripe for revolution, armed struggle can still be waged successfully. People can create the conditions for armed struggle—even if it requires provoking a moderate regime into repressive activities and then rallying the popular opposition. Third, it is the army, not the party, that must lead the revolution. Too often the party is mired in political and reformist tactics, while the guerrilla army has the daring and the commitment to take the necessary chances. Finally, Debray asserted, the revolution needs to be conducted from the countryside. The struggle must remove itself from urban activism and place itself under the single leadership of the guerrilla *foco,* regardless of how committed, active, or organized the urban movement.

These four lessons were in large part intended to challenge the political control of the Latin American Communist parties. Castro had obviously grown disillusioned with the Latin American parties' failure to fulfill their commitment to revolution. With *Revolution in the Revolution?* he was making a clear bid to the many Latin

American splinter groups that chafed under the control of the Latin American parties but lacked a clear ideological or organizational alternative. With Debray's handbook Castro was offering both.

But there was more to *Revolution in the Revolution?* than political jockeying. Castro, Debray, and Guevara seemed sincere in their belief that they were offering sound advice. Not only did it make sense deductively, they argued, but this form of strategy and tactics had proved effective in the Cuban Sierra Maestra. Had not a guerrilla *foco* of 1,500 taken on Batista's army of 50,000 and won? Finally, there is a strong mystical component to *Revolution in the Revolution?* It is a celebration of both the heroism of the Cuban *barbudo* and of the birth of the new Cuban man, freed from the corruptions and limitations of city and party and cleansed by the hardships of the *sierra* and the discipline of the *foco.*

There are several problems with Debray's arguments, not the least of which is that they misrepresented what actually happened in Cuba. Castro's victory, miraculous as it seemed, was never a military victory, in the sense that it involved a full-scale confrontation between armies. Batista's political control had grown less legitimate over the years. Eventually his army deserted, his U.S. protectors abandoned him, and he abdicated. Castro stepped in to fill the void.

This is not to deny that Castro played a major role in Batista's loss of legitimacy. The continual sniping of the guerrillas had prompted a once corrupt, but moderate, regime to become a repressive and hateful dictatorship. Castro had provoked the repression, stripped away the last shreds of Batista's legitimacy, and then offered the hope of a new and better order. It was in this way that he defeated the Batista regime—not on the field of battle. Moreover, even if Castro's band of 1,500 guerrillas had defeated Batista's army of 50,000—so the legend goes—there is no guarantee that their tactics would have worked elsewhere in Latin America, which varied widely in everything from the terrain to the racial and class makeup of the population, political and economic conditions, and degree of opposition. The United States was sworn to using any means necessary to prevent the appearance of another Cuba in the hemisphere. In spite of these realities, the Cuban leadership remained

41

committed to the strategy of armed struggle in Latin America. This commitment determined all of Cuba's subsequent political alliances.

Castro Unbound

In the spring of 1967, Havana's split with the Venezuelan Communist Party (PCV) was made public. When the Venezuelan Communists abandoned the strategy of armed struggle, Castro immediately shifted his allegiance to a splinter group of guerrillas, the MIR, led by Douglas Bravo, and sent them arms and a small number of men to help in their struggle in the Venezuelan hills. The Venezuelan Communists were angered by what they perceived as Castro's meddling in Venezuela's internal affairs. And when a Cuban fishing boat carrying a small number of Cuban and Venezuelan guerrillas was seized off the coast of Venezuela in May 1967, the PCV joined Caracas in denouncing outside interference by Cuba.

Even before the PCV denunciation, Castro had dismissed the Venezuelan Communists as defeatists and traitors to the Latin American revolution. In a March 1967 speech he went so far as to accuse the party of conspiring with the Venezuelan Government to defeat the guerrillas, in exchange for promises of legality:

> The pro-imperialist oligarchy [in Venezuela] says that we are interfering in the internal affairs of Venezuela; and the rightist [Communist] party leadership that we interfere in the internal affairs of the party in Venezuela. This is not at all a strange coincidence between reactionaries and rightists![60]

Then came the most radical breach of Communist solidarity. Castro explicitly transferred his allegiance in Venezuela, and anywhere else in the Third World where he deemed it appropriate, away from the Communist party and to any and all groups—no matter what they called themselves—that were willing to wage armed struggle:

> Our stand regarding Communist parties will be based on strict revolutionary principles. The parties that have a line without hesitations and capitulations, the parties that in our opinion have a consistent revolutionary line, will receive our support in all circumstances; but

the parties that entrench themselves behind the name of Communists or Marxists and believe themselves to have a monopoly on revolutionary sentiment when what they really monopolize is reformism will not be treated by us as revolutionary parties. *And if in any country those who call themselves Communists do not know how to fulfill their duty we will support those who without calling themselves Communists conduct themselves like real Communists in action and in struggle* [emphasis added].[61]

Finally Castro stated openly what he had alluded to since the 1966 Tricontinental Conference: Proclaiming the Communist name or having Soviet endorsement was not enough to earn the title of Communist and allegiance with Cuba. To be a *true* Communist, the Latin American parties would have to be willing to wage all-out armed struggle.

This position was probably Castro's most radical to date; it was certainly his greatest exercise in hubris. Since the earliest days of the Comintern, the Soviets had reserved for themselves the right to define who was and was not a Communist. Now the Cubans were usurping that right and applying their own criteria. This was clearly a mutiny.

There is no doubt that Castro was aware of the impact of his words, of the challenge he was presenting to both the Latin American Communists and his Soviet allies. But he found intolerable what he called the lack of "principled positions." His commitment to armed struggle transcended even considerations of discipline and loyalty to the socialist bloc. Such ideological commitment was, in his estimation, the only truly Marxist–Leninist position available:

In the name of what revolutionary principles, reasons, or fundamentals are we obliged to say that the defeatists were right, to say that the rightist capitulationist current was right? In the name of Marxism–Leninism? No! We would never have been able to say they were right in the name of Marxism–Leninism. In the name of the International Communist Movement? Were we perhaps obligated by the fact that it was a question of the leadership of a Communist Party? Is this the conception we are supposed to have of the International Communist Movement? To us the International Communist Move-

43

ment is in the first place just that, a movement of Communists, of revolutionary fighters. And those who are not revolutionary fighters cannot be called Communists.

We conceive of Marxism as revolutionary thinking and action. Those who do not possess a truly revolutionary spirit cannot be called Communists.[62]

In August 1967, the Latin American Solidarity Organization (OLAS) held its first meeting in Havana. The assembly of delegates was heavily weighted in favor of the Castroist guerrilla movements, with the Latin American Communists predominating in only three of the twenty-seven delegations. The slogan of the meeting was, "The Duty of a Revolutionary Is to Make Revolution."[63]

Of the resolutions adopted at the OLAS conference, two were highly significant. In the first, the conference openly condemned the PCV for abandoning revolutionary armed struggle. In the second, the conference criticized "certain socialist countries" for maintaining economic relations with counterrevolutionary governments in Latin America. In his closing speech, Castro made it clear that second resolution was directed at the Soviet Union and said of Moscow's recent moves to reestablish diplomatic and trading relations with Venezuela:

If internationalism exists, if solidarity is a word which deserves to be uttered, the least we can expect from a state within the socialist camp is to offer no financial and technical aid to any of these governments.[64]

THE FUNDAMENTAL CONTRADICTIONS

Castro's problems with his Soviet sponsors had actually been brewing for a long time. As important as Soviet aid was to Cuba's survival, the Cubans still did not hesitate to criticize their Soviet allies when Soviet policies appeared to diverge from Cuban ideals of internationalist behavior. The Cubans apparently saw themselves as the conscience of the socialist bloc. They publicly criticized the Soviets for failing to give adequate aid to Vietnam, for allowing the Sino–Soviet split to divert their attention from the more important struggle against imperialism, for maintaining what Cuba termed exploitative economic relations with Third World states, and for abandoning the Latin American revolution in favor of a selfish improvement of state-to-state relations in the region. The Cubans even refused to sign the joint Soviet–U.S.-sponsored Nuclear Nonproliferation Treaty, claiming that it was intended to perpetuate the global dominance of the superpowers. It was clear that the Cubans included the Soviet Union in their criticism.

Underlying the Cuban–Soviet tensions were fundamental differences in priorities. The most important foreign policy issue for the Cubans—what aficionados of Marxist jargon would call the fundamental contradiction—was the struggle between the imperialist powers and the underdeveloped states.[65] The Soviets, on the other hand, always contended that the fundamental contradiction was between the *socialist* camp and the imperialist camp. In the Soviet view, Third World struggles for national liberation and economic development were merely a subset of the larger struggle for world socialism. In other words, the primary focus of the Cubans was the North–South struggle; to the Soviets, it was the struggle between East and West.

These very different foci inevitably led to very different sets of priorities for the Cubans and their Soviet allies on almost all foreign policy issues. Two issues in particular—in addition to armed struggle—that would strain Cuban–Soviet relations throughout the 1960s were Moscow's commitment to peaceful coexistence and its limited support for Vietnam.

Starting in the early 1960s, the Soviet Union sought to moderate its relations with the United States. In the Soviet view, the threat of mutual annihilation in a nuclear war overshadowed the immediate conflict between the socialist and capitalist systems. At the twentieth Congress of the Soviet Communist Party in 1956, the Soviets proclaimed their commitment to a new program of peaceful coexistence with the capitalist powers. Thereafter, the struggle between Washington and Moscow would be peaceful and conducted solely in the political, economic, and social realms. The Soviets were con-

45

vinced that in the long run their superior economic and social system would triumph—the future of the world was socialism—*if* in the short run a nuclear conflagration could be averted.

The Cubans disagreed. Although they too were committed to avoiding nuclear war, they would not allow its threat to weaken their determination to struggle against world imperialism. The Third World, in the Cuban view, could not afford to wait for the eventual triumph of socialism. *Their* life and death battles were being fought now.

As early as 1962, the Cubans began raising some highly critical questions about the Soviet commitment to peaceful coexistence. In a communiqué issued from Havana during the January 1962 meeting of the International Organization of Journalists, Castro outlined Cuba's dissenting view of peaceful coexistence:

> The policy of peaceful coexistence is coexistence between states. This does not mean coexistence of classes. This policy does not mean coexistence between exploitation and the exploited. It is impossible for peaceful coexistence to exist between the exploited masses of Latin America and the Yankee monopolies. . . . As long as imperialism exists, international class war will exist between the exploited masses and the monopolies.[66]

By 1967, Cuban criticism of peaceful coexistence had become strident and was no longer limited to philosophical carping. Peaceful coexistence had, in the Cuban estimation, become a primary issue of policy. The military struggle against imperialism would not be limited by concerns about peaceful coexistence. In May of that year, the Cuban Communist Party issued the following statement:

> If the concept of peaceful coexistence between states with different social systems does not guarantee the integrity, sovereignty, and independence of all countries alike, large and small, it is essentially opposed to the premises of Proletarian Internationalism. What kind of peace are the Vietnamese enjoying? What kind of coexistence is the U.S. practicing with that country?[67]

At the heart of Cuba's growing opposition to peaceful coexistence was its fear that Moscow's rapprochement with Washington would mean the abandonment of the internationalist—and Cuban—cause.

The 1962 missile crisis planted the seed of doubt over the Soviet commitment. The Soviet decision to withdraw their missiles had badly shaken the Cuban leadership's faith in their Soviet protectors. The crisis and its outcome had made the Cubans painfully aware of their military dependence on the Soviets, and unsure of the fidelity of the Soviet commitment. If the Soviets could pull their missiles out of Cuba because of American pressure, what would stop them from someday pulling out of Cuba altogether? In an editorial written during the missile crisis, Che Guevara exhorted the Soviets to stand by their commitment to Cuba, no matter what the cost:

> What we contend is that we must walk by the path of liberation even when it may cost millions of atomic victims, because in the struggle to the death between two systems the only thing that can be considered is the definitive victory of socialism or its retrogression under the nuclear victory of imperialist aggression.[68]

It is interesting to note that Havana did not publish Guevara's editorial until 1968, when Cuban–Soviet differences over armed struggle had finally come out into the open.

The Cubans were extremely dissatisfied with the outcome of the missile crisis. Although a nuclear war *had* been averted, and the Cubans *had* received a pledge of no invasion from Washington, it was still not enough. In the Castro Government's estimation, the kind of political struggles and political solutions possible within the parameters of peaceful coexistence were not really solutions. They merely postponed what the Cubans believed to be an inevitable confrontation with imperialism. A year after the crisis, Guevara wrote, "There can be no bargaining, no half measures, no partial guarantees of a country's stability. The victory must be total."[69] A month later, Raúl Castro, head of Cuba's armed forces, reiterated Cuba's militant opposition to peaceful coexistence, saying, "We must never establish peaceful coexistence with our enemies."[70]

CUBA: ANOTHER VIETNAM?

Soviet policy toward Vietnam only served to justify Cuba's suspicion of peaceful coexistence and fear of abandonment. The Cubans strongly identified with the Vietnamese. As Castro was fond of pointing out, Vietnam and Cuba had much in common: Both were small states fighting for their national liberation; both were caught in a mortal struggle with the American imperialists; and both were dangerously isolated, situated thousands of miles away from their closest allies in the socialist bloc.

Vietnam was also an important symbol to the Cubans—second only to the Bay of Pigs—of the lengths that even the small and weak would go to win their independence. The phrase *Vietnam Heróico*—Heroic Vietnam—was printed on posters and painted on walls all over Cuba. Schools, clinics, and communes were all named Heroic Vietnam. Vietnamese history was a basic course taught to Cuban schoolchildren. On the Cuban calendar the year 1967 was called the "Year of Heroic Vietnam."

But Vietnam was a negative symbol as well, for it reinforced Cuba's most basic fears of American aggression and Soviet abandonment. As Havana saw it, Moscow's fear of direct confrontation with the United States was leading the Soviets to abandon the Vietnamese to the imperialists.

In a 1967 article addressed to the coordinating bureau of the Tricontinental Conference, Guevara attacked the Soviet Union, arguing that the Vietnam tragedy was the result not only of U.S. aggression, but also of the Soviet refusal to come to Vietnam's defense:

> U.S. imperialism is guilty of aggression—its crimes are enormous and cover the whole world. We already know that, gentlemen! But *this guilt also applies to those who, when the time came for a definition, hesitated to make Vietnam part of the socialist world;* running of course the risk of war on a global scale, but also forcing a decision upon imperialism [emphasis added].[71]

This letter was not an aberration for the Cubans. Throughout the 1960s the Castro regime went to enormous lengths to pressure Moscow to expand its commitment to Vietnam. In speech after speech, meeting after meeting, the Cubans alternately lobbied, pleaded with, and attacked their Soviet allies for their failure to assist Vietnam.

Castro's lectures no doubt embarrassed his Soviet allies. And Castro was no doubt aware of the risks he took. But to the Cubans these differences were not merely ideological exercises, but issues essential to Cuba's survival.

In his 1967 letter to the Tricontinental Conference, Guevara wrote that the Cubans could not afford to ignore what was happening in Vietnam, for Cuba might well be next. "It is not a matter of wishing success to the victim of aggression," Che wrote, "but of sharing his fate; one must accompany him to his death or to his victory."[72]

As basic as their differences were, and as strident as Cuba's challenges became, during the first half of the 1960s Moscow and Havana managed to moderate their conflicts, with Moscow doing much of the compromising. But by 1967, with Cuba's split with the Venezuelan Communists, these differences could no longer be ignored.

THE CUBAN MUTINY

By challenging the Marxist credentials of the Partida Communista de Venezuela (PCV) in 1967, Castro challenged not only the credentials of an individual state party, but also Moscow's criteria for endorsing Communist parties. Ultimately Castro was challenging Moscow's right to dominate the international Communist movement.

Fidel Castro was no doubt aware of the seditious nature of his position on Venezuela, and of the risk he ran. But his outrage over what he saw as the abandonment of the Latin American revolution outweighed any commitment to discipline, unity, or self-interest. A large part of Castro's willingness to take on Moscow was his growing suspicion that the Soviets might be as reformist and defeatist in Latin America as the Latin American parties had been. Not only had the Soviets continued to support the PCV after its decision to abandon armed struggle (and after its public attack on Cuba and Castro), at the same time Moscow was trying to improve its own state-to-state relations with several of the Latin American regimes that Castro was actively trying to overthrow. The Soviets had apparently abandoned their commitment to the Havana Compromise as well.

In his March 1967 speech attacking the PCV, Castro also called the Soviets to account, if somewhat indirectly. In the guise of condemning Colombia for jailing several Communist party leaders, Castro criticized Soviet overtures to Bogotá as a tacit endorsement of its repressive tactics:

> An unmistakable proof of the lack of independence of those [Latin American] governments is to be found in the recent case of Colombia, where at 6 AM, a few days ago, because of a guerrilla attack against a train, they arrested the General Secretary of the Communist Party of Colombia and all the leaders of that Party . . . *They did not hesitate a bit because at the very moment a delegation of high Soviet officials were present for the signing of a commercial, cultural and financial agreement with the Lleras Restrepo government* [emphasis added]. . . .[73]

When it became clear to Castro how far off course the socialist bloc and the international movement had strayed, he first tried to redirect his comrades with brotherly criticism, reminding them of their commitment to, and responsibility for, promoting Third World revolution. But by the time he split with Venezuela, Castro had clearly grown impatient with the deviations of the bloc. In the same speech, Castro testily reminded his comrades that the socialist bloc was:

> . . . not a church, it is not a religious sect or a Masonic lodge that obliges us to hallow any weakness, any deviation, that obliges us to follow the policy of a mutual admiration society with all kinds of reformists and pseudo-revolutionaries.[74]

By August 1967, it was clear that Castro had lost all hope of ever reforming the socialist bloc. At the opening meeting of the Latin American Solidarity Organization, Castro announced that OLAS had become the new International, the new center of revolutionary struggle. The old Moscow-based International had been left behind:

We must say that as a Marxist–Leninist party we belong to the OLAS, as a Marxist–Leninist party we do not belong to another group in the revolutionary movement, but to an organization which includes all true revolutionaries.[75]

These were brave words for the Cuban leader who, though he could claim organizational prominence in Latin America, was still irrevocably linked to the Soviet Union for military defense and economic survival. But then those were brave times. Che was fighting in Bolivia. The OLAS and the Tricontinental Conference seemed to offer new organizational vigor to the progressive Third World. And Cuba would be the head of it all. But as we shall see, subsequent events proved this vision wrong—particularly the death of Guevara in the Bolivian hills.

The Real Fight

Havana's ideological commitment to armed struggle was so strong that it was willing to stake everything on it, including its alliance with the Soviet Union. Yet Cuba's actual military presence in the region was still very modest. According to a 1967 study done for the House Foreign Affairs Committee, only four "instances of direct Cuban support to insurgent groups" in Latin America could be proved.[76] The four instances reported by the study were the following: In November 1963, several tons of weapons and ammunition were discovered in Venezuela and traced to Cuba. Throughout 1966, large quantities of small arms were sent to Guatemalan guerrillas by a Cuban support group based in Mexico. In July of that same year, an estimated twenty to thirty armed guerrillas landed on the coast of Venezuela in a Cuban-owned boat. In May 1967, another landing of Cuban-trained guerrillas, this time including several Cuban army officers, was attempted in Venezuela. Two Cuban army officers were captured and another two were killed.

The historian and journalist Richard Gott has described several other instances of direct Cuban involvement in Latin American insurgency. In May 1963, between fifteen and thirty-five Cuban-trained Peruvian students tried unsuccessfully to invade Peru from

Bolivia and establish a *foco*. In September 1963, Che Guevara may have participated in Jorge Masetti's failed attempt to invade Argentina from Bolivia. There is no doubt that three Cubans accompanied Masetti on this expedition, one of whom later joined Che in his Bolivian *foco*.[77] In mid-1967, a small band of Nicaraguan guerrillas took to the hills to begin their struggle against the Somoza regime. These early Sandinistas were said to have been trained by the Cubans.[78] The best-known Cuban attempt to export revolution to Latin America also took place in 1967, when Guevara established his Bolivian *foco*.

Cuba's material aid to the guerrilla movements was limited as well, according to a 1968 study conducted for the Senate Foreign Relations Committee. In contrast to early U.S. fears, the Soviet Union did not give Havana a blank check for its subversive activities, or for its support of guerrillas in Latin America. When the Soviets did send aid to Latin America, they tended to bypass the Cubans and to establish direct relations with cadres they could trust and control. Even then the funds and arms were limited. As a result, guerrilla groups in Venezuela, Guatemala, and Colombia, despite their strong endorsements from the Cubans, were forced to rely on kidnapping and robbery to raise money to support their struggles.[79]

Over the years, much has been made of the threat of Cuba's serving as a base for continental subversion. According to the same Senate study, Cuba has invested the most in its on-island programs for guerrilla training, political indoctrination, and propaganda. Once again, however, closer analysis reveals these programs to have been much smaller and less well organized than Washington feared, or than Cuban propaganda seemed to claim. Cuba's most significant investment was the building of a short-wave radio transmitting tower outside Havana in May 1961. Since then, Radio Havana has broadcast a steady stream of propaganda to Latin America and around the world. The programs are similar in format and intent to those of the Voice of America.[80]

There has been much confusion as well about the size of Cuba's guerrilla training programs. During the 1960s, official U.S. reports estimated that anywhere from 1,000 to 2,500 Latin American radicals were traveling to Cuba each year for ideological and military training—some 10,000 to 25,000 guerrillas in all.[81] According to Congressional testimony from the Defense Intelligence Agency in 1971, however, these numbers were greatly exaggerated. Only an estimated 2,500 Latin American leftists had been trained in Cuba during the entire period from 1961 to 1969.[82] Moreover, there has been no attempt, at least publicly, to evaluate the effectiveness of these programs in persuading graduates to stage revolutions, lean toward the socialist path or the socialist bloc, or teach the techniques for seizing power. A simple review of the failures of the Cuban-manned and Cuban-trained *focos* throughout the 1960s suggests that these training centers were not effective.

It is undeniable that internationalism and, particularly, the export of revolution were important—indeed a first priority—for Cuba throughout much of the 1960s. Not only did the export of revolution dominate Cuban propaganda and ideological statements, but the Cubans made some real and documentable sacrifices for the sake of their beliefs. First, the Cubans lost their beloved hero, Che Guevara, to the cause of continental revolution. In addition, the Cubans sacrificed the possibility of any diplomatic gains in Latin America. And, most tellingly, the Cubans were willing to place great strains on their relations with the Latin American Communist parties and the Soviet Union for the sake of continental revolution.

Given the strength of Havana's commitment to the export of revolution, it must be asked, Why were Cuba's actual attempts to implement its ideological commitments so limited? The Cubans suffered under some significant material constraints. Their economy was weak. There was very little foreign exchange. Cuba had no armaments industry and only a limited transport capability. Havana simply did not, and does not, have the resources needed for an aggressive foreign policy on the scale that its ideological commitments suggest. The current size and success of Cuba's overseas commitments in Africa are due to a great extent to the close integration of Cuban and Soviet efforts, particularly at arms supply and transport. During the 1960s, especially in Latin America, the Cubans could not depend on the Russians to provide either transport or arms to support guerrilla movements that Moscow refused to endorse.

Another major limitation of Cuban policy in Latin America was the resistance of the radical groups to accepting Cuban aid or following Cuban direction. The Bolivian Communist Party refused to send either men or arms to Che's *foco*. For this reason Guevara never had more than sixty guerrillas. If Castro's charges are true, the Venezuelan Communist Party not only rejected the Castroite guerrillas, but actually conspired against them.

Even the Castro-style guerrilla movements voiced strong doubts about Cuban domination. As early as 1966, Douglas Bravo, the leader of the Venezuelan guerrilla FALN, which was a favorite of Castro's—(Debray had described the FALN as the prototype guerrilla movement for Latin America)—questioned the applicability of the Cuban model to the rest of Latin America's armed struggles:

> Today, for example, it seems that what happened in Cuba is unlikely to be repeated in exactly the same way. Liberation movements cannot count on the factor of surprise nor on the expectant attitudes of former times. . . . In this situation it is clearly superficial to think of the Latin American struggle in terms other than those of the so-called long war. To think that the Cuban model can be copied in Venezuela is to overlook the particular conditions of the country, to act blindly without any kind of proper analysis of the situation.[83]

In September 1970, four guerrilla leaders of the Guatemalan Rebel Army Forces complained of unrest within their organization "because of the presence of Cuban fighters who are replacing Guatemalans in positions of command." [84]

Retreat from Revolution

The year 1968 was officially Cuba's Year of the Heroic Guerrilla Fighter. As it turned out, it was also the year that Cuba and the rest of Latin America questioned and reevaluated the efficacy of armed struggle and guerrilla warfare. The history of guerrilla movements in Latin America had been one of repeated failure. By 1967, when Guevara's presence in Bolivia had become world news, the guerrilla movements in Peru and Argentina had been wiped out, and the movements in Venezuela, Colombia, and Guatemala were on the run—under attack from increasingly strong counterinsurgency forces, and wracked by internal conflict and dissent. The establishment of the Latin American Solidarity Organization in Havana and the announcement of Guevara's mission to Bolivia were intended to succor these movements and resurrect the hopes of radicals around the world—and they did so temporarily. But the tragic outcome of the Bolivian *foco* and the disintegration of OLAS raised major questions in Cuba and throughout much of the hemisphere as to the prospects for guerrilla warfare in Latin America.

The hopes of Che's last *foco* symbolized the hopes of all the *focos* that had come before. Moreover, its failure was more responsible than any other single event for the Cuban decision to retreat from the export of revolution.

Guevara's Bolivian mission was actually a departure from earlier internationalist missions.[85] Its goal was to ignite a continental, rather than just a national revolution. The original plan, devised in Havana around the time of the 1966 Tricontinental Conference, was for Guevara to begin the struggle in his home country of Argentina, and revive the failed Masetti expedition of 1963. While in Argentina, Guevara was to set up close contacts with Leonel Brizola's revolutionaries in Brazil and the Peruvian revolutionaries under the leadership of El Chino. All three groups were to use Argentina as a haven and a training ground. In the spring of 1966 the plan was changed. Bolivia, and not Argentina, was to be site of the first *foco* and the headquarters for the continental revolution. From there the struggle would spread north to Peru and south to Argentina.

In November 1966, Che arrived in Bolivia. From the beginning, the major problem confronting Guevara was recruiting men for his army. Guevara had brought seventeen guerrillas with him from Cuba—mainly personal friends. Finding Bolivians proved more difficult. The Bolivian Communist Party refused to commit itself to any adventure that was not under Bolivian control. In the first months, the traditionally radical Bolivian miners seemed willing to support Guevara with money and propaganda, but were forced to renege after Bolivian President René Barrientos sent the army into the mines. From the start, the peasantry in Bolivia was wary of, and often hostile toward, the Guevaraist forces. As a result, Guevara's *foco* never grew much larger than sixty men and women.

For the first four months, Guevara's *foco* wandered the Bolivian hills, conducting drills on the techniques of guerrilla warfare and jungle survival. At the end of March, the guerrillas had their first military victory, ambushing a small army patrol of about forty soldiers. The guerrillas had not intended to engage in battle so soon, but their position had been betrayed to the army by local peasants and they had no choice. Six Bolivians were killed and seven were captured, including a major and a captain. No guerrillas were hurt. In the second week of April the guerrillas fought their second major battle. This too was a success: Eight Bolivian soldiers and two officers were killed and thirty captured. One Cuban was killed.

After the second battle the Barrientos regime and its American supporters began to take Guevara's *foco* seriously. In April the United States began to send weapons, helicopters, and advisers to Bolivia. Five U.S. military experts were sent from Panama to establish a counterinsurgency training school, where some twenty U.S. Green Berets were to train 600 Bolivian recruits and a few Cuban exiles. At the same time, the Bolivian Government declared a state of martial law in southeastern Bolivia and began to round up known members of Bolivia's many leftist groups. Whether or not Guevara was ready, the guerrilla war was about to begin in earnest.

From April to October, the guerrillas continued their hit-and-run existence, growing weaker by the day as the Bolivian army, under American tutelage, grew stronger. On October 8, 1967, Guevara's *foco*, now pared down to seventeen men, was finally surrounded in the Quebrada del Yurro canyon near the Rio Grande in southern Bolivia. During the fighting, Che was wounded in the leg and captured. A day later, on the orders of President Barrientos, he was executed. Of the seventeen guerrillas with Che in the Quebrada del Yurro, only five survived—three Cubans and two Bolivians. The Bolivians remained in the country, while the Cubans were smuggled across the *altiplano* into Chile and from there flown to

Havana, where they confirmed the destruction of the *foco* and Guevara's death.

The following summer the Castro Government released Guevara's Bolivian diaries.[86] Guevara's account of the struggle read quite differently from Debray's romantic *Revolution in the Revolution?* The hardships of the mountains, instead of cleansing and hardening the guerrillas, Guevara wrote, had worn them down. Instead of succoring the guerrillas, the peasants had turned their backs and ultimately betrayed them. The Bolivian army, with the help of the United States, had quickly learned the techniques of guerrilla warfare, and how to counter them. The story told in Guevara's diaries is one of commitment and bravery, but also one of frustration and ultimate defeat.

Havana's immediate response to Che's death was to deny that it would have any effect on the export of revolution. In his eulogy of Che, Castro directly confronted those who saw the revolutionary's death as an indictment of the strategy of armed struggle:

> Now after his heroic and glorious death some attempt to deny the truth or value of his concepts, his guerrilla theories. The master may die—especially when he is a virtuoso in an art as dangerous as revolutionary struggle—but what will surely never die is the art to which he dedicated his life. . . .[87]

Despite these words, it was eight years before another Cuban revolutionary would shed his blood in overseas combat—and then, it would be thousands of miles away in Angola.

THE OTHER INTERNATIONALISMS

The export of revolution to Latin America was not the only form of Cuban internationalism during the 1960s. All the while Havana was smuggling guns into Venezuela and guerrillas into Bolivia, the Castro Government was also sending arms and advisers to a variety of left-leaning states and movements throughout Africa. At the same time, at the summit meetings of the Third World, Havana was promoting still another diplomatic form of internationalism: a new view of Third World development based on ideals of equity and autonomy for small states, to be won through aggressive organization and bargaining. Havana's commitment to Third World development was in many ways as radical and as challenging to the traditional domination of the superpowers—in both Washington and Moscow—as any of its commitments to armed struggle.

While Cuba's often meager attempts to export revolution to Latin America were a source of obsessive concern in the United States, these other aspects of Cuban internationalism received almost no attention. There were no scholarly works, no official reports, and no Senate testimony on these other Cuban threats. This is particularly ironic in the case of Cuba's African involvements, which were substantially greater than any of its involvements in Latin America. Over a thousand Cuban advisers were sent to Africa during the 1960s, as compared to several hundred to Latin America for the same period.

There are several reasons for Washington's myopia. First, Africa was not a major foreign policy priority for the United States during the 1960s. Cuba's African commitments were either overlooked or ignored by American policy analysts as outside their sphere of influence or concern. As for Havana's radical diplomacy, Washington tended, at the time, to dismiss all Third World diplomatic efforts as merely symbolic. The days of OPEC and the North–South summits were not even imagined during the 1960s. Washington also could not grasp the idea that Castro might be taking diplomatic initiatives that were independent of, and in contradiction to, its Soviet allies. It was not until the early 1970s that Washington policy makers acknowledged the existence of a Sino–Soviet split and its potential utility for the United States. The notion of competing Cuban–Soviet interests is still not recognized today.

This myopia notwithstanding, these other aspects of Proletarian Internationalism were still important. Havana's radical ideas on Third World development, and attempts to promote them diplomatically, had become, by the late 1960s, a major source of tension in the Cuban–Soviet alliance. More recently, Havana's commitment to North–South bargaining and the redress of international disparities of wealth, resources, and power have become central concerns of such Third World organizations as the UN's Group of 77 and the Organization of African Unity. Cuba's early African involvements, in turn, lay the foundations for the commitment of some 35,000 Cuban troops to Africa by the mid- to late 1970s. Finally, both the African involvements and Havana's diplomatic initiatives had become by the mid-1970s the basis for the Castro regime's accommodation with even the most moderate Third World states, and the end of Cuba's decade of diplomatic isolation.

A Conducive Environment

Havana's interest in Africa has baffled many Americans. It seemed as though the only explanation for why a small country like Cuba, situated in the Caribbean thousands of miles away from Africa's shores, should choose to send some 18,000 combat troops to Angola was because it was acting as a Soviet pawn.[88] In fact, many purely Cuban interests were served by the African commitments. No better proof of this is the fact that the Castro Government's Africa policy predates its alliance with the Soviets, and was conducted independent of Soviet policies in Africa during much of the 1960s.

The first basis for Cuba's interest in Africa was racial. One need only walk the streets of Havana and look at the faces of the Cuban people—over 60 percent are "colored" of some sort—or listen to the music of Mongo Santamaria and his Afro–Cuban band, to realize the strength of the affinity between Cuba and Africa. More immediately, the Cuban revolutionaries felt a strong political identification with the growing number of guerrilla anticolonial movements in Africa. In many ways, these African liberation movements had more in common with the Castro regime than those in Latin America; in the early 1960s Africa was truly on the verge of a continental revolution.

This initial Cuban–African affinity was reinforced by developments of the 1960s. As guerrilla movement after guerrilla movement failed in Latin America, the FLN in Algeria, the PAIGC in Guinea, FRELIMO in Mozambique all successfully threw off the yoke of colonialism. Also, while the social democrats of Latin America were violently overthrown and replaced by rightist military juntas, leaders like Ahmed Ben Bella of Algeria, Sékou Touré of Guinea, and

59

Kwame Nkrumah of Ghana seemed (at the time) to be successfully consolidating their power.

As Cuba became increasingly isolated from its neighbors in Latin America and more dependent on the Soviet Union, Havana's diplomatic relations with the African states became its only connections outside the socialist bloc. Having lost the OAS as a platform for denouncing American imperialism and propounding their visions of an independent Third World, the Cubans turned to meetings of the Organization of African Unity and the Afro Asian People's Solidarity Organization.

Cuba's policy toward Africa in the 1960s was not that different from its early policy toward Latin America. Havana sought to promote revolution by supporting and aiding guerrilla movements while at the same time establishing more normal diplomatic relations and foreign aid programs with the progressive or social democratic governments. In Africa, unlike Latin America, this dual policy was successful. To understand why, one must consider the very different political conditions in the two continents.

First, conditions in Africa were more conducive to the kind of revolution the Cubans were promoting. In Africa, which did not begin to decolonize until the 1960s, the opposition was easily identified and organized against. Moreover, in Africa the constraints on revolution and progressive development—as well as Cuban participation—were weaker. There the Cubans did not have to contend with U.S. opposition, whether in the form of alternative aid, diplomatic isolation, or active counterinsurgency.

The Castro Government was also far less constrained in Africa by its Soviet allies. Cuban and Soviet analysts had very different expectations for Africa. As Cuba became increasingly committed to fostering what it saw as revolutionary conditions, the Soviets became equally disenchanted with prospects for revolution on the African continent. They focused their African initiatives on improving state-to-state relations.[89] While a similar divergence was the source of major frictions in Cuban–Soviet relations in Latin America, it was not a divisive factor in Africa. Because none of the African countries had active Communist parties, Cuban attempts to export revolution did not threaten any united fronts. In addition, there were no U.S. interests in Africa of the sort that caused the Cuban–Soviet tensions in Latin America. Cuban policies in Africa in the 1960s did not threaten détente.

By 1975, however, the United States had changed its mind on this issue. In that year Cuban policies in Africa became a major issue in the negotiations for a Strategic Arms Limitation Treaty (SALT). But by then Moscow had come to share Havana's analysis of conditions in Africa, and was too committed to the Angolan struggle to restrain its Cuban allies, or back down itself.

Thus, throughout most of the 1960s, Cuba had remarkable freedom of movement in Africa, and equal success in promoting its dual program: supporting guerrilla movements and building diplomatic relations with Africa's growing number of progressive regimes. This is not to suggest that Africa was completely open to the Cubans during the 1960s. Even without Washington's opposition, and with Moscow's tacit endorsement, the Cubans still had to contend with Portuguese and French interests and their well-developed counterinsurgency techniques and colonial control. In Angola, for example, despite aid from both the Soviet Union and Cuba, the MPLA won independence in 1975 only because of Portugal's decision to withdraw after its left-leaning coup, not from the success of almost two decades of guerrilla war.

African Internationalism

In 1960, Castro sent Africa its first aid shipment: arms and medical personnel for the Algerian National Liberation Front (FLN), led by Ahmed Ben Bella. The next year Cuba established its first permanent overseas military mission, a guerrilla training camp in northern Ghana. In 1962 the Cubans set up a second training camp in the newly independent Algeria.[90]

The first Cuban combat troops arrived in 1963. In early October, a Cuban merchant ship carrying small arms, tanks, and about fifty military technicians left Havana for the Algerian port of Oran on a routine aid mission. While this shipment was en route, war broke out between Algeria and Morocco over a long-contested border.

It was then that Havana apparently decided to send its first combat troops abroad to rescue the Ben Bella Government. A second and third arms shipment and a battalion of *tanquistas,* or tank troops, arrived in Oran in the last week in October. At the same time, a Cuban air transport carrying an undetermined number of troops landed at Oran. During October 1963, Castro sent a total of three to four hundred men as well as forty tanks, field artillery, and mortars to his Algerian allies.

According to reports filed at the time, the Cuban troops were never intended to, nor did they, fight Moroccans in the field. Their job was to train the Algerians to use their new equipment. The Cuban troops remained in Algeria to complete the training for at least two months after the signing of the October 30, 1963, ceasefire with Morocco.

Moscow's role in the Algerian–Moroccan border dispute has never been clearly established. In the first week of October, about the same time the first Cuban shipment left Havana, the Algerians and Soviets signed a loan agreement for industrial aid. That agreement included a promise to deliver more than 150 tanks sometime in 1964. Yet it is doubtful that the Cuban aid was sent as an advance shipment on the Soviet loan. During 1963 Cuban–Soviet relations were particularly strained in the aftermath of the missile crisis, and it is unlikely that the Castro regime would have willingly followed Soviet orders to part with such large numbers of men and material at the time.[91] Rather, it seems as though the Cubans took the initiative to send aid to Algeria. Algeria's FLN was the first African liberation movement to receive Cuban aid. And it is not surprising that the Castro regime would take further steps to ensure the survival of Ben Bella's regime, once it had successfully gained power. It must also be remembered that it was about this time that the Cubans sent their first arms shipment to Douglas Bravo's FALN in Venezuela, in direct defiance of Venezuela's Communist Party and its Moscow supporters. This was a very independent time for the Cubans.

During 1964 Havana made several diplomatic overtures to Africa. Most notably, Havana sent a major delegation to the Second Conference of Nonaligned Nations in Cairo that October. At that meeting,

Cuban President Osvaldo Dorticos committed his country to the support of international liberation struggles, saying:

> I can assure you that the people of Cuba will always be at the vanguard of the struggle, whatever the dangers and difficulties it might entail, because it is a nation of men and women who in the most tense moments of their history have responded to the call: Patria o Muerte. Venceremos![92]

In December 1964, as the Cubans were signing the Havana Compromise agreement on armed struggle in Latin America, Che Guevara began a tour of Africa. During his three-month trip he visited every left-leaning country, including Algeria, Ghana, Congo-Brazzaville, Guinea, Mali, Dahomey, Tanzania, and the United Arab Republic.[93] To each he brought the same message: The Third World states must band together politically, economically, and militarily to fight imperialism and colonialism. According to Che, Africa "was one of the most important, if not the most important, battlefields against all forms of exploitation in the world."[94]

One of Guevara's reasons for this tour was to promote the idea of Third World economic integration. Cuba was becoming increasingly isolated in its own hemisphere and needed alternative trading partners. In Ghana, Che spoke of Africa's wealth and the potential for joint development:

> Cuba has sugar, cattle and nickel; Ghana cacao, Algeria oil. If were all to unite [we could get] the most sophisticated derivative of each product and large industrial combines could be formed that would serve a substantial group of countries.[95]

Despite Guevara's ambitious vision, the African states were by and large unimpressed. Of the seven countries Guevara visited, only two—Ghana and Mali—signed a joint communiqué with the Cubans. None signed a trade agreement.

In his visit to Congo-Brazzaville, Guevara met with the leaders of the liberation movements of Mozambique, Portuguese Guinea, and Angola. Given subsequent events, it appears that Guevara promised aid to all three movements. The Cubans began sending arms to the MPLA in Congo-Brazzaville in 1965 and to Guinea in 1966.

63

Cuban instructors are said to have trained Mozambican FRELIMO guerrillas at their Tanzanian bases some time in the late 1960s as well.

As noted earlier, 1965 was a critical year for Cuba's support of armed struggle. In February Castro announced that the Cubans were ready to send troops abroad to aid liberation movements wherever they were fighting.[96] Most of Latin America, however, was off-limits, given Cuba's continued adherence to the 1964 Havana Compromise, so the Cubans turned their attention to Africa. In April 1965, Che Guevara resigned his posts in the Cuban government as well as his Cuban citizenship and left for Congo-Brazzaville to join the guerrillas fighting against the regime of Moise Tshombe in what is now called Zaire. Guevara was joined in July 1965 by 200 other Cuban fighters. Tshombe's regime was overthrown by a coup led by Joseph Mobuto, now called Mobutu Sesse Seko.

The Congolese guerrillas then asked the Cubans to withdraw so that an armistice with the new regime could be signed. Soon after, Guevara left Africa. His whereabouts remained secret until October 1966, when he surfaced in Bolivia. But Guevara's band of internationalist fighters remained in Africa and set up military missions where Angolan and Guinean guerrillas were trained to fight the Portuguese.

A Conservative Role

Africa experienced major instability in 1965 and 1966. The governments of Ben Bella in Algeria and Nkrumah in Ghana were overthrown in military coups. As a result, Havana lost not only two of its earliest and closest allies in Africa, but also both of its guerrilla training bases. These coups, coming so soon after those that deposed friendly regimes in Argentina and Peru in 1962 and Brazil and Bolivia in 1964, demonstrated graphically to Havana just how vulnerable progressive regimes were to military takeover. Castro thus turned his full attention to protecting his remaining allies in Africa.

After the coups in Algeria and Ghana, the Cubans moved their guerrilla bases to Congo-Brazzaville and Guinea and set about training those governments to resist military takeover. The Cubans sent an estimated 700 military advisers to Congo-Brazzaville in 1965. These troops first served as a personal presidential guard to Congolese President Alphonse Massemba-Debat. In addition, they created and trained a popular militia from members of Massemba-Debat's ruling party, the MNR. This militia was to be a loyal counterweight to the Congolese military.

The events of 1966 suggest that the Cubans did not act a moment too soon. In late June the Congolese armed forces revolted against the MNR's efforts to politicize the army. The coup was defeated by the Cuban guard and the Cuban-trained militia. As a result, the Cubans stepped up their training of the militia. By October 1966, the number of Cuban troops in Congo-Brazzaville had been increased to 1,000 men—about half the size of the entire regular armed forces.

This Cuban mission continued in Congo-Brazzaville until 1968, when Massemba-Debat requested a gradual withdrawal. Resentment within the army of the Cuban presence—on an institutional as well as a nationalist level—had continued unabated since the original coup attempt. The withdrawal was intended to reduce these tensions. Despite these efforts, Messemba-Debat was overthrown in August 1968. A smaller Cuban advisory group remained for another three years, serving the new President, Marien Nugouabi, until they were finally withdrawn in 1971. Throughout this period, Cuban advisers continued to train Angolan guerrillas for the MPLA at their base at Dolisie on the Congo–Cabinda border.

The 1965 and 1966 coups apparently alarmed Guinean President Sékou Touré, the longest ruling of Africa's progressive leaders (he first took power in Guinea in 1958). Nkrumah's decision to seek refuge in Guinea after the Ghanaian coup may well have brought home the growing danger of military overthrow. Thus in the spring of 1966, Sékou Touré asked for Havana's aid in building a popular militia in Guinea. Touré also requested his own Cuban presidential guard, which still exists today. At about the same time, Cuban advisers for the PAIGC arrived in Guinea to establish a guerrilla training base.

The death of Che Guevara in 1967 and the resulting inward turn to Cuban policies apparently affected Cuban policy in Africa as well as in Latin America. After Guinea, no new missions were established in Africa. By 1968 the number of men at the Congo-Brazzaville missions had dropped to fewer than 200. This left only the Guinean advisers, the Cuban guard, and a small group of military advisers working with FRELIMO in Mozambique. The Cuban presence in Africa continued at this reduced level until Havana's 1975 decision to commit combat troops to Angola.

DEVELOPMENT AND DIPLOMACY

The Castro Government's commitment to Third World liberation did not end with victory in the guerrilla struggle. It included the problems faced by the newly independent and developing states as they sought to overcome colonially imposed poverty and underdevelopment. From their own experience the Cubans knew that the task of building a truly independent political system and a self-sustaining economy was many times harder than winning a revolution.

Guevara's address to the Afro Asian People's Solidarity Organization in Algiers in February 1965 was a milestone in the diplomatic promotion of Proletarian Internationalism. Che began his speech by calling for the defeat of imperialism, and by committing Cuba and all socialist countries to support that struggle:

> There are no frontiers in this struggle to the death. We cannot remain indifferent in the face of what occurs in any part of the world. A victory for any country against imperialism is our victory, just as any country's defeat is a defeat for all. The practice of proletarian internationalism is not only a duty for the peoples who struggle for a better future, it is also an inescapable necessity. . . .[97]

Then came the substance of the speech: the economic development of the newly liberated countries, and the responsibilities of the socialist bloc. He pointed out that for each country the defeat of imperialism was really a two-stage process. First, it was necessary to overthrow colonial control with armed or political struggle. But then, to be truly free, a country must also overcome the backwardness

66

and poverty imposed by colonialism. This second task, according to Guevara, was even harder than the first. The costs of development were high, the resources of the liberated states were low, and there were many temptations to backslide into *neo*colonial relationships with the capitalist states.

Although the picture as Guevara painted it was bleak, there seemed to be some hope for the liberated states in the form of support and aid from the socialist bloc. "The development of countries which now begin the road of liberation," Che declared, "*must be underwritten by the socialist countries.*"[98] The model for these relations would be Cuba's incredibly generous alliance with the Soviet Union. This was an old theme. From the earliest days of the revolution, when Cuba first embraced the Soviet Union as its protector and defender, the Castro regime had insisted that what the Soviets were doing for Cuba they would also do for the rest of the Third World.

But it is clear from Che's speech the Cubans were not so sure their Soviet allies would see it that way. Although Guevara's audience in Algiers was a group of Third World states, his speech was clearly intended to convince the socialist bloc, and particularly the Soviet Union, that it *was* indeed their responsibility to foot the bill for Third World development. Che began with just such a pitch, reminding the Soviets that:

Each time a country liberates itself . . . it is a defeat for the world imperialist system. . . . Therefore the socialist countries are vitally interested in making these separations effective, and it is our international duty, a duty determined by the ideology that guides us, to contribute our efforts to make this liberation as rapid and thorough as possible.[99]

Guevara then went on to discuss what this responsibility would actually cost the socialist bloc—it would not be cheap. He first called on the Soviet Union to readjust its trade relations with the underdeveloped states and, in particular, to abandon what he called "exploitative economic relations" based on the free market. Like any good dependency theorist, he knew that these relations were anything but mutually beneficial. Due to the inelasticity of primary product prices and the spiraling costs of finished goods, the Third World states exchanging raw materials for the Soviet Union's industrial goods would inevitably end up with the short end of the stick:

> We believe that with this spirit the responsibility of aiding dependent countries ought to be faced and that there should be no more talk of developing "mutually beneficial" trade based on prices that the law of value and unequal international trade imposes on backward countries. How can mutual benefit mean selling at world prices raw materials which cost unlimited sweat and suffering to the backward countries and buying at world market prices the machines produced in the large automated factories of today?

> If we establish that type of relationship between the two groups of nations we must agree that the socialist countries are to a certain extent accomplices of imperialist exploitation. The socialist countries have the moral duty of liquidating their tacit complicity with the exploiting countries of the west.[100]

Guevara suggested instead that the trade policies of the socialist countries should clearly foster the development of Third World economies. Among the adjustments required would be price supports for raw materials, direct Soviet investment in nascent industries in the developing states, long-term credits repayable in goods rather than scarce foreign exchange, and a provision of appropriate technology and technical know-how, free of charge. Che completed his list of what the socialist bloc should supply with a final reference to armed struggle. For this the socialist bloc must provide arms free of charge to any people fighting imperialism:

> The aspect of armed struggle to achieve liberation from oppression of a political power must be approached according to the rules of Proletarian Internationalism. If it is absurd to imagine that in a socialist country which is at war a factory manager would demand a guarantee of payment before shipping the tanks from the factory to the front lines, it is no less absurd to inquire about the possibility of payment by a people who fight for their liberation or need those arms to defend their liberty. Arms cannot be merchandise in our

world. They should be delivered without any cost whatsoever and in quantities determined by their need and availability to those people who ask for them in order to direct their fight against the common enemy.[101]

Che finished by saying that the socialist bloc should do all this for the Third World states with no political strings attached, because it was in the interest of the socialist states to liberate any and all Third World states from the grips of imperialism. A defeat for imperialism—no matter what its political color—was a victory for socialism. In the long run, all the liberated states could be expected to turn willingly and freely to the socialist bloc, just as Cuba had. There was no reason to pressure them now.

This did not mean that the Third World states had no responsibilities. To merit such assistance, Guevara said, these states must be truly committed to ending the exploitation of man against man. Specifically, they must be willing to embark on the path of building socialism by placing the means of production in the hands of the state. Moreover, he said, those states receiving aid from the socialist bloc should not fall prey to the temptation of playing one superpower off the other. They must turn to the socialist bloc with serious respect and commitment if they hoped to progress beyond colonialism and neocolonialism.

This quid pro quo was not as crass as it might at first seem. Although Che was explicit about how the socialist bloc should aid the developing states, the responsibilities of the Third World recipients were much more ephemeral. There were no formulas to follow. That much the Cubans had learned from their own revolution. It was enough that each state should *want* to end exploitation. The rest would follow naturally:

We did not embark on the path that would end in Communism with all our steps foreseen. It was not a logical product of a predetermined ideology. The truths of socialism and the crude facts of imperialism forged our people and taught them the path which we have now consciously adopted. The peoples of Africa and Asia who move toward their definite liberation will have to take the same path sooner or later, even though today they qualify their socialism. There is only one valid definition of socialism—the abolition of exploitation of man by man.[102]

Guevara took an enormous gamble in his speech at Algiers by criticizing Soviet trade policies and demanding increased aid for the Third World. But the Cuban leadership apparently thought it was a risk worth taking—and not altogether for altruistic reasons. By 1965, it had become painfully clear to the Castro Government that its early optimism over the ease of industrial development was unrealistic. After three years of major investment in an industrial infrastructure, the Cubans were being forced to back off from heavy industry and reinvest in their hated sugar industry. Industrialization simply was not working, and Cuba's neglect of its agricultural sector—the only capital-producing sector of the economy—was pushing the Cubans deeper into debt. By 1965, it had become clear that industrial self-sufficiency, if the possibility even existed, was many years off. In the meantime, dependence on the socialist bloc could not be avoided.

The Cubans learned a disheartening lesson from their economic experience: No matter how well motivated, developing states could not succeed without the capital, technology, or know-how of the developed world. Actually this conclusion was not all that different from what Castro had been saying in Buenos Aires when he proposed his Alliance for Progress-type scheme in 1959. The difference was that now the Cubans had completely rejected the idea of Western aid, for Cuba or any other Third World state. Neocolonialism and dependency were traps, and the developing states could avoid them successfully only by cutting themselves off completely from the capitalist system.

In Algiers in 1965, Guevara made this argument subtly, warning the African states against the temptations of trying to play one bloc off against the other. For those states that still insisted on maintaining relations with the capitalist world, Che said, they must be careful and militant in order to insist on the "establishment of new relations based on equality . . . It is time to throw off the yoke, impose renegotiation of oppressive external debts, and force the imperialists to abandon their bases of aggression."[103]

By the time of the Tricontinental Conference a year later, Havana had abandoned all pretense of negotiating with the West. Imperialism, capitalism, and, specifically, the United States were condemned as the number one enemy and cause of underdevelopment in the Third World. With such an enemy, negotiation was impossible—the only appropriate response was direct opposition and struggle, and the complete support of the socialist bloc.

Cuba's position on development, like many of Havana's ideological stands of the 1960s, was clearly oriented toward furthering the interests and autonomy of the Third World states. And like many of Cuba's ideological positions formulated in the context of the North–South dichotomy, Cuba's position on development inevitably differed from, if not directly conflicted with, Soviet positions on the issue.

Certainly Cuba's advice that the Third World states cut all ties with the West and transfer their allegiance to the socialist bloc could be seen as bolstering Moscow's international standing *vis à vis* both Washington and Peking. But at the same time, the Cubans were promising far more than the Soviets were either willing or able to give. By its own admission, Moscow simply could not afford to underwrite development throughout the Third World the way it was underwriting Cuba's development no matter what Guevara, Castro, or anyone said about internationalist responsibilities. Cuba and its Soviet allies managed to avoid open disagreement for a while. But by 1968, the issue of Moscow's responsibilities to the Third World—in terms of both military and economic aid—was threatening to destroy the Cuban–Soviet alliance.

Containing the Threat:
The Origins of
U. S.–Cuban Hostilities

IT is not surprising to find a country as tiny and poor as Cuba obsessed with an enemy located just ninety miles from its shores—especially as that enemy is the most powerful country in the world.

What is surprising is that over the years the United States has been equally obsessed with Cuba. Castro's revolution challenged everything that Washington held sacred. The new domestic policies—in particular, land reform and the nationalization of foreign (mostly American) enterprises—were seen as an attack on the sanctity of private property and a dangerous precedent for the region. This sentiment prompted some extremist senators and congressmen to call for Castro's overthrow as early as the spring of 1959.

But it was the revolution's foreign policies that Washington truly could not tolerate. Castro's 1961 decision to embrace Marxism–Leninism and join the socialist bloc was in brazen defiance of the Monroe Doctrine. The new government's ability to survive American invasion and embargo, and its later efforts to export guerrilla revolution, challenged Washington's traditional authority to determine future Latin American politics.

These challenges could not—and did not—go unmet. By the mid-1960s, Washington's commitment to contain the Cuban threat had become the primary focus of American policy throughout the hemisphere.

CONSPIRACY AND TRAGEDY

Given the current state of Cuban–American relations, it is difficult to remember that Washington and the Castro regime have not always been on hostile terms. But during the first year after the Cuban revolution, both sides made a number of cautious, and apparently sincere, attempts at accommodation. Relations were not officially severed until January 1961, but even then, the split was not truly irrevocable until the April 1961 Bay of Pigs invasion.

Nor was the breakdown inevitable, although in the aftermath of the Bay of Pigs, an entire literature sprang up in the United States that described the split as unavoidable. The most partisan writers blamed either of the sides for consciously sabotaging relations. Castro, it was said, had always been a Communist—or at least a dupe of the Communists—who had temporarily concealed his hostility to the United States to give his regime the breathing space needed to solidify control and ensure Cuba's delivery into the hands of the Kremlin.[1] Others blamed the United States, whose imperialist ideology and domination by business interests made it unable to tolerate an independent revolution so close to home. These critics argued that it was not Castro's communism that precipitated the hostilities, but rather American hostility that made Castro a Communist.[2]

The most balanced analyses resisted apportioning blame. Instead, they attributed the hostilities to a "tragic dynamic" that inexorably brought these two forces into conflict. The term tragedy is from classical Greek drama, and refers to the actors' intrinsic nature that makes them "fated to perform their assigned role although they know the drama is bound to end in calamity."[3]

The claims of conscious sabotage are backed more by emotion

73

than fact. Although it undoubtedly is true that as a Cuban nationalist Castro strongly resented U.S. intervention in Cuban affairs, it is unlikely that he had any long-range plans for Cuba to become dominated by the Soviets. The fitful course of the early Cuban–Soviet alliance is evidence that Moscow was unaware of any such conspiracy.

There is no way to prove or disprove the claim that Castro was a Communist from the beginning. It is, however, useful to recall that Castro's revolution did not receive any meaningful support from the official Cuban Communist Party, the Partido Socialista Popular (PSP). Even after Castro declared his allegiance to Marxism–Leninism and began to build his own Communist party, he first purged most of the old PSP members, so that control of the new party would remain solidly in the hands of his 26th of July Movement (the original name of his guerrilla fighters, to commemorate their July 26, 1953, attack on Batista's Moncada Barracks).

Equally spurious are conspiracy theories that allege U.S. business interests as the determinants of our foreign policy. The record of Washington's early contacts with the Castro regime shows the Eisenhower and Kennedy administrations struggling with a variety of special-interest groups but striving to follow a moderate course that would satisfy American business while upholding ideals of equality and respect for Cuba's sovereignty. It is only too true that Washington often allowed its concern for American power—as well as American business—to take priority over its ideals. In Guatemala in 1954, in the Dominican Republic in 1965, in Chile in 1973, and in Cuba in 1961, the United States violated the norms of nonintervention by attacking regimes it considered hostile to its interests. Although these episodes cannot be excused, their underlying causes were much more complex than the simple need to insure American investments.

The arguments of tragic inevitability rely too heavily on the wisdom of hindsight. Given the intricacies and convolutions of Cuban–American relations, one can find evidence to support either the inevitability of conflict or accommodation. America's long history of intervention in Cuban politics, as well as the predominant role of American business in Cuba's economy, were bound to create nationalistic resentment. At the same time as this familiarity bred conflict, it also bred shared values and experiences. Cubans and Americans shared the same political ideals, legal institutions, theories of education, and even passion for baseball. The contempt that existed was more familial than xenophobic. There were many areas for potential agreement, as well as conflict.

The eventual breakdown of Cuban–American relations was the result of a series of political decisions. These decisions were made by officials in Washington and Havana who, like all policy makers, were limited by prejudices as specific as their personal idiosyncrasies and as general as their national traits. If there are any sins that can be blamed for the breakdown, for Castro it would be bravado, which often led him to forgo pragmatism for grand gestures of defiance. America's sin was intolerance, an inability to distinguish the desire for independence from actual threats to national security—particularly when that desire arose so close to our shores.

AMERICA'S HEMISPHERE

The United States has always looked at Latin America as something of its private preserve. As early as 1832, when the U.S. barely had the resources to sustain military credibility, Washington began asserting its seignorial rights with the Monroe Doctrine, which prohibited "outside" intervention in the hemisphere. The Caribbean was considered to be of particular strategic importance. As America's "third border," its sea lanes and islands had to be kept free of any powers hostile to U.S. interests. In 1825, Washington stopped Simón Bolívar, the Latin American liberator, from carrying his revolution to Cuba and Puerto Rico. As a means of preserving the regional status quo, Washington preferred Spain's colonial domination to the instability and uncertainty of an independent Caribbean. By 1898, when it had become clear that the Spanish could no longer maintain control of the region, the United States moved in to replace them, by declaring war on Spain. As a result of the Spanish–American War, Washington gained control of Puerto Rico, the Philippines, and Cuba.[4]

Paradoxically, despite Washington's professed concern with the region, Latin America never received much public attention or interest. It was as if the American public had a "psychological Maginot Line" surrounding the hemisphere. America's predominance was taken for granted. This is not to suggest that the region was ignored completely. When it was necessary, Washington moved swiftly and decisively to preserve the status quo, by sending warships to Cuba and marines to Nicaragua, orchestrating coups in Panama and Guatemala, and making sure that U.S. interests throughout the hemisphere were well defended.[5] These events, which molded the lives of millions of Latin Americans, were barely reported by the press north of the Rio Grande.

This was the situation in the mid-1950s, when Fidel Castro began his drive to overthrow the Batista dictatorship. At the time, Washington's eyes were on Moscow's growing military and economic prowess, Europe's recovering economy, and West Berlin's precarious position. While the Third World states were receiving attention for the first time, Washington's concerns were with a Czech arms deal in Egypt and wars brewing in exotic places like the Congo and Vietnam. Latin America was low on Washington's list of priorities.

In the late 1950s, the U.S. was at best ambivalent about Cuban dictator Fulgencio Batista. Washington had enthusiastically endorsed the Batista regime during its early years, preferring it to the brutal dictatorship of Gerardo Machado and the left-leaning nationalism of Ramón Grau San Martín. Washington sent Batista arms and advisers to train his army, and generally turned a blind eye to the venality and corruption that were the regime's dominant features. Later, as Batista's rule grew more repressive, some members of the State Department began to express unease. Batista was sensitive to this and to how important Washington's arms and endorsement were for his continued tenure. The Cuban dictator went to great lengths to demonstrate to Washington his concern for human rights and political freedom, and declared a general amnesty for all political prisoners in April 1955. Among those released were Fidel Castro and his brother Raúl, who had been jailed for their abortive 1953 attack on the Moncada Barracks.

The amnesty was a gesture that Batista later bitterly regretted, and one that was probably unnecessary. The following year, it became clear that the United States had no intention of withdrawing its support for Batista. Earl E. T. Smith, the new U.S. ambassador, was a bon vivant, a deep-sea fisherman, and a major contributor to the Republican Party. He was also on his first diplomatic assignment, and spoke no Spanish. He was clearly not equipped to preside over a significant change in policy.

Americans knew almost nothing about Castro and his 26th of July Movement before he came to power. This ignorance had two causes. First, Batista set up a censorship cordon to keep news of the Castro insurgency from spreading beyond the Sierra Maestra. For the first year of the struggle, many *Habaneros* did not even know whether Castro had survived the landing of the *Granma*. In addition, news of another Latin American revolution was not that unusual or important to the American public.

On February 24, 1957, Herbert Matthews of the *New York Times* temporarily excited public opinion both in Havana and in the United States when he informed the world that Castro was indeed alive, and of how he had braved the rigors of the Sierra Maestra to interview Castro in his rebel camp. Matthews was greatly impressed with Castro. He enthusiastically reported that Castro's personality was "overpowering."

"Here was an educated, dedicated fanatic, a man of ideals, of courage, of remarkable qualities of leadership . . . one got a feeling that he is now invincible."[6] Matthews also vastly exaggerated the rebels' strength and resources. During the interview Castro kept referring to "another camp," while Raúl Castro marched back and forth with the same group of men, giving the impression of a large encampment and much activity. Matthews quoted Fidel as saying, "[We] have had many fights and inflicted many losses. . . . [Batista's] soldiers are fighting badly; their morale is low, ours could not be higher." In fact, however, Castro at that moment could claim only eighteen followers.[7] Though it was a good news story, it was soon forgotten in the rush of more compelling events in more important areas of the world.

During 1957, as Batista's rule became more arbitrary and brutal, several American policy makers began to question the morality

77

and efficacy of continued U.S. support. Although the revulsion was real, it would be wrong to suggest that the opposition to Batista was anything close to a popular movement. It was the questioning by middle-level State Department officials with a "need to know" that led the U.S. to suspend arms shipments to Cuba in March 1958. But the embargo turned out to be more symbolic than real. The United States continued to deliver back-ordered arms until the following December, when Batista abdicated, and did not withdraw its military mission.

Washington's decision to withdraw support from Batista was never intended as an endorsement of Castro. By 1958, the daily reports of indiscriminate brutality and the increasing disaffection of the Cuban bourgeoisie and army had convinced policy analysts in Washington that Batista no longer had domestic control in Cuba. At the same time, Castro was a political unknown. Despite his insistence to Herbert Matthews of his intention to reinstate democracy in Cuba and his deep respect for America's political ideals, Castro's strong nationalist rhetoric and ties to the left-leaning *Auténtico* party made Washington wary. In December 1958, Washington made a last-ditch attempt to salvage the Cuban situation. William Pawley, a former U.S. ambassador to Brazil and Peru, was sent to Havana to persuade Batista to abdicate in favor of a caretaker government guaranteed friendly to U.S. interests.[8] Batista refused. Three weeks later, on January 1, 1959, he fled the island, as the rebels marched triumphantly into Havana.

Confronted with the *fait accompli*, Washington did not hesitate for long. On January 7, the United States officially recognized the new government. The announcement carefully dissociated Washington from its previous alliance with Batista. Endorsing the need for positive social change in Cuba, the Eisenhower Administration also expressed optimism that the traditionally close relations between Cuba and the United States would continue.

The American historian William Appleman Williams has written that the one thing that Washington, for all its warm words about social change, did *not* expect was for the Cuban revolution to go any further:

One is constantly and ever more strongly impressed, in reading the newspaper and magazine accounts on the Cuban Revolution, with the extent to which Americans assumed that the Revolution should— as well as would—end with the defeat of Batista. While it is too much to say that Americans were truly surprised by the idea of a revolution that aimed to change the old order, it is not too much to say that they were rapidly and increasingly perplexed and annoyed that the Cuban revolutionaries meant to make fundamental changes, and intended to go ahead with their program in the face of opposition and criticism.[9]

Williams blames this naïvete on our own history of social peace. Unlike England and the other European powers, which have had to confront the painful experiences of decolonization, the United States in 1959 was out of touch with the brutal realities—and necessities—of revolutionary change. With nearly two hundred years since our own revolution and a hundred years since the Civil War, Americans, according to Williams, seemed:

. . . to have forgotten . . . some mundane but nevertheless essential features of our own revolutions. They lasted a long time . . . they were violent and bloody, and those who opposed them suffered great losses up to and including their lives. . . .

Williams summed up the American attitude toward the Cuban revolution with the following statement: "One has the distinct impression . . . that most Americans considered it something of a personal affront that the Cubans had the gall to take their politics so seriously."[10]

Williams makes a good point about American naïvete. Time and again, Washington has underestimated the need for basic social change in the developing world, while overestimating the ease and amicability of political transitions. Whether in Cuba, Iran, or Nicaragua, this naïvete about the complexity of the revolutionary process has led first to American confusion and feelings of betrayal, and, ultimately, to resentment and open hostility on both sides.

In the case of Cuba, the situation was further exacerbated by the history of Cuban–American relations. Castro's suspicions about

American intervention made him overly sensitive to any American gesture that could be construed as critical or threatening. Even friendly advice and offers of aid were often seen as patronizing. When, after recognizing the new regime, Washington offered in a show of good faith to withdraw its military mission from Havana, Castro's response was rancorous. Requesting a withdrawal was a prerogative of the Cuban Government, not the United States. When and if the new regime decided it wanted the mission withdrawn, then it would have to leave. Castro pointed out that the mission had been of little use to Batista in his struggle against Castro. Had they taught Batista's army how to lose? "If they are going to teach us that," he said, "it would be better that they teach us nothing."[11]

Washington's traditional mixture of concern and ignorance about Latin America caused the situation to worsen. A change of regime in Cuba was expected to have a significant effect on U.S. economic interests and potentially on America's national security. On the other hand, Washington and the American public knew little about the situation in Cuba. Although Washington had supported Batista, it had paid scant attention to the nature of his rule or conditions inside Cuba. The political repression, economic stagnation, unemployment, rural poverty, and disease—all the issues that Castro said had made him a revolutionary—were unknown, or at best only poorly understood, in the United States. Beyond the issue of how Castro's programs would affect U.S. economic interests in Cuba, there was a basic ignorance among Americans about what needed to be done in Cuba. And Castro, with his particular sensitivities and resentments, was not willing to educate the Americans.

The First Clash

It did not take long for this situation to come to a head. The first clash came in early January over the issue of political trials. Once the Batista censorship was lifted, reports of earlier atrocities began to appear in the press. Day after day, the Cuban newspapers were filled with photographs of torture chambers and testimony from relatives and friends of the many thousands of Cubans who had been murdered by the Batista regime, or had simply disappeared. Demands for vengeance were heard across the island. In the first week, the situation was out of control. It has been alleged that, on their arrival in Santiago, Raúl Castro's men summarily shot 100 Batistianos. In other cities kangaroo courts sprang up to try, sentence, and execute members of the old regime. Another 100 police and army officers were said to have been executed after summary trials.[12]

Castro moved quickly to establish order. On January 10, tribunals and a clear set of legal guidelines were established. Castro, who had been educated as a lawyer, was sensitive to the traditions of due process. As a military commander he was aware of the need for orderly process. What made the situation all the more frustrating—and potentially explosive—was the fact that almost all of the most hated members of the Batista regime, including Batista himself, had fled the island. Castro knew that the Cuban people wanted revenge. He knew too that if he didn't satisfy them he would quickly lose their support. Castro must be given credit for having stemmed the tide of what could easily have turned into a reign of terror. Although the revolutionary tribunals more closely resembled court-martials than trials by peers, they were remarkably fair. Not all who were tried were convicted. And not all of those convicted were shot. For example, Batista's first cousin, a Lieutenant Zaldivar, on trial for ill treatment of prisoners, received only a year and a half in prison.[13] By mid-January, another 200 men had been executed, having been convicted of crimes such as torture and murder.

Reports of the Cuban trials raised a furor in the United States. The American press was filled with editorials decrying "blood baths" and "lynch mobs." In Washington several senators and congressmen protested what they called "Cuban atrocities." Representative Emanuel Celler (D–NY) called on the Eisenhower Administration "to publicly express horror" and bring the matter to the attention of the United Nations.[14] Senator Wayne Morse (D–Ore.) suggested that the U.S. Government express its condemnation by cutting Cuba's sugar quota or freezing Cuban assets.[15] Congressman Wayne Hayes (D–Ohio) urged the imposition of a trade embargo against the island. It is interesting to note that these suggestions were made on January 12 and 13, 1959. Less than two weeks after Castro had come to power there already were powerful, albeit unorganized, voices in Washington publicly discussing the means available for punishing the new regime. The Eisenhower Administration was more circumspect in its response. The State Department expressed its disquiet privately through its new ambassador, Philip Bonsal, and took pains to distinguish itself from the vituperative voices of the press and Congress.

Castro was either unable or unwilling to make such a subtle distinction. He was angered by the American criticisms and threats, and with bitterness he asked, Where were all the American libertarians during Batista's reign of terror? Then, in an act of defiance or supreme naïvete (probably both), Castro challenged his critics to come to Cuba and watch the trials firsthand. To make this possible, he ordered that the trial of Major Jesús Sosa Blanco and two other leaders of the Batista army be held in public, in a sports stadium in the middle of downtown Havana.

Eighteen thousand people, including several hundred foreign journalists, jammed into the sports arena. (The crowd was frenzied and kept interrupting the trial with cries of "assassin" and "kill them." The atmosphere was a mixture of carnival and the Roman Coliseum.) Under these conditions it was impossible for the witnesses to testify or the lawyers to argue. Nevertheless, Sosa Blanco was sentenced to death. The American press was horrified.[16] What was most unfortunate about this event was that the evidence indicated that Sosa Blanco was guilty of the crimes. Had the trial been conducted under normal conditions, with only a few American observers, there could have been little argument with the justice of the sentence.

Castro in the U.S.

In April 1959, Castro made his first trip to the United States as the new Cuban head of state. He came not by invitation from the U.S. Government, but rather as the scheduled speaker at the annual meeting of the American Society of Newspaper Editors. The turnout at the ASNE luncheon was unprecedented. After the meal the room had to be cleared of tables and chairs to accommodate an overflow crowd of 1,500.

When the Cuban leader entered the room the applause was scattered and awkward—many of the editors apparently had their doubts about Castro. Castro was aware of his audience's ambivalence and did his best to win them over. He began by dismissing his translator. Speaking in halting English, Castro assured the editors that he was not a Communist. No matter what they had heard, his revolution was "humanitarian" and resisted any other ideological labels. Above all, he went on to say, his revolution was committed to democratic freedom in Cuba, especially freedom of the press. "The first thing dictators do," Castro said, "is to finish the free press and establish censorship. There is no doubt that the free press is the enemy of dictatorship." By the end of the speech it was clear that even the most hard-bitten ASNE editors had been won over. The applause as he left the room was tumultuous. And the press reports the following day were glowing.[17]

The trip was clearly designed to woo the American elite. In addition to ASNE, Castro spoke to meetings of the National and Overseas Press Clubs and the powerful Council on Foreign Relations. He made special stops in New Jersey and Boston to address students at Princeton and Harvard. At the Cuban Embassy Castro hosted a posh reception for much of diplomatic Washington, an affair for which he even shed his wrinkled battle fatigues for an olive-green dress uniform complete with white shirt and tie. The change was noted approvingly the following day in the *New York Times*.[18] One accommodation he would not make, however, was to shave his beard. As he told a meeting of the National Press Club, "When we finish our jobs we will cut off our beards."[19]

Castro was particularly sensitive to the power of the American press. He held private meetings with the heads of the *New York Times,* the *New York Post* (at that time an important opinion maker), *Time* magazine, and United Press International. While in Washington he awarded medals to thirteen American journalists who had defied the Batista censorship and braved the rigors of the Sierra Maestra to interview Castro during the revolution. The list read like a "Who's Who in American Journalism."[20]

The trip was not all champagne and canapes, however. With an eye to the common man, Castro paid visits to Mount Vernon, the Lincoln Memorial, and placed a wreath at the Tomb of the

Unknown Soldier. No mention of the U.S. tradition of military intervention in Cuba was made. One night Castro managed to shake his American security guards for an after-midnight tour of Washington. At about 2 A.M. Castro and several of his companions showed up at an all-night Chinese restaurant that was a well-known haunt of one of Washington's leading radio commentators. The Cuban leader graciously granted him an interview.[21]

Everywhere he went, Castro attracted large crowds. Two thousand demonstrators chanting "Fi-del, Fi-del" met his train at New York's Penn Station; and three days later 30,000 supporters turned out to hear Castro speak from the band shell in Central Park. Ten thousand came to Harvard's Soldiers' Field Stadium to hear him speak. Castro was received enthusiastically at each rally except at Harvard, where some law students hissed him for his failure to allow due process at the much-publicized political trials. But when Castro admitted that mistakes had been made in the early days of the revolution, and assured the students that they would not be repeated, there were cheers.[22]

By contrast, Castro met few government officials during this trip. However, he held a lunch meeting with Acting Secretary of State Christian Herter, and addressed a closed meeting of the Senate Foreign Relations Committee. Herter refrained from any public statement about their talks, but the senators seemed pleased by what they had heard. Senator John Sparkman (D–Ala.) said later that Castro "made a very favorable impression." Senator George Smathers (D–Fla.) said he thought Castro was "a good man," although he did have some genuine doubts about other members of the new Cuban Government.[23]

President Eisenhower, who was in Georgia playing golf, was conspicuously absent from Washington during Castro's five-day visit. In his place, Castro met with Vice President Nixon at his Senate office and not at the White House. The meeting, at least from Nixon's end, did not go well. Nixon later wrote of his first impression of Castro, "I was convinced Castro was either incredibly naïve about Communism or under Communist discipline and that we would have to treat him and deal with him accordingly."[24] This analysis was either a testament to Nixon's unusual prescience or, more likely, the self-fulfilling nature of politics. Immediately after meeting with Castro, Nixon wrote a memo to the State Department, the White House, and the CIA suggesting that Cuban exiles be trained and armed as a reserve force in case Washington saw the need to remove Castro from power.[25]

The Escalation

Another year passed before Eisenhower acted on Nixon's suggestion, by directing the CIA in March 1960 to begin training Cuban exiles for an invasion of Cuba. During that time Washington and Havana brooked several delicate areas of disagreement. Havana protested America's harboring of Cuban war criminals and apparent toleration of exile attacks on Cuba launched from U.S. shores. Washington, in turn, protested Cuba's expropriation of American-owned land, and its alleged attempts to export revolution. Both sides complained that their honorable intentions were being consciously misconstrued and slandered in the international arena.

These issues were serious points of disagreement, and each side had legitimate claims. But disagreements need not turn into crises. The crises were the result of an unfortunate series of escalations and counterescalations for which both sides were responsible.

Washington's first disagreement with Havana began more as a matter of style than substance. Castro's penchant for hyperbole is well known. Even during the first year, when Castro was apparently still quite interested in some accommodation with the United States, he could not resist the impulse to snipe at his northern neighbor. References to the "shame and humiliation" of the 1901 Platt Amendment and other instances of American intervention in Cuban affairs peppered his speeches from the very beginning. As early as January 15, when not even Richard Nixon considered intervening against the new regime, Castro responded to American criticisms of the war trials by saying that if the Americans did not like what was going on in Cuba, they could send in the marines—in which case, said Castro, there would be "200,000 dead gringos." A day later he accused Washington of seeking to "castrate" the Cuban revolution simply because Cuba wished to be independent.[26]

The Eisenhower Administration seemed bewildered by these attacks. In a speech in the fall of 1959, the President confessed that he was "puzzled" by the Castro regime's apparent hostility. "The record of close relations between Cuba and the United States made it a puzzling matter to figure out just exactly why the Cubans would now be so unhappy."[27] Others in Washington were not so charitable. A conservative columnist, George Sokolsky, reacted to Castro's challenges saying that, "The United States needs to take a stand against every speck of a country spitting in our face."[28]

In time, the Eisenhower Administration came to regard Castro's words as a direct threat to U.S. international prestige, and to peace in the hemisphere. In November 1959, the State Department responded to Cuban charges of U.S. support for exile attacks on Cuba by accusing Cuba of a "deliberate attempt to inflame world opinion against the government of the United States."[29]

The war of words was unfortunate, but not completely without substance. The Eisenhower Administration, it is true, was still committed to a strategy of nonintervention in Cuban affairs. At the same time, the White House could not control what was being said in the press and on Capitol Hill in favor of direct intervention. Castro, in turn, cannot really be blamed for failing to distinguish between the different branches of the American policy-making elite, particularly with the recent overthrow of the Arbenz Government in Guatemala haunting him. And although Washington seemed to be sincerely committed to ending the exile attacks, it was hard to patrol every tiny air field or harbor in Florida. When Cuban exile Major Díaz Lanz bombed Cuba just weeks after having testified on Castro's links to communism before the Senate Internal Security Subcommittee, it was hard to convince Castro that no conspiracy existed.

A second area of major disagreement between Washington and Havana was land reform. On May 17, 1959, the Castro regime announced the adoption of the first Agrarian Reform Law. The law prohibited ownership of farms larger than 1,000 acres, with the exception of sugar and rice plantations producing 50 percent more than the national average. These high-yield plantations would be allowed to maintain up to 3,333 acres. It was not immediately clear what effect the law would have on U.S. holdings in Cuba.

Although most of the U.S.-owned land in Cuba was well over the acreage limit (the King ranch of Texas owned a cattle ranch in Camagüey province that covered 26,000 acres), the law included a provision that stated that foreign companies could continue holding their land if the Cuban Government determined it to be in the national interest. The law stated that no firm decisions on its implementation would be made for at least one year.[30]

Despite the law's ambiguity, the response of the American public was swift and strongly negative. The Wall Street price of Cuban sugar stocks dropped sharply. The American press immediately charged that Cuba was going Communist. According to a report in the *Wall Street Journal* in June 1959:

> So says an American business man, one of a growing number of American residents here [Cuba] who are becoming increasingly disenchanted with the policies of Fidel Castro's revolutionary government.
> Cuba's controversial new Agrarian Reform Law . . . has crystalized American opposition. . . . The harsh American appraisal here of Mr. Castro may be clouded by self-interest, it can be argued. But even though it is difficult to ascertain the truth or falsity of American charges that Castro flirts with Communism, the very fact that the accusations are being made is important. For the accusers are men who help manage $800 million of American investments in Cuba. . . .[31]

Once again, the Eisenhower Administration was more circumspect than the American public in its response to the Agrarian Reform Law. On June 11, the United States sent the Castro Government an official note of protest. The note said that Washington did not oppose the idea of land reform in Cuba, and even supported the need for adjustments in the Cuban socioeconomic structure. At the same time, the United States said it would, of course, insist on "prompt, adequate, and effective compensation" for any American land affected by the reforms.[32]

The issue of compensation—and particularly how prompt it would be—became the central area of disagreement. On June 15, Castro responded to the U.S. note saying that immediate repayment was impossible. Although in theory Castro respected the right of

American owners to expect prompt repayment, the regime just did not have the resources. Batista's corruption and the unfavorable balance of trade with the United States were blamed for Cuban insolvency. Instead, Castro offered the American owners twenty-year bonds paying 4.5 percent interest. Although the Eisenhower Administration did not insist on immediate repayment, in subsequent notes it repeated the need for "prompt" repayment, making it clear that twenty-year bonds were not adequate.

The problem of compensation for expropriated land and industry is one that the United States has had to face time and again in Latin America and elsewhere in the Third World. It is a problem with no easy solution. No developing state (particularly one that has just fought a revolution or civil war) seeking to gain control of its own resources can be expected to have the funds to reimburse foreign interests. At the same time, no U.S. Government can ignore the expropriation of U.S. property, without at least some demand for compensation. The issue is really one of how much each side is willing to negotiate the terms of compensation.

In the first months after the Agrarian Reform Law was passed, there was still room for maneuvering on both sides. As it was written, the Agrarian Reform Law did not *have* to affect U.S. holdings at all. If U.S. business interests could have shown Castro in an unthreatening way that the capital yield from the highly efficient U.S. plantations would contribute more to Cuban development than wholesale nationalization, then the Cubans might have adjudged continued U.S. holdings in Cuba to be "in the national interest."

Washington might have lent support to this process with an offer of aid and technical assistance to help the Castro regime establish a successful mixed economy. It must be remembered that, at OAS meetings over the next two years, both Cuba and the United States proposed plans for large-scale U.S. development aid for Latin America.

Even if Castro decided that nationalization was preferable to continued U.S. holdings in Cuba, there was still no need for a crisis. Washington might have extended Havana a loan to help Cuba pay off American business interests or increased the sugar quota to ensure that American business interests would be treated fairly without undue damage to the Cuban economy. With generosity and patience, Washington might well have demonstrated to Castro the many benefits of continued trade with the United States. The problem of expropriation and adequate means of compensation is one that the United States has still not resolved. Had the Eisenhower Administration worked out some amicable compromise with Cuba, Washington might have avoided subsequent crises with the Velasco Government in Peru and the Allende Government in Chile.

As it turned out, because of strong domestic and international pressures, neither Washington nor Havana seemed willing to compromise on the issue of compensation. In July 1959, the Senate Internal Security Subcommittee heard testimony from Major Díaz Lanz, the exiled head of Castro's air force, on the increasing influence of communism in the Castro regime. According to Díaz Lanz, Fidel Castro had told the major of his plans ". . . to introduce in Cuba a system like the Russians had; even better than the Russian system." With regard to land reform, Castro was alleged to have said, "I [am] going to take now the land from the people who [were] with the former government. Later on I [am] going to take the land of everybody." Díaz Lanz claimed that Castro had also told him that the regime's decision to do away with interest rates on bank loans was just the first step. "Some day the banks [would] disappear" altogether. As further evidence of Cuba's turn to communism, Díaz Lanz, with prompting from committee counsel, pointed out that the word "God" had been removed from the Cuban constitution.[33]

Díaz Lanz went on to list the names of "known Communists" in leading positions in the Castro regime. On that list were Fidel Castro, Raúl Castro, Antonio Núñez Jiménez, head of the agrarian reform, Armando Hart, the Minister of Education, Che Guevara, and David Salvador, leader of the Cuban labor movement. Subsequent research has proved most of Díaz Lanz's charges to be without basis. Most of the "known Communists" on his list were members of the July 26th Movement and not the PSP. Some, like David Salvador, were known to be committed anti-Communists and were later purged from the regime for that reason. Yet at the time, Díaz Lanz's testimony reinforced the fears raised by the agrarian reform

89

and fed greater intransigence *vis-à-vis* the Castro Government both in Washington and on Wall Street.

Castro was incensed by the press coverage given the Díaz Lanz testimony. Together with the escalation of attacks by Florida-based exiles, the United States response to the testimony seemed to convince him that any hope for a compromise with U.S. business interests was fading rapidly. Castro's pessimism became something of a self-fulfilling prophecy the following August, when he proceeded to nationalize the U.S.-owned telephone and electric power companies. These "interventions" were very popular with the Cuban public, particularly because they brought about a significant reduction in rates, and it is likely that Castro's actions had domestic political motives. Nevertheless, the effect of nationalization, along with the Agrarian Reform Law and the new progressive tax law, was to make Cuba an unattractive prospect for either U.S. investment or aid. The original year of breathing space ended with no accommodation.

The third area of disagreement was Cuba's attempts to export revolution to the Caribbean. During the Díaz Lanz testimony of July 1959, J. G. Sourwine, chief counsel to the Senate Internal Security Subcommittee, suggested that Castro's avowed intention to destroy dictatorships in the Caribbean was actually a "cover-up" for "Communist operation[s] against other Latin American countries."[34] The Administration itself did not directly comment on these policies until January 1960, when President Eisenhower responded to Cuban charges that Washington was supporting exile attacks on Cuba by saying:

> The United States record in this respect compares very favorably with that of Cuba from whose territory a number of invasions directed against other countries have departed during the past year. . . .[35]

The export of revolution did not become a policy issue until the following March, when the U.S. Department of Commerce refused to issue a license for the sale of helicopters to Cuba on the grounds that Cuba had "requested armaments far in excess of any conceivable need for self-defense." Although Washington did not directly accuse Castro of wanting the arms for offensive purposes, the State Department did issue an accompanying note suggesting that tensions in the Caribbean had increased significantly since Castro had taken power.[36]

Castro was angered by the Commerce Department decision. He claimed that the helicopters were needed to ensure Cuba's defense against exile attacks—attacks, he hastened to point out, that the United States Government was either unable or unwilling to stop.

In Chapter 2 we saw that these first attempts to export revolution were not a major part of the Castro regime's early foreign policy. All three of the attacks originating from Cuban shores in 1959 were small and poorly armed, and the degree of official support for them has never been proved. Cuban propaganda, as well as the propaganda emanating from a number of the region's right-wing governments, tended to magnify their significance, even at this date. The official U.S. response in 1959 and early 1960 was still comparatively moderate. Although several legislators—particularly members of the Senate Internal Security Subcommittee—began in 1959 to investigate allegations of growing Communist subversion in the region, the Cuban role was not yet the primary focus. However, as the Cuban–Soviet alliance grew stronger in mid-1960 and Cuba became an important topic in the presidential campaign, the issue of Cuban subversion became a principal concern of U.S. policy makers.

The Soviet Connection

Throughout 1960, relations between Washington and Havana became increasingly strained. The long-standing problems of Cuban defiance and American intolerance grew to unmanageable proportions in what were almost weekly crises. Beneath all the specifics was Cuba's new alliance with the Soviet Union.

Moscow first approached the Cuban revolution with a great deal of caution. The reasons for this caution will be discussed in detail later, but it should be noted that the Soviets did not expect Castro's revolution ever to progress beyond the stage of national independence, if it would survive at all. Long after the American press and Congress began to claim that the Cuban revolution was "going Communist," Moscow continued to have its doubts. For the first year of the revolution the Soviets avoided any direct contact with the new regime.

In February 1960, thirteen months after Castro came to power, the Soviets made their first overture, sending to Cuba a trade mission led by Politburo member Anastas Mikoyan. At the end of the ten-day visit, Mikoyan and Castro announced the signing of a trade agreement in which the Soviet Union would purchase almost five million tons of Cuban sugar over the next five years. The Soviets also promised the Cubans a $100 million credit for the purchase of industrial equipment and petroleum.

Havana saw this new alliance with Moscow as an economic necessity. Over the preceding months, the Cubans had grown increasingly uneasy about their continued economic dependence on the United States. At the time of the revolution, the U.S. was buying more than 60 percent of Cuba's sugar. Apart from the ideological issue of sovereignty, Castro was afraid of what would happen to the economy and the revolution if Washington decided to cut its sugar purchases. These fears were not unfounded. As early as January 1959, several U.S. senators and congressmen had called for economic sanctions against the new Castro regime. By January 1960, what had begun as the threats of a few anti-Castro partisans now appeared to be the official policy of the United States, as the Eisenhower Administration began to pressure Congress for the power to control the sugar import quota.[37] Even before the revolution, the Batista regime had explored alternative markets, including the Soviet Union. In 1957, Cuba sold 395,000 tons of sugar to the Soviet Union.[38] As Havana's relations with Washington became increasingly strained, Moscow must have seemed the natural alternative.

United States reaction to the Cuban–Soviet trade agreement was strong and negative. All prior claims that Castro was a dupe of the Communists seemed confirmed. The irony was that Washington knew all along that Cuba had no other choice. The day after Mikoyan arrived in Cuba, the *Wall Street Journal* published an article outlining Havana's tough economic position and Moscow's likely role:

European and U.S. credit sources are cracking down on Cuba and the Cubans have no other place to go than Russia. . . . Russia probably will extend credit or barter because she is aggressively seeking markets.[39]

What disturbed Washington in February 1960 was not merely that Cuba was trading with the Soviet Union—the United States was doing that. The problem was that Cuba was trading with the Soviet Union on top of all its other problems with the United States. By trading with Moscow, Havana had deprived Washington of one of its most effective weapons against Castro: the threat of economic sanctions.

During 1960, the issue of Cuba's trade with the socialist bloc resurfaced time and again, becoming uglier and more confused in each instance. In April 1960, when the Cubans announced the signing of a trade agreement with Poland, several U.S. senators proposed that the United States retaliate by cutting its aid to Poland. The idea was topsy-turvy: The proposed punishment was directed against Poland, rather than Cuba or the Soviet Union. At the same time, the U.S. was trading with all three, so why punish Poland because it was trading with Cuba, who was trading with the Soviet Union? The response was not analytical, but merely emotional. The Administration resisted.

The Cubans seemed enchanted with their new-found power to stir things up in Washington. In April Guevara published an article in the Cuban military magazine, *Verde Olivo,* in which he gloated:

Sometimes we even thought it was rather pompous to refer to Cuba as if it were in the center of the universe. Nonetheless, it is true or almost true. If someone doubts the revolution's importance he should read the newspaper. "The U.S. threatens Poland because of the Pact with Cuba." Man, we're strong and dangerous. We have poisoned the American environment and threatened the sweet democracy of Trujillo and Somoza so now the champions of freedom threaten Poland because it signed an agreement with Cuba. . . .

Oh it is so great and comfortable to belong to such a strong world power as dangerous as Cuba![40]

Although the situation did have its light side, the negative effects of the trade agreement on Washington's attitude toward Cuba must not be underestimated. A month after Mikoyan's visit, President Eisenhower ordered the "organization, training, and equipping of Cuban refugees" for a possible invasion of Cuba.[41] After a year of repeated commitments to nonintervention in Cuba, Eisenhower had finally decided to take Nixon's advice.

The Final Conflict

The action set in motion by the February Cuban–Soviet trade agreement finally came to a head in June over the issue of Soviet oil. As part of the trade agreement, the Soviets had agreed to sell the Cubans a significant amount of crude oil—about a third of Cuba's annual consumption. The deal was particularly attractive to Havana because it was repayable in sugar and would not require any additional demands on Cuba's almost depleted financial reserves. At the time, the regime already owed the British and American oil companies operating in Cuba some $50 million.

At the time of the trade agreement, Havana had informed the oil refineries of its plans to import Soviet oil. The Cubans had no doubt that the American and British refineries would refine the Soviet crude oil. But, in early June, less than three weeks before the first delivery, the foreign oil companies informed Castro they would *not* refine the Soviet oil. In a public speech, Castro warned the companies that either they would do so or "accept the consequences." As usual, Castro did not mince words:

> Don't let them say afterwards that we attacked them, confiscated them or occupied them. The government accepts the challenge, and the companies must decide their own fate.[42]

Despite Castro's warnings, when the oil finally began to arrive at the end of June, the oil companies refused to refine it. The Castro Government's response was swift and predictable. On June 29, it seized the Texaco refinery in Santiago de Cuba, and then the Standard Oil and Shell refineries.

Washington's response was equally swift. On July 6, the Eisenhower Administration cut Cuba's sugar quota by 700,000 tons. After months of wrangling with Congress for the power to set the import

94

quota, the Administration had finally prevailed—one day before the arrival of the Soviet oil. As he had promised, Castro responded to the cut in the sugar quota by seizing all of the American mills.

At this point, the Soviets stepped in to bail out Havana, and offered to increase their own purchase of Cuban sugar by 700,000 tons. Two days later, on July 9, Khrushchev solidified Moscow's commitment to Cuba by promising that Soviet missiles would defend Cuba against a possible American intervention. In scarcely more than a week, the worst-case scenario had come true: The Cubans had expropriated American oil refineries and sugar mills and apparently placed themselves solidly within the socialist camp.

There can be little doubt that Washington knew what was coming. The oil companies felt they had no choice but to refine Soviet oil, because, as one executive put it, "If we didn't take it we would be taken over. So what would we gain?"[43] And Castro had given the United States adequate warning about the takeover of the sugar mills as well. "We can lose our sugar quota and they can lose their investments," he said in a June 24 speech.[44]

From the sequence of events, it might appear that Washington actually wanted to precipitate a crisis. Although the Administration denied this, Washington did appear to expect that the sudden loss of American business would force the Cuban economy and the Castro Government to collapse. The Americans did not think the Cubans could run the refineries by themselves—an attitude similar to Britain's view of Egypt after Gamal Abdel Nasser nationalized the Suez Canal. Washington also doubted that the Castro Government would find an alternative market for the sugar in time to forestall disaster.

It has also been suggested that Washington had actually been planning to play the sugar card for a long time, but when the congressional authorization finally came, the Administration needed a cover. Without some crisis, a cut in Cuba's sugar quota would be seen throughout the hemisphere as economic aggression. For this reason, Washington is said to have directed the oil companies to reverse their decision and refuse to refine the Soviet oil. The expropriations that were all but guaranteed to follow would give Washington the pretext to cut the sugar quota.[45]

In retrospect, the obvious question is, Why didn't Washington expect Cuba to turn to Moscow immediately? There was no doubt that the Soviets had both the technical know-how to help the Cubans maintain the refineries and the capital to buy the surplus Cuban sugar. Ever since the Cuban–Soviet trade agreement of the previous February, one of Washington's worst fears had been that Soviet trade with Cuba would erode Washington's ability to use economic sanctions.

Nevertheless, it seems that for the first few years of the Cuban–Soviet alliance—until the missile crisis of 1962—Washington consistently underestimated Soviet will in Cuba. When reading accounts of the missile crisis, one is struck by the fact that no one in the intelligence agencies, the military, the State Department, or the White House ever expected the Soviets to send missiles to Cuba. Such a challenge to American supremacy in our own backyard was unthinkable. Later, Washington consistently erred in the other direction, by overestimating Soviet interest, influence, and power in Latin America. Both attitudes led to dangerous policy mistakes.

AN ELECTORAL ISSUE

Much to the surprise of both candidates, Cuba became an important issue in the last days of the presidential campaign of 1960. Neither candidate had had much experience with Latin America. Kennedy, while still a student, had toured Latin America some twenty years earlier; as Vice President, Nixon had visited the region more recently. But his experience of being stoned and spat on by mobs in Venezuela and Peru was something he would rather have forgotten. Until the fall of 1960, the two candidates were content to ignore the issue of Cuba. When pressed, both supported Eisenhower's official policy of nonintervention.

But starting in September 1960, Democratic campaign strategists began to report that Cuba was becoming an important issue for the American public. Kennedy would have to take a stand. The historian and former Kennedy adviser Arthur M. Schlesinger, Jr. reports that, at first, Kennedy refused to use Cuba as a campaign issue. He was not sure that the Eisenhower Administration was really to blame. According to Schlesinger, as the campaign progressed, "politics began to clash with Kennedy's innate sense of responsibility. . . . he began to succumb to temptation." The Cuban issue seemed too good to pass up. Kennedy was still unsure about how Eisenhower could have saved Cuba. But as the candidate told his staff one day, "What the hell, they never told us how they would have saved China."[46]

On September 10, the Senate Internal Security Subcommittee released a report that made Kennedy's task easy. According to the report, which was based largely on the testimony of U.S. Ambassadors Earl E. T. Smith and Arthur Gardner, his predecessor in Havana, the Eisenhower Administration had failed to heed early warnings about Communist influence in Cuba. Cuba, they said, had been handed over to the Communists much the same way China had been handed over to the Communists a decade before.[47] Kennedy seized the opportunity. In an October 6 speech on Latin America, he claimed that the Eisenhower Administration had "lost Cuba" and as a result had opened the hemisphere to Communist infiltration.[48]

If red-baiting was to be the strategy, Nixon would not be outdone. A week and a half later, in a speech to an American Legion convention in Miami, the Vice President described the Castro regime as "an intolerable cancer." "I say that our goal must be to quarantine the Castro regime. A number of steps can be taken to do this and are planned."[49] The next day the White House announced the imposition of an almost complete embargo on U.S. trade with Cuba. There is no doubt that the embargo was a political expedient to prove that the Republicans were capable of being tough with Castro. Unfortunately, nobody in Washington at the time seemed to be looking beyond the electoral campaign. The possibility that a U.S. embargo might actually increase Cuba's dependence on Moscow was not even discussed, at least publicly.[50]

Kennedy rejected the new embargo as a classic case of "too little too late." He claimed that the Cuban situation required a much stronger response—the United States must abandon its previous course of nonintervention, and give aid to the anti-Castro forces both in Cuba and in exile.[51]

Nixon called the Kennedy proposal "shockingly reckless" and a "direct invitation for the Soviet Union to intervene militarily on the side of Cuba."[52] His response was more than slightly hypocritical. The Vice President had made a similar proposal some sixteen months earlier, immediately after meeting with Castro in Washington. There was also no doubt that in October 1960 Nixon knew that exactly such a plan was at that moment being implemented in the mountains of Guatemala, where CIA-trained Cuban exiles were preparing to invade Cuba. For once, access to official secrets was more of a hindrance than an advantage in a presidential campaign.

Thus, in retrospect, it is clear that both Kennedy and Nixon were committed to using economic and military means to remove Castro. Why were both so hostile to Castro's continued rule? Two themes run through their statements on Cuba. First, both Kennedy and Nixon considered Cuba's growing military and economic alliance with the Soviet Union an unacceptable breach of the Monroe Doctrine and a concrete threat to American security. Second, the issue of Cuba's potentially harmful influence on the rest of Latin America was becoming a primary concern.

It is important to note that during the first year of the revolution, American critiques of Cuba centered on the *domestic* failings of the Castro regime: political trials, land reform, press censorship, and the alleged role of the Communist party in the new regime. Now the *international threat* posed by Castroism had moved to the forefront of U.S. concerns. There are several likely reasons for this shift in focus. First, Cuba's deepening alliance with the Soviet Union had raised—really for the first time in American history— the specter of international communism in the Western hemisphere. At the same time, Washington was growing increasingly uneasy about the stability and reliability of its Latin American allies.

The crux of the matter is that while Washington had become increasingly concerned about the influence of Castroism on the hemisphere, its primary concern at this time was not *Cuban* policies of active subversion—which in 1960 were negligible—but rather the vulnerability of the hemisphere itself. Once the "psychological Maginot Line" was breached by the Castro revolution, American policy makers began to look at conditions in Latin America with a freshly critical eye. The poverty and underdevelopment so long taken for granted now made Latin America look dangerously vulnerable to the influences of Castroism and international communism. On October 21, in the last of the televised presidential debates, Kennedy took particular notice of this problem. Referring to the recent visit to Cuba by Brazilian presidential candidate Jânio Quadros, Kennedy asked, with no small pique:

> Can any American looking at the situation in Latin America feel contented with what's happening today when a candidate for the presidency in Brazil feels it necessary to call not on Washington during the campaign, but on Castro in Havana, in order to pick up the support of Castro supporters in Brazil?

Nor, said Kennedy, was this an isolated case:

> Castro is only the beginning of our difficulties throughout Latin America. The big struggle will be to prevent the influence of Castro spreading to other countries—Mexico, Panama, Brazil, Bolivia, Colombia.

If the United States wished to counter the Castro influence, according to the presidential candidate, it would have to reformulate its policy toward the region as a whole. Kennedy spoke of the need:

> . . . to provide closer ties to associate ourselves with the great desire of these people for a better life if we're going to prevent Castro's influence from spreading throughout Latin America. . . . His influence is growing mostly because this administration has ignored Latin America. You yourself said, Mr. Vice President, a month ago, that if we had provided the kind of economic aid five years ago that we are now providing, we might never have had Castro.
> Why didn't we?[53]

These words embodied both the vision and the folly of the Alliance for Progress. The vision was that a better life for all Latin Americans was the best way to serve U.S. interests. The folly was the first premise for the provision of that aid: the prevention of another

Castro. Kennedy would have done better had he asked, If the United States had provided the early Castro regime with the type of aid it was now offering the rest of the hemisphere, would *Castro* have become such a threat to U.S. interests?

Given the level of the polemic of the electoral campaign, the eventual severing of U.S.–Cuban relations in early January 1961 was somewhat anticlimactic. The months after the election were much like those preceding it. Florida-based exile attacks went on unabated, while news of a CIA training camp for Cuban exiles in Guatemala continued to be leaked to the American press. At the same time, Cuba's ties with the socialist bloc grew even closer. In the end of December, Cuba renewed its trade agreement with Moscow, increasing the Soviet commitment to purchase Cuban sugar to some 1,700,000 tons. China would buy an additional million tons, while the other socialist bloc countries would purchase some 300,000 tons in the coming year.[54]

Castro had become obsessed, in the last months of 1960, with what he was convinced was an impending U.S. attack on Cuba. On January 4, 1961, in a speech to the UN, Cuban Foreign Minister Raúl Roa formally charged the United States with conspiring to overthrow the legitimate government of Fidel Castro. According to Roa, the Eisenhower Administration planned to move within the next few weeks before the inauguration to present the new Administration with a *fait accompli.*[55]

Two days earlier, as Castro addressed an anniversary celebration in Havana, a bomb exploded in the crowd. Castro's immediate response demonstrated just how fearful he had become. "It is the U.S. embassy," he charged, "that is paying the terrorists to put bombs in Cuba." The embassy was the very wellspring of counterrevolution within Cuba, and Castro would no longer permit it to operate. He ordered the U.S. embassy to reduce its staff to eleven people within thirty-six hours.[56]

President Eisenhower responded the next day by severing all relations with Cuba. According to Eisenhower, Castro's decision to reduce the American embassy staff was to "have no other purpose than to render impossible the conduct of normal diplomatic relations" with Cuba. Furthermore, according to the President, this was "only the latest of a long series of harassments, baseless accusations, and vilifications. There is a limit to what the United States in self-respect can endure." Eisenhower concluded his statement by saying, "Our sympathy goes out to the people of Cuba now suffering under the yoke of dictatorship."[57]

As it turned out, Eisenhower was actually extending to the Cuban people more than just his sympathy; he was also offering guns and training to a group of 1,300 Cuban exiles in Guatemala. Castro had been right. An invasion of Cuba was planned. He was wrong only about when it would come. The Eisenhower Administration, having charted the course for the Bay of Pigs some two years earlier, would leave its implementation to its successors.

FROM CONCILIATION TO CONFLICTS

Havana greeted the Kennedy Administration with cautious optimism. On January 21, the day after Kennedy's inauguration, Castro ostentatiously removed the Cuban armed forces from a state of emergency, saying:

> We have no resentment of the past, but we will wait for the action of the Kennedy Administration. We will be glad for a rectification of the U.S. policy toward Cuba, but we will wait for action, not words.[58]

Despite the belligerence of Kennedy's campaign rhetoric, Castro seemed willing—almost eager—to give the new President the benefit of the doubt. He specifically expected Kennedy to call off the impending invasion.

But Kennedy did not call off the Bay of Pigs operation. On April 16, 1961, some 1,300 CIA-trained Cuban exiles in American-surplus planes and boats left Nicaragua to invade Cuba and liberate their countrymen. The Cuban people were ready for the invaders—the militia had been on alert for much of the previous two years—but not for liberation. Within forty-eight hours, it was over. One hundred and fifty of the invaders were killed, and almost 1,200 were taken prisoner. Throughout Cuba, the victory at the Bay of Pigs was celebrated as a great triumph over American imperialism.

Sixty-three years after the Spanish–American War, Martí's score with the United States was finally settled.[59]

Why Kennedy decided to go ahead with the Eisenhower Administration's plans for the invasion has been the topic of much debate. Bureaucratic inertia and domestic political pressure undoubtedly contributed to the decision, but Kennedy's own hostility to what he thought was a Moscow-dominated regime should not be underestimated. Indeed, during the campaign it was Kennedy and not Nixon who first spoke of the need for stronger measures against Castro, such as arming opposition forces both within Cuba and in exile.

Yet despite his hard line, Kennedy was apparently ambivalent about the proper means to destabilize the Castro Government. In particular, he was concerned about how direct American military intervention in Cuba would affect U.S. standing in the hemisphere. As a result, Kennedy decided that American support for the invasion would have to be covert: We would provide the exiles with arms and training, and even some old bombers repainted with Cuban air force insignia, but no direct military involvement, air support, naval cover, or back-up ships.

This choice of soft-line tactics to implement a hard-line policy doomed the exercise from the beginning. However, seen in the proper historical context, these tactics are less irrational, if still misconceived. Seven years earlier the United States had successfully "destabilized" the Arbenz regime in Guatemala simply by training and arming Guatemalan exiles, without committing American resources to the actual battle. Washington's real failure was in thinking that the situation in Cuba was similar to that in Guatemala. This faulty view may well have been the result of bureaucratic inertia—generals are always fighting the last war—as well as a concrete failure of American intelligence, which consistently underestimated the degree of local popular support for the Castro regime. The latter problem plagued American policy toward Cuba for the rest of the decade.

Further evidence of Kennedy's hostility toward Cuba is that the failure of the Bay of Pigs invasion did not dissuade him from considering a future policy of intervention. Speaking before the annual convention of the American Society of Newspaper Editors (the same group Castro addressed two years earlier) three days after the Bay of Pigs debacle, Kennedy denied any U.S. involvement in the invasion, but did not repudiate the actual policy:

> Any unilateral American intervention, in the absence of an external attack upon ourselves or an ally, would have been contrary to our traditions and to our international obligations. But let the record show that our restraint is not inexhaustible. Should it ever appear that the inter-American doctrine of nonintervention merely conceals or excuses a policy of nonaction—if the nations of the hemisphere should fail to meet their commitments against outside Communist penetration—then I want it clearly understood that this Government will not hesitate in meeting its primary obligations which are to the security of our nation![60]

Kennedy went on to give three reasons why the policy of nonintervention could no longer restrain the United States. This speech is important because it reveals Kennedy's attitude toward Cuba, and also his Administration's attitude toward the Third World in general. The speech is one of the earliest and clearest statements of Kennedy's commitment to containing the spread of communism in the Third World.

First, according to Kennedy, the traditional norms of nonintervention could no longer apply because the forces of international communism posed a threat to the free world unlike any seen before:

> If the self-discipline of the free cannot match the iron discipline of the mailed fist—in economic, political, scientific and all other kinds of struggles as well as the military—then the peril to freedom will continue to rise.

Second, he said what was at stake was not just America's security but the security of the entire hemisphere:

> The American people are not complacent about Iron Curtain tanks and planes less than ninety miles away from their shore. But a nation of Cuba's size is less a threat to our survival than it is a base for subverting the survival of other free nations throughout the hemisphere.[61]

Once again, Kennedy failed to give any details of actual Cuban subversion to substantiate this point, instead focusing on the vulnerability of the Latin American states. This tack not only expressed the substance of Kennedy's concern, but also had the additional benefit of deflecting any Latin American charges that Kennedy was resurrecting the "Big Stick."

Finally, said Kennedy, the Cuban threat was not an isolated phenomenon, nor was it limited to the Western hemisphere. Rather, it was part of a new and insidious campaign of international subversion that preyed on the vulnerabilities and weaknesses of people throughout the Third World:

> Power is the hallmark of this offensive—power and discipline and deceit. The legitimate discontent of yearning people is exploited. The legitimate trappings of self-determination are employed. But once in power all talk of discontent is repressed, all self-determination disappears, and the promise of a revolution of hope is betrayed, as in Cuba, into a reign of terror.[62]

This struggle for the hearts and minds of the Third World could not be won merely by virtue of our superior military capability. Rather, this was a new battle demanding new strategies and commitment from the entire Free World, whether the battle was being fought in Cuba or South Vietnam:

> We dare not fail to see the insidious nature of this new and deeper struggle. We dare not fail to grasp the new concepts, the new tools, the new sense of urgency we will need to combat it—whether in Cuba or South Vietnam. And we dare not fail to realize that struggle is taking place every day, without fanfare, in thousands of villages and markets—day and night—and in classrooms all over the globe.

The United States, said Kennedy, would not let one failure like the Bay of Pigs diminish its commitment to contain and defeat this new international threat. In fact, he proposed quite the opposite:

> We intend to profit from this lesson. We intend to reexamine and reorient our forces of all kinds—our tactics and our institutions here in this community. We intend to intensify our efforts for a struggle in many ways more difficult than war. . . . I am determined upon

our system's survival and success, regardless of the cost and regardless of the peril![63]

The outcome of the Bay of Pigs invasion directly affected the roles that Havana, Moscow, and Washington would play in the missile crisis some eighteen months later. For Havana, the Bay of Pigs demonstrated just how vulnerable Cuba was to U.S. attack, and how much it needed a strong alliance with the Soviet Union to guarantee its defense. For Moscow, as we shall see in more detail, Cuba's ability to survive the invasion was proof that Fidel Castro's revolution was a risk worthy of a major military and diplomatic investment. Finally, the failure of the invasion solidified Washington's hostility to Castro, and convinced Kennedy that to safeguard both national security and his own political fortunes no half-measures toward Cuba would do.

THE CRISIS TO END ALL CRISES

In late July 1962, the CIA began to report an unusual amount of activity in Cuba: Soviet specialists were streaming in by the thousands; Soviet ships carrying construction equipment and as yet unidentified weaponry were arriving almost daily at Cuban ports; and new construction was proceeding at a number of military sites.[64] After reviewing the data, CIA analysts reported that Moscow was upgrading Cuba's air defense system by installing a network of surface to air missile sites. Although Washington was concerned about the increasing Soviet military presence on the island, there was also agreement that the United States could not oppose these defensive measures, especially so soon after the Bay of Pigs invasion.

Throughout August and early September, regular U-2 overflights of Cuba continued to report increased construction activity on the island. But none returned with evidence that the missiles were anything but defensive. In mid-September, President Kennedy warned the Soviets in both public and private communications that although the U.S. had no evidence of anything but defensive weaponry on the island, if Cuba were "ever to become an offensive military base," the United States would do "whatever must be done to protect its own security and that of its allies." Khrushchev sent back several messages assuring Kennedy that the armaments in Cuba were "designed solely for defensive purposes" and that he, Khrushchev, would do nothing to undermine Kennedy's position before the upcoming November congressional elections.

All the while, Washington continued to receive reports from the Cuban refugee community of nuclear missile sites under construction in Cuba. But intelligence analysts tended to be skeptical of these charges, as similar reports had been coming in at a fairly consistent rate for more than a year and a half, and none had yet proved to be true. The CIA was not sure its sources in Cuba were capable of distinguishing an "offensive" from a "defensive" missile. And since the Bay of Pigs, the intelligence community was not sure it could trust its refugee contacts.

Others in Washington, however, took the refugee reports more seriously. Senator Kenneth Keating (R-NY) had hinted darkly throughout the summer about an impending crisis in Cuba. In early October, he announced that the Soviets were building offensive missile bases. Although Keating's charges definitely applied pressure on the White House to get more conclusive evidence, at the time most observers tended to dismiss them as merely political and self-aggrandizing.

In late August, Kennedy ordered that the number of U-2 surveillance flights over Cuba be doubled. In mid-October, they finally hit the jackpot. A U-2 flying over western Cuba brought back photographs of an unusual amount of construction going on in San Cristóbal. That evening, the CIA brought National Security Assistant McGeorge Bundy the shocking news: The Soviets were building launch sites for medium and long-range ballistic missiles in San Cristóbal; one missile was already visible on the ground. The worst had finally happened: The Soviets were turning Cuba into a base for nuclear missiles just ninety miles from American shores.

When Bundy relayed the news to Kennedy the next morning, the President reacted angrily. As Schlesinger reports, the President asked, If Khrushchev would pull this after all his protestations and assurances, how could he be trusted at all?[65] Kennedy then called a meeting of fifteen of his closest advisers to discuss his options.

For the next six days, this "Executive Committee" (or ExCom, as it was later dubbed by the press) met in total secrecy in the White House. The President did not want to tip his hand to either the Russians or the American public before he was ready to take a stand. The responses that were discussed ranged from diplomatic negotiations to a military strike against Cuba. The one option that was never considered was allowing the missiles to remain in Cuba.[66]

In the beginning, a majority of the committee favored an air strike against the missile sites as the only solution. The missiles would be destroyed, and the Russians, and the rest of the world, would once and for all see the seriousness of our intent. Pentagon experts were brought in to outline the technical problems of an air strike. The experts informed the committee that the sort of limited, or "surgical," air strike they had been discussing would not be enough. The CIA could not be certain that all the sites had been identified, and it would be dangerous to leave known Cuban air bases untouched. The Pentagon recommended a much larger air strike to destroy both missile sites and military bases. This action would ensure American security and might also lead to Castro's downfall. Here was a perfect opportunity to make up for the Bay of Pigs; a chance to use hard-line tactics that few of our allies would fault. The logic of the Pentagon experts, as several members of the ExCom later reported, was compelling.

But there were equally compelling arguments against an air strike. Even a limited air strike would kill Russian technicians and might provoke Moscow into a nuclear response. A major air strike of the sort called for by the Pentagon would kill thousands of Cuban civilians and bring international condemnation from even our closest allies. With this one action, the United States would be branded as the aggressor.

In the end, the ExCom chose diplomatic negotiations coupled with a naval "quarantine" of all military shipments into Cuba. This course had numerous advantages. It would give Khrushchev time to consider his response and minimize the chances of a reactive

107

attack against either the U.S. or Berlin. Over time, the pressure could be increased, by broadening the selective blockade to include nonmilitary items essential to Cuba's functioning, such as oil. And if the Russians refused to negotiate, the United States was still left with the option of a military strike.

From the size of the military buildup simultaneously taking place in Florida, it is clear that Kennedy considered a military confrontation likely. Under the cover of a long-planned amphibious exercise off the Florida coast, some 40,000 marines and another 100,000 army troops were deployed.

Speaking on national television on October 22, eight days after the U-2 flight first brought back evidence of San Cristóbal, President Kennedy informed the American people and the Russians of his decision. "The purpose of these bases," the President said, "can be none other than to provide a nuclear strike capability against the Western Hemisphere. . . . capable of striking Washington, D.C., the Panama Canal, Cape Canaveral, Mexico City. . . . [and] most of the major cities in the Western Hemisphere ranging as far north as Hudson Bay, Canada, and as far south as Lima, Peru." This, Kennedy said, the United States could not accept. The missiles would have to be removed from Cuba.[67]

Kennedy seemed almost as concerned about the fact that the Russians had lied about the missiles—he recounted their many denials in great detail—as about the missiles themselves. Such deception, he said, could not be tolerated in a world where the threat of nuclear annihilation existed.

Kennedy then outlined what he called the *initial* steps he was taking to ensure the missiles' removal. Besides ordering a naval quarantine of all offensive materials shipped into Cuba, he was asking the Organization of American States and the United Nations to take the necessary steps to condemn the Soviet action. He was also stepping up U.S. surveillance of Cuba, and was increasing the number of American troops stationed at Guantánamo base in Cuba.

Kennedy then warned the Soviets that it would "be the policy of this Nation to regard any nuclear missile launched from Cuba against any nation in the Western Hemisphere as an attack by the Soviet Union on the United States, requiring a full retaliatory response upon the Soviet Union." Kennedy called on Khrushchev "to halt and eliminate this clandestine, reckless, and provocative threat to world peace. . . . [and] abandon this course of world domination."[68]

From the perspective of the crisis's fortunate outcome, there is a tendency to assume that world reaction to Kennedy's speech was unanimously favorable. It is true that most countries endorsed Washington's position, but not without expressing their misgivings. The British and Italians were particularly skeptical. The traditionally conservative British *Economist* suggested that it might not be worth risking a nuclear showdown for what it called "a shipment of Russian arms." The left-leaning *Manchester Guardian* even went so far as to suggest that the Russians might actually have the right to place missiles in Cuba. Hadn't the United States placed missiles of its own on the Soviet borders? In the end, and particularly after Ambassador Adlai Stevenson's dramatic performance at the United Nations, the allies lined up behind the United States.[69] But it is important to recognize that even in 1962 there were voices in Europe questioning the right of the superpowers to base nuclear missiles wherever they pleased.

Moscow made no reply to the Kennedy speech. For four excruciating days the world held its breath. The first ray of hope appeared on Thursday, October 25. U.S. surveillance planes over the Atlantic reported that half of the Soviet ships en route to Cuba had turned around and were now heading for home. But still there was no reply from Khrushchev. When the first Soviet ship, a tanker, entered the quarantine zone that same day, several of Kennedy's advisers urged the President to take a strong stand. Kennedy, however, wanted to give Khrushchev more time, and he ordered the blockade ships to let the tanker pass.

On Friday, October 26, word finally came, but in a very roundabout way. Alexander Fomin, a middle-level bureaucrat in Moscow's Washington embassy, called John Scali, a State Department correspondent for ABC News, and asked if they could meet immediately.[70] Over coffee at the Occidental Restaurant in Washington, Fomin told Scali that he thought there might be a way out of the crisis. If Khrushchev removed the missiles in Cuba and promised never again to place offensive weapons on the island, would the United States in turn promise publicly not to invade Cuba? Scali told Fomin that he did not know. Fomin pleaded with him to get an answer as soon as possible.

Scali returned to the State Department, where he delivered Fomin's message to Roger Hilsman, who was the Department's Director of Intelligence and Research. Hilsman then called Secretary of State Dean Rusk, who carried the news to the President. After discussing the Soviet proposal with the Executive Committee, the President directed Rusk to tell Scali to get in touch with his Russian contact and tell him that the Americans were interested in his proposal. At 7:30 that evening, Scali passed the word along to Fomin in the coffee shop of Washington's Statler Hilton Hotel. Two hours later, a cable arrived from Khrushchev that made the deal official.

The story has one further twist. The following morning Radio Moscow broadcast a second letter from Khrushchev that reversed much of the previous evening's cable. The broadcast stated that the Soviets were now offering to remove the missiles from Cuba in exchange for Washington's removal of offensive missiles from Turkey.

Once again, the more hard-line members of Kennedy's committee urged the President to attack Cuba. Khrushchev, they said, had betrayed Kennedy's trust once more. While the negotiations dragged on, the missiles in Cuba were still being assembled. But Kennedy resisted once again. He would, his brother Robert and others recalled, not provoke a nuclear confrontation until all alternatives had been exhausted. In the afternoon of October 27, Attorney General Robert F. Kennedy came up with one last plan. He suggested that Kennedy ignore Khrushchev's second message and accept the first. The President agreed that his brother's plan was worth trying and that evening sent Moscow a letter offering to trade a no-invasion pledge in return for the removal of the Soviet missiles. No mention was made of the Jupiter missiles in Turkey.[71]

The next morning, Sunday, October 28, Khrushchev's answer arrived. Construction of the missile sites in Cuba would stop immediately. The arms would be dismantled and sent back to the Soviet

110

Union. Negotiations on monitoring the process would start immediately at the United Nations. The crisis was over. The Soviets tried to put the best face possible on the situation, claiming the American no-invasion pledge as a great diplomatic victory. There is no doubt that both sides felt a strong sense of relief.

Missile Fallout

Havana was not pleased by the outcome of the crisis. Indeed, from beginning to end, the whole crisis was one long exercise in humiliation for Castro. The obvious exclusion of Castro from the Kennedy-Khrushchev negotiations was a major blow to the Cuban leader's pride and a painful demonstration of Cuba's impotence in the face of big-power negotiations.

Castro did not take the exclusion lightly. He resisted the process every step of the way. At the beginning of the crisis, on October 23, the day after Kennedy's speech, Castro publicly denied that either the Cubans or the Soviets would ever consider withdrawing their missiles. Cuba, he said, had the right to possess any and all arms it desired. If the U.S. imperialists insisted on denying Cuba that right, the Cubans would be willing to defend it—no matter what the cost. Contemplating the potential outcome of such a confrontation, Castro said, "It calms us to know that the aggressors will be exterminated. It calms us to know this." As for Soviet solidarity in such a confrontation, Castro was sure that the Soviet position would be, "serene, exemplary, a genuine lesson to imperialism, firm, serene, laden with arguments, with correct thinking."[72]

As it turned out, the Soviets did not live up to Castro's expectations. Although the Kremlin's leaders were armed with argument, they were also not eager to see anyone exterminated. Moscow *would* negotiate. Over the next several days, while the Soviets and Americans struggled desperately to find some terms for accommodation, Castro tried his best to force a confrontation. On October 27, Castro rejected a bid from UN Secretary General U Thant that the Cubans be party to the negotiations, insisting again that Cuba's right to control its own defense was nonnegotiable. At the same time, Castro tried to up the stakes, by issuing a warning that any combat plane

111

trying to enter Cuban air space would be fired on. Shortly thereafter, an American U-2 was shot down over Cuba. Neither Kennedy nor Khrushchev acknowledged the incident.[73]

By October 28, it had become clear to Castro that the Russians were willing to go to almost any lengths to avoid a military confrontation with the United States. Castro tried to launch a last-minute salvage operation by issuing his own list of five conditions for a missile withdrawal. These conditions included an end to the blockade, an end to U.S. subversion within Cuba, an end to U.S-funded exile attacks against Cuba, an end to U.S. overflights, and a complete withdrawal of U.S. forces from the Guantánamo naval base.[74] That same day, Khrushchev agreed to withdraw the Soviet missiles from Cuba. In his letter to Kennedy, Khrushchev made no mention of Castro's five conditions.

As the Soviets and Americans moved back from the brink, the Cubans continued to resist the inevitable. Castro commented grudgingly on the crisis's outcome, saying that "an armed conflict has been avoided, but peace has not been achieved."[75] And in a final act of defiance, Castro refused to permit UN observers to enter Cuba to monitor the dismantling of the missiles, as Khrushchev and Kennedy had agreed.

The Cubans came through the missile crisis committed to one thing above all: As Castro vowed, "Never again in the chess game of power" would Cuba be found "playing the docile pawn."[76] The Cubans also emerged with some major questions about their alliance with the Soviet Union. In particular, from that point on, Havana would be suspicious of any Soviet attempts at accommodation with Cuba's enemies. The missile crisis had taught Castro a bitter lesson: that the Russians, or at least Khrushchev, did not have what Castro called the *cojones* to stand up to the United States.[77]

RETHINKING THE BALANCE

The missile crisis raised the most basic questions about the international balance of power and the future of peaceful coexistence. In this the crisis had much more to do with relations between

Moscow and Washington than it did with Havana. Certainly both the United States and the Soviet Union saw it that way, in choosing to conduct all the negotiations in the missile crisis without consulting Castro. This fact may well have contributed to the happy outcome. Washington's relations with Havana, as described earlier, had always been ham-fisted. When reading the accounts of the crisis, one is impressed with the restraint shown by Washington, with the nuances and subtleties of Washington's negotiating style. Despite their diametrically opposed interests, both Kennedy and Khrushchev seemed committed to finding the basis for a compromise. One wonders how different the course of Cuban–American relations might have been had Castro and Eisenhower or Castro and Kennedy been willing to exercise such forbearance. But the stakes in the missile crisis were much, much higher.

A second point is that the missile crisis established a series of important precedents that would substantially define future relations among Havana, Moscow, and Washington. The missile crisis confirmed once and for all Washington's hostility toward Havana. If there was no turning back for the Cubans after the Bay of Pigs, the breaking point for Washington came with the missile crisis. The crisis was worse than any of the worst-case scenarios that were worked out at the time of the Cuban-Soviet trade agreement. Not only had Cuba gone Communist, allied itself with the Soviet Union, and become a base for hemispheric subversion, it had almost succeeded in becoming a nuclear outpost for the Soviet Union.

Having raised that awful specter, the missile crisis also laid it to rest. As a result of the crisis, Moscow agreed that it would never again try to place offensive weapons of any kind in Cuba. That agreement was tested and reconfirmed in 1970, when it was discovered that Moscow was building a nuclear submarine base in Cienfuegos Bay on the southern coast of Cuba. Washington protested that this was an unacceptable breach of the missile crisis accord, and Moscow backed down, halting construction on the base.

The missile crisis also established the precedent of "linkage." Henceforth, all major issues of disagreement between Washington and Havana would be linked directly to relations between Washington and Moscow. This strategy worked very effectively in the missile crisis and the Cienfuegos affair. It has, unfortunately, had much less success in issues in which Moscow plays a less central role in the disputed policy. In these cases, linkage has not curtailed Cuban policies, and has gravely strained Washington's relations with Moscow.

Two examples should make this point clear. In 1975, when Havana sent troops to Angola, Washington threatened to abandon the SALT negotiations unless they withdrew. The Cubans did not withdraw, and the U.S. went ahead with the negotiations anyway. Not only was there loss of face in Washington, but the strategy also seriously jeopardized the outcome of the SALT talks, by undermining the credibility of Washington's "hard-line" position while raising doubts about the sincerity of Washington's commitment to arms control. An even more ridiculous example of the failure of linkage came in September 1979, during the crisis of the so-called Soviet "combat brigade." The Carter Administration—now under pressure from Capitol Hill—tried to link the SALT negotiations to the removal of some 2,500 Soviet soldiers from Cuba. These troops had been there since the days of the missile crisis, and neither Moscow nor Havana was willing to accede to Washington's demand. The White House was forced to back down, and the SALT treaties suffered another setback on the Hill.

Underlying this strategy of linkage has been the assumption that Moscow can always and easily determine Havana's policies. This was not true during Cuba's 1960s phase of exporting revolution, and it is apparently not true today, despite the increasing warmth of the Cuban–Soviet alliance. As we will see, Moscow has certain levers that it can use to pressure Havana when necessary; but using these levers so strains the Cuban–Soviet alliance that Moscow has been careful not to overuse them. There is no doubt that the Soviets *could* have removed the 2,500 troops from Cuba, or even forced a Cuban pullback in Angola, had they wanted to. But as much as the Soviets may have wanted to salvage the SALT negotiations, they apparently valued their alliance with the Cubans even more.[78] After the missile crisis, the Soviets became very careful about provoking Castro's anger.

Everything But Invasion

The missile crisis established one further precedent with long-range implications for Cuban–American relations: the American "no-invasion pledge." As part of his agreement with Khrushchev, Kennedy promised that if the Soviets withdrew their missiles from Cuba, the Americans in turn would not intervene militarily against Cuba. This did *not* mean that Washington was now willing to tolerate the Castro regime. In fact, over the next decade Washington used every means at its disposal short of direct military intervention to destabilize Cuba.

Washington's chief weapon against Cuba thus became the trade embargo. The embargo was expected to cripple Cuba's economic development. Economic failure was in turn expected to discredit the Cuban model for the rest of Latin America, and lead to severe discontent and opposition to the Castro regime from within. It was also hoped that the embargo, by increasing Cuba's economic dependence on the Soviet Union, would ultimately lead to Moscow's disaffection with Castro.

When the embargo was imposed by the Eisenhower Administration in October 1960, one of then-Senator Kennedy's chief criticisms was that it would not work if it were only limited to trade with the United States:

> I believe that if any economic sanctions . . . are going to be successful, they have to be multilateral, they have to include the other countries of Latin America. The very minute effect of [the U.S. embargo] on Cuba's economy, I believe Castro can replace those markets very easily through Latin America, through Europe, and through Eastern Europe. If the United States had a stronger prestige and influence in Latin America it could persuade, as Franklin Roosevelt did in 1940, the countries of Latin America to join in an economic quarantine of Cuba. That's the only way you can bring economic pressure on the Castro regime. . . .[79]

After the missile crisis, one of the Kennedy Administration's primary diplomatic goals was to convince the other Latin American states to join in the embargo against Cuba. This was no easy task.

115

As Kennedy had noted, American prestige in Latin America was low, whereas Castro still retained considerable influence. The sight of the United States threatening tiny Cuba tended to generate more sympathy for Havana than for Washington.

It was not until July 1964 that the OAS finally adopted sanctions against Cuba. The decision was due less to Washington's success than it was to Havana's failure. By 1964, the region had begun to experience a severe shift to the right that was due in part to the fear of Castroism. In addition, Castro had managed to alienate many of the region's moderate leaders with his increasingly strident internationalist rhetoric, and a few ill-conceived attempts to export revolution. The immediate pretext for the levying of sanctions was the interception of a shipment of Cuban arms to guerrillas in Venezuela.

The sanctions, when finally imposed, went far beyond a suspension of trade. They included the severing of all diplomatic and commercial relations, the suspension of all sea and air service to Cuba, and the establishment of passport restrictions on travel to and from Cuba.[80] In addition to placing severe political and economic pressures on the Castro regime by isolating Cuba from its hemispheric neighbors, the sanctions would have the added benefit, in Washington's view, of *isolating the Latin Americans* from Castro's influence. Washington considered Castroism contagious, and was unsure whether Latin America had sufficient resistance.

Despite its official commitment to noninterventionism, Washington unofficially continued to engage in a variety of covert actions intended to destabilize the Castro Government. The 1976 investigations of the intelligence services by the Senate Select Intelligence Committee, headed by Senator Frank Church (D-Idaho), uncovered evidence of a variety of subversive activities and "dirty tricks" by the CIA, including supplying millions of dollars worth of arms to opposition forces within Cuba, aiding exile attacks against Cuba, and even orchestrating a series of bizarre attempts to assassinate Castro using botulism toxin, booby-trap sea shells, and even a poison fountain pen.[81]

Even though the United States was restrained from attacking

Cuba directly by its accord with the Soviet Union—and its fear of a nuclear confrontation—Washington never really accepted the permanence of Castro's rule. "I don't accept the view that Mr. Castro is going to be in power in five years," President Kennedy said in 1963.[82] The expectation was that at some point a local uprising would overthrow Castro and rid Cuba of Communist domination. Until that happened, Washington would refuse to recognize the Castro regime and do everything in its power—and within the parameters of the missile crisis accord—to succor and aid those "democratic forces."

ALLIED FOR PROGRESS

With the Cuban issue "on hold," Washington now turned its full attention to the task of preventing other Cubas in Latin America. As early as the spring of 1960, the Eisenhower Administration acknowledged the need to step up American aid to the region to ensure successful and stable development. The Administration authorized spending $350 million for the initial capitalization of the Inter-American Development Bank and another $500 million for a fund for social development programs known as the Social Progress Trust Fund. While the White House denied that the infusion of American assistance had anything to do with developments in Cuba, most Latin Americans, who referred to it as "the Fidel Castro Plan," knew better.

For years, at least since World War II, Latin American economists, academics, and politicians (even Castro) had petitioned the United States for development assistance, for a program like the Marshall Plan. Each time Washington turned down the requests, saying the situation in Latin America was very different from that in Western Europe. The Marshall Plan had been essential to America's national security. If the U.S. did not get the shattered European economies back on their feet, there would be nothing to stop Moscow from overrunning France and Germany, as it had so recently overrun Czechoslovakia and Romania. Luckily, Latin America was in no such danger.[83]

117

Thus, although Washington was willing to acknowledge Latin America's need for foreign capital, the most it offered was that the region try to attract *private* American investment. Until the Eisenhower Administration decided to invest in the Inter-American Development Bank in the summer of 1960, U.S. aid to Latin America was limited to "financing exports of U.S. equipment, to long-term sales of agricultural commodities, and to a modest technical assistance program for demonstration and training in health, education and agriculture";[84] in short, only aid that would further American economic interests in the region. By bringing the Cold War into the hemisphere, the Cuban revolution would change all that.

The Kennedy Administration made no bones about the role Cuba played in its decision to reformulate U.S. policy toward the region. As a candidate, Kennedy had publicly linked the need for Latin American development—embodied in an *Alianza para el Progreso*—with the need to contain the spread of Castroism.

Schlesinger tells the story of how the Alliance for Progress got its name.[85] Throughout the campaign, Kennedy repeatedly scored the Republicans for their failures in Latin America. When the time came for Kennedy to unveil his own plans for the region, the candidate wanted a symbol that would fire the imaginations of both the American voter and our Latin American allies—a symbol or a phrase as grand as Roosevelt's Good Neighbor Policy.

Richard Goodwin, a Kennedy staffer fresh from Harvard Law School, was given the task of finding such a symbol. Sitting in a campaign bus traveling through Texas in September 1960, Goodwin came across a Spanish-language magazine named *Alianza,* or Alliance. He knew he was half way there. Goodwin then called Karl Meyer, an editorial writer specializing in Latin America for the *Washington Post.* Alliance was a good start, but an alliance for what? Meyer in turn called Ernesto Betancourt, an early Castro supporter now in exile in Washington. Betancourt made two suggestions: Alliance for Development—*Alianza para el Desarollo;* or Alliance for Progress—*Alianza para el Progreso.* When Meyer called back, Goodwin knew there was no contest. Kennedy, never known for his linguistic ability, would never be able to pronounce *Desarollo. Alianza para el Progreso* was the clear winner. (The *el* was later dropped, making it grammatically incorrect but even more euphonious.)

Kennedy's plans went far beyond those envisioned by his predecessor. In fact, the only American foreign aid program comparable to the Alliance for Progress, either before or since, was the Marshall Plan. When the full contours of the Alliance were finally unveiled at the August 1961 OAS meeting in Punta Del Este, the U.S. representative, Treasury Secretary C. Douglas Dillon, spoke of a U.S. investment of some $20 billion in Latin America in the decade to come.

The charter of Punta del Este outlined a series of objectives for the Alliance for Progress. The primary goal was an economic growth rate of "not less than 2.5 percent per capita per year" in each of the Latin American states. This growth rate was to be the engine that moved forward all of the region's needed social and political development. The Alliance's second goal was a more equal distribution of each country's wealth. A third goal was diversification of exports, and movement away from single-crop dependency. A fourth objective was a solid program of industrialization that would use the region's vast natural resource base and also put to work the enormous pool of un- and underemployed. A fifth objective was an improvement of agricultural productivity, so that the region might begin to feed itself. To achieve this, the charter not only promised aid and technology but also spoke of the need for widespread agrarian reform. In addition, to raise the quality of life for all Latin Americans, the charter promised improved health care, provision of social services, and education.[86]

There is no doubt that each of these goals was admirable if Latin America was ever to overcome its underdevelopment. Indeed, some of the goals of the Alliance—such as agrarian reform and the equalization of income—were downright radical. They were also consistent with the type of social welfare concerns that characterized the programs of the New Frontier and the Great Society. But charity and altruism were not the only reasons for Washington's new commitment to regional development. As Kennedy pointed out time and again, the United States really had no other choice. The status quo in Latin America could no longer be maintained. As Kennedy put it, "those who make peaceful revolution impossible make violent revolution inevitable."[87]

Containing the Threat

Although the Alliance's long-range goal was to make Latin America invulnerable to communism by fostering its economic and social development, its planners did not ignore the more immediate security threats. The Alliance for Progress was really only half of Washington's new Latin American policy. The other half, the development of an advanced system of regional military security, was pursued with equal if not greater fervor.

In 1960, President Eisenhower had established the "southern command" in the Canal Zone. Previously, the U.S. armed forces had only three continental commands: Europe, the Middle East, and Asia. The addition of a southern command was testimony to Washington's increasing concern about Latin American security in the wake of Castro's revolution. Kennedy's election led to a new dimension in Washington's security planning: counterinsurgency.

In his early years in the Senate, Kennedy had downplayed the idea of a Communist threat in Latin America. Speaking in Puerto Rico in December 1958, just weeks before Castro seized power, the Senator warned of the danger in thinking "that all Latin American agitation is Communist-inspired—that every anti-American voice is the voice of Moscow—and that most citizens of Latin America share our dedication to an anticommunist crusade to save what we call free enterprise."[88] Once he became President, and was beset with the problems of Cuba, Laos, Berlin, and Vietnam, Kennedy soon forgot his own advice.

Immediately after his election, Kennedy directed Goodwin to set up a Latin American task force to develop concrete policy suggestions to go along with the still rhetorical Alliance for Progress. Adolph Berle, one of the authors of Roosevelt's Good Neighbor Policy, was to serve as chairman; its six members included Goodwin and several leading academics and regional policy makers, all with strong ties to Latin America's democratic left. It soon became clear that even among these sophisticated and liberal policy analysts an anti-Communist fervor had taken hold.

The task force report, submitted in early 1961, desc\
goal of any Latin American policy as to prevent "the in\
and necessary Latin American social transformation" from
captured by "overseas Communist power politics." The Comm\
goal in the region, according to the report, was "to convert Latin
American social revolution into a Marxist attack on the U.S. itself."
The peril, the report continued, "resembles, but is more dangerous
than, the Nazi-Fascist threat of the Franklin Roosevelt period and
demands an even bolder and more imaginative response."[89]

That response would, of course, entail extensive American aid
and political direction aimed at basic economic and social development in the region. But, as the report emphasized, "good wishes
and economic plans do not stop bullets or hand grenades or armed
bands." The United States would have to take a strong military
stand to contain the Communist threat in Latin America.[90]

Kennedy himself was something of an *aficionado* of guerrilla
warfare. He had read the works of Mao Zedong and Guevara,
and had become convinced that guerrilla warfare was becoming
one of the primary threats to U.S. interests and to the future of
the entire free world. It was also a threat that the United States,
despite its superior military fire power, was singularly unprepared
to confront. As we have seen, after the Bay of Pigs, Kennedy warned,
"We dare not fail to grasp the new concepts, the new tools, the
new sense of urgency we will need to combat it—whether in Cuba
or South Vietnam."[91]

Kennedy's concern was not shared by his generals, who preferred
the sophisticated and expensive technology of conventional warfare
to the homemade weapons and self-taught tactics of guerrilla warfare. Overriding considerable professional resistance, Kennedy ordered the generals to retool. They were to study carefully the works
of Mao and Guevara and develop the means for containing the
new threat. The Special Warfare Center at Fort Bragg (originally
designed to train a small number of soldiers for behind-the-lines
missions in the event of another world war) was upgraded and
expanded, and its graduates were awarded the "green beret" as a
symbol of their new elite status. In the fall of 1961, a Counter-
Insurgency Committee led by General Maxwell Taylor was formed

to coordinate the new counterinsurgency offensive: New weapons would be developed, training manuals would be rewritten, a whole new philosophy of warfare would emerge.

Nor was this new fervor limited to the military. Under the direction of Walt W. Rostow, economic historian and Deputy Assistant to the President for National Security Affairs, courses on guerrilla warfare methods were added to the curriculum of the State Department's Foreign Service Institute. At the same time, the Special Forces were given training in economic development and public administration. The traditional boundary between civil and military functions was discarded. According to Rostow, guerrilla warfare was a pathological response to economic underdevelopment in the Third World. To contain the guerrilla threat, counterinsurgency planners would thus have to address not only the military strategy of guerrilla warfare but also the root economic, political, and sociological causes. The essential lesson of guerrilla warfare, whether one read Mao and Guevara or Rostow, was that politics and warfare could not be kept separate.

Washington's obsession with guerrilla warfare was quickly transmitted south. Between 1962 and 1969, some 20,000 Latin American military officers stationed at the U.S. Army School of the Americas in the Canal Zone were trained in the techniques of counterinsurgency and domestic pacification. Thousands more were trained at the Special Warfare Center at Fort Bragg, North Carolina, the Inter-American Defense College in Washington, D.C.,[92] and by U.S. military missions attached to the Latin American military academies. Washington also provided the Latin American military forces with the most sophisticated, newly developed counterinsurgency technology: helicopters, defoliants, and napalm.

At the same time, hundreds of civilian American advisers were dispatched to the region to supervise a myriad of nonmilitary development projects: developing internal communications systems, building new roads and new dams, advising farmers on agricultural techniques and police forces on the latest in law enforcement methods. Although most of these advisers were what they claimed to be—genuine civilian technicians concerned solely with improving the quality of life in Latin America—others used their embassy affiliations to monitor and direct the counterinsurgency efforts. It must be remembered that almost all the civilian advisers had received some training in counterinsurgency before being sent to the region.

The United States did not limit its counterinsurgency role in Latin America during the 1960s to advice, education, and supply. When it was deemed necessary, U.S. advisers and troops were sent to help the struggle to contain communism. In 1965 alone, the U.S. Special Forces "made fifty-two special anti-subversive missions in Latin America, including parachute drops into guerrilla zones."[93] Over the next three years, the Green Berets served in antiguerrilla missions in Guatemala, Bolivia, Venezuela, and Nicaragua. It was the Green Berets who trained and assisted the Bolivian Rangers, who captured and killed Che Guevara.

Washington's export of counterinsurgency was much larger, better funded, and of wider reach than any of Havana's attempts to export revolution. This involvement in Latin America, however, received almost no press coverage in the United States. The American public, increasingly concerned about the escalating war in Vietnam, apparently had no time for the much smaller guerrilla wars brewing so close to home.

Mixed Reviews

Washington's dual program of security and development had mixed results, but succeeded in its primary goal of preventing additional Cubas in the hemisphere. Indeed, until the 1979 Sandinista revolution in Nicaragua, not one pro-Marxist revolution succeeded in Latin America. The two democratically elected pro-left regimes that did come to power—Quadros in Brazil in 1960, Allende in Chile in 1970—were soon replaced by right-wing military juntas friendlier to the United States.

The development goals of the Alliance for Progress were less successful. By almost every quantitative and qualitative indicator of development, the Alliance was a failure. In terms of economic growth, the region as a whole did not reach the target of 2.5 percent per capita until 1968, with some individual states notably lagging behind. As for income distribution, a 1968 UN study reported, "little if any change in [the] structure of gross income inequality" in the region. Industrialization did increase significantly during the Alliance decade. However, because highly capital-intensive industry was chosen, rather than labor-intensive, unemployment in Latin America was not reduced. The same is true of agricultural productivity.[94] According to the *Rockefeller Report on the Americas* released in 1969, "while overall food production is going up, food production per person, due to the population explosion, is estimated at 10 percent less than it was at the end of World War II."[95] The tentative attempts at land reform also failed to keep up with the increase in the number of peasants seeking land. The plans to improve health care, education, and housing also have not lived up to the charter's expectations.

Why the Alliance failed so dismally has been the subject of much debate. The reasons offered include poor planning, corrupt implementation, the failure of the United States to provide the promised aid, too much emphasis on investments that either served U.S. interests or the interests of politically sound allies, the use of "inappropriate" technology, and the suggestion that the task itself was just too great.[96]

Some critics also blame the Alliance's failure on American unwillingness to make the necessary economic sacrifices and to take the necessary political risks. In the economic realm, it promised disinterested aid, clearly intended to foster Latin American development rather than serve U.S. economic interests. In the political realm, the Alliance promised to support the development of Latin America's democratic left. The democratic left, it was felt, was the only group in the region that would make the economic and social changes necessary to stave off left-wing revolutions. But when it came time to implement these radical programs, Washington balked, returning to its traditional role of supporting U.S. economic interests and conservative political regimes.[97]

Harmful "Side Effects"

The real tragedy of the Alliance was its failure to preserve democracy in Latin America. Although the security component of the program did manage to prevent the Latin American democracies from falling prey to left-wing revolutions, it could not defend the region's democracies against the attacks of the Latin American *right*. Between 1964 and 1973, coups led by right-wing military officers overthrew democratic regimes in Brazil, Argentina, Uruguay, and Chile. Today, some form of military rule still prevails in these nations.

The reasons for the rise of right-wing authoritarianism in Latin America are varied and complex and are the subject of an entire literature within Latin American studies that analyzes "bureaucratic authoritarianism."[98] Some of the causes that have been suggested are internal economic dynamics, the "bunching" of demands for distribution and participation, the fear of Castroism, and Washington's active intervention on the side of conservatism.[99]

One theory suggests that the United States actually taught the Latin American militaries—albeit unknowingly—to seize power in their countries.[100] The United States has traditionally trained many of Latin America's military elite, both at military academies in the United States and through military advisory missions assigned to a number of the region's leading military schools, such as Brazil's Escola Superior de Guerra. Previously, one of the main goals of the U.S. training had been to teach the Latin American militaries democratic ideals, especially the need to keep civilian and military life separate. It was hoped that American tutelage would keep a new generation of Latin American "men on horseback" in the barracks and out of the presidential palaces.

But after 1961, the need to contain the Communist threat in Latin America took precedence over all other concerns. In fact, the new counterinsurgency curriculum actually undermined the earlier training on the separation of civil and military roles. As Yale political scientist Alfred Stepan has pointed out in his study on the emergence of military rule in Brazil, the United States began "urging the Latin American military to become more deeply involved in all stages of society in order to wage an effective campaign against internal war." This urging, Stepan says, "implicitly encouraged a deeper involvement of the military in politics, and . . . can be considered a contributing factor in the creation of military regimes."[101]

The new training gave the Latin American military elite not only the means to seize power but also a justification, a belief in its competence to rule, and a new sense of mission. These were not the *caudillos* of old seizing power for personal gain, but rational technocrats in uniform committed to their new role of "nation builders." At the military academy they learned how the myriad difficulties of economic underdevelopment—corruption, special interests, and poor planning, as well as Communist subversion—stood in the way of stable development. But under the careful guidance of a military elite, trained in public administration and economic planning as well as counterinsurgency, the country would not only be able to contain the Communist threat but also get back on the track of sound economic and political development. Although the counterinsurgency curriculum never explicitly told the military it should seize power, the logical inference was often implicit. And it was precisely this sense of mission that led the military to seize power from democratically elected governments in Brazil in 1964, Argentina in 1966, and Chile in 1973.

It is doubtful that U.S. planners were aware of the political implications of their curriculum, at least not in the beginning. Men like Kennedy, Rostow, and Bundy were all committed to democracy. The whole point of the counterinsurgency training, they argued, was to give the democracies the necessary tools to defend themselves. Nevertheless, a close reading of the academic literature produced during this period—a good deal by the supporters of the Kennedy and Johnson Administrations—reveals a strong antidemocratic and proauthoritarian, particularly military authoritarian, bent.

In somewhat oversimplified form, the argument of many of the new development specialists was as follows: In the increasingly chaotic Third World, the military was the logical choice to lead the development process. The military was rational, technically trained, uncorruptible, and had a sense of mission. More than any other group it could bring order to chaos and make the necessary sacrifices to put these countries on the road to development.[102] If in the process some members of society were deprived of their democratic rights, that was unfortunate, but perhaps necessary. As one leading development expert put it, in many modernizing countries "the primary problem is not liberty but the creation of a legitimate public order. Men may, of course, have order without liberty, but they cannot have liberty without order. Authority has to exist before it can be limited, and it is authority that is in scarce supply in those modernizing countries where government is at the mercy of alienated intellectuals, rambunctious colonels, and rioting students."[103]

DIRECT INTERVENTION

Only the most radical and manichean of conspiracy theorists would suggest that U.S. intervention was the sole cause of the right-wing military coups in Latin America. Yet there is conclusive evidence that Washington did use aid, loans, as well as covert intervention not only to support conservative Latin American regimes and private economic interests, but actually to destabilize the democratic-left regimes of Goulart in Brazil and Allende in Chile.

The story of Washington's covert involvement in the Chilean coup is well known.[104] During the 1960s various U.S. administrations funneled over $13 million in covert funds to Chilean political groups and media to prevent Allende's election. After he finally won the presidency in 1970, Washington's opposition and level of intervention increased. The strategy chosen by the Nixon Administration to depose the new Popular Unity regime was one of economic strangulation. Acting in close concert with top executives of the International Telephone and Telegraph Corporation (ITT), Washington systematically cut off the Allende regime's access to international credits from both public and private lending sources. Washington also used political and economic influence to cut off critical supplies of spare parts and machinery to Chile. In 1973 the Nixon Administration even dumped U.S. copper reserves on the world market to drive down the price of Chile's major source of foreign exchange.

At the same time Washington continued to pour millions of dollars into political organizations that opposed the Allende Government. The most notable recipient of Washington's largesse was the truckers' union whose strike brought the crisis to a head. This large influx of covert funds had the additional effect of further distorting Chile's already severely inflated economy. Throughout the crisis Washington kept in close contact with the Chilean military elite, actually increasing aid to the Chilean armed forces at the same time that it cut off all support for the Chilean Government.

In September 1973—apparently with the full knowledge and support of the Nixon Administration—the Chilean military overthrew the democratically elected government of Salvador Allende. After the coup the left-wing press in Latin America and the United States was filled with charges of American complicity. It was not, however, until 1976 and the Church Committee's investigations of the abuses of the intelligence agencies that the full story of Washington's involvement in the overthrow of Salvador Allende became public knowledge in the United States.

The story of the American role in the 1964 military coup against Goulart is less well known. According to Alfred Stepan, the United States played an important, but not conclusive, role in the Brazilian coup.[105] Stepan argues that Washington's primary contribution was the creation of a political and intellectual predisposition to coup among the Brazilian military elite. Stepan says that Washington then reinforced that predisposition with a selective aid program intended "to weaken the Goulart government . . . and to strengthen the military government of General Castello Branco who succeeded Goulart." Much like the Nixon Administration's Chile policy a decade later, the Johnson Administration suspended all grants to the Brazilian Government, while significantly increasing economic and material support to Goulart's political and military opponents. This policy was known in the Johnson State Department as strengthening "islands of sanity" in Brazil. Stepan also says that Washington's military attachés in Brazil—men with strong personal and professional ties to the Brazilian military elite dating back to World War II—let it be known that the United States would not oppose a military coup against the Goulart Government.

Phyllis Parker in *Brazil and the Quiet Intervention* argues that the Johnson State Department was prepared to take a more active role in the coup.[106] A U.S. aircraft carrier was stationed off the Brazilian coast throughout the crisis, and a special task force was established at the State Department to monitor and, if necessary, direct events. The reason the intervention remained quiet, according to Parker, was that there was no need for a more active involvement. The indirect pressures did their work. Washington certainly made no attempt to mask its delight after the coup. President Johnson's congratulations to the new junta reached São Paulo even before the deposed President Goulart was out of the country.

The Brazilian case is important not only because it was the first of the new type of technocratic military coups trained and aided by the United States, but also because it suggests that the Allende coup was not an aberration. Much of the breast beating that followed the revelations of American covert involvement in Chile was accompanied by claims that it was a symptom of the peculiar Nixon pathology, along with the secret bombing of Cambodia and the abuses of Watergate. The Brazilian coup suggests that it was not. In the campaign to contain the Communist threat in Latin America such abuses were standard operating procedure for every American Administration since John F. Kennedy and the Bay of Pigs.

THE CUBAN OBSESSION

The most serious failure of Washington's Latin American policy during the 1960s was its repeated sacrifice of developmental goals in favor of security concerns. The Alliance for Progress was originally intended to assist and reinforce progressive change throughout the hemisphere. As President Kennedy frequently stated, peaceful revolution under the aegis of the Alliance was the only way to defend Latin America from violent revolution under Communist domination. Over time, however, many of Washington's policy makers became increasingly unable to distinguish between these two types of change, and in the end chose to oppose change altogether. Underlying this basic shift in American attitudes was a growing obsession with Cuba and Castro's attempts to export revolution to Latin America.

It must be remembered that Cuba's early efforts to export revolution were not of major concern to U.S. policy makers. The Eisenhower Administration's hostility to the Castro regime was based on the radicalization of Cuba's *domestic* policies and on Castro's penchant for anti-American propaganda. Only after Cuba's alignment with the Soviet Union during the Kennedy Administration did Washington become seriously concerned about the international possibilities of Castroism. But even then, Kennedy's concern was more with the strength of the Cuban example and Latin America's vulnerability than with any concrete Cuban attempts to export revolution. But by the mid-1960s, Washington seemed to have become obsessed with the Cuban export of revolution, and with the means to contain that threat.

When one considers the force of the American response, the remarkable fact is that throughout the 1960s no more than a few hundred Cubans fought in all of Latin America. Why did Washington so consistently overestimate the strength of the Cuban threat? There are several possible explanations. First, Cuba's alliance with the Soviet Union was proof enough that the Cuban threat was real and dangerous to U.S. interests. Washington took its Cold War rhetoric so seriously that it overlooked the facts that Cuban resources were severely limited, that there were never more than a few hundred Cuban guerrillas, and that the Russians had refused to underwrite Cuba's internationalist policies.

At the same time, the alleged Cuban threat was only a part of Washington's growing obsession with international Communist subversion. It must be remembered that Kennedy originally justified the Bay of Pigs invasion by claiming that Cuba was only the first step—the first domino—in what was an international plot by Communist forces to exploit and subvert national liberation movements and ultimately challenge the very survival of the free world. So global a threat had to be taken seriously.

Washington also seemed to take Cuban rhetoric far too literally. When Castro pledged to turn the Andes into the Sierra Maestra of Latin America, various administrations apparently believed he could do it. The best example of Washington's credulity is the report on the 1966 Tricontinental Conference prepared for the Internal Security Subcommittee of the Senate Judiciary Committee. In it the Cubans were blamed for almost every major and minor instability in the hemisphere. In Puerto Rico alone, the Cubans were said to be the source of student riots:

> Chronic riots at the university of Puerto Rico are attributed to student agitators following instructions from Cuba's government-controlled subversive student organization, the University Student Federation;

drug trafficking:

> Cuba has also become an important way-station for the transfer of drugs from Red China to Puerto Rico and thence to the mainland of the United States. . . . the sale of drugs, particularly heroin, in the United States and other Free-World countries provides a considerable amount of foreign exchange by which Cuba finances guerrilla activities . . . ;

and acts of sabotage:

> Sabotage, little reported and less understood in the mainland United States has taken and is taking its toll in Puerto Rico. . . . Targets [are] mainland U.S. companies—Levittown Construction Co., Barker's Department Store, Woolworth's, the Bata Shoe Factory and Bargain Town.

Moreover, according to the report, Cuban subversion in Puerto Rico was part of a larger Cuban–Soviet "Master Plan" to gain control of the Caribbean:

> Geographically, Cuba, Haiti, the Dominican Republic and Puerto Rico extend in that order in a straight line across the Caribbean from the tip of Florida to the Leeward Islands. Under Communist control, and appropriately equipped militarily, the latter three could effectively block sea and air approaches to northern South America and the Panama Canal. Cuba alone virtually commands the access routes to the Gulf of Mexico and Central America. This is the political and strategic significance of Puerto Rico in the Communist master plan for the Western Hemisphere.[107]

As one reviews this report on Cuban subversion, three aspects stand out as particularly representative of Washington's misperception of the Cuban threat. First, the report consistently overestimates Cuba's ability to challenge American domination of the hemisphere. According to the report, "Cuba has a proved record of success in penetrating Latin America,"[108] although no concrete examples of successful Cuban guerrilla missions are offered. The fact that every one of Cuba's attempts to export revolution to Latin America failed is not mentioned.

In addition, the report consistently overestimates Soviet support of Cuban international revolutionary activities. The report states that "Latin America is a major target of Communist expansion" and that Havana was Moscow's chosen headquarters for hemispheric subversion.[109] As we shall see, neither assertion was true.

Finally, the report directly expresses in clear language Washington's frustration and humiliation at its apparent inability to contain the Cuban threat:

> It is humiliating enough to have the international Communist conspiracy seize control of a country only 60 [sic] miles from American shores, and maintain itself in power despite all the pressures we have thus far brought to bear. It becomes a thousand times as humiliating when that country is transformed into a headquarters for international revolutionary subversion while the OAS and the mighty United States of America look on helpless and apparently incapable of any decisive action.[110]

A MYTH IS BORN

For all its concern with the Cuban threat, Washington remained remarkably ignorant of Cuba's actual foreign policies. Throughout the 1960s, as American scholars published book after book on Cuban domestic policies, Cuba's relations with the socialist bloc, and the theoretical aspects of Havana's attempts to export revolution, there was not one study of Cuba's foreign policies in either Latin America or Africa. American policy analysts similarly avoided the subject, preferring innuendo to facts in their regular appearances before congressional subcommittees. As one observer grimly noted in 1970:

> . . . although American policy for the last decade has been dedicated to repressing liberation movements in Latin America, not a single

serious study of any of these movements has appeared in the United States. The American taxpayer is thus paying for his army to crush movements of which he has virtually no knowledge.[111]

A decade has done little to change the state of Cuban studies. Although numerous books have been written on Cuba since 1970, and there has been strong interest in Cuban foreign policy since the 1975 Cuban involvement in Angola, scant information and misinformation on Cuban policies in Latin America still predominate—whether they be allegations of Cuban subversion in Guatemala in 1961 or in El Salvador in 1981.

Allegations of a Cuban threat have apparently served the political interests of a variety of American policy makers for the past twenty years. Kennedy spoke of the need for a program like the Alliance for Progress, claiming it was the only way to meet the Cuban threat in Latin America. In fact, the Cuban threat Kennedy spoke of was more symbolic than real. But when it came time to sell the Alliance to Congress, symbolic Cubans were not enough to justify a multibillion-dollar allocation. Real Cubans and a real military threat were the only way. This psychology unfortunately reinforced belief in the sort of misinformation and misinterpretation that to this day characterize American pronouncements on Cuban foreign policy.

The myth of the Cuban threat also served a wide variety of political interests in Latin America. For the left, Castro's revolution heralded the beginning of a new era of Latin American revolutions. The belief that the Latin American left could not only depend on Cuba for inspiration but also for some direct military support was an invaluable propaganda tool. Exercises like the Guevara Bolivian *foco* thus received coverage in the left-wing press far beyond its size or chances for success.

The right also found the myth of the Cuban guerrilla an invaluable tool for mobilizing support. The Cuban threat became a justification for crackdowns on domestic opposition and an important bargaining chip for those demanding U.S. military aid. In fact, the Cuban threat was so useful that even when there were no Cubans invading, the right was willing to invent them. In May 1961, the Guatemalan government protested to the Inter-American Peace Committee of the OAS that Cuban troops were being trained in Mexico for an invasion of Guatemala, and that Raúl Castro himself had traveled to Mexico to inspect the troops. The Mexican Government denied the allegations, and an OAS investigation could find no traces of Cuban guerrillas. Yet the Guatemalans continued to allege a Castro plot to return Arbenz to power, and used the opportunity to round up opposition members in the cities.[112] Thus, the myth of the Cuban guerrilla seemed to take on a life of its own.

idel Castro, center, his brother Raúl, far left, and members of the July 26 Move-
ent leaving the Isle of Pines Prison after a year and a half of imprisonment
llowing the abortive attack on the Moncada Barracks.

he Guevara, Fidel Castro, Calixto García, Ramiro Valdés, Juan Almeida in
ierra Maestra campaign against Batista, 1958.

Cuban exile prisoners captured during Bay of Pigs invasion, 1961.

Castro, on his first visit to Washington as head of state, leaves Vice President Richard Nixon's office after a two hour and twenty minute meeting in April 1959. Not long afterward, Nixon circulated a memo recommending the creation of an anti-Castro exile force.

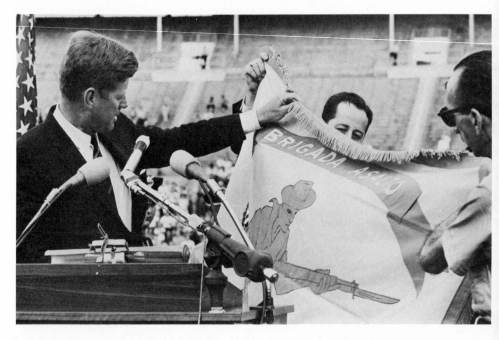

Twenty months after the failure of the Bay of Pigs invasion, President John F. Kennedy receives the combat flag of the Cuban exile brigade from recently released prisoners of war at a ceremony at the Miami Orange Bowl in December 1962.

UN Ambassador Adlai Stevenson (right) telling Soviet delegate Valerian Zorin that "we have proof and will show it to you," unveils U.S. reconnaissance photographs of intermediate-range missile sites in Cuba during October 25, 1962, emergency session of the UN Security Council.

U.S. Navy patrol plane and destroyer monitor a Soviet freighter as it leaves Cuba with what appeared to be canvas-shrouded missiles in November 1962.

Castro visits with Soviet Premier Nikita Khrushchev, right, and USSR President Leonid Brezhnev at Khrushchev's estate outside Moscow in April 1963.

American troops battle rioters in Santo Domingo during 1965 U.S. intervention in the Dominican Republic.

Che Guevara in Bolivia in 1967. Bottom photo shows Guevara with French writer
Régis Debray, right, and Bolivian guerrilla known as "el Chino," far left.

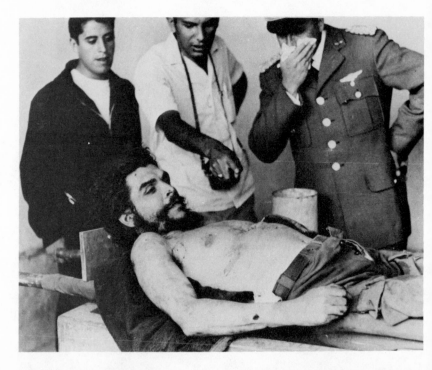

Bolivian officer and newsmen peer at body of guerrilla leader Che Guevara after his execution by the Bolivian army in October 1967.

Castro and Chilean President Salvador Allende during Castro's November 1971 visit to Chile.

Cuban soldiers train with MPLA forces near Cabinda, Angola, in 1976 as the Angolan civil war raged.

Somali forces display a young Cuban soldier captured during 1977 Ethiopia-Somali war over the Ogaden.

Fidel Castro addresses the UN General Assembly, October 1979.

Orlando José Tardencillas, nineteen, a Nicaraguan guerrilla brought to Washington to bolster U.S. assertions of Cuban and Nicaraguan involvement in El Salvador, tells a March 1982 press conference that he was not trained in Cuba and acted on his own.

Uneasy Allies: Cuba
and the Soviet Union

FIDEL Castro's revolution caught the Soviet Union by surprise. Moscow had always downplayed the significance of Third World revolutions by claiming the conditions in the underdeveloped nations were not right. With no industry, no proletariat, and no Communist party, how could these countries be expected to build a true Communist society? Moscow was particularly skeptical about the prospects for a Latin American revolution. Latin America, in Soviet eyes, was irrevocably part of Washington's sphere of influence. Castro's revolution was not expected to survive.

The Cuban revolution proved the Soviets wrong on both points. Not only did Castro stage an independent revolution on the doorstep of the United States, he then transformed it into a genuinely socialist revolution. Not only was Castro's the first such revolution in the Western hemisphere, it was also the first popular revolution in the socialist bloc since Mao's revolution in China a decade before. The Cuban example demanded a complete reordering of Moscow's most basic theoretical and ideological assumptions.

Neither was Castro satisfied with leaving that challenge implicit. In speech after speech, meeting after meeting, Castro demanded that his Soviet allies acknowledge the revolutionary potential of the Third World and make a major commitment to fostering its revolutions. During most of the 1960s, Moscow chose to ignore Castro's challenges—refusing to engage in a polemic with the Cubans, and also refusing to increase its commitments to the Third World.

When it became clear to Castro that his ideological critiques had failed, he actually went so far as to question Moscow's right to lead the international movement. This was a challenge that the Kremlin would not tolerate. Castro no longer debated theory, he threatened Moscow's fundamental notions about bloc loyalty and discipline. Steps would have to be taken to control Castro. By 1968, it looked as if the Cuban–Soviet alliance, and possibly Castro's revolution, might be destroyed.

THE SOVIETS AND THE THIRD WORLD

When Castro seized power in Havana in January 1959, Soviet attitudes toward the Third World were in a state of flux. During the Stalin years, Moscow had generally ignored the national liberation movements in Africa and Asia, dismissing their antiimperialist ideologies as rhetoric and their leaders as puppets of Western imperialism.[1] With Stalin's death and the overhaul of Soviet policies, the Kremlin's new leadership began to show a new interest in and optimism about the Third World. At the 1956 Congress of the Soviet Communist Party—site of Khrushchev's famous "secret speech" denouncing the abuses of Stalinism—the First Secretary described the anticolonial wars in Africa and Asia as "development[s] of world-historical significance."[2] At the very least, the demise of colonialism would lessen the power of the Western imperial camp. At best, in the long run, the new nationalist leaders (or, more likely, their descendants) would throw their lot in with the socialist camp.[3]

Moscow's optimism about the Third World was part of a new, much broader optimism toward what Soviet theorists called the "changing correlation of international forces." Soviet development of an inter-continental ballistic missile, the successful launching of Sputnik, and the unprecedented growth rate of the Soviet economy during the 1950s convinced Moscow's leaders that a worldwide triumph for socialism was inevitable—if a long way off. In the interim, Moscow would now have the means not only to defend its own borders, but also to stem the tide of Western imperialism. In Moscow's view, the new terms of peaceful coexistence would restrain Washington from intervening militarily against the new crop of left-leaning regimes coming to power in the Third World.

Peaceful coexistence would also require Moscow to exercise caution in its foreign policies. The goal of coexistence was above all to avoid a direct military confrontation with the United States, and to give the Soviet economy the breathing space needed for its development and for the eventual eclipse of capitalism. In terms of Soviet policies in the Third World, this meant economic aid and political support appropriate to Moscow's new interest and optimism. But it also called for a great deal of restraint when it came to possible military commitments that might force a confrontation with the United States.

A Theory of Convenience

During the mid- to late 1950s, the Kremlin's theorists began to outline a new theory of Third World development that encompassed both Moscow's new optimism for the Third World and Moscow's need to limit its military involvement in liberation struggles. In November 1960, at the Moscow Congress of the Eighty-One Communist Parties, Soviet theorists unveiled the new doctrine of "National Democracy" to describe the type of limited progress the Soviets expected in the Third World, and the type of states Moscow intended to aid. It must be emphasized that what were termed National Democratic states were regarded "progressive" because of their natural opposition—born of their struggle against colonialism—to Western imperialism. They were not, however, expected to become Communist states at any time in the near future. They had no industry, no proletariat, and, most importantly, no Communist party leading their struggle. Moscow did expect, however, that

137

the National Democratic states would stay free of Western domination—limiting Western investment and refusing to join Western military alliances—and cultivate political ties with the socialist bloc while beginning the painstaking process of social development at home.[4]

It must also be emphasized that Moscow expected the transition to socialism in a National Democratic state to take a long time, requiring first the development of an industrial base and an industrial class. It would also occur without violence. The Soviets could thus afford to concentrate their aid to these states on long-range economic development and avoid short-term military confrontations. The forces of history seemed to reinforce the needs of peaceful coexistence—at least doctrinally. One of Moscow's most dramatic commitments to a National Democratic state was the 1958 loan of $500 million to Nasser's Egypt for the building of the Aswan Dam.

The theory of National Democracy was developed primarily to address events in Africa and Asia, not Latin America. Latin America had traditionally been last on Moscow's list of priorities.[5] Before 1961 the prestigious Soviet Academy of Sciences did not even have a department to study Latin America, while it had whole institutes devoted to Africa and Asia. Of all states in the developing world, conditions in Latin America were thought to be least auspicious for either Soviet influence or socialist development.

Above all, Washington's vigilance against Communist infiltration was known to be unbending. The 1954 U.S.-orchestrated overthrow of Guatemala's Arbenz Government—merely on the suspicion of Communist sympathies—made that fact utterly clear. In addition, according to Soviet theorists, the nature of the Latin American class structure made any form of progressive revolution unlikely. Because of the long history of American investment in Latin America, these states had both a highly developed middle class and a well-entrenched oligarchy with strong ties to the United States that would oppose any progressive revolution. The only hope for change in Latin America, according to Soviet theorists, was in the development of an independent, national bourgeoisie whose interests were not inevitably tied to American capital. Although Moscow directed the local Communist parties to improve its ties with the local bourgeoisie and to encourage any and all nationalist movements, it did not anticipate any success in Latin America in the foreseeable future.

An Unexpected Revolution

What first impressed the Soviet observers about Castro's revolution was its obviously anti-American tenor. The revolution, however, had little immediate effect on Moscow's conservative analyses of Third World development.[6] At best, Castro might be expected to limit American domination of the Cuban economy while starting some progressive changes—such as agrarian reform—at home. The Soviets had no expectation that within two years of the revolution Castro would declare himself a Marxist–Leninist and seek Cuba's admission to the socialist bloc. As far as Moscow was concerned, neither Cuba's class structure nor its proximity to the United States would allow Castro's revolution to develop to the socialist stage. Finally, and most tellingly in Moscow's opinion, Castro was not, nor had he ever been, a member of a Communist party.

In his memoirs, Khrushchev tells a story about his own early doubts about Castro:

> The leaders of the Cuban revolution go up to heaven; Saint Peter comes out to meet them as God's official representative and orders them all to line up. Then he says, "All Communists, three steps forward!" Guevara steps forward; Raúl steps forward; so does someone else. But all the rest, including Fidel, stay in line. Peter glares at Fidel and shouts, "Hey! you, the tall one with the beard! What's wrong, didn't you hear what I said? All Communists three steps forward!"

"The point of this story," the former premier goes on to say, "is that while Saint Peter and everyone else considered Fidel a Communist, Fidel himself did not. He thought Peter's command didn't pertain to him."[7]

Moscow approached the Cuban revolution with a great deal of caution—even more caution than it was simultaneously exercising in Asia or Africa. Throughout 1959, the Soviet press described developments in Cuba in friendly terms, but was also careful not to imply any offer of possible Soviet support.[8] On several occasions

139

the Soviet press spoke of Cuba's precarious geopolitical situation, and warned of the danger of a repeat of the Guatemalan tragedy. But as they denounced U.S. plans for military intervention, the Soviets avoided any suggestion that they would come to Cuba's defense.

Despite Moscow's growing optimism about the improving balance of international forces, it apparently did not feel that its new power to counter American imperialism extended to Latin America. At the very least, Moscow was not yet willing to test its new strength for the sake of a regime it did not believe could ever become a member of the socialist camp.

At the same time, Moscow may well have feared that any sign of Soviet support for Castro might actually provoke Washington to a military intervention. Throughout 1959 and much of 1960, Moscow repeatedly denied charges that Castro was a Communist, contending that anyone who asserted otherwise was merely trying to incite an American attack on the new regime.[9]

Beginning in early 1960, Moscow began to show a greater optimism about the future of the Cuban revolution, and its own possible role. The Castro Government had survived its critical first year in power without a U.S. intervention. Domestically, the new regime was implementing a growing number of progressive policies, including a sweeping agrarian reform, while successfully building popular support. Castro even allowed the Cuban Communists to participate in the new government, if only on a local level. By 1960, Cuba had become the ideal National Democratic state.

The Soviets made their first real overture to the Castro regime in February 1960, when Mikoyan led a Soviet trade fair to Cuba. That same month Moscow made its first ideological commitment to the revolution. Speaking before the Indian Parliament in New Delhi on February 12, 1960, Khrushchev announced that, "Our sympathies have always been with and will always be with countries like Cuba who defend their national and economic independence through arduous struggle." Continuing in general terms, Khrushchev said, "The Soviet Union has always given and will continue to give disinterested aid and support to all countries in their struggle for freedom and independence, in their struggle against economic backwardness."[10] There was nothing concrete about Khrushchev's statement. Its significance lies only in the fact that after a year of carefully avoiding even a suspicion of Soviet involvement in Castro's revolution, Moscow had apparently decided to express its "disinterested support." Even then, another three months passed before Moscow and Havana established official diplomatic relations.

A Slip of the Lip?

The pace began to pick up significantly during the last weeks of June 1960, as U.S.–Cuban relations deteriorated rapidly. First the Soviets bailed Cuba out of the refineries/sugar mill crisis. Then, in the second week of July, Khrushchev made a startling military commitment to Cuba, warning the United States that any intervention in Cuba might lead to attack by the Soviet Union:

> It would be wise not to forget that the United States is no longer at an inaccessible distance from the Soviet Union. Figuratively speaking, should the need arise, Soviet artillerymen can support the Cuban people by missile fire if the aggressive forces from the Pentagon dare intervene in Cuba.[11]

One must ask why, after a year and a half of qualified endorsements and only the most nebulous commitments, all intended to soothe American nerves and limit Moscow's responsibility to Havana, should Khrushchev now decide to throw all caution to the wind? In less than two months, Moscow had gone from simply recognizing Cuba to chancing a nuclear confrontation with Washington over Castro's survival.

Moscow's new hard line on Cuba was only part of a more general hard line on international affairs adopted during the spring of 1960. That May, U.S.–Soviet relations took a severe downturn when Khrushchev abruptly canceled a long-planned summit meeting after an American U-2 spy plane was shot down over Soviet territory. Less than a month later, Khrushchev lashed out at China, his other major rival. At a Bucharest Conference of Communist parties, he denounced as treasonous Peking's increasingly vocal opposition to Soviet leadership of the socialist bloc.

At this time, Moscow apparently began to realize the significance of the Cuban revolution for its international prestige *vis à vis* both these rivals. Castro's revolution, if it survived, would refute Peking's claim that the Soviets had lost their revolutionary touch, and at the same time would deal a major blow to Washington's traditional domination of the Western hemisphere. In a June speech, Khrushchev declared that the Cuban revolution was one of "the most portentous historical events in recent times and one of the most notable events in modern history."[12] At a press conference the following month—just three days after his statement about the Soviet missiles—Khrushchev announced that the Monroe Doctrine was now officially dead. "The only thing left to do with the Monroe Doctrine," he gloated, "is to bury it, just as you bury anything dead, so it will not poison the air."[13]

Despite all these signs, it would be wrong to suggest that Moscow's new commitment to Cuba was the culmination of any long-range plan to subvert the Castro Government and pry it away from the Western bloc. It was more likely that the events of July 1960, initiated by Washington's refusal to refine Soviet oil and escalated by Castro's nationalization of the U.S. refineries, overtook Moscow and forced a quick reaction—or, some would say, overreaction. Khrushchev, of course, was notorious for his temper and hyperbole.

For months after the July missile speech, Moscow tried valiantly to bring its commitment to Cuba back from the nuclear brink. While continuing to promise "the necessary aid" for Cuba's defense, Khrushchev did not repeat the missile part of the threat. When asked by Cuban journalist Carlos Franqui in an October 1960 interview to explain the extent of Moscow's commitment to Cuba's defense—a question undoubtedly preoccupying the entire Cuban leadership—Khrushchev was diplomatic and ambiguous:

Franqui: The imperialists say that the Soviet government's statement on the possibility of using missiles in case of armed aggression against Cuba has a purely symbolic meaning. What do you think? *Khrushchev:* I would like if such a declaration on the part of the enemies of the Cuban revolution would be merely symbolic. This would require that the imperialists not transform their threat of intervention in Cuba into military action. In that case there would be no need

142

to verify the meaning of our statement about armed aid to the Cuban people against aggression. Is this clear?[14]

Much about Soviet foreign policy remained unclear after the July missile speech. Previously, Moscow had only promised its nuclear capability to the defense of the socialist bloc states. Now it was broadening that commitment to include a state that it claimed was not socialist and nowhere near becoming socialist. The first question was, How much could Cuba rely on the Soviet Union? Could Havana now expect economic and military aid on a level comparable to that enjoyed by the socialist bloc? Furthermore, what did the commitment to Cuba mean for Soviet policies toward other progressive or National Democratic states in the Third World? Could they too expect the Soviet Union to guarantee their defense under the Soviet nuclear umbrella? And, finally, what did Moscow's commitment to Cuba mean for the future of peaceful coexistence? Was Moscow bringing the military component back into the U.S.–Soviet competition?

Moscow tried to avoid these questions by claiming that its commitment to Cuba was really no different from earlier commitments to other National Democracies, such as Egypt in 1956, or Iraq in 1958. But despite Moscow's claims, the commitment to Cuba was different precisely because it included the mention of missiles. In seeking to deescalate the Cuban issue, Moscow appealed to both Washington and Havana to exercise prudence.

Most important, having made its commitment to Cuba, Moscow tried to temper the policies of its new ally, counseling Havana to take a course of moderation at home and in its dealings with Washington so as to avoid direct confrontation. Specifically, the Soviets pressed Castro to maintain economic ties with the United States, and counseled Havana against wholesale nationalization at home. Cuba would have to maintain a substantial private sector in order to avoid the bottlenecks and imbalances that would inevitably be part of an abrupt transition to a centralized economy. Not incidentally, Moscow wanted to avoid Cuban requests for even more aid from the socialist bloc. The Soviets also seemed reticent to commit themselves to any other revolutions in Latin America. Castro's frequent promises to turn the Andes into the Sierra Maestra of Latin America were not repeated in Moscow.

This last point deserves particular attention. From the beginning of the Cuban revolution, Moscow tried to play down the importance of armed struggle for Castro's victory or for other revolutions in Latin America. Although the Soviets were quick to point out the significance of the Cuban model for the rest of Latin America, Moscow focused on the nonviolent aspects of Cuba's radicalization, particularly the implementation of agrarian reform. Like Havana, Moscow also expected the Cuban revolution to become a rallying point for progressive forces throughout the Latin American continent. But unlike Havana, the Soviet leaders hoped that the wave of sympathy for Cuba and against the United States would lead to the formation of broad united fronts with the liberal bourgeoisie, rather than further polarization. Once again, the basis of this disagreement was the issue of the imminence of radical change. Moscow expected that the transition to socialism in Latin America, though aided by the Cuban revolution, would still be a long and predominantly political process, the first step being the formation of united fronts. Calls to turn the Andes into the Sierra Maestra would only end in polarizing and alienating the potentially progressive nationalist bourgeoisie while increasing the chance of direct American military intervention.[15]

Castro Unbound

As it turned out, Havana heeded none of Moscow's cautionary advice. Spurred by revolutionary fervor at home and the euphoria of having snubbed the United States and lived to tell the tale, Castro further radicalized his revolution in the fall of 1960 with a wholesale nationalization of the Cuban private sector. At the same time, the Cuban press was filled with calls to arms in Latin America. The final escalation came in April 1961, when Castro announced that the Cuban revolution was socialist.[16] There were no ticker tape parades in Moscow to greet the news. Khrushchev later said that he was confused by Castro's announcement, which served only to increase internal opposition to his regime as well as Cuba's vulnerability to American attack. "As far as personal courage was concerned," Khrushchev said, "his position was admirable and correct. But from a tactical standpoint, it didn't make much sense."[17] The Soviet press did not report Castro's speech, and it was another year before Moscow would acknowledge Cuba's shift to socialism.

Moscow was apparently startled and quite displeased by Castro's refusal to follow the course of moderation it advised. Castro's shift to socialism made the Soviet Union, as well as Cuba, more vulnerable to U.S. attack. If Cuba really were socialist, then no qualifications, no "figuratively speakings," no quiet disclaimers could limit Moscow's commitment to Cuba's future defense. There can be little doubt that Castro chose to announce his turn to socialism precisely to remove the ambiguity about Moscow's commitment. The announcement was made on April 16, 1961, one day *after* American-based exiles began bombing Cuban cane fields and one day *before* the landing of 1,300 Cuban exiles at the Bay of Pigs.

The ideological problems of Havana's turn to socialism, while seemingly arcane, must not be minimized, for they are founded in important strategic issues. Until Castro's April speech, Cuba had been an almost ideal National Democratic state. As such, it was a testimony to the vitality of the antiimperialist movement and the new-found strength of the socialist bloc, which could take credit for forestalling the aggressive advance of American imperialism through the deterrent value of peaceful coexistence. The latter issue, of course, had been seriously muddied by Khrushchev's precipitous promise of missile protection the previous July, but since then Moscow had tried to gloss over that point and get Cuba back on the track of being a National Democratic state.

But in order for the Soviet Union to benefit fully from Cuba's status as a National Democratic state, Cuba would have to remain one for a long period of time. The essence of National Democracy was not only the inevitable triumph of socialism, but the long duration of the transition. *Because* the transition to socialism was not imminent—and depended on a painstaking process of internal development—there was no need for the Soviets to overcommit their resources. *Because* the transition to socialism was not imminent, there was also no need for the United States to feel threatened and risk a confrontation with the Soviet Union. If, however, Cuba could make the transition from National Democratic state to socialist state in only two years, then the doctrine of National Democracy as well as the nature of the Soviet Union's responsibilities to Cuba and the rest of the Third World would have to be reevaluated.

SOVIET MISSILES

The Soviets resisted making a decision on the ideological issues for another two years. In the interim, however, the international situation was heating up—spurred by increasing U.S.–Cuban hostilities—and Moscow would have to address the strategic issues. Sometime during the first half of 1962, the Kremlin decided to recognize Castro's turn to socialism and commit itself fully to Cuba's defense by placing Soviet missiles on the island. Moscow, however, refused to make a commitment about the future of socialism in any of the other National Democratic states, such as Egypt, Iraq, or Algeria, or its potential responsibilities to these states. These decisions were clearly linked. Had Moscow committed missiles to Cuba's defense without recognizing Cuba's socialism, it would have laid itself open to demands for similar protection from other National Democratic states—vastly multiplying the opportunities for a confrontation with Washington.

It was not a perfect solution. By recognizing Cuba's transition to socialism, Moscow clearly discredited much of its touted theory of National Democracy. Moscow also opened the door to other states that might wish to follow Castro's route, declaring themselves socialist in order to finesse Soviet support. Moscow was still, however, left with the right to refuse to recognize these states, although to do so would put it in the uncomfortable position of denying the imminence of socialism in the Third World. Several other Third World states had already declared themselves socialist without Moscow's recognition or commitments to their defense.

If the Soviets *could* limit their decision to the Cuban case, then Moscow might actually get some real benefits from recognizing Cuba's socialism and backing that recognition with Soviet missiles. The most obvious payoff was the prestige of having a socialist revolution in the Western hemisphere so close to the U.S. Of course, the Soviets would never have endorsed Castro's turn to socialism if they did not believe that the revolution was going to last. Two events during 1961 made the Soviets much more optimistic about Cuba's future. First, the failure of the Bay of Pigs invasion demonstrated the regime's popular support and resilience. And Castro's announcement in December 1961 that he had become a Marxist–Leninist and would be one "until the last days of my life" did much to allay earlier fears about Castro's lack of an ideological base.

But the benefits of acceding to Cuban socialism and sending missiles far exceeded the breaching of the Monroe Doctrine. By boldly placing missiles so close to the United States, the Soviets believed that their strategic position would improve significantly, and that they would regain the psychological advantage lost the year before when Washington discovered that the missile gap actually favored the United States. Khrushchev later said that placing missiles in Cuba was intended to redress more than just the balance of power:

> The Americans have surrounded our country with military bases and threatened us with nuclear weapons, and now they would learn just what it feels like to have enemy missiles pointing at you; we'd be doing nothing more than giving them a little of their own medicine.[18]

This strategy also gave Moscow new ammunition in the Sino–Soviet struggle. By recognizing Cuba's socialism, Moscow would discredit Peking's line that socialist revolutions were impossible under peaceful coexistence. By giving Cuba missiles, Moscow would refute Peking's charges that the Soviets had lost the will to hold off U.S. imperialism and lead the international movement.

Despite the many possible benefits, the choice of strategy turned out to be unfortunate. Washington discovered the Soviet installations in Cuba before the missiles became operational, and decided to confront Moscow directly. In a crisis that brought the world closer to a holocaust than any other event since the development of nuclear weapons, Khrushchev was forced to back down and withdraw his missiles.

The costs of that capitulation in terms of Moscow's international prestige *vis à vis* both Washington and Peking was enormous. As we know, it also placed grave strains on Moscow's relations with Havana. With hindsight, it is easy to condemn the Soviet decision to place missiles in Cuba as foolhardy—certainly it was considered as such by even Khrushchev's closest colleagues and successors.

Nevertheless, it is useful to consider briefly the other alternatives open to Moscow at the time. Having committed themselves to Cuba's defense, the Soviets then had to establish the means. Had Moscow given Cuba a bilateral treaty or admitted Cuba to the Warsaw Pact (an almost impossible feat given the distance and the logistic and supply problems), it would have even fewer alternatives. If the United States attacked Cuba, then Moscow would either have to attack the United States or welsh on its treaty. The danger of the latter course for the Soviets' Eastern European allies should be obvious. On the other hand, giving Cuba missiles of its own would have strongly deterred American attack, and might have kept the conflict—had it occurred—in the Western hemisphere. As Khrushchev is reported to have told the Supreme Soviet in December 1962, the placement of missiles in Cuba was intended to make the imperialists understand that if they invaded Cuba, "the war which they threatened to start stood at their own borders."[19]

It is also useful to consider what might have happened had the missiles become operational before the United States discovered them. There is no doubt that this was Moscow's plan: to present Washington with a *fait accompli.* (The Soviets had gone to unusual lengths to prevent premature discovery of the installations. It appears that even the Soviet ambassador in Washington, Anatoly Dobrynin, was not told about the missiles, to make his denials more convincing.) It is more likely that Moscow would not have backed down, had the missiles been operational. Khrushchev believed that the Americans were too liberal, too soft to fight.

But from the start of the crisis, Kennedy was clear on one point: The presence of Soviet missiles in Cuba was unacceptable.[20] If Moscow refused to back down, Kennedy was ready to take the step of nuclear confrontation. But *had* Khrushchev been right, and Kennedy the one to back down, then the psychological gains for Moscow would have been enormous. The result probably would have been a vast proliferation of Soviet military commitments throughout the Third World. Certainly both Washington and Moscow would have conducted the Vietnam War very differently. Moscow might well have turned into the crusading internationalist that both Havana and Peking had demanded.

As it turned out, Moscow managed to salvage a commitment from Washington not to invade Cuba. But with Cuba's defense assured by Washington's diplomatic commitments rather than Moscow's superior military capability, the Soviets would be far more careful about making similar military commitments to the Third World in the future.

THEORY CATCHES UP

Despite the chastening experience of the missile crisis, Moscow apparently did not lose its optimism about the future of socialism in the Third World. In 1963, Soviet theorists updated their doctrine to reflect that optimism, and unveiled the theory of "Revolutionary Democracy." This new theory suggested that the transition to socialism in Third World states might come sooner than the Soviets had originally predicted, and might even come about under the leadership of non-Communists: The progressive military, the intelligentsia, the peasantry, and the petty bourgeoisie might play the role of the vanguard party.[21]

The most surprising aspect of the new doctrine was the admission that a Communist party is not always necessary for a successful socialist revolution—a notion that refuted a basic and previously irrevocable tenet of Marxism–Leninism. The Soviet theorists got around this revisionism by suggesting that in the current world, given the increasing strength of the socialist system, the socialist bloc could ". . . in a material, moral, and political context play the role of the proletarian vanguard."[22]

The theory of Revolutionary Democracy was obviously developed to address the theoretical/ideological problems posed by Cuba's abrupt transition to socialism. It also enabled the Soviet Union to claim a good deal of credit for the Cuban phenomenon. Yet it is unlikely that the Soviets would have based a new doctrine on the Cuban case had they not expected similar successes elsewhere in the Third World. During 1963 and 1964, the Soviets used the term Revolutionary Democrat to describe the left-leaning regimes in Algeria, the United Arab Republic, Ghana, Mali, and Guinea.[23]

Two points are worth noting in terms of the strategic implications of this new theory. First, although Moscow was now willing to recognize several Third World states as socialist or on the path to becoming socialist, Moscow did not promise any of these states the sort of defense commitment it had given Cuba. There was never any mention of Soviet missiles to defend Egypt, Algeria, or Guinea, nor was there clear commitment as to how much aid any of these states could expect from the Soviet vanguard.[24] Moscow was apparently willing to help educate the Revolutionary Democrats, training cadres in Moscow at the Patrice Lumumba University and sending Soviet technical and political advisers to Africa. The Soviets also were willing to send a limited amount of economic aid to the Revolutionary Democratic states, particularly to help develop industries in the state sector. But nowhere did Moscow make the sort of economic commitment comparable to the aid/trade relations it worked out with Cuba.

The second notable point is that Moscow applied the term Revolutionary Democracy only to regimes already in power. Although Moscow was now willing to admit the revolutionary potential of several Third World states, it was apparently not interested in fomenting any additional revolutions. The latter point is particularly significant in terms of Soviet relations with Latin America, where no states other than Cuba were considered Revolutionary Democracies. Thus, despite Moscow's growing optimism about the future of socialism in the Third World in general, and in Cuba particularly, the Soviets still had no intention to become deeply involved in Latin America.

A TEMPORARY INFATUATION

We have already discussed the 1964 Havana Conference of the Latin American Communist Parties in great detail. The most significant outcome of that conference was the Havana Compromise, under which Moscow and the Latin American parties agreed to endorse the strategy of armed struggle in six Latin American countries. Several explanations have already been offered for Moscow's decision to endorse armed struggle, including Moscow's desire to undercut China's role in Latin America, prevent a confrontation between Cuba and the Latin American parties, and even limit and moderate Castro's increasingly strident commitment to armed struggle in Latin America.[25] But when the Havana Compromise is viewed in the context of events in Africa and Moscow's adoption of the theory of Revolutionary Democracy, some credence must be given to the possibility that Moscow, at the time, had caught at least some of Castro's enthusiasm about the possibilities of armed struggle.

It is difficult to ascertain the Kremlin's true feelings about Latin America during this period. Moscow's subscription to the Havana Compromise and subsequent endorsements of particular guerrilla movements found in the pages of *Pravda* during 1964 and 1965 were a striking departure from its previous policy, which was either to ignore the issue of armed struggle or mention it as the least favored route to political change in the region. At the same time, however, there was little evidence of any substantial material support from the Soviets behind their ideological commitment. In fact, the only documented instance of Soviet aid to Latin American revolutionaries was the March 1965 capture in Venezuela of two Italian Communist messengers carrying some $330,000 apparently intended for the revolutionary wing of the Venezuelan Communist Party. Even the most alarmist of those who have written on Soviet subversion in the hemisphere have been hard pressed to produce further evidence of Soviet aid to Latin America during this period. One writer refers to, but offers no evidence of, Cuban-transferred Soviet arms being sent to Latin American revolutionaries, as well as the training of Latin American guerrillas in the Soviet Union and Bulgaria.[26] There is no doubt that whatever arms Cuba sent to Latin America during the 1960s originated in the socialist bloc, since Cuba had no armaments industry of its own and was under an embargo by the world's other major arms producers. But even if these arms were sent under Moscow's direction, the shipments were still very small.

Moscow's Retreat

Moscow began to back off from even this limited commitment to Latin American revolution in early 1966. S. R. Rashidov, the Soviet representative to the January 1966 Tricontinental Conference, made a rousing speech endorsing the future of international armed struggle.[27] However, at the same time in capitals around the world, Soviet officials privately disclaimed their commitment to armed struggle as a viable strategy for political change. When the Uruguayan Government angrily summoned Moscow's ambassador in Montevideo to the Foreign Ministry to explain Rashidov's speech, the Soviet ambassador assured the Uruguayans that Rashidov spoke as "a private citizen" and not as an official of the Soviet Government.[28]

There were several indications during the months before the Tricontinental Conference that the Soviet leaders once again questioned the efficacy of armed struggle in particular, and, more generally, the revolutionary potential of the Third World. In October 1965, Moscow hosted a conference celebrating the thirtieth anniversary of the 1935 Seventh Comintern Congress. At the historic Seventh Congress, Soviet leaders had urged the adoption of united front strategies to contain the spread of fascism in Europe. At the 1965 anniversary conference, leading Soviet theorist B. T. Rudenko drew a direct parallel between contemporary conditions in Latin America—most notably, America's new aggressiveness as presaged by the Dominican invasion—and those in Europe during Hitler's rise to power. According to Rudenko, the principal task in Latin America under such conditions was "to assemble all democratic and progressive forces. Latin American Communists are fighting precisely to attain this great and noble goal, to unite around themselves broader and broader popular masses."[29] Compromise and not confrontation was the best way to contain the new American threat.

There are several explanations for Moscow's decision to back off from its earlier commitment to armed struggle. As was mentioned earlier, events in Latin America—both the new American hard line and the defeat of several Cuban-backed guerrilla movements—made

152

Moscow increasingly skeptical of the guerrilla movements' prospects for success, and wary of provoking the United States into further policies of reaction.

Several other events, in particular a series of defeats in Africa, may have been equally responsible. As it turned out, Moscow's retrenchment in Latin America was really only part of a wider revision of Soviet optimism about the future of socialism in the Third World. Beginning in 1965, Soviet theorists began to admit that the Revolutionary Democratic states were running into some severe problems, particularly in the economic realm. The transition to socialism—originally said to be underway—was once again expected to take much longer than anticipated. The overthrow of two important Revolutionary Democratic leaders, Algeria's Ben Bella in June 1965, and Ghana's Nkrumah the following February, shocked Moscow and led to a complete revision of the theory of Revolutionary Democracy in 1966.[30]

Moscow now argued that earlier theorists had been entirely too optimistic in their estimation of the revolutionary consciousness and leadership abilities of the Revolutionary Democratic leaders. As the recent setbacks in Africa demonstrated, it was highly unlikely that any Third World leader untrained in the precepts of Marxism–Leninism and lacking the support of a developed working class would be able to effect a successful and genuine transition to socialism.[31] Generalizing even further, the Soviets now announced that they saw very little chance for socialist revolution anywhere in the Third World, given the current level of reaction both at home and internationally.

One further domestic component may have played a central role in Moscow's retrenchment. A major reason offered for Khrushchev's ouster in the fall of 1964 was that he had gravely damaged the Soviet economy. Among the "hare-brained schemes" that came under particular criticism were Khrushchev's ill-fated plan to develop the "Virgin Lands," and his overextension of Soviet military and economic aid commitments to the Third World. In a *Pravda* editorial issued one year after Khrushchev's overthrow, Moscow announced its intention to limit its foreign aid responsibilities, and to concentrate instead on the much-needed development of the Soviet domestic economy.

In contrast to earlier theories that suggested the Soviet Union could act as the international vanguard, training and guiding Third World leaders in the direction of socialism, the *Pravda* editors now asserted that "The Socialist countries could not substitute for other detachments of the liberation struggle." The editorial reeled off the traditional argument for Soviet conservatism in the Third World: The Soviets could not "forcibly impose their will on other peoples." Such a course would certainly lead to "the unleashing of a thermonuclear world war." But in a new twist the editorial also claimed that such policies were no longer economically sound. Rather than dispose of Soviet surpluses, foreign aid programs actually diverted funds and equipment that were urgently needed by the socialist countries for their own development.[32]

This position was made official policy at the Twenty-third Party Congress the following spring when the Kremlin's leaders announced that their goal had become the development of the Soviet economy. In language reminiscent of Stalin's commitment to "Socialism in One Country," the Soviet leaders announced that their primary international task was to build their own economy so they could then aid the world revolutionary struggle more effectively.[33]

This change in policy did not mean that the Soviets would now withdraw from the Third World; just the opposite, in fact. In 1966, the Soviets initiated a new policy toward the Third World that has been aptly characterized as a strategy of "counterimperialism."[34] According to this new strategy, Moscow would now focus its attention on those Third World states and movements that demonstrated either strategic or economic importance for the Soviet Union, rather than those that appeared to follow a progressive path. Economic relations with Third World states would be used to improve Moscow's own economic position.[35]

The Kremlin's new leadership now moved quickly to establish diplomatic relations with a wide variety of Third World states with a range of political hues and international alignments. In Africa, the Soviets opened relations with such conservative states as Ethiopia, Upper Volta, Morocco, Zaire, and the Ivory Coast. The Soviets also sought to improve relations with governments traditionally considered irretrievably in the U.S. sphere, such as Turkey, Iran, and Pakistan.

At the same time, the Soviet Union also made some unprecedented advances in Latin America. In 1966, Moscow began political negotiations with Colombia, Venezuela, and Bolivia; trade negotiations with Chile, Ecuador, Uruguay, and Costa Rica; and extended a $100 million credit to Brazil's right-wing military regime.[36] A year later, it gave the liberal Frei government in Chile a credit for $57 million.

The Soviet success in Latin America was, more than anything else, due to the new receptivity of the Latin American states. Many of Moscow's new contacts in the region were actually initiated by the Latin Americans. By the late 1960s, the Cold War scare created by the Cuban revolution had begun to wear off. In this period of thaw, many of the Latin American states once again had begun to chafe at the bonds of American domination. Recognizing the Soviet Union or taking advantage of Soviet offers of economic aid or trade was one sure way for even the most conservative Latin American leader to mobilize nationalist sentiment by appearing to defy the United States.

The increasingly public split between Moscow and Cuba over the issue of armed struggle in Latin America made such a policy even easier. Compared with Fidel and the Castroite guerrillas, the Soviet Union and its local Communist party allies seemed moderate, perhaps even a moderating influence on the Latin American left. As one observer noted, the Raúl Leoni regime in Venezuela began to court the Soviet Union precisely at a time when it was embroiled in a bitter dispute with the Castro regime and trying desperately to destroy Douglas Bravo's Cuban-backed guerrillas. Opening relations with Moscow was ". . . a way of accentuating the tension between the [Venezuelan] guerrilla movement and the Communist Party on the one hand, and between the Soviet Union and Cuba on the other, while proving to the country that it was not under the thumb of the United States."[37]

A COLLISION COURSE

By 1967, Moscow and Havana were on a collision course. The Soviets had come full circle in their perception of Latin America, and indeed much of the Third World, rejecting these regions as potential arenas for revolutionary struggle. At the same time, Moscow began to show a strong interest in building diplomatic and economic relations with many nonrevolutionary states. But the Cubans took the diametrically opposite position. By 1967, Havana had decided that revolution, armed struggle in particular, was the only strategy for change in Latin America. Havana rejected all attempts at political accommodation with even liberal regimes as a betrayal of the revolutionary cause.

This disagreement was not new. From the earliest days of the Cuban–Soviet alliance, the Cubans had tried to commit Moscow to the support of Third World revolutions, starting with their own. Over the years they had limited success with the Soviets. Yet, Cuban–Soviet relations had remained basically cordial and mutually supportive, and, as evidenced by the 1964 Havana Conference, willing to reach at least formal compromises.

The debate might have remained cordial indefinitely had the Soviets continued passively to disagree with Cuba: paying lip service to revolution in Latin America, while at the same time resisting any serious commitment of resources or political capital. But by 1967, the Kremlin had developed other interests in the region beyond merely placating Havana. A growing number of Latin American regimes had begun to make diplomatic and economic overtures to Moscow. And Moscow was receptive.

It was Moscow's public willingness to place state interests over the interests of international revolution that Castro could not abide. And, as we have seen, the Cuban leader did not tend to mince words. He began by attacking the Latin American Communist parties—and, by implication, the Soviet Union—for reformist and defeatist tendencies and for colluding with Latin America's right-wing regimes. By late 1967, Castro had gone so far as to challenge Moscow's right to head the international movement.

It was the latter issue that the Kremlin would not tolerate. Although Moscow could abide Cuba's ideological divergence on issues such as armed struggle in Latin America (and in some instances may have actually benefited from it), it could not tolerate direct Cuban attacks. One of the main reasons Moscow originally took on the burdens of supporting and defending the Cuban revolution was Castro's utility to Moscow in the Sino–Soviet split. Over the years, Moscow repeatedly—if with only varying degrees of success— tried to use Castro to isolate Peking from the Latin American movements, and in general to improve its standing in the Third World. One of Moscow's more overt acknowledgments of Cuba's importance in its struggle with the Chinese came in a 1963 *Pravda* editorial in which the author rhetorically asked:

> Why is it that our Chinese comrades stubbornly ignore the approval given by the Cuban leaders to the Soviet government's policies which they consider a policy of fraternal solidarity and genuine internationalism?[38]

Thus, for the sake of Castro's endorsement, Moscow had been willing to accept more ideological divergence from Cuba than from any other country in the socialist bloc. Once it began to look as though Havana were not merely going to disagree with Moscow but actually publicly attack Moscow's policies and even threaten to secede from the socialist bloc, then it was time for action.

The Velvet Glove

What is remarkable, given the stridency of the Cuban challenge, was the mildness of the Soviet response. Moscow's leaders have never been known for their tolerance of ideological diversity, let alone insubordination, from any member of the bloc. When the Chinese refused to toe Moscow's line, the Soviets pulled out all their economic and technical aid, even going so far as to take back the blueprints for partially completed factories. The resulting disruption of China's industrial development was enormous. In Hungary in 1956, and Czechoslovakia in 1968, Moscow's punishment was even more decisive, as Soviet tanks literally rolled over all dissent.

But with Havana, Moscow used no strong-arm tactics. Rather, the Soviets first sought to restrain Cuba through ideological critiques. It is interesting to note that Moscow even refused to get directly involved in a battle of polemics with Havana. Their shouting matches with the Chinese no doubt made the Soviet leaders wary of repeating the experience with Castro. Instead, the Soviets criticized Cuba's positions indirectly, opening the pages of *Pravda* to several Latin American and European Communist leaders who wished to criticize the Cubans.

There was nothing indirect about these leaders' charges. Terms such as adventurist, unscientific, emotional, tragic, and disruptive were used to characterize the Cuban theories and policies. On the eve of the first meetings of Castro's new Latin American Solidarity Organization, *Pravda* printed an article by Chilean Communist Party leader Luís Corvalán, who rejected the idea of continental revolution as adventurist, inappropriate for the conditions in Latin America, and ultimately disruptive of the international movement. According to Corvalán, the problem with movements advocating armed struggle was their lack of a solid Marxist–Leninist base:

> The revolutionary current which emerges on a petit-bourgeois base usually underrates the proletariat and the Communist parties, is more disposed toward nationalism, adventurism, and terrorism, and sometimes permits anti-Communist and anti-Soviet attitudes.[39]

Although Corvalán never mentioned the Cubans by name, this description leaves no doubt. Corvalán urged the Latin American proletariat to unify and resist this adventurist current.

An article by Rodolpho Ghioldi, a long-time leader of the Argentine Communist Party, published in *Pravda* in October 1967, was even more violent in denouncing the Castro line. Although Ghioldi also avoided mentioning Castro by name, referring instead to "petty bourgeois nationalists under the influence of Maoism and its related currents," there was no doubt about whom he was writing. Ghioldi first directed his criticism against Debray and the Cuban theorists of armed struggle who insisted that the particular conditions of Latin America called for new theories and new strategies of revolution. According to Ghioldi, these theorists were seeking merely to justify their own revisionism and increase their personal power.

"Since Marxist–Leninist theory does not justify their actions, down with the theory." Ghioldi then responded to the Cuban charge that the Soviet Union was not providing adequate aid to Vietnam and other Third World revolutions, by saying that such belligerence was "proposing a dangerous game of war." Ghioldi concluded his attack by describing the Guevarist commitment to continental revolution as a "dangerous revival of the Trotskyite thesis concerning the impossibility of building Communism in one country."[40]

When these criticisms-by-proxy failed to restrain Castro, the Soviet leaders began to print some ideological critiques of their own. Once again, it must be emphasized that the Soviets never named the Cubans as the source of the wrong-headed theories, attributing them instead to the Mao group, Trotskyites, and a whole pantheon of enemies. Soviet theorists first took issue with Castro's view that the fundamental contradiction was the struggle between imperialism and the underdeveloped world, by describing it as "essentially a bourgeois theory which splits the international alliance of revolutionary forces."[41] Cuban claims of armed struggle as the only strategy for Latin America were rejected as artificial and naïve, as Moscow warned of the danger of regarding Latin America as something uniform, "without taking into account the national particularities and specific conditions of each country."[42] As for the Cuban idea that revolutions could be exported, the Soviet theorists replied:

> Every genuine revolution is without a doubt the domestic business of the people who make it. Marxists are convinced that the implantation of revolutions from outside will not give the desired result. A revolution can only be victorious and its results lasting only if the ideas of the revolution represent the country itself and continue to be held by the majority of the population.[43]

Debray's attack on the primacy of the Communist party came in for special criticism. The Soviet theorists who, as authors of the theory of Revolutionary Democracy, had once proclaimed that a revolution was possible without the vanguard role of the party, now denied that possibility with equal vehemence:

. . . . with the intensification of the attacks of U.S. imperialism on the honor and sovereignty of the Latin American peoples, any underestimation of the role of the Marxist–Leninist Party of the working class in the national liberation struggle, any weakening of the Communist parties, and even more, any splitting of their ranks, whatever motives may lie behind it, would bring irremediable damage to the vital interests of their countries and people.[44]

Finally, the Soviets responded to Havana's calls for increased Soviet aid for both Third World revolution and development by reasserting that the primary duty of the socialist states was to build their own economic base. Then, in a statement undoubtedly intended to remind the Cubans of their own precarious economic situation, the *Pravda* editorial said that "Not only positive examples of the Socialist countries have their influence on the revolutionary processes proceeding in the world but also failures, difficulties, and errors."[45]

The greatest blow to Cuban pride must have come in late 1968, when the Soviets celebrated the first anniversary of Che's death by printing a copy of Guevara's Bolivian diaries with a highly critical introduction. According to Moscow, the Guevara *foco* had failed because it lacked popular support. Then, in a move that Castro had so often used against Moscow, the introduction concluded by quoting Lenin back to Fidel, saying, "We do not need hysterical outbursts. We need the measured treads of iron battalions of the proletariat."[46]

These ideological criticisms failed to produce the desired effect; the Cubans refused to moderate any of their positions. If anything, the means that Moscow had chosen—using other parties to criticize the Cubans—made Castro even more strident in his attacks. In his closing speech to the Latin American Solidarity Organization, Castro lashed out against the "disgusting conspiracy" led by the "reactionary mafia of the revolutionary movements." He accused the Latin American Communists of wanting to drive a wedge between Moscow and Havana, of trying to "create a conflict and have the Socialist camp join the imperialist blockade against Cuba as well."[47]

An Inside Job

Having failed to restrain the Castro regime through ideological criticism, Moscow's leaders next may have tried to restrain the Cubans through covert political pressure. In late January 1968, Havana announced the arrest of a "microfaction" of forty-three state officials and party members on charges of treason to the revolution. Among the list of their seditious activities, the microfaction was accused of "presenting calumnious data about the plans of the Revolution to officials of foreign countries with the intent of undermining the international relations of Cuba with other governments. . . ."[48]

According to a report made by Raúl Castro to the Party's Central Committee, sometime in 1965, Aníbal Escalante, a leader of the old Cuban Communist Party, began to contact many of his former associates to discuss what he felt as growing opposition in Cuba to the Castro regime's policies. The microfaction opposed voluntary labor in agriculture, the predominance of moral over material incentives in the industrial sector, and, above all, the commitment to armed struggle in Latin America.[49] The microfaction was particularly concerned about what they saw as an increasingly anti-Soviet bent in the Cuban ideology.

The members of Escalante's microfaction, according to Raúl Castro, began to gather documents on the Cuban economy and pass them secretly to officials in the Soviet Union, Czechoslovakia, and East Germany. Their goal was to convince the Soviets and Cuba's other socialist trading partners to apply economic pressure in an attempt to force a change in policy. Raúl even hinted that the microfaction had gone so far as to suggest that these pressures be used to replace Fidel as the leader of the Cuban revolution.[50]

The Cuban public and the world was first informed of the existence of the microfaction in August 1967. At a meeting of the Latin American Solidarity Organization—the site of Castro's most seditious attacks on the Soviet Union—the Cuban leader told the delegates that the Latin American Communist parties were not the only parties plagued with "pseudorevolutionaries." Cuba, too, he said, had a "microfaction" of "old resentful sectarians" opposed

161

to "all the concepts of the revolution" who tried to "instill their unhealthy ideas, their resentful ideas into the old and tried revolutionaries."[51] It is interesting, however, that the members of the Escalante microfaction were not arrested until December 1967, some five months after Castro's speech. Whether the Cuban authorities waited because of the possible international repercussions has never been established.

Moscow's role in the Escalante affair is unclear. There can be no doubt that Escalante was well acquainted with members of the Soviet Central Committee and a true believer in Moscow's legitimacy as leader of the international Communist movement. Escalante's youthful training as a member of the Moscow-dominated PSP had firmly established his allegiance. He had renewed his contacts with the Eastern block in 1962, when he was purged from Castro's new party on charges of seeking to dominate it for the PSP, and was sent to Czechoslovakia for three years of exile. However, it has never been established whether Moscow contacted Escalante first in an effort to restrain the Cubans from inside the party, or Escalante independently contacted his old allies in the Eastern bloc. But it is undeniable that Escalante had sufficient reason to resent Castro and initiate such a plan on his own.

Both Havana and Moscow went to great lengths to play down the international aspects of the Escalante affair. The Central Committee report on the microfaction exonerated all foreign officials and governments of any complicity. The Soviet press reported the Escalante affair but made no comment.

The Big Squeeze

While Moscow was cleared of all charges of conspiring with the Escalante microfaction, it appears that the Kremlin was simultaneously applying pressures of its own on Castro. There is a great deal of confusion about the nature and extent of Soviet economic pressures on Cuba in 1968, as well as about how explicit the Soviets were in demanding a Cuban *quid pro quo*. The most extreme account is offered by two Cuban defectors—members of the elite Cuban intelligence service, the Directorio General de Inteligencia (DGI)—

who sought asylum in the United States in the late 1960s, early 1970s.[52] Both arrived with tales of Soviet economic blackmail and a secret agreement in which Castro ceded Cuba's autonomy in return for Moscow's guarantee of continued economic support.

Orlando Castro Hidalgo was granted asylum in the American embassy in Luxembourg in March 1969. In October 1969, Castro Hidalgo testified before the Senate Internal Security Subcommittee on the growing Soviet domination of Cuba. The defector began his testimony by describing himself as a Cuban patriot who had faithfully served Castro and the Cuban Communist Party from the earliest days of the revolution. From 1967 until his defection, he had worked as an intelligence officer in the Cuban embassy in Paris. When asked why he defected, he replied that since mid-1968, "the Cuban revolution has delivered itself as a colony to the Soviet Union."[53]

According to Castro Hidalgo, sometime in late 1967 the Soviets threatened to cut off economic support to Cuba unless the Castro Government stopped publicly attacking Soviet policies and abandoned its efforts to export violent revolution to Latin America. To demonstrate their seriousness, the Soviets supposedly cut back oil deliveries to a trickle and for several weeks suspended all shipments of critically needed industrial goods. The Castro Government held out for a few months, but finally the economic pressures became too much, and they gave in to Moscow's demands. At that time, said Castro Hidalgo, the Cubans were forced to sign an agreement with the Soviets "under which the Cuban government [was] forced to cede its sovereignty in exchange for Soviet economic aid."[54]

As part of the agreement, the former intelligence officer said, the Soviets promised to restore previous aid and "increase considerably their technical assistance" to Cuba, sending an additional 5,000 technicians to help develop the Cuban military and industry. The Soviets also promised to increase their shipments of raw materials and volume of purchases to help overcome Cuba's huge balance of payments deficit.

In return, Castro Hidalgo said, the Cubans promised to refrain from publicly criticizing either the Soviet Union or the Latin American Communist parties and to turn their foreign policy decisions over to Moscow and to Moscow's agents to Cuba, the Russian-trained DGI members. In the future, he said:

Cuba will faithfully follow Soviet policy when basic Soviet interests are involved. Where basic Soviet diplomatic and commercial interests are not involved, the Cuban government will be permitted to undertake revolutionary adventures.

Castro Hidalgo then summed up Cuba's predicament by saying that "The Soviet economic strangulation of Cuba must be very intense for a revolutionary like Fidel Castro to have to accept Soviet direction of Cuba's foreign policy."[55]

Other less extreme accounts suggest that Moscow did not cut back on either aid or oil supplies to Cuba, but merely refused to increase its deliveries of oil to Cuba beyond 2 percent at a time when Castro requested an increase of 8 percent. By taking this route, the Soviets did not try to destroy the Cuban economy, but merely to demonstrate their own power by limiting the Cuban economy's ability to grow.[56]

There is an excellent reason for all the confusion: Neither Moscow nor Havana ever went public with their problems. The most detailed accounts of Soviet pressure and Cuban response have been given by two Cuban defectors who had strong personal and political reasons to play up the amount of Soviet pressure and the degree of Cuban capitulation in testimony to U.S. Senate committees that were already convinced that Cuba was a satellite of the Soviet Union.[57]

Because of the confusion and distortion, it is necessary to spell out what little is known about this critical phase of Cuban–Soviet relations. First it is clear that the Cuban–Soviet trade negotiations for 1968 were a long and tortuous process—begun early in the fall of 1967, the negotiations were not completed until the spring of 1968. The Cubans were undoubtedly aware early in the game that they would have a tough time with the Soviets. They began to ration gasoline as early as October 1967. There can also be no doubt that Castro was aware of the political implications of Soviet economic pressure. In a March 1968 speech, Castro spoke of the desire for "maximum independence" from foreign aid and of the political vulnerability of economic dependence, saying:

We have known the bitterness of having to depend to a considerable degree on things which come from the outside and how that can become a weapon and at least create the temptation to use it against our country.[58]

There is also no doubt that Cuba was extremely vulnerable to such pressures. In 1967, a record year for Cuban oil production, the Cubans produced only 2.3 percent of the oil they consumed. What made the Soviet oil cutback even more galling was that at the same time that Moscow was squeezing Havana, the Soviet press reported yearly production so high that the Soviet Union was increasing its petroleum exports to Brazil and Argentina, two of Cuba's sworn enemies.[59]

Yet despite these pressures, the Cubans did not immediately back down. In April 1968, Castro announced an agreement with Romania—another dissenting member of the socialist bloc with a penchant for challenging Soviet dominance—[60] for personnel and equipment to develop Cuba's oil resources.[61] That May, in the face of continued Soviet pressure, the Cubans took another strong anti-Soviet stance, denouncing the Nuclear Nonproliferation Treaty, jointly sponsored by the Soviet Union and the United States, as superpower collusion against the small states. Six years after the 1962 crisis, missiles were still a sore point for the Castro regime.

But Cuba's resistance to Soviet pressure did not last much beyond the summer of 1968, when Castro is said to have signaled a new Cuban–Soviet accommodation by endorsing the Warsaw Pact invasion of Czechoslovakia. At the same time, Havana began to back off from its commitment to armed struggle in Latin America. As we shall see, there were many other reasons—beyond Soviet economic pressure—for Cuba to reevaluate its position on Latin American strategy. On close analysis, even Castro's endorsement of the Czech invasion is not so complete a capitulation as it first appeared. Nevertheless, starting in the summer of 1968, Cuba and the Soviet Union began a new period of accommodation and alignment.

CUBA'S POWER

It is interesting to speculate about what the Soviet Union would have done had Castro *not* backed down. Although Cuba was extremely vulnerable to economic coercion, it would be wrong to overestimate either Cuba's weakness or the Soviet Union's strength in this dispute. It is clear from both the stridency of the Cuban challenge and the mildness of the Soviet response that, despite its complete economic dependence on the Soviet Union, Cuba retained bargaining power throughout.

Over the past decade, international relations theorists have tried to explain the phenomenon of small state power. One concept particularly appropriate to the Cuban case is Albert Hirschman's "dependency management," which suggests that under certain conditions small states can have a great deal more power in an alliance with a large state than originally expected, given the inequalities of size, resources, and military capabilities. According to Hirschman, at the policy-making level, negotiating skill, political conditions, even the strength with which the interests are held may gain the dependent or client state more power to choose than the overall structure of inequality would suggest.[62]

David Ronfeldt of the Rand Corporation has put an even finer point on one particular category of small state power with his notion of "superclients."[63] In a comparative study of the U.S. alliance with Iran under the Shah and Cuba's alliance with the Soviet Union, he writes that the very fact of being recognized publicly as the client of a superpower gives all client states some leverage. If the client is strategically located, like Cuba or Iran, its leverage is so great that it becomes a superclient. Having invested international prestige as well as having made a concrete and often large commitment of resources, the superpower has a strong interest in maintaining and defending the client state—particularly if it has no other client in a comparably strategic location.

Although it is playing a dangerous game, the client always has the alternative of threatening its own collapse to ensure that it gets what it wants out of the alliance. An analogy that may be a little too prosaic for international relations theory is that of the

166

small child who threatens to hold his breath if he does not get his way. Of course, for both child and client state there is always the danger that the parent or patron will ignore such a threat, leaving the client or child either to commit suicide or back down, thus losing its bargaining power once and for all. Although the leverage is real, it cannot be used lightly or often.

The Soviet Union is not the only superpower to have staked its world reputation on its ability to defend a client state and found the client state calling the shots. The same phenomenon also made it difficult for Washington to control its allies in South Vietnam. Any pressure on Saigon to control corruption or limit domestic repression undoubtedly would have been rejected as endangering the war effort. This turnabout also kept the U.S. Government fighting in Vietnam long after the war had become a major political liability at home.

The Soviet Union has been particularly vulnerable to such leverage in its alliance with Cuba because of a Soviet ideological idiosyncrasy, which takes as a basic premise the notion of the "irreversibility of socialist revolutions." Once a state has become socialist, it cannot revert—regardless of whether the cause is external attack, internal political pressures, or economic failure. This belief appears to be even more compelling for the Soviets than the domino theory has been for the United States. After all, the United States finally did withdraw from Vietnam. The commitment to irreversibility led the Soviets to invade Hungary in 1956, Czechoslovakia in 1968, and Afghanistan in 1979, and underlies the current crisis in Poland. This commitment also led Moscow to sustain its level of support to Cuba, even as the Castro regime became increasingly critical of Soviet policies.

Because of this commitment, it is doubtful that the Soviets would have cut Cuba off completely—even if Havana had not backed down. Basically, the Soviet Union could not afford to destabilize the Castro Government. The costs in terms of Soviet international prestige *vis à vis* Peking, Washington, and the Third World would have been intolerable.

Though the point about the irreversibility of socialism is useful for understanding the Cuban–Soviet alliance, it should not be overgeneralized. It is not certain that other Soviet leaders before Brezhnev and Kosygin would have responded in the same way to Cuba's challenges. Stalin obviously felt no hesitation about cutting Tito off completely from Soviet support—even if that meant forcing Yugoslavia into the capitalist camp. Similarly, Khrushchev—despite the lessons of Yugoslavia—did not hesitate to withdraw his support from China in an equally hostile and abrupt manner when the Maoist leadership dared to challenge his control of the international movement.

It is still not certain that Brezhnev and Kosygin, even with the failures of Yugoslavia and China to haunt them, would have responded with the same restraint had they been dealing with a renegade Communist state other than Cuba. Cuba's symbolic value (in terms of both the Sino–Soviet and U.S.–Soviet competitions), Cuba's geopolitical value, and Castro's remarkable bargaining ability may well have made Cuba an exception.

This is also not to suggest that the Soviets were without bargaining power of their own. As we have seen, they used that power in a restrained but ultimately effective manner—giving enough aid to keep Castro in power and to prevent him from seeking any other patron, but limiting that aid enough so there would be no doubt about the Soviets' ability to define the limits of Cuba's growth. As Castro was forced to admit in a speech in early 1969, Cuba had little hope of becoming economically self-sufficient in the near future.[64]

5

The Great Retreat:
Castro's Harsh Realities

O N August 20, 1968, 200,000 Warsaw Pact troops invaded Czechoslovakia. Three days later, a grim-faced Fidel Castro went on Cuban national television to discuss the events. The Warsaw Pact invasion, said Castro, was a "flagrant" and "illegal" violation of Czech borders. Nevertheless, Castro continued, the invasion was also necessary. Under the leadership of Alexander Dubček, Czechoslovakia was "moving toward a counter-revolutionary situation" and directly into the "arms of imperialism. . . . It was absolutely necessary, at all costs . . . to prevent this from eventually taking place," even if the price was Czechoslovakia's national sovereignty.[1]

The immediate reaction to Castro's speech, both within Cuba and internationally, was shock and confusion. *Why* would Castro, the nationalist, champion of the underdog, defender of the rights of the Third World, endorse a big power's attack on a small state? It seemed a complete reversal of Cuba's internationalist ideals. Over the next two years, Castro took several equally surprising stands: He retreated from his commitment to armed struggle, abandoned

169

his criticism of the Latin American Communist parties, and acknowledged Moscow's leading role in the international movement. When the Czech speech was viewed in the context of these other ideological reversals, one explanation emerged: Castro had finally caved in to Soviet pressure. It was only a matter of time, the argument went, before Castro *had* to realize that Cuba is, after all, only an island—small, weak, and dependent—and it was trying to play an autonomous role in international affairs that was elusive at best. By the early 1970s, almost every expert on Cuban politics seemed to agree that Castro's days as a crusading internationalist were over.[2]

CUBA'S DEPENDENCE

Various explanations were given for Castro's new docility, ranging from overt Soviet blackmail to a subtle shift in bargaining leverage between Moscow and Havana. Despite the variations, all the explanations shared two basic assumptions. First, the changes in Cuban foreign policy, beginning with Castro's endorsement of the Soviet invasion of Czechoslovakia, were the direct result of *external* pressures placed on Cuba by its Soviet allies. The second, and corollary, assumption was that as long as Cuba remained dependent on the Soviet Union, these changes would be irreversible.

The most extreme form of the dependence argument was offered by two Cuban defectors who arrived in the United States soon after the Czech invasion with lurid tales of Soviet economic blackmail that included a secret pact, in which Castro sold Cuba's sovereignty for continued Soviet economic support.[3]

Moderate observers eschewed the idea of a literal secret pact while keeping the notion of Cuban capitulation to Soviet pressure. In the late 1960s, they argued, the Castro regime suffered several major policy defeats. Che Guevara's death in Bolivia in 1967 discredited Havana's radical foreign policies. The failure of the much-touted 1970 drive to produce ten million tons of sugar completely undermined the Castro regime's guerrilla-style domestic policies. As a result of these failures, according to veteran Cuba-watcher Carmelo Mesa-Lago, the Cuban model "suffered a mortal blow, Castro's strength and prestige were eroded and the Soviet Union increased its bargaining power." At that point, "the only real alternative open to Castro was to yield to the Soviets. He would have to relinquish part of his power and Cuba its independence, but he and the revolution would continue." Castro's endorsement of the Czech invasion was the first step in his capitulation.[4]

It is true that after 1968 the Cubans did make several significant policy changes. Most notably, they abandoned the idea of exporting revolution to Latin America. But the simple calculus of dependence that has been so widely accepted does not tell the whole story.

Free Will

Castro's endorsement of the 1968 invasion of Czechoslovakia was not nearly as complete a capitulation as the observers suggest. The Cuban leader had good reasons to endorse the invasion, apart from a need to pay off his Soviet allies. Although Castro was known as a defender of the rights of small states, he was by no means a liberal when it came to internal politics. It is likely that Castro honestly opposed the reforms of the Prague spring and considered the Soviet invasion necessary to preserve communism in Czechoslovakia. (By 1968, all the Alexander Dubček-style civil libertarians in Cuba had long been jailed or forced into exile.) With his endorsement, Castro warned his internal opposition that he would not hesitate to take similarly brutal measures to guarantee the survival of socialism in Cuba.

Castro also used the August 23rd speech to reassert many of his radical ideas about the export of revolution and Moscow's responsibilities to the Third World. In Czechoslovakia, Castro said pointedly, the Warsaw Pact states had done what was painful but absolutely necessary to preserve socialism. What disturbed him was that these same states could simultaneously be so short-sighted about Latin America:

> We have disagreed with, been displeased at, and protested against the fact that these same countries have been drawing closer economically and culturally to the oligarchic governments of Latin America. . . .[5]

To be consistent, Castro argued, the Brezhnev Doctrine's commitment to the defense of socialist revolutions would have to be extended to include Latin America as well. If the Soviets must remove the counterrevolutionary regime in Prague, then they must also withdraw their support from the "reformist" and counterrevolutionary Latin American parties. If the Soviets must intervene against the "rightist" regime in Czechoslovakia, then the Cubans must be allowed to intervene against the regimes in Latin America.

If the Soviets had to send troops to defend socialism in Czechoslovakia, Castro said, then they must also be counted on to send troops to defend socialism wherever it is threatened, no matter what the cost.

> Will Warsaw Pact troops also be sent to Vietnam if the Yankee imperialists step up their aggression against that country and if the peoples of Vietnam request that aid? Will they send the divisions of Warsaw Pact troops to the Democratic People's Republic of Korea if the Yankee imperialists attack that country? Will they send the divisions of the Warsaw Pact to Cuba if the Yankee imperialists attack our country, or even in the case of the threat of a Yankee imperialist attack on our country, and if our country requests it?[6]

It is important to understand that the Cubans felt very differently about Soviet troops and tanks than did their allies in the Eastern bloc. Although the Czech invasion was a brutal reminder to the Romanians and Poles of exactly how vulnerable they were to Soviet military domination, the Cubans, situated thousands of miles away, felt no such fear. For Havana, the primary threat was *American* invasion and abandonment by Moscow.

Although Castro's decision to endorse the Warsaw Pact invasion seemed inconsistent with Cuba's commitment to the sovereignty of small states, Castro did his best to make that endorsement consistent with, and to reinforce, many of Cuba's other internationalist interests. As ever, Castro's support did not come cheaply.

A Measured Retreat

There are various explanations for Castro's subsequent decision to abandon the export of revolution to Latin America. A brief review of these theories is not intended to substitute any one of them for the more widely held dependence approach, but only to suggest that Cuba's decision to abandon the export of revolution to Latin America was not as necessary, as inevitable, or—most importantly— as irreversible as some experts have suggested.

The simplest explanation for Cuba's decision to stop exporting revolution to Latin America is that the policy was not working. The repeated defeats suffered by the Venezuelan guerrilla leader Douglas Bravo in Venezuela in the mid-1960s cast serious doubts, even in the minds of the most radical Cuban leaders, on the relevance of the Cuban brand of revolution for the rest of Latin America. The execution of Guevara in Bolivia completely discredited the strategy.

Second, by the early 1970s Cuba could no longer afford an independent foreign policy. Overcoming failures in its domestic development programs demanded the republic's full resources and Castro's complete attention. In the 1960s, the Cubans not only tried to pursue an independent foreign policy, but also tried to develop their economy according to what they considered an appropriately revolutionary model: relying on moral rather than material incentives, and seeking to improve productivity through guerrilla-like offensives and sacrifices. These development policies produced nearly as much conflict with the Soviets as did Cuba's foreign policies. By 1970, the development policies had failed just as soundly.[7]

Third, new policy options became available in the early 1970s. The election of the socialist Allende regime in Chile and the appearance of a left-oriented military junta in Peru gave the Cubans a new chance to end their isolation without overthrowing hostile regimes.

These developments in Latin America placed a new premium on the issue of national sovereignty. It was one thing for the Cubans to ignore the sanctity of national boundaries when they had no diplomatic relations in Latin America to maintain. Now a growing number of states were seeking to normalize relations with Cuba, and so Havana had to respect conventional international behavior.

One can also explain the changes in Cuban domestic policy after 1970 without relying so heavily on the dependence paradigm. This is not to suggest that the Soviets did not pressure the Castro regime to rationalize both its economic and foreign policies, nor is it an attempt to minimize Cuba's susceptibility to Soviet influence. But unlike the dependence argument, this argument suggests that Soviet pressure was only one variable—albeit a very important one—in the calculation of Cuban policy.[8]

By 1970, the Kremlin's leaders were not the only observers to recognize that Cuba's domestic policies were not working. On July 26, in a nationally televised speech, Castro announced the failure of the 1970 drive to produce, as the slogan went, "ten million tons" of sugar. The harvest had yielded a record 8.5 million tons—almost double the previous year's production, but that was not enough. Castro had promised his people they would reach the ten-million-ton mark; he had staked his reputation on it. More important, he had staked the Cuban economy on it, diverting manpower and scarce resources from other sectors, wreaking incredible havoc with the entire economy.[9]

One Cuban editor remembers 1970 as:

> the hardest year of the revolution—much harder than anything in the early years of the embargo and rationing. . . . There was nothing in the stores to buy, not thread to sew on a button, or even a button. Everyone made sacrifices believing the campaign would succeed. And that was the hardest of all. It didn't.[10]

In his anniversary speech, Castro acknowledged these problems and took full responsibility for the drive's failure.

> We are going to begin . . . by pointing out the responsibility which all of us and I in particular have for these problems. . . . I believe that we cost the people too much in our process of learning. And unfortunately our problem . . . is our heritage of ignorance.[11]

He then offered to resign. The crowd, with a roar, rejected his offer.

It is unlikely that Castro expected any other response. Indeed, it could be argued that the speech was staged precisely to elicit that endorsement. Nevertheless, the significance of the experience should not be underestimated. Castro learned a very hard lesson from the "ten million tons" debacle: No matter how pure the consciousness of the Cuban revolutionaries, no matter how committed the people, the material constraints on Cuban development were formidable.

In the months that followed, the need for sober realism and sound planning became a major theme of Castro's speeches. Speaking to a December meeting on basic industry, Castro warned:

> Let us not do as we have done so often, when we got an idea . . . putting it into practice without further ado, only to discredit the idea because . . . it was taken directly from the brain to the world of reality where it died for lack of minimal conditions. . . .[12]

No doubt a similar learning process was taking place in Castro's understanding of the Cuban–Soviet relationship. In 1968, Castro learned that he could push his Soviet allies only so far and still retain their support. With the failure of the 1970 harvest, Castro realized that Soviet economic support would be indispensable for the foreseeable future. Havana would have to adjust its policies to guarantee Moscow's continued backing.

Castro was acutely aware of how his new docility would look to the rest of the world. Speaking in the spring of 1970, he attacked what he called "a whole plague of pseudo-revolutionaries" who had criticized the growing closeness of the Cuban–Soviet alliance. "We spoke of how decisive Soviet support had been to us . . . and there are some who don't even approve of our mentioning this." These critics, Castro claimed, lived in "imaginary and hypothetical worlds." Cuba, he said, could no longer afford such luxuries. "The world of today is very complex—a very difficult world. There are no easy solutions to any problems."[13]

The newly pragmatic Castro was saying that Cuba had no choice but to adjust its policies and draw closer to the Soviet Union. He did *not* say, however, that Cuba would have to abandon forever all hopes for autonomy. Castro had bargained for and won Cuba's freedom in the past—choosing his own policies independent of his Soviet allies and even in opposition to them—while remaining economically dependent on the Soviet Union. There might be another time when Castro could trade on Cuba's unique strategic and ideo-

175

logical position. How he would use that autonomy, when the time came, remained to be seen.

NEW ATTITUDES: ARMED STRUGGLE
AND PEACEFUL CHANGE

After 1968, Cuban ideology underwent a major revision. Some of the basic—and most defiant—precepts of Cuban internationalism were replaced by more moderate, pro-Soviet attitudes. As dramatic as they were, these changes did not take place overnight. Several years passed before the contours of Cuba's new conservatism emerged. Even then there were a number of skewed lines, such as Havana's continued commitment to guerrilla warfare in Africa. At the time, most observers tended to dismiss such pronouncements as merely rhetorical. But after some 18,000 Cuban troops were sent to Angola by mid-1976, such statements were taken more seriously.

One of the most dramatic changes was in Havana's commitment to armed struggle in Latin America. After years of ridiculing the Latin American Communists for their "fatalism" and cowardice, Castro began to express doubts about the immediacy of the Latin American revolution. In July 1969, he said:

> We are not impatient, we are not in a hurry. We will wait while one by one they break with the past, while one by one they develop their revolutions. How long will we wait? For as long as necessary— ten, twenty, thirty years if necessary—though nobody thinks even remotely that it will take that long.[14]

The following April, he took an even more surprising position when he acknowledged the possibility of different roads to progressive change. Although he had once claimed that the only way to overcome the bonds of imperialism and neocolonialism was through Cuban-style armed struggle, Castro now conceded that the Cuban model of *focismo* might not be universal. Different circumstances may well require different strategies:

> Cuban support does not necessarily have to be expressed in favor of guerrilla movements. . . . There will not be two revolutions that

176

will develop in the same way, new possibilities and new forms will appear.[15]

Castro then tried to remove himself even farther from the adventurism of the late 1960s. In the future, he warned, Havana would apply very strict criteria to any guerrilla movements seeking Cuban aid:

> . . . Cuba has never refused nor will she ever refuse support to the revolutionary movement. But this is not to be confused with support for just any faker . . . [just] because some have put out their signs claiming to be revolutionaries. And the saddest thing about it is that in some cases we have believed them. And some of them we have even known.[16]

The tragic defeats suffered by Cuban-backed guerrilla movements in Latin America—particularly Che Guevara's death in Bolivia in 1967—undoubtedly played an important role in Havana's disillusionment with armed struggle. But there was a bright side to the change as well: the apparent success of Salvador Allende's democratically elected Popular Unity regime in Chile.

From the beginning, Castro was aware that Allende's government was a challenge to the Cuban model of revolution through armed struggle and to Cuba's self-proclaimed role as the vanguard of Latin America. When he arrived in Santiago in late November 1971, Castro spoke to the cheering Chilean crowds with uncharacteristic humility:

> We aren't holding our Revolution up as a model. . . . We don't claim that we are free of defects, that we haven't made any mistakes. . . . It would be ridiculous for us to tell you: "Do as we have done."[17]

At the end of his trip, Castro paid Allende and the Chileans an even greater compliment, saying that he had not come to Chile to teach but to learn. He had come to see:

> something extraordinary. . . . Something more than unique: unusual! It is a revolutionary process practically the first in humanity's history . . . in which revolutionaries are trying to carry out changes peacefully.[18]

Yet despite his obvious pleasure at Allende's success, Castro was still not convinced that Allende's commitment to democratic institutions such as free elections and a free press was the right course for Chile. With chilling foresight, Castro warned Allende that it was too easy for these tools to be used to undermine the revolution: Peasants could be divided from workers, and the middle class turned against the revolution. In the sort of struggle Allende was waging, Castro said, "the odds are against the revolutionaries; [they] are not equal to the reactionaries."[19]

The brutal military coup that overthrew Allende in mid-September 1973 seemed to prove the soundness of Castro's warning. The Cuban leader was outraged. He blamed the United States for organizing and funding the coup, and declared that the new Pinochet regime would forever be the enemy of all the Cuban people. To this day the Cuban press is filled with regular attacks on the Chilean junta. Nevertheless, Castro did *not* offer to underwrite a movement to overthrow Pinochet. In the mid-1960s, Cuba had responded to the right-wing turn in Latin America with a new militancy of its own. A decade later, Havana no longer considered Cuban military opposition a viable option.[20] In the spring of 1976, Castro officially rejected any exporting of revolution to Latin America, saying, "No Latin American country, regardless of its social system, has any reason to fear the Cuban armed forces."[21]

The Diplomatic Option

By mid-1969, Havana had begun to show renewed interest in diplomatic and trade relations with its Latin American neighbors. Whereas Castro had once condemned Soviet overtures to Venezuela and Colombia as collusion and a selfish betrayal of internationalist solidarity, the newly pragmatic leader had come to consider links to Latin America essential if Cuba were ever to overcome its dependence and underdevelopment. In a 1969 interview, Cuban economist and soon-to-be deputy prime minister Carlos Rafael Rodríguez said:

It would be much easier for Cuba to import some of the raw materials and manufactured goods it needs from countries that lie 100 to 500

miles from its ports, instead of having to transport such goods over
5,000 or 6,000 miles, given similar economic arrangements. . . .[22]

At first, Castro would only consider diplomatic relations with
governments that were officially committed to revolutionary change
at home and were solidly anti-American in international outlook—
in other words, Peru. As early as mid-1970, however, Castro had
relaxed his criteria to the point of considering diplomatic relations
with any Latin American state that was willing to act independently
of the United States.[23] By the mid-1970s, Havana had reestablished
relations with more than a dozen of its hemispheric neighbors.

Havana's new commitment to diplomacy was apparently accompanied by a cutoff of aid to the Latin American guerrilla movements.
This cutoff is difficult to document. Cuban aid to the Latin American
guerrillas was always limited. According to a House Foreign Affairs
Committee report issued in 1967, only "four instances of direct
Cuban support to insurgent groups" in Latin America—in total
several tons of arms and a few hundred men—could be proved.[24]
It would be difficult to detect any decrease in such a small amount
of aid. Nevertheless, a Senate Foreign Relations Committee report
issued four years later described Cuban support for Latin American
insurgency at the time as "minimal."[25]

Perhaps a better indicator of the shift in Cuban aid policies is
the response of Havana's previous allies. Early in 1970, Venezuelan
guerrilla leader Douglas Bravo attacked Castro by name and accused
the Cubans of abandoning the continental revolution in favor of
selfish concerns about their own economic development.[26]

Bravo's charges notwithstanding, Havana's decision to abandon
the export of revolution did not mean Cuba had abandoned all
interest in the region. If anything, after 1970 Cuban aid to Latin
America actually increased. The difference was that Cuba's new
aid programs were predominantly humanitarian rather than military, and were directed to official state governments rather than
guerrilla movements.

Cuba sent its first aid, earthquake relief, to Peru in 1970. Cuban
medical and construction brigades were among the first on the scene
and played a visible and important role in relief efforts. Over the

next three years, Havana sent similar aid to Nicaragua, Honduras, and Guatemala in the wake of devastating earthquakes.[27] By the mid-1970s, Cuban technical and military advisers, as well as hundreds of doctors, teachers, and construction workers, had become involved in development programs in Jamaica, Guyana, Grenada, and St. Lucia.

Although the actual monetary value of the Cuban aid programs was limited, the payoff was high, in terms of international goodwill. Havana's willingness to send help to Nicaragua—the home of one of Castro's oldest enemies, Anastasio Somoza—seemed to validate Castro's claims of genuine and "disinterested" concern for the plight of all Latin Americans regardless of their form of government. The long-term benefit in terms of Cuban popularity in postrevolutionary Nicaragua was unexpected but welcome. To many in the hemisphere, such good works signaled that Cuba's days as an international outlaw were over.

A Question of Style?

The change in Cuban policy after 1968 that has been noted most often was Havana's increasingly cordial attitude toward the Soviet Union. Throughout the 1960s, Castro had been bitterly critical of his Soviet allies. His most common complaint was that the Soviets were not doing enough for the Third World; they were not living up to their internationalist responsibilities, whether in Vietnam, Venezuela, or Cuba. By the early 1970s, all had changed, as Castro stopped attacking the Soviets and became one of Moscow's staunchest supporters.

What changed was not Soviet policies. Moscow was no more willing to underwrite democratic socialism in Chile in 1973 than it had been willing to support armed struggle in Venezuela in 1967. The Soviets stood by as Washington and the multinationals moved to starve out the Allende regime.[28] What changed after 1968 was Cuba's attitude. This shift, more than any other, exposed Havana to charges of hypocrisy and betrayal. However, as in the case of the Czech endorsement, there were a number of possible explanations for Havana's new positions—apart from the need to pay off Moscow. Confronted with its economic failures at home and military defeats abroad, by the early 1970s Havana appeared to have developed some of Moscow's natural caution. Despite the fiery rhetoric of Proletarian Internationalism, it began to look like neither Moscow nor Havana could stage an international revolution, regardless of the sincerity of their desires. In the context of newly lowered expectations, Moscow's continued generous support for Cuba must have seemed deserving of Havana's full endorsement.[29]

It is possible to explain the other major shifts in Cuban ideology by using similar calculations of Cuban interest. Cuba's increasingly vocal hostility to China—while clearly supporting Moscow in the Sino–Soviet split—can be traced to the Castro Government's militant years, when Havana saw Peking as a rival for the allegiances of the Latin American guerrilla left. In turn, Cuba's decision to endorse détente can be explained as a result of Cuba's abandonment of guerrilla warfare. During the mid-1960s, Havana rejected peaceful coexistence, saying that the time had arrived to confront imperialism in the Third World through armed struggle. But with defeat after defeat in Latin America, the Cubans were forced to abandon their hopes for immediate revolution. In this context, peaceful coexistence begins to look more rational and more desirable. If you are sure to lose a war, it is better not to fight.

Havana's growing domestic security may well have contributed to its new tolerance for coexistence. Washington seemed to be sticking to its half of the 1962 bargain, and an American military attack on Cuba seemed unlikely. Exile attacks had also decreased significantly. By the mid-1970s, Havana even seemed to have caught some of Moscow's earlier optimism about the correlation of international forces. The American defeat in Vietnam and the victory of the MPLA in Angola shortly thereafter seemed to convince Havana that history actually was on the side of socialism. If this were true, then the Cubans were willing to be as patient as their Soviet allies. In the short run they were willing to coexist with imperialism if the victory of socialism in the long run was guaranteed.

As for Havana's increasingly zealous promotion of Moscow's interests in the Nonaligned Movement and other Third World forums, it must be remembered that as critical as the Cubans were of Soviet policies during the mid-1960s, they never counseled the

Third World states to seek alternative trading partners or allies. After 1970 the Cubans continued to believe that the only hope for the Third World lay with the socialist bloc. Only now Havana appeared to be more realistic about what the Soviets could and could not offer the Third World, and thus was much less critical of Moscow.

If there are so many sound, nationalistic reasons for the changes in Cuban policy after 1970, why do most observers prefer to explain these changes as the result of Soviet pressures? Certainly Havana's critics—whether in the policy-making, scholarly, or journalistic communities—would naturally gravitate to the former explanation. To describe Cuba as a mere pawn of the Soviet Union makes any American attempt to oppose Cuban policies and any American attack on Cuba look legitimate.

But even an observer sympathetic to the Cuban revolution finds it hard to avoid the impression of Soviet domination—because the changes in Cuba were so great and so abrupt, and because the docile tone of the new Cuban rhetoric was so different from the Castro regime's earlier style.

Hypocrisy is no stranger to diplomacy and certainly no stranger to the socialist bloc, which has a censored press and a penchant for rewriting history. This sort of rhetoric is significant only in its point of origin: Cuba, for much of the 1960s, spoke freely and often very critically of its alliance with the Soviets. Reading the Cuban press today, it is hard not to think of Cuba as a satellite state.

The change in rhetoric is important because it symbolized a new attitude in Havana, and a greater willingness to conform to the parameters of bloc membership. As part of its new maturity, Havana apparently became more realistic about what it could achieve by directly criticizing its Soviet allies. Charges of collusion and betrayal did not stop Moscow from pursuing diplomatic relations in Latin America. All that the charges accomplished was to focus Soviet pressure on Cuba.

After the late 1960s, the Castro regime apparently decided that a quieter form of diplomacy—a mixture of outward cordiality and back-room negotiations—was the best way to gain Soviet support for its policies. By the mid-1970s, such a strategy had begun to pay off, as Cuba embarked on another course of revolutionary internationalism in Angola—this time with Soviet backing.

THE TURN EASTWARD

Havana's new policies began to show a definite payoff by the early 1970s. The most immediate and obvious benefit was improved relations with its Soviet allies. The economic pressures Moscow had put on Havana were lifted at about the time of Castro's endorsement of the 1968 Czech invasion. Over the next few years, as Havana began to tailor both its foreign and domestic policies according to Moscow's precepts, Soviet economic and military aid to Cuba increased substantially.

Castro's decision to endorse the Warsaw Pact invasion of Czechoslovakia was undoubtedly important to his allies in the Kremlin. Moscow had been vehemently attacked by the West for the Czech invasion—which was expected. What was not expected, however, was the volume of criticism voiced by Communist parties in Western Europe, the Third World, and within the socialist bloc itself. Romania's Communist leadership would not commit its Warsaw Pact troops to the invasion, and even went so far in its opposition as to refuse to allow Bulgarian troops to cross or fly over Romanian territory on their way to Prague.[30] An endorsement from Fidel Castro, given his reputation for honesty and independence when it came to bloc matters, was thus invaluable to the Soviets.

But Moscow was not just looking for another yes man. Its disagreements with Havana, it must be remembered, went well beyond ideological debates on the nature of revolution and included such concrete issues as how Havana was using—or misusing—Soviet aid. Cuba's economic failures were particularly disappointing to the Soviet Union. First, they were embarrassing. How could the Soviets claim Cuba as a great revolutionary success and a model for the Third World if the Cubans couldn't even feed themselves? At the same time Cuba's economic failures were costly—too costly for the Soviet Union, which was experiencing major economic problems at home. Castro's decision to rationalize Cuba's economic practices after 1970 was thus very important to the Soviet Union and deserving of both ideological and material support.

None of these changes took place overnight. Between 1969 and 1972 there was a slow but steady realignment of Cuba's international relations as Havana tested new policies and as its allies and enemies tested new responses.

Moscow had never publicly admitted it was having problems with Havana—at least not directly—and it was equally circumspect about acknowledging any reconciliation. In December 1969, more than a year after Castro's endorsement of the Czech invasion, Radio Moscow commented on the state of Cuban–Soviet relations in a cautious but ultimately positive tone:

> . . . it would be wrong to say that all is ideal in our relations. The main thing is that in every course of historical development our countries are together side by side. . . . The events in Czechoslovakia and the position adopted by the Communist Party and Revolutionary Government of Cuba on this completely confirm this. For this reason we must be able to rapidly overcome the strange and casual things that sometimes arise in Soviet–Cuban relations.[31]

Although Moscow's language was carefully veiled, there was little doubt about what "strange and casual things" the Kremlin wanted overcome: Castro's critical challenges to Moscow's foreign policies and Cuba's repeated economic failures. It was time for the Cubans to set aside their internationalist pretensions and start concentrating on problems at home. According to an article in *Pravda* in the fall of 1970:

> . . . Cuba's main contribution to the world socialist system and the general revolutionary process now lies in economic building and creating a developed socialist society on this base. . . .[32]

It took time for Castro to convince the Soviets that his commitment to change was sincere. He took his first step in July 1970, when he admitted that the "ten million tons" campaign had been a fiasco, and pledged a complete overhaul of the Cuban economy. In December of that year, Cuban economist Carlos Rafael Rodríguez led a delegation to Moscow for meetings with economists from the Soviet Central Planning Board. That same month, the Cuban–Soviet Commission of Economic, Scientific, and Technical Collaboration was formed. Moscow also announced that it would delay the adoption of a new Cuban–Soviet trade agreement until the Joint Commission had an opportunity to study fully the Cuban economic situation.[33]

Over the next year, Soviet and Cuban economists shuttled between Havana and Moscow. In the fall of 1971, Soviet Premier Alexei Kosygin arrived in Havana for a series of meetings with Fidel and Raúl Castro, Cuban President Osvaldo Dorticós, and the increasingly important Rodríguez. At the end of his stay, Kosygin and Castro issued a joint communiqué describing their "complete mutual understanding" on a range of international and domestic issues.[34] Upon returning to Moscow, Kosygin announced that negotiations toward a new Cuban–Soviet trade agreement had begun.

Even then, one further step remained to be taken before the new economic plan was unveiled. In July 1972, Havana proved its commitment to the Soviet economic line by petitioning for admission to Comecon, the Moscow-dominated Council for Mutual Economic Assistance. There is a great deal of confusion about whether or not the Cubans wanted to join Comecon or would benefit from it. Cuba's admission to Comecon has been described by some observers as a Soviet concession: Moscow promised Havana that its future economic well-being would be guaranteed by the socialist bloc. It has also been described as a Cuban concession: Castro gave control of his country's economy over to Soviet planners.[35]

This loss of control, according to one analyst, was more than a symbolic issue. The Comecon plan is based on a model of specialization of tasks—or comparative advantage—that would keep Cuba producing sugar rather than diversifying exports.[36] And it is true that Cuba today is as dependent on sugar exports as it was before the revolution. Whether Cuba's Comecon membership has prevented diversification, however, is not clear. The Castro regime failed to diversify the Cuban economy during the thirteen years preceding Cuba's admission, as had Castro's predecessors. In any case, Castro

185

apparently was not completely satisfied with the step and left Moscow five days before the Comecon meeting. Carlos Rafael Rodríguez remained to make the formal request.

In December 1972, the new Cuban–Soviet economic agreement was finally signed. Although it took two years, it was worth the wait. Under the terms of the new agreement, the Soviet Union would pay Cuba a substantially higher price for its exports—the price paid for Cuban sugar alone would almost double. The agreement also promised increased technical aid to help Cuba mechanize its sugar harvest, develop its nickel production and textile industry, and improve its oil refineries. Finally, the agreement deferred the repayment of the Cuban debt for thirteen years.[37] Like so many underdeveloped countries in both the capitalist and socialist worlds, Cuba had fallen into the debt trap, each year borrowing more and more to pay the spiraling prices for manufactured goods, and watching its debt grow and compound to a point where it could barely meet the interest payments. It has been estimated that by 1972 Cuba owed its Soviet allies close to $4 billion.[38] Moscow's decision to suspend interest charges on this debt and defer payments on the principal until 1986 was crucial if Cuba was ever to resolve its economic problems.

Better Defense

Moscow's satisfaction with the new Cuban line was expressed in military terms as well. Ever since Khrushchev backed down in the 1962 missile crisis, the Cuban leadership had felt uneasy about Moscow's military commitment to Havana. Almost every major Cuban policy statement—whether a critique of Soviet policies in Vietnam or an endorsement of Soviet policies in Czechoslovakia—included a reminder of Soviet responsibilities for Cuba's defense. With the improvement in Cuban–Soviet relations after 1968, Moscow took several steps clearly calculated to allay these fears.

In July 1969, a Soviet naval squadron paid its first visit to Cuba. The squadron was composed of two diesel-powered submarines, a submarine tender, a guided missile cruiser, and two guided missile destroyers. Over the next nine years, Soviet naval squadrons made nineteen visits to Cuban ports.[39] Each time the quality of the ships was upgraded. Although these visits posed no real threat to the United States, their symbolic importance was enormous, and the message to both Havana and Washington was clear: The Soviet Union now had the capability to defend Cuba against any American attack. At the same time, the Soviet naval maneuvers had the additional benefit of asserting Moscow's right and will to operate openly and freely in the Caribbean.

Moscow tried to take these points one step further the following summer, when it began to build a base for Soviet nuclear submarines in Cienfuegos Bay on Cuba's southern coast. Washington first learned of the base in late August 1970, when a U-2 overflight reported an unusual amount of construction activity on one of the islands.[40] By mid-September, U.S. intelligence had definitive proof: Photographs taken on a September 16 overflight showed new barracks, administrative buildings, a soccer field, and a Soviet nuclear submarine tender moored in the bay. Photographs of the mainland showed a new dock, fuel storage depot, and a major communications facility still under construction. The entire complex was guarded by antiaircraft missiles and surveillance radar. There was no doubt that Cienfuegos was to be a permanent Soviet submarine base.

Washington had been ambivalent about the earlier Soviet naval visits. On the one hand, the precedent being established was obviously distasteful to the Nixon Administration, which was solidly committed to containing the spread of Soviet power, especially in its own backyard. On the other hand, the Administration felt it could hardly claim that the Soviet naval visits were illegal or an act of belligerence—the Caribbean was, after all, international waters. But the Cienfuegos base was something else again: The installation of Soviet offensive weapons in Cuba—whether missiles or submarines—was an unacceptable breach of the 1962 missile accord.

At a press briefing on September 25, 1970, National Security Adviser Henry Kissinger made Washington's position clear. "The Soviet Union," he said, "can be under no doubt that we would view the establishment of a strategic base in the Caribbean with the utmost seriousness."[41] At the same time, Kissinger did not publicly accuse the Soviets of actually building a base. Both Nixon and Kissinger wanted to give Moscow the room to withdraw gracefully this time. In private meetings with Soviet Ambassador Anatoly Dobrynin, Kissinger was much more direct. The United States knew the Soviets were building a base in Cienfuegos Bay, he told Dobrynin, and would not tolerate it.

Kissinger's technique of "quiet diplomacy" worked. On October 13, the Soviet Government issued a statement that said:

> The Soviet Union has not built and is not building its military bases in Cuba, and is not doing anything that would contradict the understanding reached between the Governments of the USSR and the United States in 1962.[42]

U.S. overflights that week showed that Soviet subtender had left Cienfuegos.

Unlike the missile crisis, Castro did not protest the Soviet capitulation in the Cienfuegos affair. There are several possible explanations for this new docility. Having learned its lesson in 1962, Moscow may have warned Castro beforehand about making any untoward comments. Or, given his experience with the 1968 oil deliveries, Castro may well have been wary of pushing his Soviet allies again. It is also possible that this time Castro may have been afraid of provoking a confrontation between Washington and Moscow. As one Cuban Communist Party official later described it:

> In 1962 we were all for a confrontation. . . . We were sure our own country was going to be destroyed anyway. By 1970, having survived much longer than we ever expected, we felt differently.[43]

A final explanation could be that by 1970 Castro had actually grown more secure about his relationship with the Soviets and their commitment to Cuba's defense. Even without the submarine base Havana felt that it could depend on Moscow. There was no need to protest the withdrawal.

One further difference between the missile crisis and the Cienfuegos affair was that this time Moscow did not back down completely. Although the Soviets withdrew the submarine tender from its permanent moorings in Cienfuegos, the tender continued to operate in the Caribbean until the following January. In December another Soviet naval squadron arrived in Cuba, and in February a new submarine tender arrived in the Caribbean. Once again the message was clear: Although the Soviets had agreed to dismantle their base in Cuba, they had no plans to withdraw from the Caribbean.

At the same time, the Soviets helped the Cubans to develop their own defensive capability. In November 1969, Soviet Defense Minister Marshal Andrei A. Grechko arrived in Cuba for talks with Cuban military leaders. Six months later, Cuban Defense Minister Raúl Castro paid a return visit to the Soviet Union. Although their talks were private, apparently some agreement was reached to upgrade Soviet military aid to Cuba and increase the number of Soviet technical and military advisers assigned to the Cuban armed forces.

Very little hard information is available on Soviet military aid to Cuba. Neither Havana nor Moscow ever publish their military agreements. In 1970, Castro claimed that Soviet military aid to Cuba through 1969 had had an estimated worth of $1.5 billion.[44] At the First Party Congress six years later, Castro described Soviet military assistance to Cuba as worth "several billions."[45] The United States intelligence services' efforts to monitor the sort of weaponry Moscow has provided to Cuba have disclosed that a majority of the matériel transferred during the 1960s was second-line equipment with a solely defensive capability. After 1970, however, Moscow significantly upgraded the quality of Soviet equipment, sending Cuba several hundred new tanks, armored personnel carriers, reconnaissance missiles, antitank missiles, and even some new self-propelled antiaircraft guns.[46] In January 1972, the Cuban navy doubled its antiaircraft capability, receiving several Soviet missile-carrying launches. Three months later, the Cuban air force received ten to fifteen MIG-23s, Moscow's most advanced fighter interceptor at the time. But the Soviets still did not give their Cuban allies either air or naval equipment to transport medium-to-heavy weaponry off the island or for the large-scale movement of troops. If the Cubans were planning to use their upgraded forces in any military engagements off the island, they would have to depend on their Soviet allies to get them there.

There remained one other commitment that Moscow refused to make: admitting Cuba to the Warsaw Pact. Havana's position on the issue has never been discussed publicly, and can only be surmised. Cuba's membership would not come without definite cost. As a member of a military alliance, Cuba would lose all claims to nonalignment. But this seems to be a price the Cubans were willing to pay for guaranteeing their defense. In a speech delivered on April 22, 1970—when his brother Raúl was in Moscow negotiating military aid—Fidel Castro reaffirmed the strength of Cuban–Soviet military ties:

> We shall never break our political ties with the Soviet Union or even what they call military ties. On the contrary. So far as we are concerned we will always be ready to increase our military ties with the Soviet Union.[47]

The following August, Castro repeated his commitment to increased military ties with the Soviets, saying, "We repeat, our disposition is to establish, if possible, even more ties with [the Soviet Union]."

From these statements it would seem that Castro was lobbying the Soviets for admission to the Warsaw Pact or some formal military agreement. For reasons we have already discussed in detail, Moscow was not willing to fulfill Castro's request. It could not take the risk of ever having to confront the United States over the issue of Cuba's defense. Even after 1970 and the shift in the Castro Government's policies, concessions remained that the Soviet Union would not make to its Cuban allies.

END TO ISOLATION

Paradoxically, many of the changes in Cuban policy that brought Moscow and Havana closer together also improved Cuba's diplomatic standing in the West, particularly among its Latin American neighbors. Cuba had begun the 1970s totally isolated in the hemisphere. Despite Castro's avowed intention to improve diplomatic relations in the region, most states continued to fear Cuban subversion. The image of the Cuban guerrilla was hard to shake.

But in February 1970, at a conference of the Inter-American Economic and Social Council in Caracas, President Rafael Caldera of Venezuela and Prime Minister Eric Williams of Trinidad and Tobago took the first step toward reuniting Cuba with the rest of

Latin America by calling for a resumption of diplomatic and trade relations with the Castro Government. The resolution was defeated by a majority of the member states, but for the first time in a decade the issue was definitely back on the agenda of hemispheric politics.

Over the next year, Castro's efforts to woo his neighbors began to make progress. In November 1970, the new Allende Government in Chile renounced the OAS sanctions and established relations with Cuba. In May 1971, on his way home from Chile, Castro made short stopovers to meet with the leaders of Peru and Ecuador. These trips obviously paid off. By year's end, Ecuador's Galo Plaza, the OAS secretary general, endorsed Cuba's request for readmission, and General Juan Velasco, the Peruvian head of state, invited Cuba to attend the Lima meeting of the Group of 77—a new coalition of developing nations committed to redressing world economic inequalities.[48]

In 1972, the Castro Government's diplomatic overtures showed increasing signs of success. In the spring, Peru introduced a bill in the OAS to lift the ban on trade with Cuba and to permit member states to reestablish diplomatic relations. Although this motion was also defeated—seven for, thirteen against, three abstentions—the divided vote reflected the success of Cuba's diplomatic courtships and marked a clear departure from the unanimity that had marked the imposition of sanctions eight years before. Despite the motion's defeat, Peru went ahead and independently established relations with the Castro Government the following July.

In December 1972, four of Cuba's Caribbean neighbors—Barbados, Guyana, Jamaica, and Trinidad and Tobago—dramatically broke with the OAS ban and jointly established relations with Cuba.[49] Havana's diplomatic efforts gained further ground in the spring of 1973, when Argentina's Peronist President, Héctor Cámpora, decided to reopen relations and extend Cuba a $1.2 billion credit to buy agricultural and road-building equipment. Another important step was taken the following summer when Argentina's new economics minister announced that Argentine subsidiaries of U.S.-owned corporations would be required to sell to Cuba. In the face of strong pressure from Buenos Aires, the U.S. Treasury Department granted three American auto companies a special release from the embargo on Cuban trade in April 1974.[50] The hated embargo was finally breached—and a Latin American state had forced Washington to do it. The Cubans were delighted.

By the mid-1970s, Cuba had established itself as a solid member of the international community. Attempts to diversify Cuba's trading partners beyond the socialist bloc were received favorably by almost every Western state, except the United States. In 1974, 45 percent of Cuba's exports were sold to Western governments, up from 24 percent at the beginning of the decade.[51]

Cuba's bilateral trade agreements increased more than five-fold between 1970 and 1975. No doubt the fact that Cuban sugar sold on the world market in 1974 at an average price of almost 30 cents a pound made Cuba look especially attractive. In December 1974, the Spanish Government extended Cuba a $900 million trade credit, and within the first five months of 1975, Cuba received credits of $350 million from France, $155 million from Canada, and $580 million from England.[52] Cuban bids for hard-currency loans were also well received in the European financial markets. A 1975 offering on the London Eurocurrency market raised $100 million for the National Bank of Cuba.[53] Castro's policy of reconciliation paid its most gratifying—if not most remunerative—dividend in mid-summer 1975, when, in a decision by sixteen of its twenty-one members, the OAS abolished the economic and political bans against Cuba.

THWARTED RAPPROCHEMENT

Some form of rapprochement with the United States would have been a logical corollary to Cuba's newly moderate foreign policy. In 1974, Havana and Washington did make a number of cautious overtures, which culminated in a series of secret meetings to discuss terms for reestablishing relations. But these efforts were abandoned less than a year later after Cuban troops were committed to the Angolan civil war.

Whether one sees Moscow or Havana as the principal architect of Cuba's new foreign policy, there is no doubt that improved relations with the United States would have benefited all concerned.

The most immediate benefit for Havana would have been access to American markets. Although the U.S. embargo never actually succeeded in starving out the Castro Government, it severely stunted Cuba's economic growth.[54] The socialist bloc has tried to take America's place, buying as much sugar and nickel as Cuba can produce and selling industrial goods and petroleum to Cuba at very favorable prices. But the sheer distance over which these goods must be transported has made the relationship disadvantageous. Other economic problems facing the Cubans include a shortage of foreign exchange—almost all Cuban–Soviet trade is conducted in barter—and dissatisfaction with the quality of advanced technology in the Soviet bloc. Finally, no matter how fraternal the relationship with the Soviets, given their history, the Cubans must beware of placing their economic well-being in the hands of a single state.

Since the early 1970s, Havana has tried to diversify its trading partners, seeking new markets in Latin America, Western Europe, and Japan. The Castro Government's growing acceptance in Latin America, in defiance of the OAS sanctions, has had great political significance. But most Latin American states unfortunately have little to offer Cuba economically. Most produce raw materials and have little need for Cuban sugar (many produce sugar themselves) and little to offer Cuba in terms of advanced technology or capital.

At the same time, Havana began to have some success in courting West European and Japanese markets and investors, particularly after the world market price for sugar tripled in 1974. But the costs of shipping even to Western Europe were steep for Cuba. Further hampering Havana's efforts to expand its trade base was the large amount of Western European capital tied up in U.S.-based multinational corporations; few states have been willing to challenge the U.S. embargo. In addition, many Western European lending sources—both public and private—follow the U.S. lead when choosing investments. Thus a resumption of trade relations with the United States would not only have given Cuba access to American markets and capital, but also would have improved Cuba's financial standing internationally.

Another benefit of rapprochement would have been an increased sense of military security for the Castro regime. Despite the American "no-invasion pledge" of 1962, throughout the 1960s and 1970s Havana continued to fear an American attack. The findings of the Senate Select Intelligence Committee's 1976 investigation of the CIA suggest these fears were not unfounded.[55] Cuba's distrust of the U.S. has remained so great, however, that even if some form of rapprochement with the United States were feasible, it would still be quite a while before Havana would be willing to lower its guard. As Castro declared in 1974, "Our defense can never rest on the good faith of the imperialists."[56] Nevertheless, rapprochement with the United States remains a necessary first step if the Cubans are ever to start demobilizing their highly militarized society.

Though it may seem paradoxical, Moscow would also have benefited from improved relations between Havana and Washington. A resumption of Cuban–American trade would have meant a reduction in the substantial economic burden on Moscow created by Cuba's almost total dependence. Since 1960, when the Soviet Union replaced the United States as Cuba's primary trading partner, mentor, and protector, the Soviets have poured billions of dollars into Cuba. As one observer described it, Soviet assistance "has meant far more than simply helping Cuba develop a little faster a little better." Since 1962, "Cuba has had a deficit economy saved from bankruptcy only by Soviet aid."[57]

The Soviet Union has managed to keep the Cuban economy afloat with a mixture of direct aid grants and an elaborate system of price supports and trade subsidies. Moscow buys Cuban sugar and nickel at prices well above the world market price and sells Cuba petroleum at below free-market rates. For example, in 1966, when the world market price for sugar was at a low of 1.86 cents a pound, the Soviets were buying Cuban sugar at 6.17 cents a pound. In 1974, when the world price for oil jumped to $11.58 a barrel, the Soviet Union sold Cuba its petroleum for $3.19 a barrel.[58] It has been estimated that between 1960 and 1976 Soviet economic assistance to Cuba exceeded $8 billion. This does not include the cost of Soviet military aid or technical, educational, and developmental assistance programs, whose value was estimated to have reached another $3 billion by the mid-1970s.[59]

Certainly, a resumption of Cuban–American trade could not have been expected to make much of a dent in a deficit that size. But, as we noted above, access to American markets would be an important first step toward Cuba's gaining broader access to other Western markets—and thus sources of foreign exchange—as well as public and private lending agencies. This access would be essential if Cuba were to reduce its economic dependence on the Soviet Union.

Another important benefit for Moscow of improved Cuban–American relations would have been a reduction in Soviet–American tensions. There is no doubt that over the years the Soviets have benefited greatly from Cuba's anti-American stance. Castro's dramatic break with the United States and subsequent alignment with the socialist bloc was an enormous boost for the Soviet position in the Cold War. The problem is that Moscow has not always been able to control its Cuban allies. And at times like the 1962 missile crisis, Castro's vituperative anti-Americanism has dangerously strained Moscow's program of peaceful coexistence.

A Cuban–American rapprochement would also have solved one of Moscow's major strategic dilemmas. Always underlying the Cuban–Soviet alliance has been the unspoken question of how far Moscow would be willing to go to defend Cuba against an American attack. Should Cuban–American hostilities ever escalate to open confrontation, Moscow would be in the untenable position of either having to abandon its Cuban allies and completely lose its international credibility, or face a nuclear confrontation with the United States. Both Moscow and Washington recognized the danger of this situation early on, and tried their best to defuse it with the missile crisis accord. But Castro was never a party to this agreement. At the time he rejected it as big power collusion. Therefore, so long as there is the potential for a Cuban–American confrontation, there remains a potential for a Soviet–American confrontation. A rapprochement between Cuba and the United States would do much to remove that danger.

Moscow's desire for a Cuban–American rapprochement does, however, have some natural limits. The Soviets would certainly not want Cuban–American relations to improve to the point where Havana was considering switching its allegiances or even using the threat of defection to improve its bargaining position.

What will happen to Cuba when Castro is no longer leading the revolution is less certain. Moscow's reaction to a post-Castro leadership that pursued some form of what Castro calls "tropical Titoism"[60] or, even worse, a return to capitalism, cannot be predicted. To "lose" Cuba would certainly be an enormous blow to Moscow's prestige and to the prestige of the entire bloc. Whether Moscow would be willing to risk a confrontation with Washington and send troops to "discipline" its erstwhile allies is a question that future policy analysts may well have to confront. In the near future, any form of Cuban–American rapprochement will be limited by Havana's continued commitment to socialism and dependence on the Soviet Union.

First Steps

By the early 1970s, both Havana and Moscow had good reason to consider improving relations with the United States. After Richard Nixon's dramatic 1972 visit to the People's Republic of China, they also reasonably expected a positive reception in Washington.

Whatever the possible benefits for Cuba, Castro was not going to rush into a rapprochement with the United States. His pride and the distrust born of two decades of hostility were too great. The first sign that the Cuban leader was even considering improving relations with Washington came during his 1971 visit to Chile. At that time Castro stated that a revolution in Washington would not be necessary for Cuba and the United States to reestablish relations. All that was needed was the leadership of a U.S. President of "wide vision and broad understanding." Unfortunately, Castro hastened to add, such a President was not currently available— Richard Nixon, Castro vowed, would never visit Havana.[61]

While in Chile, Castro also outlined two preconditions necessary for Havana even to consider reopening relations with Washington: first, an end to the war in Vietnam, and, second, an end to U.S. interventions in Latin America. At a press conference the following May in Sofia, Bulgaria, Castro added two more items to the list. Before Cuba would begin talks, he said, the United States would have to end its illegal embargo and withdraw from the naval base in Guantánamo. It is difficult to decide which was more significant:

196

Castro's willingness to discuss conditions for rapprochement, or that the preconditions outlined were almost impossible for Washington to meet.

Washington's attitude mirrored Havana's. The Nixon Administration was officially committed to dealing "realistically" with governments of all types—whether they be the right-wing authoritarian junta in Brazil, the left-wing authoritarian junta in Peru, or even the Communist leadership in Peking. As far as Cuba was concerned, the Nixon Administration was willing to be realistic to the point of accepting the permanence of Cuba's socialism.

But Washington's tolerance for the Castro Government still only went so far. Two U.S. preconditions would have to be met before the Nixon Administration would consider reestablishing relations with Cuba: Havana would have to cut its military ties with the Soviet Union and abandon its subversive activities in Latin America.[62] The American preconditions—in their intransigence—bore a striking resemblance to the Cuban preconditions.

With time, both sides began to soften their positions. In early 1974, Secretary of State Henry Kissinger indicated that Washington was now willing to drop its demand that Havana cut all military ties with the Soviet Union. All that remained was the requirement that Cuba abandon its efforts to export revolution to Latin America. This was really not much of an obstacle, since Havana had voluntarily foresworn the export of revolution four years earlier. All that Washington had to do was recognize that declaration.

On the Cuban side, one of Havana's major preconditions was met in February 1974, when the United States signed the InterAmerican Conference of Foreign Ministers' pledge to a policy of nonintervention in the hemisphere. Like Havana's avowed rejection of the export of revolution, this pledge required some faith on the beholder's part. Another of Havana's preconditions was met the following year in April, when the United States withdrew its forces from Vietnam.

Despite this obvious progress, relations between Washington and Havana remained deadlocked throughout Nixon's second term. The only notable movement was the signing of a Cuban–American anti-hijacking agreement in February 1973.[63] With Nixon's resignation in the summer of 1974, the prospects for improved Cuban–American relations brightened significantly. On many occasions during the Nixon years, Kissinger had expressed his interest in normalizing relations with Cuba. The Secretary of State's interest in Cuba was supported by a wide variety of American legislators, including not only liberals, such as Senators Edward M. Kennedy (D–Mass.) and George S. McGovern (D–S. Dak.), but also conservatives such as Sen. Robert Byrd (I–Va.), who in 1974 urged a reevaluation of U.S. policies toward Cuba, guided by "enlightened self-interest."[64] However, the personal animosity shared by Nixon and Castro (which, it must be remembered, dated back to 1959) made any overtures difficult.

During the Ford Administration, personal animosity was no longer a problem. Kissinger was eager to exploit the nascent diversity of the Communist world and to probe the strengths and weaknesses of the Cuban–Soviet relationship. His Cuban policy was also part of a new concern for the growing strength of Third World alignments—dramatically brought home to the United States by the 1973 OPEC oil embargo.

In the fall of 1974, Kissinger sent a message to Havana that the time for discussion was finally ripe. Havana responded positively, sending two envoys to meetings in Washington and New York in November. These secret meetings went on for almost a year. The discussions focused on resolutions to the legacy of long years of nonrecognition: the trade embargo, compensation for $1.8 billion in U.S. property expropriated after the revolution, release of $30 million in Cuban assets frozen by Washington, release of political prisoners in Cuba, reunion of Cuban families, and the status of Guantánamo Bay Naval Base in Cuba.[65] There is no doubt that these issues were difficult, and each potentially a major stumbling block. But as the U.S. experience with China later proved, no issue was insurmountable if the will to negotiate and compromise was there.

However, Cuba's involvement in the 1975 Angolan civil war abruptly ended the talks and all hope for a U.S.–Cuba rapprochement. The commitment of some 18,000 Cuban combat troops was viewed in Washington as a direct challenge to U.S. power and influence in the Third World. Washington threatened to suspend the recognition talks if Cuba did not immediately withdraw from Angola. Castro refused, saying that Cuba's practice of internationalist solidarity in Angola was a sovereign right and not subject to negotiation. "At that price," Castro said, "there shall never be any relations with the United States."[66] The Cuban envoys went home.

Dogs in the Manger

Not all of Cuba's allies were satisfied with the new line. In particular, several of Havana's previous revolutionary comrades began to accuse Castro of selling out the Latin American revolution in favor of Cuban self-interest. The problem facing the Cubans in Latin America was similar to one the Soviets had confronted just a few years earlier. In the early 1970s, Latin America was still filled with revolutionary movements, many claiming allegiance to socialist and even Castroite ideals. But the years had shown that, despite their ideals, these revolutionary movements had little chance of ever coming to power. At the same time, several Latin American regimes—in many cases, the same ones under attack by these revolutionaries—had begun to express an interest in reestablishing diplomatic and trading relations with Cuba. What was Havana to do? Back the revolutionaries who were bound to fail? Or further its own state interests while waiting for more revolutionary times? It is clear which route Moscow chose when it found itself in a similar quandary, and as a result was severely castigated by its Cuban allies for "betrayal" and "collusion" in Latin America. Now, only a few years later, Castro had made the same analysis of the situation in Latin America and had come to the same decision.

Like Castro before them, the Latin American guerrillas could not contain their outrage. Hugo Blanco and Héctor Béjar, two pro-Castro Peruvian guerrillas, were especially vocal in their criticism of Cuba's new policies—particularly after Castro enthusiastically endorsed the Peruvian junta that had imprisoned them. Blanco, a sworn opponent of the new junta, criticized Castro for thinking that socialism could prevail in Peru without armed struggle. This was the same criticism Castro had repeatedly made of his comrades in the Latin American Communist parties. Blanco was so disillusioned that he bitterly claimed that even during the late 1960s, when Cuba was still promoting a revolutionary line, Cuban material aid never lived up to Cuban promises.[67]

Upon his release from prison, Héctor Béjar, unlike Blanco, became an enthusiastic supporter of the new Peruvian junta. But he too was critical of Castro, in particular of Cuba's growing dependence on the socialist bloc. The Cuban–Soviet alliance, he claimed, was no different from Cuba's earlier dependence on the United States, and was just as stifling to the true Cuban national spirit. In words reminiscent of Castro's early days of revolutionary nationalism, Béjar claimed that the Peruvian way of seeking aid from both the capitalist and socialist states was the only way to a pure revolution. Peru, he claimed, had replaced Cuba as the revolutionary vanguard of Latin America.[68]

Douglas Bravo's criticisms of the new Cuban line were probably the most dramatic and the most telling. In December 1970, Bravo also accused Castro of selling out the Latin American revolution in favor of Cuba's own selfish economic concerns. It must be remembered that Bravo was the leader of the Venezuelan revolutionary FALN when it broke with the Venezuelan Communist Party over the issue of armed struggle. In order to support Bravo, the Castro regime had dramatically repudiated the Venezuelan Communists, claiming that since they were unwilling to make a revolution they were not truly Communists. It was also because of Bravo that Cuba had challenged Moscow's right to lead the international movement. By supporting the Venezuelan Communists against Bravo's FALN, Castro said, the Soviets had proved they also were not truly committed to international revolution. And it was for Bravo and those like him that Cuba had broken with Moscow and set up its own International, the Latin American Solidarity Organization. Now Bravo was claiming that Havana had made the same mistakes as Moscow by recognizing many different routes to progressive change, and by seeking improved diplomatic relations with the ruling Latin American regimes. As a result, Bravo said, Cuba could no longer claim to be the leader of the international struggle or the vanguard of the Latin American movement.[69]

Many loyal revolutionaries in Cuba had their doubts about the new line. According to one party leader who left his foreign ministry post after 1968, "some of us believed that Bolivia was another Moncada . . . a temporary setback, not an end to the struggle."[70] Most Cubans refused altogether to discuss the policy changes. No public debate was allowed.

Cuba's new policies met one further challenge from an unexpected source—the Nonaligned Movement. Cuba's influence in the Nonaligned Movement began to increase significantly in the early 1970s. By choosing diplomacy over the export of revolution, Castro had won diplomatic acceptance of Cuba from most of the group's members. At the same time, the movement as a whole was moving closer to Cuba with its increasing emphasis on North–South issues. Throughout the 1960s, Cuban delegates had spoken to the Nonaligned Movement summits about the need to redress international economic inequalities, for commodity price supports, to renegotiate loans, and to lower trade barriers. At the time, however, most of the nonaligned states were more concerned with the possibility of a nuclear war between the superpowers, and with building some form of peaceful coexistence. But by the early 1970s, the world had changed. Détente seemed to endure, and the 1973 OPEC oil embargo had moved international economic issues to the top of the Third World agenda. The nonaligned states were now ready to listen to the Cubans.[71]

Paradoxically, Cuba's commitment to the export of revolution— although it was opposed by a majority of nonaligned states—was seen as proof of Cuba's independence. The Soviets opposed the Cuban line on Proletarian Internationalism, nuclear nonproliferation, and a host of other international issues—so Cuba had to be independent. By the early 1970s, however, a growing number of states had come to see nonalignment as the test of true independence. Havana's statements about the "natural alliance" between the socialist bloc and the Third World—once seen as Cuba's bid for Soviet aid to the Third World—now appeared to be proof of the Castro Government's dependence on the socialist bloc. At the 1973 conference in Algiers, Cuba's right to continue as a member of the Nonaligned Movement was challenged by two leaders of the new bloc of radical and nonaligned states, Cambodia's Norodom Sihanouk and Libya's Muammar Qadaffi. According to Qadaffi:

We are against Cuba's presence in this Conference of Nonaligned Nations. There is no difference between Cuba or for that matter Uzbekistan and the Soviet Union itself.[72]

A Significant Exception

The changes in Cuban foreign policy in the early 1970s were dramatic, but their significance should not be exaggerated. In particular, Cuba's alleged retreat from Proletarian Internationalism was not nearly as complete as has been suggested by most observers. Havana's support for revolutionary movements in Africa, for example, continued unabated. When these policies are viewed in the context of Cuba's later involvements in Angola and Ethiopia, Cuba's continued support for the African liberation movements during the early 1970s looks less like the exception and more like the rule.

Throughout the early 1970s, Havana continued to express its support for the strategy of armed struggle for Africa. In a speech to the UN, delivered in early October 1970, Cuban delegate Ricardo Alarcón announced that Cuba was committed to aiding "the just struggles of the peoples of Guinea-Bissau, Angola, Mozambique, Zimbabwe, Namibia, and South Africa."[73] When Fidel Castro made a tour of Africa eighteen months later, he met not only with the usual heads of state but also with leaders of several revolutionary movements. In a joint communiqué issued with Algeria, Cuba promised the "most resolute" and "efficient" aid to revolutionary fighters in Guinea-Bissau, Cape Verde, Mozambique, and Angola.[74]

These were not empty promises. Evidence of Cuba's African involvements during these years is meager, since the Cubans only began to acknowledge their support for African revolutionaries after their mid-1975 involvement in Angola. Yet, throughout the early to mid-1970s Havana apparently continued to aid African liberation movements. Havana sent both technical and military advisers, doctors, and a limited amount of weapons. After Castro's 1972 African tour, two new Cuban military missions were established in Sierra

Leone and equatorial Guinea—each with an estimated 100 advisers. Over the next three years, Havana set up technical missions in Somalia, Algeria, and Tanzania as well.[75]

It is true that the number of Cuban advisers stationed at these African missions was cut back from a mid-1960s high point of over a thousand to several hundred by the early 1970s. Nevertheless, it must be remembered that during the mid-1960s there were never more than a few hundred Cubans fighting in all of Latin America. The Cuban presence in Africa during the supposedly isolationist period of 1970 to 1975 was thus comparable to the Cuban presence in Latin America during the most activist years of revolutionary export.

There is one further anomaly about this period of alleged Cuban isolationism: Cuba's growing military presence in the Middle East. In early 1973, several hundred Cuban advisers were sent to South Yemen to help train both the Yemeni army and Marxist Dhofari guerrillas fighting in Oman. When the Shah of Iran sent an expeditionary force to crush the Dhofari rebellion in late 1973, Havana quickly increased the number of Cuban advisers in Yemen to an estimated 600 to 700.[76]

But perhaps the most dramatic of Cuba's overseas military involvements during the early 1970s (and the one about which the least is known) was Cuba's support for Syria in the 1973 Yom Kippur War. All sources agree that during the conflict Cuba committed a significant number of troops to Syria—somewhere between 500 and 750, according to Western estimates.[77] Israeli intelligence, however, contended that some 4,000 Cubans were airlifted to Syria at the start of the 1973 conflict and remained there until 1975, when they were reassigned to Angola. Reports on the role played by the Cuban troops in Syria also vary greatly. One Israeli intelligence report claimed that the Cubans were part of an infantry brigade that never saw active combat. Another Israeli report contended that the Cuban troops were part of a tank brigade that took part in the fighting on the Golan Heights. Still another claimed that the Cubans served in an armored brigade, on commando raids, and even flew missions in Syria's Soviet-provided MIG jet fighters.[78]

Whatever the numbers or the role played, there is no doubt that the Cuban involvement in Syria was important. This was only the second time in the entire history of Cuban internationalism that the Castro Government decided to commit regular troops to overseas combat, rather than send volunteers to play an advisory role. In the first instance, Havana sent some 400 troops to help the Algerians in the 1963 Algeria–Morocco border war. And, as one expert noted, the commitment of Cuban combat troops to Algeria and Syria established a clear precedent for Cuba's subsequent involvements in Angola and Ethiopia:

> The policy guidelines were unchanged since the first such commitment (Algeria, 1963): a friendly progressive state faced with a serious external threat to its security. This same decision rule . . . continued to govern Cuba's deployment of combat troops abroad throughout the 1970s.[79]

Although the rest of the world may have been shocked by the commitment of some 18,000 Cuban combat troops to Angola by mid-1976, for Havana it was not a radical change in policy. All that was really different about Angola was the size of the Cuban commitment.

A POPULAR MISPERCEPTION

With the benefit of hindsight, Cuba's involvements in Africa and the Middle East during the early 1970s look very significant. At the time, however, Cuba's stated commitment to the African liberation movements was dismissed as mere rhetoric by most observers, who predicted that the days of Cuban internationalism were irrevocably over. Cuban commitments to the Middle East were not even mentioned in most studies. Throughout the 1960s, these same observers had consistently played down the significance of Cuba's African involvements in favor of Cuban activities in Latin America. With the commitment of Cuban troops to Angola, however, both the predictions of Cuban isolationism and the regional bias of Cuban foreign policy studies had to be abandoned.

There was, however, no need for the experts to reject the basic paradigm of Cuban dependence. No matter that Havana's links to the Angolan guerrillas could be traced back to Che Guevara and the most radical and independent days of Cuban internationalism; in 1975, Cuban troops in Angola clearly were promoting Moscow's interests. If anything, the commitment of Cuban troops to Angola was pictured as further proof of Cuba's dependence on the Soviet Union.

With time, the experts rejected that argument, placing greater emphasis on the many genuine Cuban interests served by the Angolan involvement. These interests ranged from Cuba's traditional ties to the MPLA to the new institutional needs of the Castro regime—in particular, the need to employ Cuba's recently professionalized armed forces. But even then the experts would not jettison the dependency model. Although they now argued that Cuba's foreign policy choices were autonomously chosen—the Czech endorsement notwithstanding—they continued to insist that Moscow was still calling the shots in most other major areas of Cuban policy. That was the price Cuba had to pay for Soviet aid after the 1970 economic disasters. If this argument contained a logical inconsistency, no one was willing to admit it.[80]

Whatever the nuances of the expert analyses, there was no changing the minds of the American public. Whether it was *U.S. News and World Report,* which described Castro as Moscow's "cat's paw," or Senator Daniel Patrick Moynihan (D-NY), who would later call the Cubans the "Gurkhas of the Russian Empire," it was popular consensus that the Cubans were in Africa for one reason and one reason only: Moscow had sent them there.[81]

This attitude was hardly surprising, and certainly did not need counterarguments replete with sophisticated social science paradigms about economic dependence and constraints on national autonomy. Ever since Cuba opted for communism in the early 1960s, it was the popular U.S. view that Cuba under Castro was a Soviet satellite. The Cuban–Soviet alliance—indeed the entire socialist bloc was known to be monolithic—was controlled from Moscow with no chance for opposition or dissent. The possibility that Cuban efforts to export revolution to Latin America during the 1960s were carried out not only independently of Moscow, but actually in spite of Moscow's protests, simply did not fit the American world view.

The possibility that the Cubans had gone to Angola on their own seemed equally spurious—particularly because everyone knew that Moscow was backing the Angolans. Thus by the time of Cuba's 1975 involvement in Angola, whether one relied on the expert view of a once-autonomous Cuba gone dependent, or the popular view of Cuba as a long-standing Soviet satellite, there was really only one logical explanation for the Cuban presence in Angola: Cuba was in Angola to pay off its Soviet masters.

The strange thing was that of all the Castro Government's concessions to the Soviets after 1970—and there were many—the one policy that had *not* changed was Cuba's support for the African liberation movements. In fact, if there had been any radical change, it was in *Moscow's* policy toward Africa, not Havana's.

As early as 1959, the Soviets began supporting the Popular Movement for the Liberation of Angola, as well as a number of other African liberation movements. In 1970, V. Solodovnikov, director of the Soviet Institute of African Affairs, acknowledged publicly that the Soviet Union was providing the MPLA with "considerable quantities of military equipment, various armaments, ammunitions, means of transportation, and communications equipment." He also acknowledged that MPLA military and political cadres were being trained in the USSR.[82]

Unlike the Cubans, however, Moscow had never sent Soviet troops to Africa to help in guerrilla training or fighting. And all the evidence suggests that Cuba's commitment of weapons, advisers, and internationalist fighters to Africa during the 1960s was completely independent. Moscow's decision in late 1975 to join forces with Havana, airlifting Cuban troops to Angola in Soviet transport planes, and arming Cuban troops with Soviet weapons once they arrived, was thus a significant change in Soviet policy. In Angola, Moscow actually seemed to be following Havana's lead—not the other way around.

6

A Global Threat:
Angola to Central America

HEROIC VIETNAM was one of the first Cuban ships sent
to Angola. On board were a few hundred men, jeeps, and
about 200 tons of gasoline, though the ship was over twenty years
old and never meant to transport troops or heavy equipment. In
fact, it was purchased as a cruise ship by the Batista dictatorship,
and after the revolution it was turned into a floating school. But
in the spring of 1975, when Agostinho Neto, head of the Popular
Movement for the Liberation of Angola (MPLA), first asked for
aid in Angola's widening civil war, the Cubans had no other way
to get their men and arms to Africa. *Heroic Vietnam* and two
merchant ships were hurriedly pressed into service.[1]

The Castro Government's first contingent in Angola consisted
of 230 military advisers. Within nine months, the number of Cubans
in Angola had risen to almost 18,000.[2] Two years later, in late
1977, Havana sent another 17,000 troops to Africa, this time to
help Ethiopia turn back an invasion from Somalia. By 1979, the
Cuban presence in Africa included an estimated 35,000 combat

troops and almost 10,000 economic and technical advisers.[3] At the same time as it was expanding its African commitments, Havana began once again to turn its attention to Latin America, sending arms to the Sandinistas in Nicaragua, and teachers, doctors, construction workers, and military advisers to the new left-wing regimes in Jamaica, Grenada, Guyana, and St. Lucia.

For Cuba, extensive overseas involvements were not new. Havana first established links with the MPLA, the Sandinistas, and many other African and Latin American movements during the radical days of the 1960s, when its goal was, as the slogan went, to "create many Vietnams." But the internationalism of the late 1970s was very different. As the revolution matured, so did expectations of what was possible both at home and abroad. Cuba no longer tried to export revolution; rather, its policy was to support existing revolutions. In Africa it backed recognized regimes and movements— the same regimes and movements supported by the mainstream Organization for African Unity (OAU). In Latin America, sensitive to its earlier failures in the region, Havana was even more circumspect and refused to get involved militarily. Cuba sent no troops and only a limited amount of arms to support the Nicaraguan revolution; even more important, Havana's backing for the Sandinistas was seconded by Venezuela, Costa Rica, Panama, and Mexico.

Not even during the most romantic days of the 1960s could the Castro Government have imagined such diplomatic approval and practical success. With Havana's help, the MPLA came to power in Angola in late 1975 and since then has managed to retain that power, in the face of many challenges, including repeated invasions from South Africa. With Cuban support, the Ethiopian regime turned back Somali forces in 1977 and consolidated its control over the disputed Ogaden region. And with Cuban backing, the Nicaraguan Sandinistas made the second successful socialist revolution in the Western hemisphere, when they overthrew the Somoza dictatorship in July 1979. It was a victory Havana had waited twenty years for. At the same time, Castro appeared to be making unprecedented diplomatic gains. In 1976, Cuba was elected the next head of the Movement of Nonaligned Nations. Although Havana's ascendant position was challenged by both the left and the right,[4] there was no doubt that by the late 1970s, Cuba's reach had become truly international.

AFRICA: A NEW DEPARTURE?

The Havana leadership did not originally see the Angolan involvement as a new departure for Cuban foreign policy.[5] The initial commitment of just over 200 advisers to Angola in the spring of 1975 was no different from other Cuban advisory missions established in Africa during the supposedly quiescent early 1970s. If anything, the original Angolan mission was smaller than their missions in Sierra Leone, equatorial Guinea, South Yemen, and Somalia.[6]

Available evidence further suggests that the eventual escalation of the Cuban commitment was the outcome of a series of incremental decisions. It was more of a reaction to a rapidly changing military and international situation—specifically, an invasion from South Africa—than the result of conscious decision by Havana to embark on a new phase of military involvement in the Third World.

ANGOLA'S COMPLEX SCENARIO

The story of the Angolan civil war is a complex one. Its players include Portugal's Salazar and Caetano dictatorships, two factions within the Portuguese armed forces, three Angolan guerrilla groups, Cuba, the Soviet Union, the United States, the People's Republic of China, and the front-line African states of Zaire, Zambia, and South Africa.[7]

At the time of the revolution, three major guerrilla movements were fighting for control of Angola: the MPLA, the National Front for the Liberation of Angola (FNLA), and the National Union for the Total Independence of Angola (UNITA). The movements were separated more by ethnic, territorial, and language barriers than by ideology. These natural differences had been magnified over the years by Portuguese colonial policy aimed at weakening indigenous opposition. Press censorship, travel restrictions, and constant police harassment combined to create an environment of mutual

209

suspicion where petty jealousies and tribal rivalries obscured what should have been a shared commitment to Angolan independence. As one expert described the liberation movements:

Their leadership ranks would have been thin in any case, coming as they did from the politically aware portions of a tiny elite (only one to five percent of the population were literate). But they were additionally handicapped by travel restrictions, police harassment and lack of funds. Their ranges of action, life-spans and political vision were limited. Thus they remained parochial; most were unable fully to transcend the bounds of primary ethnic or regional loyalties, or of class and racial ties.[8]

The differences were further exacerbated by the intervention of foreign powers, such as the Soviet Union, China, and the United States, who, by providing arms, aid, and advisers to the various guerrilla movements, superimposed the divisions of the Sino-Soviet competition and the Cold War on the Angolan struggle for independence.[9]

The fighting began in 1961 during the first wave of Africa's wars of decolonization. During the first decade, the guerrillas scored very few successes against the Portuguese. They spent most of their time fighting each other, rather than their colonial masters. It was not until the spring of 1974, when the Caetano dictatorship in Lisbon was overthrown by a group of democratically minded military officers, that independence became a possibility. The new Portuguese regime in Lisbon—particularly the increasingly strong and left-leaning Armed Forces Movement—was eager to rid itself of the burden and the embarrassment of its colonial past.[10]

Although the Angolan struggle attracted international interest from the beginning, the amount of aid each movement received fluctuated enormously over the years according to the political concerns of their sponsors as well as the fortunes of the movements. In the early 1960s, Peking made serious overtures to both the FNLA and UNITA, sending arms and technical advisers. The upheavals of China's Cultural Revolution (1966–1970) forced Peking to cut back its international commitments.[11] Thus, for most of the late 1960s, the FNLA was forced to rely solely on Zaire for its armaments while UNITA operated completely without external support.

Soviet aid to the MPLA also waxed and waned according to Moscow's constantly changing evaluation of Africa's revolutionary potential. On two separate occasions—once in 1963 and again in 1974—Moscow canceled all aid to the MPLA when it looked as though they were losing the war. Briefly, in 1973, Moscow even sent arms to the rival FNLA after one of Neto's lieutenants, Daniel Chipenda, defected to the FNLA.

Although Havana's ideological commitment to the MPLA remained more consistent, the volume of material aid fluctuated over time. From a peak in 1966 of several hundred advisers helping to train MPLA guerrillas, the number of Cuban advisers assigned to the MPLA was reduced to only a handful by the early 1970s. It is not clear why this cutback took place. It could have been part of a broader Cuban retrenchment in the early 1970s as Havana grappled with its flagging economy. Or perhaps after the 1968 ouster of Congolese President Alphonse Massemba-Debat neither the MPLA forces nor their Cuban advisers were considered welcome by their Congo-Brazzaville hosts.

There is much uncertainty as to how many Cubans remained in Congo-Brazzaville after the 1968 coup. Some analysts argue that the Cubans withdrew immediately, while others contend that a small number stayed to train MPLA guerrillas at least until 1971. In 1970, when the MPLA moved its bases from Congo-Brazzaville to Zambia, some Cuban advisers apparently went with them.[12] How many Cubans remained with the MPLA during the early 1970s has never been established. What is clear, however, is that the Zambian regime did not support the MPLA, and any Cuban advisers stationed with the MPLA in Zambia were forced to work undercover. No matter how ideologically committed to the MPLA Havana may have been, conditions in Africa in the early 1970s were not conducive to a major Cuban intervention.

While Moscow, Peking, and Havana all jockeyed for position in Angola during the 1960s, Washington held back. Traditionally, the United States had paid little attention to Portuguese Africa. In 1961, the Kennedy Administration declared its support for the self-determination of the Portuguese colonies and briefly flirted with the idea of sending aid to the FNLA (FNLA leader Holden Roberto had visited the U.S. in 1959 seeking American support). But the Administration reversed that position a year later, after Portugal threatened to withdraw from NATO. Good relations with the dictatorship of Antonio Salazar and, specifically, continued U.S. access to refueling bases in the Azores were apparently too important to jeopardize. Kennedy's decision was reaffirmed by the Nixon Administration in 1969, when a major review of U.S. policy toward southern Africa ruled out the possibility of a "black victory at any stage" in the Portuguese colonies.[13] The CIA, however, tried to hedge its bets in Angola and placed Roberto on a personal retainer for much of the 1960s. But no official commitment was made.[14]

A Mad Scramble

The April 1974 coup against the Caetano dictatorship—and the subsequent decision by the Armed Forces Movement to divest Portugal of its colonial holdings—set off a mad scramble for influence in Angola. As early as June, Chinese arms and military advisers for the FNLA began to arrive in Zaire—Angola's neighbor to the north and a long-time supporter of the FNLA. A month later, the United States began shipping arms to Roberto through Zaire as well. By November, the Soviets had also resumed their shipments of arms to the MPLA.

The new Portuguese regime hoped to withdraw from Angola in an orderly fashion. In January 1975, it hosted a meeting of the three guerrilla leaders—Neto, Roberto, and Savimbi—in Alvor, Portugal, to discuss the means of ensuring a peaceful transition to independence. According to the "Alvor Agreement," Angola would be administered by a transitional government representing all three movements under Portuguese leadership until the withdrawal, which was set for November 11, 1975. A single national army made up of forces from all three movements was to be formed during the transition period, and open elections were scheduled for October 1975 to choose the postcolonial Angolan government.[15] All three guerrilla leaders signed the agreement, and a formal truce was declared.

Despite Lisbon's optimism, the situation in Angola made a peaceful transition almost impossible. The three Angolan guerrilla movements were more accustomed to fighting each other than they were to fighting the colonialists. Now that the Portuguese were withdrawing, the factions' differences were greatly magnified. At the same time, the interests of the three superpowers served to widen these divisions even further. Although Peking, Moscow, and Washington all officially endorsed the Alvor Agreement, unofficially they began to send large quantities of arms and aid to their respective clients. If the peace would be broken—which it was less than three months after the Alvor meeting—they wanted to make sure their allies emerged victorious.

In January 1975, while the guerrilla leaders were meeting in Alvor, the "Forty Committee" of the U.S. National Security Council, at the urging of the CIA and under the direction of Secretary of State Henry Kissinger, authorized a covert grant of $300,000 to Angola's FNLA.[16] Washington had been slow to recognize the importance of Angola; now it seemed shocked into a strong showing.

For Kissinger, more than just the future of Angola was at stake, although Angola's strategic location on the shipping lanes of the South Atlantic was mentioned from time to time. The entire balance of power rested on the outcome in Angola. According to Kissinger, Angola was a test of U.S. strength and willingness to back up its global commitments in the post-Vietnam era. It was a test of U.S. resolve to resist Soviet expansionism. Testifying before the Senate Foreign Affairs Committee's Subcommittee on Africa in January 1976, Kissinger explained the U.S. interest in Angola. "The Soviet Union" he said, "must not be given any opportunity to use military force for aggressive purposes without running the risk of conflict with the United States."[17]

Neither Moscow nor Peking was as straightforward as Washington concerning its motivations in Angola. Each touted the ideological purity of its client's struggle rather than its own geopolitical concerns. Yet, there is little doubt that for both powers a primary motivation in Angola was to deny each other increased influence. For Moscow, the challenge was twofold. First there was the Sino-Soviet struggle, which had been escalating in Africa ever since the late 1960s. In addition, there was the traditional U.S.-Soviet competition in the Third World, made even more pressing by prospects of a U.S.-Chinese alliance against the Soviet Union.

Nothing makes these big power concerns clearer than the ease and rapidity with which all three switched allegiances. In 1974, Moscow sent aid both to Neto's MPLA and Daniel Chipenda's splinter group. That same year, Peking sent aid to both the FNLA and UNITA, and after Chipenda split from the MPLA and joined the FNLA, Peking found itself supporting Chipenda as well. Washington also approached its alliances pragmatically, ultimately backing both the UNITA and FNLA forces in their attempts to defeat the Soviet-backed MPLA.

In this game of musical chairs, only Havana remained constant in its commitment to the MPLA. It is unclear whether this was due to a higher ideological commitment, strong personal ties between Castro and Neto, or the fact that with limited resources Havana could not even consider playing two ends against the middle. Still, Havana, which lacked both an arms industry and advanced transport capabilities, limited its support for the MPLA during the first year of the Civil War—until May 1975—to ideological pronouncements.

THE ANGOLAN WAR

In this context of spiraling international pressures, the Alvor truce did not hold for long. In March 1975, emboldened by the influx of U.S. arms, the FNLA opened an attack against MPLA forces in the Angolan capital of Luanda, and began a drive to expel the MPLA from the northern territories bordering on Zaire. At the end of March, Zaire sent 1,200 soldiers across the border into Angola to back up the FNLA offensive.

At the same time, Soviet aid to the MPLA increased enormously, and Havana made its first commitment to the MPLA in the civil war. In March, massive amounts of Soviet military supplies began to arrive in Angola by both air and sea. In May, Cuban military commander Flavio Bravo arrived in Angola for talks with MPLA leader Neto. According to Neto, the MPLA did not lack arms— in fact, they were flush with Soviet weaponry. What it lacked was the know-how to use them. In June, 230 Cuban advisers arrived and opened four MPLA training camps.[18]

There is some confusion about both the cause and effect and the sequence of events. Analysts sympathetic to the MPLA blame the outbreak of fighting on the influx of Western arms to the FNLA. According to William LeoGrande, it was only *after* the March FNLA offensive that the MPLA began to seek increased aid from the Soviet bloc. LeoGrande writes, "The MPLA responded to this escalation of fighting by seeking additional aid from both the USSR and Cuba. The Soviets quickly stepped up their flow of arms. . . ."[19]

Jiri Valenta, in a study highly critical of Soviet expansionism in Angola, argues the opposite. The Russian arms were the first to arrive and caused the violation of the truce:

> It is against this background—the delivery of Soviet military supplies to the MPLA and the power struggle among the three factions— that the crisis that developed in Angola in the spring and summer [of 1975] should be viewed. The massive Soviet military supplies to the MPLA reached Angola in March and April, several months before U.S. shipments of military supplies began to reach the FNLA through Zaire.[20]

It is almost impossible to prove either case, since records of covert arms shipments are hard to come by, and the facts are often further obscured by the desire of the analysts to lay blame. It is safest to note that throughout the spring of 1975, the three guerrilla movements in Angola, aided and abetted by an increasing flow of arms from their international sponsors, escalated the conflict.

Fighting abated for a brief period in June, as the Portuguese struggled vainly to revive the Alvor truce. But by early July, the civil war was raging again, with the Soviet-supplied and Cuban-advised MPLA forces scoring significant victories against their opponents. By mid-July, the MPLA had regained Luanda and had begun a major campaign to win control of the rest of Angola's provincial capitals in time for the Portuguese withdrawal in early November.

The increasing strength of the MPLA led to two major realignments in the summer of 1975. First, FNLA and UNITA formally joined forces in order to defeat the MPLA. At the same time, they made a joint appeal for outside aid. In mid-July, the National Security Council's Forty Committee authorized a major increase in U.S. aid to the Angolan insurgents and a program of covert CIA involvement. Given the code name of Operation Feature, the CIA program was to recruit mercenaries to fight with FNLA and UNITA forces inside Angola, while sending its own personnel to train guerrilla forces in Zaire. Over the next six months, Operation Feature supplied UNITA and FNLA forces with over $30 million worth of armaments.[21]

Once again bolstered by the promise of Western aid, the FNLA launched a second offensive on Luanda in mid-July. Three weeks later, South Africa joined the fight, sending troops across the Namibian border into southern Angola.[22] The South African leadership claimed that they were interested only in protecting their Cunene River hydroelectric projects on the Angola-Namibia border. In fact, however, their interest far exceeded the defense of the Cunene River dams. The Government in Pretoria wanted nothing less than the total defeat of the MPLA.

The South African Connection

South Africa's objections were based first on the MPLA's alliance with the Soviet Union. Pretoria feared nothing more than a Soviet takeover of southern Africa. Pretoria believed even more firmly than Washington that Angola was only the first step in a grand Soviet design of world conquest. In addition, the MPLA was allied with the South West Africa People's Organization (SWAPO)—the guerrillas fighting to overthrow the South African regime in Namibia to the south of Angola. Thus, by supporting the FNLA–UNITA forces, the South African Government was helping to install a moderate—read anti-Soviet—government in Luanda, while destroying its own Namibian insurgents. There is no better proof of South Africa's broader interest than its mid-August establishment of training bases for FNLA and UNITA guerrillas in Angola and Namibia.[23]

At this time the MPLA turned again to its Soviet allies, sending a delegation to Moscow in August to ask for additional arms and military advisers.[24] What happened at those meetings has never been disclosed, but it appears that the Soviets were unwilling to send advisers. Arms, yes, but Soviet troops or advisers were a risk that Moscow was unwilling to take. The MPLA then asked Havana for additional men to help train the MPLA. In the first week of September, three Cuban merchant ships, including *Heroic Vietnam,* set sail for Angola. By mid-October, the number of Cuban advisers stationed in Angola had risen to an estimated 1,500.[25]

The fighting raged on throughout September and October. Armed with Soviet weapons and trained by Cuban advisers, the MPLA forces managed to retain control of Luanda in the face of repeated FNLA and Zairean attacks. With November and the day of the Portuguese withdrawal rapidly approaching, the FNLA and UNITA forces began to panic. If they could not dislodge the MPLA from the capital by the time of independence, the MPLA would be able to claim *de facto* control of Angola.

At this time the South African regime apparently decided it had to get directly involved. On October 23, 1975, between 5,000 and 10,000 crack South African troops invaded Angola.[26] The South Africans were well armed and well trained, and the MPLA was no match for them. On November 11, the day of Portugal's withdrawal, the South African forces were less than 200 miles from Luanda, and once again Zairean troops invaded Angola from the north.

The Cubans claim that they decided to commit combat troops to Angola only after South African regulars intervened.[27] Within a week of the South African invasion, four Cuban transport ships had left for Angola. An airlift of Cuban troops began a week later on November 7. By December, some 400 troops per week had begun to arrive in Angola. By January, the rate had jumped to 1,000 per week. Between November 1975, when Havana first began committing combat forces, and March 1976, when the South Africans began to withdraw, between 15,000 and 18,000 Cuban troops were sent to Angola.[28]

By mid-December, the MPLA, with Cuban help, was able to halt the South African advance in the south and the Zairean-FNLA offensive in the north. By late January, the South African troops pulled back to their original positions just north of the Angola-

Namibia border. At this time, joint Cuban-MPLA forces directed their full strength to the north. By the middle of February the FNLA had also retreated back across the border into Zaire. By March, the MPLA, with Cuban support, had won control of Angola.

Although Cuban military support was essential, the Angolan war was not won solely on the battlefield. An enormous amount of diplomatic jockeying lay behind the MPLA victory, and diplomatically, the South African troops, rather than the Cuban troops, made all the difference.

First, it was because of the South African intervention on the side of the FNLA–UNITA that the MPLA won the essential endorsement of the Organization for African Unity. The OAU had consistently advocated a negotiated settlement of the Angolan civil war, refusing to endorse any guerrilla group and warning repeatedly of the dangers of outside intervention. With the South African invasion, the OAU reversed that position completely. The OAU's revulsion toward Pretoria's apartheid regime far outweighed its fear of Soviet meddling. On January 22, 1976, the OAU condemned the South African invasion of Angola, while making no mention of the much larger Cuban presence. Two weeks later, the OAU admitted the MPLA-led People's Republic of Angola to its ranks.[29]

Second, it was partly because of the South African intervention that the United States was forced to cut back its aid to the FNLA–UNITA forces. In December 1975, while the South African invasion was being condemned internationally, the extent of U.S. involvement in Angola was made public. Immediately the U.S. Senate, under the leadership of Senator Dick Clark (D-Iowa), moved to cut off all U.S. aid to Angola[30] and any *de facto* alliance with South Africa.

There were actually several reasons why the Clark Amendment passed the Senate, among them strong fears that Angola could become another Vietnam. Kissinger had originally sought covert funds for Angola through the Forty Committee precisely because he feared that a public request would cause a confrontation with the Congress—and he was right. At the same time, there was strong congressional resentment of the Forty Committee's authorization of covert funds for Angola, which was seen as an unnecessary abuse of executive privilege that flouted Congress's exclusive constitutional right to declare war.

Finally, this U.S. decision to cancel aid to the FNLA–UNITA is said to have played a major role in Pretoria's subsequent decision to withdraw from the fighting. Secretary of State Kissinger denied that there had been any U.S. collusion with South Africa. The South Africans, however, told a very different story, claiming that Washington had pledged to provide all necessary arms and aid to ensure an MPLA defeat if South Africa were willing to commit its troops to the fighting.[31] Pretoria publicly blamed its decision to withdraw from the Angolan fighting on Washington's default on this agreement. Whether this alliance was *de facto* or *de jure*, Washington's aid cutoff no doubt played a large role in Pretoria's decision, as did several South African defeats at the hands of the Cubans and mounting public opposition within South Africa.

Thus, by the end of January 1976, the FNLA–UNITA forces had been deprived of diplomatic recognition by the OAU, arms from the United States, and logistical and military support from South Africa. Bereft of international support, the FNLA–UNITA forces were handily defeated by the Cuban-MPLA forces.

A SOVIET PLOT?

The degree of Cuban-Soviet coordination in the Angolan civil war has never been ascertained. Most American observers assume that the Cubans were sent to Angola as Moscow's proxy. The Cubans, however, deny this, claiming that the decision to commit both military advisers and eventually regular combat troops was made in Havana. In an April 1976 speech, Castro said, "Cuba made its decision completely on its own responsibility." The Soviet Union, according to Castro, was "extraordinarily respectful and careful in its relations with Cuba. A decision of that nature could only be made by our party."[32]

There are several good reasons to believe that Havana's role in Angola was voluntarily chosen. The strong historical precedents include the Castro regime's traditional ties to the MPLA, dating back to the mid-1960s, and its more recent commitment of hundreds of military advisers to Africa and several thousand Cuban troops to Syria. Certainly the dispatch of thousands of troops to Angola was much larger than any of Cuba's earlier internationalist missions, but if the Cubans' claim is true, they never planned to make such a large commitment to that country. Only after South African troops entered the fight did the MPLA and Castro begin to realize the need for the larger commitment. It was necessary for the Cubans either to send the troops or watch the MPLA be destroyed.

Certainly the Soviet Union had no reason to oppose Cuba's involvement. Historically, Moscow had a strong interest of its own in an MPLA victory. Moscow supported the Angolan guerrillas long before Che Guevara ever made contact with Agostinho Neto on his 1965 tour of Africa, indeed well before Castro came to power in Havana. But Soviet support for the MPLA had been erratic over the years. And it must be remembered that at the time of the Portuguese coup, Moscow had suspended all aid to Neto's forces and had begun to court Daniel Chipenda's rival faction. At that time—if only briefly—Moscow and Havana were actually on opposite sides of the struggle, with Havana supporting the MPLA.

Even after the Soviets revived their support for the MPLA in November 1975, Moscow remained cautious in its commitments to the MPLA—certainly more so than Havana. It is useful to recall that in August 1975, when the South Africans first crossed the border into Angola and Neto turned to the Soviets for help, Moscow agreed only to increase arms shipments, not to send military advisers. It was after that rebuff that Neto turned to the Cubans, asking for and receiving at least 500 advisers from Castro's personal guard, known as the Prime Minister's Reserve Troops.[33]

It is always possible, of course, that Moscow, for the sake of international opinion, had made it seem that it was Havana's decision to commit Cuban troops to Angola while Moscow was really calling the shots. But this would have been a very dangerous game to play, since it severely limited both the amount of aid and its speed of delivery to the MPLA. Moscow's feigned hesitancy might have cost the MPLA the war.

In early November, when the South Africans and the FNLA

had Luanda virtually surrounded, Havana was forced to transport its much-needed reinforcements to Angola in leaky merchant ships and obsolete commercial airplanes. The Soviets had never supplied Cuba with military aircraft capable of transporting troops or heavy equipment great distances, although they had provided such equipment to other allies, including Egypt, India, Syria, Iraq, Poland, Yugoslavia, and Algeria.[34] Whether this was because Moscow did not trust the Castro Government or for some other reason can only be imagined. Even after the Russians began shuttling Cuban troops to Angola in Soviet transport planes in early December, their air support was erratic. The flights were suspended on several occasions over the next few months, after Moscow received official protests from Washington. The Cubans were then forced to rely on their own completely inadequate transport facilities during what were some of the most pressing moments in the Angolan civil war.

Although Havana apparently chose to send troops to Angola of its own free will, it is unlikely that the Cubans would ever have made such a strong commitment had their allies in Moscow actively opposed it. The Cuban leadership learned a harsh lesson about the costs of opposing Moscow from the 1968 oil deal. Since 1970, the Cubans had learned some equally important lessons about the benefits of cooperating with their Soviet allies. It is doubtful that Havana would have been willing to jeopardize these benefits or risk Moscow's wrath, regardless of its emotional and historical ties to the MPLA.

Although the true cause and effect may never be known, the historical record suggests that at the beginning of the civil war, Moscow passively tolerated Cuba's predominantly ideological support for the MPLA, while it waited on the sidelines to see which of the guerrilla movements it would support. In the middle of the conflict, Moscow and Havana were both supporting the MPLA, Moscow with arms and Havana with advisers, but their efforts did not appear to be centrally coordinated. By the end of the conflict, Moscow was actively supporting the Cuban involvement, flying Cuban troops to Angola on Soviet transport planes and arming them with Soviet weapons on their arrival.[35]

THE BIG PAYOFF

Although Havana may have backed into its new activist role in Angola, the rewards for that role were very real—so real, in fact, that most observers predicted that the Angolan involvement was only the beginning of a new global era in Cuban foreign policy.

In Angola, Havana was able to pursue a wide variety of interests, many of which had lain dormant since Castro gave up trying to export revolution to Latin America in the late 1960s. Havana's aid successfully brought the MPLA to power, fulfilling a long-standing internationalist commitment, while helping to defeat representatives of Cuba's enemies—the United States, South Africa, and Zaire. The public pride and euphoria in Cuba at the time of the Angolan victory can only be likened to that which followed Cuba's victory at the Bay of Pigs. It is interesting, however, that Castro was apparently unsure of how the Cuban public would receive the Angolan involvement and waited until April 1976, when victory was certain, to publicly announce the commitment of Cuban troops.[36]

By helping bring the MPLA to power in Angola, Havana also helped to promote the interests of other left-leaning movements in the region. Despite the alarmist predictions of Washington and Pretoria, the MPLA victory did not inevitably lead to a Communist takeover of southern Africa. On the other hand, the presence of a leftist regime in Luanda did further both the strategic and diplomatic positions of the guerrilla movements in Zimbabwe and Namibia. Angola provided these guerrillas with arms and a safe haven. Even more important, the MPLA victory sent a clear message to both the Rhodesian and South African regimes that the forces of change in southern Africa could no longer be resisted. This may well have contributed to the subsequent willingness (if only temporarily, in Pretoria's case) to compromise on both Zimbabwe and Namibia.

Another legacy of the Angolan involvement has been Havana's strengthened ties with Moscow. Trade relations between the two have improved steadily over the past six years. Even more significant is the improvement in Soviet military aid. For the first time since the Soviets withdrew their missiles from Cuba, the Cubans have received the most advanced military technology Moscow has to offer. In November 1978, the State Department confirmed that Cuba had received an estimated fifteen to eighteen MIG-23F fighter planes.[37] At a time when the Soviets actively sought an arms limitation treaty with the United States, this was a bold and dangerous move. Although U.S. officials believed that these planes were not modified to deliver nuclear weapons, several members of Congress saw this shipment as a direct violation of the 1962 U.S.-Soviet agreement prohibiting the deployment of offensive weapons in Cuba, and threatened to use the issue of the planes to obstruct Senate passage of the SALT treaty. Moscow's willingness to jeopardize the treaty at a time when the SALT agreements still seemed viable suggests an unprecedented Soviet desire to strengthen ties with Cuba.

Another benefit of Cuba's involvement in Angola was Havana's apparent success in committing the Soviets to a more active role in Africa. From the earliest days of their alliance with the Soviets, the Cubans have alternately cajoled, lectured, and castigated their Soviet allies in an effort to enlist their support for such Third World struggles. In the mid- to late 1970s, it began to look as though Havana was finally getting its way.

Cuba also appeared to have recovered much of its lost prestige with the Third World. Three years after Sihanouk and Qadaffi tried to have Cuba ejected from the 1973 Algiers Conference of the Nonaligned, the Cubans were not only secure among the members of that conference, but were cast in a leadership role. In 1976, at the Fifth Conference of the Nonaligned Nations in Colombo, Sri Lanka, the Cubans were unanimously and publicly commended for their role in Angola. The role played by the Soviets was not even mentioned specifically:

> The Conference congratulated the Government and people of Angola for their heroic and victorious struggle against the South African racist invaders and their allies, and commended the Republic of Cuba and other States which assisted the people of Angola in frustrating the expansionist and colonialist strategy of South Africa's racist regime and its allies.[38]

Then, in the *coup de grace,* Cuba was chosen to host and chair the next nonaligned summit.

This is not to suggest that the Angolan involvement was without costs. The most immediate was the suspension of the 1975 Cuban-U.S. rapprochement talks. For Washington, Cuba's involvement in the Angolan civil war was a challenge to U.S. influence in the Third World, and a betrayal of the spirit of rapprochement. President Gerald Ford angrily warned Castro that either Cuba would withdraw its troops from Angola or give up all hope of normalizing relations with the United States.[39]

The Cubans were both confused and angry at Washington's response. They could not understand what their support for the MPLA had to do with U.S.-Cuban relations. Washington had no historical interest in Africa, whereas Havana certainly did. And if the United States expected complete isolationism from the Cubans in return for its diplomatic recognition, that was a price Havana was not willing to pay.[40]

For a brief period it looked as though U.S.-Cuban relations might be set back even further—to the point of a return to open hostilities. In 1976, amid rumors of an impending Cuban involvement in Namibia, Secretary of State Henry Kissinger actually threatened the Castro Government with direct U.S. retaliation should Havana increase its military presence in Africa.[41] Any military action against Cuba would have clearly violated the 1962 U.S.-Soviet agreement, and it is not clear whether Kissinger was bluffing. In any event, the Secretary never got the chance to prove his mettle because the Cubans never went into Namibia. By the time of Havana's next major military commitment in Africa—Ethiopia in 1977—Kissinger was no longer in office, and Washington, under the leadership of Jimmy Carter, had a new Cuba policy.

At the outset, the Carter Administration appeared to be much more tolerant of the Cuban involvement in Angola. Angola was a special case, Carter officials argued. It was not part of some grand Soviet design to dominate Africa. At one point, UN Ambassador Andrew Young went so far as to describe the Cubans as a "stabilizing force" in Angola. With time, however, and particularly after the commitment of some 17,000 Cuban troops to Ethiopia, the Carter Administration reversed that attitude, accusing the Cubans of being pawns of the Soviet Union in Africa and halting all efforts at normalizing relations with Havana. Once again, Cuba expressed confusion and anger about the change in Washington's attitude. Havana had never claimed that Angola was a special case nor promised to avoid future internationalist commitments in Africa. Since then, the issue of Cuba's involvement in Africa has remained one of the primary stumbling blocks to any attempt to find a Cuban-U.S. rapprochement.

There was one additional drawback to the Angolan assistance that was apparently unanticipated at the time of Havana's original commitment: Sending troops to Angola proved to be much easier than bringing them home. The Angolan civil war was substantially over by March 1976, when Havana announced its intention to begin withdrawing its troops. By early 1977, the number of Cuban troops there had dropped from its estimated peak of between 15,000 and 18,000 to 12,000.[42] But as it turned out, the MPLA victory celebrations were premature. Throughout 1977 and 1978—indeed, until the present—the MPLA continued to fight running battles with South African-supported UNITA forces based in southern Angola.

Even after its victory, the MPLA faced internal political problems as well. In May 1977, a faction within the MPLA led by Nito Alves challenged Agostinho Neto for leadership of the party and almost succeeded in toppling him in a coup attempt.[43] Beset by internal divisions and continued harassment from FNLA, UNITA, South African, and Zairean forces, Neto requested Cuban reinforcements. By the end of 1977, the number of Cubans stationed in Angola had returned to and actually surpassed earlier levels, peaking at an estimated 19,000.

Cuba's Vietnam?

American observers have suggested that there have been far-reaching domestic costs to the Cuban involvement, referring to Angola as Cuba's Vietnam. Reports from Cuba of an economic downturn and growing public disillusionment have been attributed to Cuba's involvement in Africa. This overly-simple analysis underestimates the emotive and ideological support for internationalism in Cuban society, and the pride felt by most Cubans at their army's repeated military victories. Moreover, the recent questioning and

225

opposition within Cuba can be traced more accurately to domestic problems, particularly the continuing economic failures. It is interesting that of the hundreds of Cuban refugees interviewed during the 1980 Mariel boat lift, the complaints all focused on economic privation, lack of jobs, limits on personal freedom, *not* on the Castro regime's foreign policies.[44] Whether Cuba's economic failures can be traced to its adventurism in Africa is not clear. It appears that Moscow has been willing to foot much of the bill.

Yet it would not be surprising if Havana's involvement in exercises as long and as costly as commitments in Angola and Ethiopia *had* provoked some negative reaction within Cuba. Although information is scarce, because of Cuba's strict press censorship, it appears that some Cuban business managers have raised questions about the effects on productivity of the large commitment of Cuban reserve forces overseas. Not only have the enterprises lost workers—more than half of the almost 20,000 Cubans sent to Angola were reservists—they have also had to pay the salaries of the reservists out of the enterprise budgets. In a speech to the First Party Congress in the end of 1976, Castro addressed this problem, if somewhat obliquely, saying, "It is necessary to combat the occasionally exaggerated notion as to who cannot be dispensed with in production."[45]

There also seemed to be a growing disaffection on the local level toward military service. In the same Party Congress speech, Castro called for a change in attitude toward the military:

. . . correcting a situation in which military service far from appearing and being presented as a great honor is used by parents and teachers to intimidate young men and students who do not study and by the organizations themselves as a threat and a means to punish undisciplined youths.[46]

One expert has also suggested that troop insubordination may have become a problem as a result of Angola. To support this argument, Jorge Domínguez notes that, for the first time in twenty years, *Verde Olivo,* Cuba's popular military magazine, carried a detailed discussion of military disciplinary procedures soon after the commitment to Angola.[47]

The reasons for this new resentment of the military are not clear.

The explanations include specific disaffection toward serving in Africa, disaffection toward serving overseas for prolonged periods—a new experience for Cuba's armed forces—and a more general disaffection toward military service that seems common to all armies when they are not actively defending their own homes. Economic conditions in Cuba have not enabled the Castro Government to offer the sort of incentives for military service that are currently available in the U.S. In the First Party Congress address, Castro also spoke of the need to improve the salaries, housing, and general living conditions of the Cuban armed forces.

In the past, the Castro Government has shown a remarkable ability to survive and mobilize popular support. Although the Angolan involvement has had its costs—many of which have only become clear over time—the benefits outweigh them. The most basic lesson in 1976, when Cuba was still feeling the first flush of the MPLA victory and its election to head the Nonaligned Movement, was that the Cubans could pursue a new, more active role in Africa and satisfy a wide variety of interests at home, in the socialist bloc, and in the Third World. Whether the impetus was Moscow's or Havana's, all sides predicted that Angola was only the beginning of a new era of Cuban military involvement throughout Africa and perhaps throughout the Third World.

ETHIOPIA: A NEW LESSON?

In November 1977, Cuba was given an opportunity to put the Angolan lesson into practice—in Ethiopia. But this time the benefits were not so clear. The Cubans successfully defended the Ethiopian regime against an invasion from Somalia, and further cemented their relations with the socialist bloc by guaranteeing the stability of another strategically located pro-Soviet regime. But Cuba's involvement in Ethiopia also greatly strained its relations with many Third World and Western governments, and raised serious doubts about the validity of the Angolan lesson for Cuba's future foreign policy choices.

The sequence of events that led to the commitment of some 17,000 Cuban troops to Ethiopia is similar to the Angolan story. Cuba's

227

relationship with the Dergue, Ethiopia's military regime, was established in February 1977 after Colonel Mengistu Haile-Mariam seized power. Havana moved quickly to solidify its alliance with this new Marxist-Leninist regime. That same month, a Cuban military delegation led by General Arnaldo Ochoa, a veteran of the Angolan conflict, arrived in Addis Ababa for a week of consultations with the Ethiopian leader.[48] In March, Castro followed with an unpublicized two-day visit. His visit came at the end of a seven-week tour of Africa that included stops in South Yemen, Mozambique, Angola, Algeria, and, significantly, Ethiopia's traditional rival, Somalia.

In early May, the first Cuban military mission arrived in Ethiopia. It consisted of some 200 military and technical advisers. Its purpose, as in Angola and many other African states, was to train the Ethiopian People's Militia to use their newly acquired Soviet weaponry.[49] According to Havana, that was *all* the Cubans wanted to do in Ethiopia. But again, international events forced a larger role.

A major invasion by Somali forces across the border into the Ogaden region of Ethiopia in November 1977 led the Cubans to commit some 17,000 men to help defend their new allies. Castro described that decision in a speech the following March:

> Initially we decided to send a few dozen, maybe a few hundred advisers to teach the Ethiopians how to handle Soviet weapons. . . . If the Ethiopians had had a little more time they would have learned how to handle all those tanks, artillery pieces, and other modern weapons! We, along with other Socialist countries, would have contributed to training personnel. But the critical situation created by the invasion in late November led the Ethiopian government to make an urgent request that we send tank artillery and aviation specialists to help the army to help the country, and did so. . . .[50]

Even after the Somali invasion, Havana, Moscow, and Addis Ababa all denied that Cuban troops were fighting in Ethiopia, claiming that Soviet and Cuban "technical and medical personnel" were helping with the defense efforts.[51] Only after the Somali invasion had been turned back did Castro publicly acknowledge the full extent of the role played by Cuban pilots, and artillery and motorized infantry units.[52]

A Difficult Situation

Despite the success of its involvement in Angola, Havana was at first apparently hesitant to commit so many troops to Ethiopia. This reluctance can be explained by the specifics of the Ethiopian situation. The first quandary that Havana faced in Ethiopia was that of shifting alliances. Cuba's ties to Somalia actually predated its ties to Ethiopia; Cuba sent a military mission to Somalia in 1974. Traditionally, alignments on the Horn of Africa had been divided between the two superpowers: Somalia looked to the socialist bloc for arms and aid, Ethiopia to the United States. The pattern was broken in 1974 when the regime of Haile Selassie was overthrown in a leftist military coup. After the coup, the United States tried to continue its twenty-year relationship with the Ethiopians. As the new regime moved Ethiopia steadily to the left, however, that alliance became increasingly strained. In December 1976, the Soviet Union—ever mindful of Ethiopia's Red Sea ports—reportedly offered to replace the United States as Ethiopia's chief arms supplier. Four months later, in April 1977, Addis formally cut its ties with Washington.[53] A month later, Cuban advisers began arriving in Ethiopia.

For the next six months, Havana and Moscow found themselves supporting both Somalia and Ethiopia. Although this gave the socialist bloc unprecedented access to the strategic Horn of Africa, it was not an easy position to maintain. Ethiopia and Somalia are both self-proclaimed socialist states. They are also traditional enemies caught in a long-standing territorial dispute. The Somalis claim that the ethnically Somali Ogaden region of Ethiopia is rightfully a part of their country. They are sworn to regain it, and have said they will go to war with Ethiopia to do so. The socialist revolution in Ethiopia did nothing to change Mogadishu's attitude toward the Ogaden.

Though the situation was ticklish, for a while it looked as though the Cubans and Soviets might succeed in walking a tightrope between the disputing parties, and thereby gain absolute strategic superiority on the Horn of Africa and the Red Sea. The Cubans reportedly attempted a reconciliation of their two allies. Appealing to socialist solidarity above territorial gain, Castro is said to have arranged a secret meeting between the two sides in Aden in March 1977, proposing a plan for a federation of the Horn.

But by late spring, it was evident that such efforts at negotiation had failed, as the Somalis stepped up their attacks on the Ogaden. Moscow then took a more direct route, cutting back arms supplies to Somalia. By July, Soviet pressure had become so obvious that the Western powers—notably France and the United States—offered the Somalis military aid for defensive purposes (these offers were withdrawn after Somalia invaded Ethiopia). A month later, Moscow openly accused the Barre regime of acts of aggression in the Ogaden.[54] In November 1977, Somalia officially severed its ties with the socialist bloc over the issue of the increasing flow of Soviet arms to Ethiopia. All Soviet diplomats and both Cuban diplomatic and advisory personnel were expelled. Although the Somalis shifted their international alignments, they did not abandon their socialism.

It is a basic tenet of Cuban ideology that internationalist responsibilities take precedence over narrower state interests or bloc commitments. This was the premise behind Havana's acrimonious split with Moscow over Douglas Bravo and the Venezuelans a decade earlier. Siding with the Ethiopians against the Somalis simply because of the shift in bloc alignments—when both are socialist states—would be a similar violation of the principles of internationalism. Thus, only after the Somalis had invaded Ethiopia and violated the even more basic tenet of national sovereignty could the Cubans justify a full commitment to Ethiopia against Somalia. Any earlier action would have been hypocritical. Even after the invasion, Havana was apparently hesitant to admit the full extent of its involvement in the Ethiopian-Somalian conflict.

The nature of the Ethiopian leadership also gave pause to Havana. Ethiopia is ruled by a military junta notorious for its brutality. If there was any lesson that the Cubans should have learned from their failure to negotiate a settlement on the Horn of Africa, it was that neither the ties of internationalist solidarity nor the ties of military dependence could guarantee common interests between allies, or even a willingness to compromise Moscow had learned that lesson from Havana a decade earlier.

Havana's fear that it might not be able to control its Ethiopian allies may explain Castro's refusal to acknowledge Cuba's participation in the war in the Ogaden until he was certain that Ethiopia would not try to invade Somalia. Even after the war was over, with the Ethiopian militia solidly in control on its own side of the border, Havana apparently continued to distrust its Ethiopian allies.

The Eritrean Problem

Havana's serious problems with its ally, the Ethiopian Dergue, began only after the victory in the Ogaden and centered on the issue of Eritrean independence. Eritrea is a northwestern province of Ethiopia that borders on the Red Sea. Whereas most Ethiopians are Coptic Christians, the Eritreans are Moslems. Since the early 1960s, the Eritreans have been fighting to secede from Ethiopia.

When Haile Selassie was emperor, the Marxist branch of the Eritrean front received support from many left-leaning states, including Cuba and the Soviet Union. When the socialist Dergue seized power in Ethiopia in 1974, the bloc of Eritrean supporters was thrown into confusion. Havana and Moscow broke with the Eritreans, while the pro-Soviet regimes in Syria, Algeria, and Iraq continued their support. At the same time, the more conservative branch of the Eritrean front gained new support from Saudi Arabia, Egypt, and Iran—all countries committed to opposing the Dergue and containing what they saw as a growing Communist influence on the Horn of Africa and the Red Sea.

After the defeat of the Somali invaders, Ethiopia turned the full force of its Soviet-equipped, Cuban-trained army on the Eritreans. From the beginning, the Cubans refused to become involved. Cuba's vice president, Carlos Rafael Rodríguez, stated publicly that Eritrea was an internal Ethiopian problem for which Cuban aid could not be used. He urged the Ethiopians to seek a political solution.[55]

But the Dergue rejected a political solution. At the end of April 1978, it mounted an all-out offensive on the Eritrean front, deploying a reported 35,000 troops.[56] At the same time, Ethiopia's Colonel Mengistu traveled to Havana, where he was awarded the Playa Giron medal and lobbied for Cuba's support in Eritrea:

231

Having triumphed in the East and gained the upper hand over the international reactionary force, the Ethiopian revolution has not yet defeated the plotting of the secessionist groups in the North that are now guided by, organized and supported by imperialism and Arab reaction. . . . I have absolute confidence that the people of revolutionary Cuba and the progressive forces of the world will support our struggle to overcome the secessionists.[57]

But the people of revolutionary Cuba did *not* want to get involved. Castro responded by endorsing Ethiopia's right to "defend its territorial integrity and its unity against Eritrean secessionists," but he refused to commit Cuban aid or Cuban troops to the Eritrean front.[58] Havana also did not withdraw its estimated 17,000 troops. Their continued presence on the Somali border freed the Ethiopian militia to move against Eritrea.

The Eritrean battle raged during the spring and summer of 1978. Throughout, charges of active Cuban involvement filtered out of Eritrea. The reports were often confused. Cuba's presence was said to range anywhere from a small number of Cuban pilots flying Soviet fighter planes[59] to mechanized columns of from 500 to 6,000 Cubans actually engaged in fighting.[60] Havana denied any active participation in Eritrea. As yet, no such participation has been proved. But Havana's credibility had been sorely strained by the earlier denials of an active role in the Ogaden. The continued presence of 17,000 Cuban troops on the Ogaden border suggested at least tacit Cuban support for the Mengistu offensive.

Regardless of Cuba's actual role in Eritrea, these allegations placed new strains on the Castro Government's relations with many of its allies. By the end of June, Cuba had reportedly received strong warnings from Algeria, Yugoslavia, Portugal, and even Angola to stay out of Eritrea.[61] By the July 1978 meeting of the Nonaligned Movement, Cuba's alleged role in Eritrea had become one of the underlying issues in a growing movement to boycott the upcoming Havana summit and have Cuba ejected from the organization.

The problems Havana faced in Ethiopia were not new to the Ethiopian situation or to the Cubans. They were issues that any state must confront while trying to pursue a consistent foreign policy in the face of the ever-shifting alliances of the Third World. In Cuba's case, these difficulties were exacerbated by Havana's desire to pursue foreign policies that were not only consistent with its ideology of internationalist responsibility, but that also managed to combine and balance the interests of its two constituencies in the socialist bloc and the Third World. When viewed from the perspective of Cuba's long history of internationalist missions, the *absence* of such policy problems in Angola suggests that the Angolan involvement was an anomaly and that the Angolan lesson was not really applicable to Cuba's foreign policy decisions elsewhere in the Third World. From the start, the lesson of Ethiopia was that if the diplomatic conditions were not right, an overseas military commitment could have grave costs.

A DIPLOMATIC SETBACK

In the summer of 1978—only two years after the resolution praising Cuba's involvement in Angola was adopted unanimously by the Conference of the Nonaligned Nations in Sri Lanka—the presence of Cuban troops was again a major topic at the meetings of the Third World. But this time conflict, rather than accord, lay beneath the discussions.

The lines were drawn early. At a meeting of the Organization for African Unity in mid-July, the Somalis attacked the Cuban presence in Africa, claiming that the Cubans were merely pawns of the Soviets. The Somalis then moved to have the Cubans ejected from the nonaligned conference planned for the following month in Belgrade. Similar positions were taken by a variety of West-leaning states, including Egypt, Mauritania, and Zaire. This offensive received counterattacks from the Soviet-leaning states in Africa: Mozambique, Ethiopia, and Libya (the same Libya that wanted Cuba expelled from the Nonaligned Movement three years earlier). The latter states first defended Havana's and Moscow's right to be in Africa, and then launched a counteroffensive, charging that the French and Belgians had shown imperialist and neocolonialist intentions in Africa by airlifting peacekeeping troops to Zaire's

Shaba province the previous May. The interchange was predictable. As one delegate reportedly summed it up: "Those who have Cuban troops attacked the West. Those with French troops attacked the Cubans."[62]

The most serious questions for Havana's relations with the Third World were raised by the Nigerians, who took a third, truly nonaligned position on the Cubans in Africa. Nigeria's President Olusegun Obasanjo began his speech by thanking the "Russians and their friends" for their support in Africa. He pointed out that they had been "invited into Africa for a purpose," and that in each country they "intervened as a consequence of the failure of Western policies." But Obasanjo went on to warn the Russians and Cubans not to "overstay their welcome . . . lest they run the risk of being dubbed a new imperialist presence in Africa."[63]

Two significant points emerged from the Nigerian's speech. First, the continued presence of more than 30,000 Cuban troops in Africa was becoming a source of concern to the nonaligned states. Second, the Cubans were no longer seen as acting independently of the Soviets in Africa. When the 1976 Colombo Conference passed the resolution on Angola, it was the Cubans who were thanked. Now, two years later, the situation was reversed. The Russians got first billing, and the Cubans were referred to as "their friends."

This pattern was repeated the following month at the nonaligned conference in Belgrade. A number of West-leaning states spoke of boycotting the upcoming Havana summit and of ejecting Cuba from the movement. Cuba's position was supported by several Soviet-leaning states. The nonaligned position was taken by Yugoslavia and India.[64]

Yugoslavia and India, like Nigeria, are truly nonaligned states. Both are founders of the Movement of Nonaligned Nations. Both states have managed to maintain their relations with the two blocs while remaining outside either bloc. Their interests are thus beyond reproach in such debates, and both were highly critical of the presence of Cuban troops in Africa.

India advocated peaceful resolutions to the conflicts in Africa, warning of the danger to nonalignment posed by the presence of outside troops:

The rights of national self-defense cannot be questioned. We should not allow a situation to develop which will lead to a vicious cycle of external military dependence or involvement. If we do we may well bring the Cold War in by the back door, having all but succeeded in defeating it frontally.[65]

Belgrade also counseled the African states to look for peaceful resolutions that would keep the bloc conflict out of the Third World. In addition, Yugoslavia returned to an earlier point of contention with the Cubans: the issue of the supposed "natural alliance" of the socialist bloc and the nonaligned Third World. An official government news release issued during the conference was highly critical of the Cubans:

Struggling against neutralism, they propose another equally unacceptable extreme—the unity of the nonaligned countries with the Socialist Bloc—representing quite a definite alignment.[66]

Riding the euphoria of victory in Angola, Cuba's motions to redefine the meaning of nonalignment at the 1976 conference had been generally ignored. By the 1978 conference, however, such efforts were coupled with the tensions of the Ethiopian situation and once again provoked a drive to have Cuba ejected from the Nonaligned Movement. The conference host, Yugoslavia, prevented a direct confrontation by skillfully maneuvering to table all of these motions. It appears, however, that it did so more to preserve the unity of the movement, which it had founded, than out of a conviction that Cuba was truly nonaligned. Each criticism of Cuba was tempered with a plea for unity and the warning that the movement had, over the years, "only grown and never diminished in size."[67]

What Had Changed?

What had changed since Angola? Why was Cuba suddenly on the defensive? The answer is simple. Two years earlier, the Third World saw the Cubans as acting independently of the Soviet Union in Angola. Now, in the eyes of almost all involved, the Cubans— whether on the battlefields of Africa or in the meeting halls of the UN—were seen as representatives of, and proxies for, the Soviet

235

Union. Cuba's interests were no longer acknowledged as independent. The history of Cuba's independent and revolutionary policies in Latin America and Africa seemed to have been forgotten. There are a number of reasons why this change took place. First, the Ethiopian situation seriously tainted Cuba's reputation for independence and ideological commitment. Even if Havana did hesitate before committing itself to Ethiopia, and for all the right reasons, its eventual commitment seemed motivated by the expediency of bloc alignment.

Once the judgment had been made that Cuba was merely serving Soviet interests in Africa, subsequent deeds—no matter how ideologically pure—could not redeem the Castro Government's reputation for independence. There can be little doubt that *Moscow* wanted the Ethiopian Dergue to defeat the Eritreans. The Eritrean war was costly and obviously had sapped the strength and resources of the Dergue (not to mention increasing the Dergue's economic and military demands on Moscow). Even more important, Eritrea had Ethiopia's only ports on the Red Sea. Yet, despite the strong political and strategic reasons for supporting an Ethiopian victory, the Cubans still refused to get involved.

Havana's decision to stay out of the Eritrean conflict *should* be objective proof of the independence of its foreign policy decisions and its sensitivity to the opinion of the Third World. The decision has *not* been interpreted that way mainly because of Cuba's lagging stature in the Third World. It is also influenced by the fact that more than a year after the victory in the Ogaden, some 17,000 Cuban troops remained in Ethiopia, if not in Eritrea. Havana's protests that the troops remained solely because of the continued Somali threat seemed to fall on deaf ears.

With time, the continued presence of Cuban troops in both Angola and Ethiopia became Havana's major problem with its Third World allies. By 1983, more than six years after they first entered Angola, an estimated 35,000 Cuban troops remain in Africa. They remain because the fighting continues.[68] Reports from Cuba suggest that on several occasions the Castro Government has tried to extricate itself from Angola. Yet the continued instability of the MPLA regime's territorial control and the repeated attacks from UNITA forces and South African troops have required the continued presence of Cuban troops. Havana has learned a hard lesson in Africa, the same lesson that Washington learned in Vietnam: In the Third World there are no quick victories.

The problems faced by the Cubans at the 1978 nonaligned conference were really no different from those they faced at the 1973 Conference of the Nonaligned Movement. The Third World still defines nonalignment as independence from *both* blocs (as chimerical as that may be for most Third World states). But Cuba still pursues policies that reinforce rather than deny the impression that it is working for the Russians. Whether or not Havana actually follows Moscow's orders is not the point. Rather, the question is one of appearances. In fact, it could be argued that the Cubans did *too* good a job in Angola by getting Moscow actively involved— the independence of their interest and involvement in the Third World has been overshadowed by the Soviet presence.

The continued presence of Cuban troops in Africa had one further cost: It did significant damage to Cuba's financial standing in the West. Trade credits and hard currency loans, which mushroomed during the mid-1970s—spurred on by the soaring price of sugar— began to dry up after the Ethiopian involvement. In November 1979, an approved and publicly announced Swiss-backed Eurocurrency loan for $18 million was precipitously withdrawn by its manager, Singer and Friedlander, after a series of articles highly critical of the Castro Government's policies in Africa ran in a Swiss newspaper.[69] The banks had not had the same reaction to the Angolan involvement. But then, the world market price for sugar in 1974 was 30¢ per pound, 300 percent higher than it was in 1979.

LATIN AMERICA: A SECOND CHANCE

By the late 1970s, Havana had learned various lessons about foreign policy. In Angola, the Cubans learned that they could take a strong internationalist stance, support a traditional ally, and at the same time improve their relations with both the socialist bloc and the Third World. But in Ethiopia, Havana was forced to revise that lesson. If diplomatic conditions were not right, such overseas military commitments could also seriously damage Cuba's international position. Cuba had watched its standing with the nonaligned states fluctuate from the brink of expulsion from the movement to leadership and back again. Such a volatile history only underlined the need for caution and shrewd diplomatic calculation when making any foreign policy decision. Thus, when there were new opportunities for Cuban internationalism in Central America and the Caribbean in the late 1970s, Havana weighed its options carefully.

Latin America has always been Cuba's primary area of interest, whether for historic, ideological, economic, or strategic considerations. It must be remembered that Havana only abandoned its hopes for a Latin American revolution in the late 1960s, after watching movement after movement suffer crushing defeats at the hands of U.S.-backed counterinsurgency forces. Even then, it was not certain that Castro would have stopped trying to export revolution to Latin America had his Soviet allies not objected so strenuously. Whatever the cause, by the early 1970s, Castro was forced to admit that conditions in the region were not ripe for revolution.

By the late 1970s, the situation seemed to be changing. U.S. influence in the region had been declining steadily throughout the decade. After years of vigilance, the struggles of the Cold War and the need for U.S. protection seemed to be less of a concern to the region's growing number of nationalist leaders. Even the most right-wing Latin American regimes had begun to chafe at Washington's control, particularly after the Carter Administration sought to moderate their domestic policies through the human rights campaign, or block access to American nuclear technology or arms. Havana was an unwitting benefactor of this shift, as one by one the Latin American states broke with the Washington-imposed OAS ban and established relations with Cuba.

For the conservative regime in Barbados, recognizing Cuba was a cheap and easy way to assert its independence from Washington and appease its own left-wing nationalists without making any substantive policy changes. Although Barbados established relations with Cuba in 1972, since that time its contact with the Castro Government has been minimal. There are regularly scheduled flights between Havana and Barbados's capital of Bridgetown, and Havana may also have sent Barbados a few agricultural technicians. But when Cuba began to airlift troops to Angola in the fall of 1975, Barbados refused to allow Cuban aircraft to refuel there en route to Africa.[70]

Not all of Cuba's new alliances were so superficial. Indeed, by the late 1970s, Havana had established close relations with a small but growing number of left-leaning regimes in the Caribbean. Jamaica was undoubtedly Cuba's closest new ally. Since 1972, when Michael Manley was elected Prime Minister, Jamaica had moved steadily leftward. Manley's ideology was not Communist, but a personal mixture of nationalism, socialism, and radical populism. But like Castro, Manley was deeply concerned about the issues of small-state development and passionately committed to Third World unity.

Manley was also an enthusiastic supporter of the Castro Government's new international role. In the spring of 1976, Manley strongly endorsed Cuba's involvement in Angola: "We regard Cuban assistance to Angola as honorable and in the best interests of all those who care for African freedom."[71] The Cubans were delighted with this new ally so close to home. Jamaica and its struggle against U.S. domination became a regular topic for Cuban writers. When Manley visited the island in 1975, he was greeted with as much fanfare as any leader from the Eastern bloc.

Guyana's turn to the left occurred at about the same time as Jamaica's. The current Guyanese Government of Forbes Burnham came to power in 1964. Burnham's predecessor, Cheddi Jagan, was a Marxist and one of Castro's first allies in the region, having visited Cuba in 1961. For the first six years of his rule, Burnham tried to undo most of Jagan's work by promoting capitalism in Guyana, inviting foreign investment, and breaking relations with Cuba. But by the early 1970s, faced with mounting domestic unrest and the growing strength of Jagan's left opposition, Burnham made an abrupt about-face. In 1970, he declared Guyana a "cooperative republic," nationalized a good percentage of Guyana's foreign-owned enterprise, and committed his regime to an autonomous and nationalist foreign policy. Two years later Guyana broke the OAS ban and reestablished relations with Cuba. At the time of the Cuban involvement in Angola, Guyana was at the forefront of UN efforts to condemn South Africa's intervention. During the troop airlift, Cuban planes were allowed to refuel in Guyana despite heavy pressure from the United States.[72]

Havana was undoubtedly pleased yet ambivalent about Guyana's support. Burnham's abrupt turn to the left—including his recognition of Cuba—was viewed as an opportunistic attempt to coopt Jagan's left-wing following. Castro's real loyalties, both historically and ideologically, were with Jagan. At the same time, Castro could not afford to refuse Burnham's support. *Any* diplomatic ties in the region were preferable to the sort of isolation Cuba had suffered for the preceding decade. Therefore, soon after the Angolan episode, Cuba and Guyana signed a number of economic and technical agreements providing Cuban aid to develop Guyana's sugar industry.

During 1979, two new Caribbean regimes were added to Cuba's camp. In March, the conservative regime of Eric Gairy in Grenada was ousted in a left-wing coup led by Maurice Bishop and his New Jewel movement. At the same time, newly independent St. Lucia, under Deputy Prime Minister George Odlum, began to move to the left. Both Bishop and Odlum publicly expressed interest in closer ties with Havana and Cuban aid.

For these new left-leaning regimes, establishing relations with Cuba has had a significance far beyond the exchange of ambassadors or the receipt of aid. First, there appears to have been a genuine personal bond between Castro and these new Caribbean nationalists. Although Washington saw Castro as a tinhorn dictator and Soviet puppet, the view from the Caribbean—and a good part of the Third World—revealed something very different. Fidel Castro was a nationalist hero, liberator, and leader who dared defy the multinationals and Washington—and win. And if Castro had to sell a good deal of Cuba's soul to the Soviets in the process, that was the sort of compromise that the leaders of small states could understand.

One must also remember that in 1979 the extent of Cuba's domestic economic problems and internal unrest was not widely known. Indeed, to most observers, Cuba looked like a glittering success. It was independent of Washington, its economy appeared to be growing, its people were fed, clothed, educated, and employed. Its leader was internationally respected as the head of the Nonaligned Movement. And, as St. Lucia's Odlum put it, the Caribbean was, "going through a period of searching for its own structures and systems."[73] In 1979 the Cuban model looked more than viable.

For these regimes, opening relations with Cuba was also an avowal of independence from the United States, an emotionally and politically gratifying nose-thumbing to Washington's traditional domination of the region. This interpretation helps explain the often ostentatious displays of affection for Castro and the Cuban way. In the fall of 1979, as Castro finished his address to the United Nations, Grenadan leader Maurice Bishop rushed to the podium to embrace Castro. The gesture was caught by television cameras and broadcast all over the world. Although Bishop's affection for Castro was no doubt genuine, the symbolic significance of the embrace went far beyond their personal relationship.

Finally, playing the Cuban card also seemed to be a calculated bid for international aid—from Cuba, from the United States, or preferably both. The leaders of tiny countries like Grenada and St. Lucia—whose combined population is less than a quarter of a million—knew that they had little to offer the United States and little hope of garnering significant U.S. aid. But by ostentatiously recognizing Cuba, visiting Havana, and inviting Cuban technicians and advisers, there was a good chance of arousing U.S. interest and perhaps even support. It had happened before in Latin America during the Alliance for Progress, so why not now in the Caribbean? At the very least these states would benefit from Cuban aid.

On several occasions, Caribbean leaders have gone fishing for Western aid and used Cuba as bait or vice versa. In March 1980, Jamaica's Michael Manley paid a surprise visit to Cuba immediately after a particularly difficult series of negotiations with the International Monetary Fund had fallen through.[74] There is little doubt that the two were related. Similarly, Grenada's Bishop turned to Havana after a visit to Canada failed to produce the funds for a new Grenadan airport. The bid to Cuba was more successful. In February 1980, Bishop announced that Cuba was sending some 300 construction workers, machines, and about $10 million worth of materials to begin work on the new airport.[75]

CUBA IN THE CARIBBEAN: REALITY
AND MYTH

There is no doubt that Castro was pleased and flattered by all the attention. After twenty years of isolation and treatment as the pariah of the Western hemisphere, Cuba was finally coming into its own, and in its own Caribbean. But no matter how pleased the Cubans were, they were still unsure about what role they would play. In the 1960s Havana had learned some very harsh lessons about overestimating the strength of revolutionary movements and underestimating the strength of the opposition. Havana had also learned that its own support could actually increase the amount of opposition a struggling regime or movement might face. The widespread negative reaction to the Ethiopian involvement may also have made Havana wary of any move that could further jeopardize its hard-won diplomatic gains, especially in the hemisphere. Even the suspicion that Cuba was back in the business of fomenting revolution in Latin America could send Havana back out into the cold. At the same time, there was little to suggest that Moscow had changed *its* mind about the revolutionary potential of the hemisphere. Although the Castro Government was undoubtedly interested in nurturing this new leftward trend in the Caribbean, the Cubans were also wary of becoming too involved.

Thus, at the end of the 1970s, Cuba continued its earlier Latin American policies: staying out of the internal politics of its neighboring states and relying primarily on humanitarian aid to maintain and improve its diplomatic standing. In Guyana, the Cubans constructed a fishing port. In Jamaica, an estimated 350 Cuban advisers helped build schools, dams, and a waterworks, while some forty Cuban doctors worked feverishly to fill the gap created by the loss of scores of Jamaican doctors fleeing Manley's creeping socialism. To Grenada the Cubans sent a fishing trawler—Grenada's first— while an estimated 300 construction workers (highly valued in Cuba, where housing is the principal shortage) helped build an international airport.[76] As they did in Africa, Cuban military advisers also helped train the militias of their new allies. Some thirty to forty Cuban military instructors were sent to Grenada to help train

242

its 1,200-man People's Revolutionary Army. A small number of Cuba's 500 advisers in Jamaica were assigned to Jamaica's security forces.[77] On the whole, however, Cuba's commitments to the Caribbean were self-consciously overt and constructive.

But no matter how mundane and humanitarian Havana's aid to the Caribbean seemed, there were still many in the United States who were determined to prove the continued existence of a Cuban threat. According to these observers, Havana's humanitarian moves were actually just window dressing concealing a Cuban plot to subvert these governments and turn them into Soviet pawns. The Caribbean, which was variously referred to as America's "backyard," "front yard," and "soft underbelly," was no longer secure. Cuban advisers in Jamaica were actually there to help train the Jamaican military and secret police as a prelude to Manley's imposition of a totalitarian regime. Cuban construction workers in Grenada were building an airport, not to improve Grenada's tourist trade, but to provide Cuban and even Soviet planes with a new strategic base on the continent. Cuban teachers in Guyana were not there to improve Guyana's literacy rate but actually to indoctrinate Guyanese children in Marxist ideology, just as Cuba had indoctrinated its own children.[78]

In official testimony, U.S. security analysts tended to play down the Cuban threat. Testifying before the Subcommittee on Inter-American Affairs of the House Committee on Foreign Affairs in the spring of 1980, Martin Scheina and Col. Ralph Martinez-Boucher of the Defense Intelligence Agency both denied that the Cuban-built airport in Grenada would constitute a security threat to the United States. The testimony is worth quoting since it demonstrates the interplay of popular myth and official reality:

Mr. Fox [*Minority staff counsel*]: One recent article, reporting on the airbase that Cuba is helping build in Grenada, suggested that it might play some future strategic role for the Soviets. The suggestion is that it would be large enough to handle the Backfire or other type of long-range combat aircraft.

Do you see any validity to that kind of an argument?

Col. Martinez-Boucher: No; I do not think it is valid at all.

Mr. Friedman [*staff director*]: Are you saying you see no military use for that airport?

Mr. Scheina: I would like to say one thing. If the airfield is going to handle international civilian air traffic, it very likely may have a runway which is of sufficient length to handle the Backfire. . . .[79]

Although the experts did not think that the airport would be used for strategic purposes, there really was no way of proving otherwise.

The Carter Administration subscribed to the popular view. After his early years of tolerance, Carter, like so many of his predecessors, came to believe that the Cubans were a real threat to United States security who would have to be contained—forcibly, if necessary. In the fall of 1979, at the height of the tempest-in-a-teapot "troop crisis," the Carter Administration issued a new position paper on Cuba entitled Presidential Directive 52. PD 52 reflected the same mentality of containment that had dominated Washington's Cuba policies for the previous two decades. Its goal was to limit the Cuban threat, first by discrediting Cuba in the eyes of the Third World, second by pressuring Moscow, and third by escalating Washington's military presence in the region.[80]

On October 1, 1979, Carter ordered that a rapid deployment force be created for the Caribbean in Key West, to be known as the Caribbean Contingency Joint Task Force.[81] The following March, a U.S. aircraft carrier was sent to the Caribbean on a "show the flag" visit. A complex series of military maneuvers in the Caribbean was planned for the following May, including a televised landing of marines at the U.S. Guantánamo Base in eastern Cuba. Washington was clearly back in the business of waving the big stick, with no guarantees that its policies would be any more successful now than they had been in the past.

Grenada, St. Lucia, and Guyana are all small countries with little strategic importance. Guyana's population in 1979 was just under a million, and Grenada and St. Lucia together boasted less than a quarter million people. They have no oil, no precious metals. Guyana's principal product is sugar, St. Lucia produces bananas and coconuts, and Grenada's primary export is nutmeg. As former British colonies, they have no historic ties to the United States.

One would not expect Washington to be particularly concerned about events in any of these states—certainly not enough to resurrect the Cold War in the Caribbean.

But a curious phenomenon was at work in Washington in 1979. After years of ignoring the Caribbean and taking America's predominance for granted, Washington officials began to talk with increasing unease about a leftward trend in the area. "Caribbean dominoes" became common parlance. U.S. newspapers and magazines were filled with headlines like "Powder Keg at Our Doorstep" and "Revolutionary Winds in the Caribbean." Americans who were barely aware of events in Brazil and Argentina or even neighboring Mexico now became conversant, if only temporarily, with the intricacies of domestic politics in Dominica, St. Lucia, St. Vincent, and Grenada. And though observers were hard pressed to say how, the consensus remained that Castro was somehow behind it all.

The sequence of events that led to this sudden flurry of concern about the Caribbean is strikingly similar to the events preceding Washington's sudden concern for Latin America in the early 1960s. In the years before the Cuban revolution, Washington had basically ignored Latin America, taking its strategic predominance for granted. After Castro's revolution, however, U.S. policy makers suddenly turned the full force of their attention on the region. What they saw scared them: poverty, inequality, repression, and crushing underdevelopment. Latin America was suddenly seen as vulnerable to revolution. The United States would have to act immediately, lest the rest of Latin America follow Castro's course. The Alliance for Progress and the extensive security assistance programs were brought into existence to meet that challenge.

Of course Latin America did not suddenly become ripe for revolution in 1960. Its poverty, its underdevelopment, all of it had been there for decades. Nor had the Cuban revolution made any serious changes in the conditions in Latin America. Castro certainly never had the means to create revolutionary conditions where none had existed. What had changed in 1960 was *Washington's* attitude toward Latin America. As a direct result of the Cuban revolution, Washington had come to see that poverty and underdevelopment had the potential to produce revolution in Latin America and be-

245

come a concrete threat to America's future security. In itself, this new concern was not bad, and it was time for the United States to pay some attention to, and take some responsibility for, its less fortunate neighbors. What was unfortunate, however, was that it took an alleged strategic threat to mobilize that concern and justify the cost of humanitarian programs like the Alliance for Progress. Because as soon as that concern was mobilized, predominantly strategic solutions were pursued. The Cuban threat—which was little more than symbolic—took on a life of its own. And as we have seen, the need to contain the threat not only justified the cost of the Alliance for Progress, in the end it took precedence over the Alliance and a commitment to democracy and development in the region.

In 1979, the U.S. was in danger of replaying that sequence in the Caribbean. This time it was not one major event such as the Cuban revolution that set the ball rolling, but a series of smaller events: Manley's growing closeness with Castro, the leftward turn in Guyana, and the socialist coup in Grenada set off the alarms. Once again, Washington turned its attention to the region and was shocked to find persistent poverty, inequality, and repression just beyond its own borders. The Caribbean was pronounced ripe for revolution. After the Sandinista victory in Nicaragua in July 1979 and the "discovery" of a Soviet combat brigade in Cuba the following September (the brigade had been there for nearly two decades), many in Washington were convinced that the revolution had begun.

Three years later most of these fears about the Caribbean seem to have been groundless. Despite continued Cuban aid, Grenada and St. Lucia have not become Soviet bases. Under Forbes Burnham, Guyana has made still another about-face and is solidly back in the capitalist camp. Burnham and Castro are no longer talking. Meanwhile, in Jamaica, Michael Manley was defeated in free elections by conservative leader Edward Seaga. Seaga was on record as committed to dismantling everything that Manley and his Cuban henchmen created and returning Jamaica to capitalism and the Western bloc. After his electoral defeat, Manley quietly left power, and the 500 or so Cuban advisers stationed in Jamaica—whatever their role—were withdrawn peacefully.

By contrast, three years later Washington's worst fears about Central America do seem to be coming true. The left-wing Sandinistas are solidly in control of the ruling directorate. El Salvador is in the midst of a brutal civil war, Guatemala is on the brink of explosion, and Honduras does not seem to be far behind. Central America today truly seems ripe for revolution. But even there the Cuban role has been limited.

THE NICARAGUAN REVOLUTION

The revolution in Nicaragua created a new set of opportunities and quandaries for Havana's foreign policy. Castro and the Somoza dynasty have always been enemies. In 1961, President Luís Somoza, father of Anastasio, lent his ports for the use of Cuban exiles in the Bay of Pigs attack. Somoza is said to have bid the invaders godspeed at the docks, admonishing them to "bring back some hairs from Castro's beard."[82] In the mid-1960s, Castro tried to return the favor by providing arms and training to the fledgling Sandinista guerrillas. Thus, both history and emotion bound Havana to the Sandinista cause.

But by 1978 there were strong political reasons for Cuba to exercise caution in Nicaragua. Castro was on record as having abandoned the export of revolution to Latin America and to be interested solely in building good diplomatic relations in the hemisphere. Any false moves in Nicaragua and Cuba could easily destroy almost a decade of diplomatic progress.

As a result, the Cubans played only a very limited role in the Nicaraguan civil war. According to a CIA report issued in May 1979, three months before the Sandinistas came to power, Havana avoided any direct military involvement in Nicaragua that might have led to a confrontation with Washington or jeopardized Cuba's delicate political relations in Latin America.[83] The Castro Government sent no troops to fight in Nicaragua, and only a small amount of arms—two planeloads of light weapons, according to the CIA report. Instead, Havana chose to limit its role in the Nicaraguan revolution primarily to that of political adviser.

During 1979, as the struggle in Nicaragua escalated, Castro met with the leaders of the Nicaraguan opposition on several occasions to discuss political and strategic matters. According to the same U.S. intelligence report, the Cuban leader gave surprisingly moderate advice at these meetings. First, he urged the opposition leaders to set aside their ideological and historical differences and forge a unified directorate. Castro is said to have personally spent some forty-eight hours trying to hammer out a compromise among the three main factions. To make it stick, he told the new directorate that evidence of their continuing unity was a prerequisite for any Cuban support—arms, money, or ammunition. Obviously, Castro had learned an important lesson during the 1960s, when internal divisions were as much responsible for the defeat of Latin America's revolutionary left as any counterinsurgency efforts. In a July 1980 speech in Cuba, Sandinista leader Jaime Wheelock acknowledged Castro's central role in unifying the Nicaraguan opposition:

. . . and when for some reason amidst our difficulties, we had our differences . . . the support and advice of our brother Fidel was of great importance for the Sandinista's unity which was the unity of the whole people and was the guarantee of the Sandinista revolution.[84]

Castro also urged the Sandinistas to play down the Marxist nature of their programs and to form a broad united front with members of the Nicaraguan business, professional, and landowning communities that opposed Somoza. This was a radical departure for Castro, who, during the 1960s, had vehemently condemned as "collusion," defeatism, and a betrayal of the Latin American revolution any efforts by the Latin American Communist parties to form such alliances. By 1979, a united front had become a practical necessity if the Sandinistas were ever to succeed in marshaling enough support to topple the Somoza dynasty. Nor was Castro's commitment to the united front merely tactical. Even after Somoza's overthrow, Castro would continue to advise the Sandinistas to work in concert with Nicaragua's business, professional, and landowning classes to rebuild the country. By 1979, the Cuban leader had come to hold some significantly different attitudes about what was necessary both to make a revolution and to run a country. The practical realities of political coalition-building and economic management were taking precedence over issues of so-called revolutionary purity.

Castro's tactical advice to the Sandinistas was equally cautious. The Cuban leadership apparently shared the Sandinistan conviction that armed struggle was the only way to oust the Somoza dictatorship. At the same time, the Cubans were not sanguine about the prospects for an immediate victory, cautioning the Sandinistas in the spring of 1979 to prepare for a prolonged struggle. In particular, Castro warned against expending limited resources on dramatic but doomed frontal attacks on the Nicaraguan National Guard, counseling them instead to concentrate their efforts on hit-and-run actions. Attacks fashioned after Castro's own 1953 assault on the Moncada Barracks were rejected. Once again, Castro spoke from the bitter experience of the 1960s, when heroic *putschism* led to repeated tragedy for the Latin American revolutionaries.

Havana began to send arms to the Sandinistas only after the Revolutionary Directorate had unified and Castro had doled out his advice of compromise, patience, and restraint. Even then, Cuban material commitments were very small: two or three planeloads of light weapons, according to U.S. intelligence reports. It has been charged that, during the final Sandinista offensive of June and July 1979, Havana significantly increased its deliveries of arms and may even have sent some military advisers to fight alongside the Sandinistas. At the time Havana denied this. Since then, however, the Sandinistas and Cubans have made oblique references to Cuban military aid during the final offensive. During a 1980 visit to Cuba, Wheelock thanked the Cuban people for "their concrete solidarity":

> . . . when that people was ready to fight with stones and even with their own teeth to overthrow the dictatorship, we again had the concrete solidarity of the people of Cuba and of Commander Fidel Castro. For we know that revolutions are not made with teeth.[85]

Havana apparently overcame its caution in Nicaragua for sound diplomatic reasons. By the time of Cuba's military commitment, the Sandinistas had received the endorsement of many of the region's leading liberal nations, including Costa Rica, Venezuela, Mexico, and Panama. The amount of arms sent to the rebels by these regimes far surpassed Cuba's military aid to the Sandinistas. In many ways, the situation in Nicaragua repeated the Cuban experience in Angola. The Cubans were able to help a revolutionary group they had begun supporting during the early 1960s, and at the same time satisfy the current interests of a wide variety of allies in the socialist bloc and the Third World—in particular, the oil-exporting states of Mexico and Venezuela. Yet even under these auspicious conditions Havana still did not send troops to fight in Nicaragua.

HAVANA SUMMIT: A DREAM DEFERRED

The 1979 Havana summit conference of the nonaligned should have been a triumph for Fidel Castro. For years Castro had dreamed of becoming a major Third World leader. Even when the Third World was barely aware of itself as a political entity, Castro diligently orated and sought to organize any chance he got for Third World unity and political action. The Cuban leader promoted Third World interests even when it jeopardized his alliance with the Soviet Union, as it often did during the early years of the revolution. By the mid-1970s, in the wake of the OPEC embargo, everyone—North, South, East and West—had come to see the Third World as a viable and important political entity. Thus, when Cuba was chosen in 1976 to chair the next nonaligned summit, Castro undoubtedly felt that his dream had come true. The Third World was becoming a major political force in the world, and Cuba was going to be its new leader.

By the time the nonaligned conference was convened in Havana three years later, however, everything had changed. OPEC had not sided with its Third World brethren, and used its new-found power solely to enrich itself. The OPEC price hikes, instead of giving the Third World new influence, were actually hurting the less developed countries more than they were hurting the industrialized states. Spiraling oil prices only increased the less developed countries' dependence on the Western banks, as they were forced to borrow more and more to finance their oil bills. At the same time, Cuba's position in the Third World—in the aftermath of the

250

Ethiopian involvement—had deteriorated significantly. For months preceding the September meeting in Havana, the Western press was filled with predictions that the conference would be boycotted, or Cuba censured, or Castro relieved of his position as chairman of the movement.

Castro thus convened the opening session of the nonaligned summit on a note of conciliation rather than exultation. In his speech he spoke forcefully about the problems of imperialism and underdevelopment confronting the Third World and left little doubt as to which countries should be held responsible. Yet he avoided any mention of the natural alliance thesis that had caused Cuba so much trouble at earlier conferences. Instead, he emphasized the need for unity and accord among the movement's members in their joint struggle against imperialism and the growing world economic crisis, and promised that Cuba would not use its position as chairman of the movement "to try to impose our radicalism on anyone."[86]

The Havana conference came off with barely a hitch. But it was clear throughout that Castro was playing catch-up. In the past he had never hesitated to use his position to impose his ideas on his allies. In the summer of 1979, however, Castro was obviously unsure of Cuba's standing in the Nonaligned Movement and reluctant to provoke any conflict that might endanger Cuba's position as the leader of the movement for the next three years.[87]

Cuba's problems with the Third World became more acute after the Soviet invasion of Afghanistan in December 1979. Moscow's decision to send 30,000 troops into Afghanistan to prop up Babrak Karmal's puppet regime was widely condemned. Like the response to the socialist bloc invasion of Czechoslovakia eleven years earlier, protests came from regimes of different political colorations and from all parts of the world. This was not an issue of East versus West, or communism versus capitalism. It was the issue of a superpower imposing its political will on a small state through the use of brutal military superiority. When a motion condemning the invasion was raised at the United Nations in mid-January 1980, it passed overwhelmingly. Of the ninety-one nonaligned nations, only nine refused to condemn Moscow. Cuba was one of those nine.[88]

The comparison between the Afghanistan vote and Havana's endorsement of the Czech invasion was unavoidable. To all observers, Cuba once again seemed to betray its most basic internationalist commitment to the rights of small states. And again Havana seemed to be knuckling under to Soviet pressure. What made it all that much worse this time was that Cuba was now the head of the Nonaligned Movement. Whatever doubts had been brewing among the members since the 1973 Nonaligned Conference, when Castro first proclaimed his commitment to the socialist bloc, now came spewing forth. The charges made in 1973 by a few critics such as Qadaffi and Sihanouk now seemed to be the growing consensus: Cuba's nonalignment was a sham. Immediately after Cuba lost its bid for a seat on the UN Security Council.

As chairman of the Nonaligned Movement, Cuba's candidacy should not even have been challenged. Instead, Colombia chose to vote against Cuba, and the election was deadlocked after 156 ballots. To save Castro further embarrassment, two of the leading nonaligned states, India and Nigeria, convinced both Havana and Bogotá to withdraw from the running, and Mexico, a long-time Cuban ally, was elected.[89] Nevertheless the defeat was seen as a major setback for Castro and Cuba.

It is likely that Havana foresaw the effects of supporting Moscow. During the debate on the Afghanistan condemnation, Cuba's UN ambassador, Raúl Roa, acknowledged as much, saying, "As far as Cuba is concerned, this debate poses a need to take a stand in the face of an historic dilemma." Moreover, Roa was careful in his speech not to endorse the Soviet intervention. Instead, he said that Cuba would not vote to condemn the Soviet Union because to do so would be the same as endorsing U.S. imperialism—and that Cuba would not do:

> We will not vote against socialism. . . . we are well aware of what socialism and what imperialism mean, and we fully appreciate the historic role of both the Soviet Union and U.S. imperialism. We therefore cast our vote today against that imperialism. . . .[90]

No matter how Talmudic the explanation, the effect was the same. By not condemning the invasion of Afghanistan, Havana was seen as endorsing it.

Most of the explanations for Castro's endorsement of the Czech invasion do not obtain in the case of Afghanistan. The explanation of external pressure does not apply. In 1980, Cuba's need to pay off the Soviet Union was much less pressing than it was in 1968. Havana was no longer defying Moscow in Latin America or anywhere else. If anything, Havana had become Moscow's staunchest ally, whether at the meetings of the Nonaligned Movement, or on the battlefields of Angola and Ethiopia. Havana also did not need to endorse the Afghanistan invasion to guarantee Moscow's continued economic support. Moscow's economic commitments to Cuba were secure in 1980, and had been since 1972, when Cuba joined the Council for Mutual Economic Assistance. Nor did Havana need to support the invasion to reinforce Moscow's military responsibilities to Cuba. By 1980, Moscow's military commitment to Cuba was also no longer in doubt.

The explanation of internal political pressures also does not apply. Castro backed the Czech invasion by arguing it was necessary to defeat the forces trying to reinstate capitalism in Czechoslovakia. By endorsing the invasion, Castro was warning his own internal opposition that he would not hesitate, if necessary, to take similarly brutal measures in Cuba. The Cubans made no such argument about preserving socialism in Afghanistan. In fact, their public statements at the time made no mention of the situation in Afghanistan. Privately, Cuban diplomats admitted that the Soviet invasion was "unfortunate" and a "mistake"—one that would be costly both in terms of resources and lives and in terms of the international prestige of Moscow and the entire bloc.

What defined Cuba's position at the United Nations was a straightforward issue of bloc loyalty. Although the Afghanistan situation was complex, the UN vote was not. For Cuba, it was a simple matter of supporting its friends through a particularly difficult period, and opposing its enemies.

It is not clear whether Havana would have taken the same position during the more radical 1960s, when issues of small state solidarity frequently took precedence over East–West loyalties. But in 1980, when Moscow was not only solidly committed to Cuba's defense, but also providing crucial support for Cuba's internationalist missions abroad, Havana's loyalty to Moscow was much less in doubt. Why the Cubans did not abstain from the vote—if they thought the Soviets had made a mistake—is an interesting question. Certainly Moscow should have understood that Cuba's standing in the Nonaligned Movement—as well as a seat on the Security Council—hung in the balance. Havana's value to Moscow would have grown enormously had it won that Security Council seat.

Cuban officials dismiss this idea by saying that the Security Council seat was in doubt even before the invasion. For months, Washington had lobbied steadily against Cuba's election, and had apparently been making headway. At the time of the invasion, the anti-Soviet sentiment in the UN was so strong that it really did not matter how Cuba voted. Moreover, say the Cubans, the damage from the vote was grave, but it was not irreparable. Although Cuba lost its bid for a seat on the Security Council, Castro was not removed from his position as head of the Nonaligned Movement, Cuba was not expelled from the Movement, and no states cut diplomatic relations. As usual, the Third World proved more forgiving—or more expedient—in its attitude toward Cuba.

CUBAN TROOPS AND CUBAN INFLUENCE

Since the mid-1970s, Havana has scored a remarkable number of foreign policy successes. Cuban troops brought one socialist regime to power in Angola and helped keep another socialist regime in power in Ethiopia. Cuban advice and a limited amount of arms helped bring a third socialist regime to power in Nicaragua. At the same time, Havana began to expand its diplomatic influence, sending political, military, and technical advisers, construction workers, engineers, teachers, and doctors to help a wide variety of left-leaning governments in Central America, Africa, Southeast Asia, and the Middle East. According to CIA estimates, by 1979 Cuba had some 35,000 troops and another 13,000 civilian advisers stationed overseas.[91]

This widespread Cuban presence has been the source of grave concern in Washington. To assess the true impact of Cuba's international presence, it is not enough simply to count the number of Cubans stationed abroad or even to tally the number of Cuban-backed victories. First, one must ask how much tangible influence the presence of Cuban troops or advisers has had on any state. Then, one must look closely at how Havana has used whatever influence it has gained. Have the Cubans tried to turn any of these states into a Soviet pawn? Or does Havana have another agenda?

The amount of influence the Castro Government has been able to exercise has actually varied a good deal from state to state. In Angola, where Cuba has some 19,000 troops stationed and another 7,500 civilian advisers,[92] Havana's influence has been considerable. Above all, Havana has had enough influence to keep the MPLA in power in Luanda despite repeated attacks from opposing guerrilla groups, hostile neighbors, and factions within the ruling MPLA. By contrast, in Ethiopia, where some 12,000 Cuban troops are still stationed, the Cubans have been unable to influence either domestic or foreign policies. Cuban attempts to replace the Dergue's military authoritarianism with a more open, civilian-based political party failed miserably. In both states, the presence of Cuban troops is essential to the regime's survival. It is not clear why Havana's influence varies so markedly.

In May 1977, MPLA President Neto came close to being over-thrown in a coup led by Nito Alves, one of his lieutenants. Neto was saved only by the presence of Cuban troops, which fought side-by-side with MPLA troops still loyal to him. Alves's faction opposed Neto's leadership on a wide range of ideological and politi-cal issues. Alves wanted to socialize the entire Angolan economy— a sort of Angolan War "Communism"—whereas Neto was commit-ted to maintaining a mixed economy. Alves was committed to a black nationalist ideology, whereas Neto's regime was avowedly multiracialist. And finally, Alves wanted Angola to seek a much closer alliance with the Soviet Union, whereas Neto preferred to maintain Angola's nonaligned status.[93]

Havana and Moscow found themselves on opposite sides in this split. Despite the extreme radicalism—and some would say ideologi-cal purity—of Alves's position, Havana's loyalties were with its old ally, Agostinho Neto. Moscow, on the other hand, is said to have given Alves its tacit endorsement at the very least. Moscow's relations with Neto had always been touchy; some say Neto was too independent for the Kremlin's taste. Although the Soviets supposedly knew about the planned coup weeks in advance, they did nothing to stop it or to help defend Neto. Moscow did not even inform Havana that its ally was threatened. When the coup attempt finally came, Havana's troops fought side by side with MPLA loyalists while Moscow sat on the sidelines.

Significantly, although Havana had enough power to decide who would rule in Luanda, when the time came Havana did not exercise its influence to place the most radical faction, or the faction that was most closely allied with Moscow, in power. In Angola, at least, the Cubans did not seem interested in turning the MPLA into a Soviet pawn.

Although the MPLA obviously owes its existence to the continued presence of some 19,000 Cuban troops, Havana's influence has not been complete. On at least two important occasions, the MPLA leadership has taken positions contrary to Havana's wishes. How many private disagreements have occurred can only be imagined. In March 1977, several thousand Katangan guerrillas invaded Zaire's Shaba province from their bases in northern Angola. Havana immediately denied any knowledge of or support for the action. The invasion came at a particularly bad time for Cuba, just as Castro was embarking on a major diplomatic tour of Africa, a tour intended to deemphasize Cuba's military presence in Africa. The invasion also made Angola much more vulnerable to Zairean attack and prevented Cuba from continuing its planned troop withdrawals.

Luanda, on the other hand, had good reason to support the invasion. A year earlier, in March 1976, Angola and Zaire signed a peace treaty in which Luanda promised to restrain the Katangan rebels if Zaire cut off all support of the FNLA. Zaire did not keep its part of the bargain, and by early 1977 not only was the FNLA still active in Zaire, but Zairean Government troops were also involved in regular forays across the border into Angola. Several observers have suggested that Luanda may have decided to back the Katangan invasion in order to teach Zaire a lesson.[94] Luanda either did not consider, or ignored, the fact that this would jeopardize Havana's diplomatic interests in Africa as well as place further strains on Cuba's already over-extended military.

In the summer of 1978, the Angolan leadership once again broke with the Castro Government—this time publicly—when it advised the Cubans against any involvement in the Eritrean civil war. Although Havana had not yet made a decision about Eritrea, the public embarrassment it felt at being lectured by Luanda must have been very real. Castro had always thought of himself as the revolutionary conscience of the socialist bloc; now Agostinho Neto seemed to want to usurp that position. Thus, whereas Cuban support had been essential to the MPLA's survival, Havana's influence in Luanda had been nowhere near complete. Not only had Angola not become a Soviet pawn, Cuba apparently was unable to turn Angola into a Cuban pawn.

There are some striking similarities between the Cuban–Angolan relationship and the Soviet–Cuban relationship. In both cases, a "small" state, dependent on a militarily superior power for its survival, has managed not only to carve out its own foreign policy, but has actually challenged its patron on issues of correct revolutionary conduct. There is no small amount of irony in this situation for Havana.

The bottom line in any discussion of the Castro regime's influence in Angola is how the MPLA has used its Cuban-backed power. Despite its large debt to the socialist bloc, the MPLA has not turned Angola into a traditional Soviet satellite. On international issues Angola has clearly aligned itself with the socialist bloc. In January 1980, Angola was one of the nine nonaligned states to vote against the UN condemnation of the Soviet invasion of Afghanistan. At home, however, Gulf Oil rigs in Cabinda province have not been expropriated and continue to pump as Cuban troops stand guard. Luanda has also refused Moscow's requests for military bases.

Havana has been able to exercise far less influence in Ethiopia. Even though the Dergue's survival depends on the continued presence of some 12,000 Cuban troops, the Castro regime has had several serious policy conflicts with the Mengistu regime. Havana split with Addis Ababa on the issue of Eritrea, urging the Ethiopians to seek a political rather than military solution. Havana also tried to moderate the role of the military in Ethiopia's domestic politics, urging Mengistu to form a civilian political party. When this suggestion fell on deaf ears, the Cubans are said to have smuggled a popular opposition figure, Negedde Gobeze of the All Ethiopian Socialist Movement, back into the country to help set up a civilian party. Gobeze was caught by the Dergue, and some heated words were apparently exchanged between the Ethiopians and the Cubans. Immediately afterward, the Cuban ambassador to Addis Ababa was called home.

Why Havana has had so little influence in Ethiopia, despite the large size and importance of its military presence, can only be surmised. It is true that Havana's ties to the Ethiopian Dergue were established only recently and were much weaker than its historical ties to the MPLA, which date back over a decade. At the same time, Havana's involvement in Ethiopia was mediated by Moscow from the beginning. Unlike the Angolan war, in which Cuba and the Soviet Union established their relations with the MPLA independently, throughout the Ethiopian conflict Moscow was calling the shots—advising the Dergue, flying Cuban soldiers in on Soviet planes, arming the Cuban soldiers once they arrived, and directing all military operations from a Moscow-staffed command. Whether the Soviets have had any greater success in influencing their Ethiopian allies is unknown.

Of all the states that Cuba has aided, it has undoubtedly been able to exercise the greatest influence in Nicaragua. During the revolution, Castro played the role of elder statesman, military strategist, and political adviser to the Sandinistas. Since July 1979, when the Sandinistas took power, the Cuban advisory role has increased. Although intelligence reports vary, it appears that today there are stationed in Nicaragua somewhere between 2,500 and 5,000 Cuban civilian advisers, building hospitals, teaching school, and organizing social welfare programs. Two Cuban-sponsored programs that have received particular attention in Washington are the Sandinista literacy campaign and the organization of local revolutionary defense committees. Both are modeled closely after programs implemented by the Castro Government in Cuba in the early 1960s and will undoubtedly have long-range effects on the political socialization of the Nicaraguan people. According to a recent State Department report, there are also 1,500 to 2,500 Cuban military and security advisers now working in Nicaragua, advising the Nicaraguan internal security forces and helping to transform the Sandinista guerrilla forces into conventional armed forces.

Since 1980, Nicaraguan officials have shuttled regularly between Managua and Havana, seeking Cuban advice and direction. In July 1980, Castro spoke at the Nicaraguan revolution's first anniversary celebrations; his address attracted more than 100,000 enthusiastic Nicaraguan listeners.[95]

Both publicly and privately, Castro's advice to the Nicaraguans, according to Cuban Foreign Ministry officials, continues to be remarkably moderate. Despite Washington's early fears, Castro has not counseled the Sandinistas to nationalize all foreign industry, cut ties to the West, and follow Cuba into the socialist bloc. Instead of autarky and revolution, Castro has told the Nicaraguans to adopt a moderate course—a nonaligned position abroad and a mixed economy at home. As one observer noted, Castro's advice to the Sandinistas has been so pragmatic "and often so divorced from expected Marxist ideology, that a friend of his recently declared: 'In the old days, he probably wouldn't have taken it himself.' "[96]

Castro has warned the Sandinistas against too much economic centralization and the dangers of building an overly bureaucratized state structure. In particular, Castro has urged the Sandinistas to maintain a free market system and avoid rationing. These cautions apparently derive from what Castro sees as his own Government's failures. Havana has long acknowledged its severe economic problems, but apparently did not suspect the amount of local disaffection demonstrated by the 1980 exodus of over 100,000 citizens. Since then, Castro has tried to deal with particular problems at home, including reorganizing and streamlining the cumbersome Cuban state bureaucracy—particularly in the social service sectors—and resurrecting local private enterprise, hoping to overcome food shortages by allowing free agricultural markets to open all over the island.

Politically, Castro continues to advise conciliation among the diverse factions of Nicaraguan society. He has urged the Sandinistas to maintain good relations with the business community and the private landowners—two groups he forsook early in his own revolution, when he implemented wholesale nationalizations of industry and land. As Castro explained to a Cuban audience in July 1980—just a week after his return from Nicaragua—the Nicaraguan revolution was an experiment based on a multiclass alliance:

> In Nicaragua there is a new revolutionary project, in the sense that what they have in mind at this stage is national reconstruction with the cooperation of everybody. As they announced on July 19th, they also aim to put into effect an agrarian reform covering lands standing idle, they're also trying to stimulate private industrialists who have remained in the country and middle-level farmers—who were capitalist farmers—to contribute the utmost to national reconstruction. This in itself is a new experience in Latin America.

Although Castro was quick to point out that Nicaragua's multiclass alliance and mixed economy was *not* socialism, it was, said Castro, a genuine revolution:

> Now then, is there a revolution in Nicaragua or not? There is real revolution in Nicaragua. And does the existence of the bourgeoisie or private property mean that there's a bourgeois revolution there? No! There's no such thing as a bourgeois revolution in Nicaragua. In Nicaragua there is, in the first place, a people's revolution whose main strength is found in the workers, the peasants, the students and the middle strata of the population. The people's revolution conducts the process, so that the right thing be done at the right moment.[97]

In another radical break with his own past, Castro has also endorsed the role of the Catholic church in Nicaragua's revolution. In the same speech, Castro explained, "Nicaragua is a country where religious feelings go far deeper than they did in Cuba. Therefore, the support given to the revolutionary movement by these religious sectors is very important." But Castro's endorsement of the church obviously went far beyond the specific circumstances in Nicaragua. Castro's earlier dogmatic rejection of religion as an instrument of class repression has recently been replaced by a new appreciation for the strength and progressive potential of the Latin American church:

> If the revolution in Latin America were to take on an antireligious character it would split the people. In our country the Church was, generally speaking, the Church of the bourgeoisie, of the wealthy, of the landowners. This is not the case in many countries in Latin America where religion and the Church have deep roots among the people. The reactionary classes have tried to use religion against progress, against revolution, and in effect they have achieved their objective for quite a long time. However, times change, and imperialism, the oligarchy, and reaction are finding it more and more difficult to use the Church against revolution.[98]

Castro even seems to have adopted some of the new liberation theology. Despite the obvious incongruities with his own strong commitment to Marxist–Leninist orthodoxy, Castro even went so far as to describe Christianity as "the religion of the poor" and "religion of the slaves," saying:

> . . . there is no doubt that the revolutionary movement, the socialist movement, the Marxist–Leninist movement, would benefit a great deal from honest leaders of the Catholic Church and other religions returning to the Christian spirit of the Roman slaves. What's more, Christianity would benefit along with socialism and Communism.
>
> And some religious leaders in Nicaragua asked us why strategic alliance, why only strategic alliance; why not speak of unity between Marxist–Leninists and Christians.
>
> I don't know what the imperialists think about this. But I'm absolutely convinced the formula is highly explosive.[99]

Castro continues this tone of moderation and conciliation in discussing the international situation as well, telling the Sandinistas to keep open their political and economic ties to the West in general and the United States in particular. In a July 1979 speech, Castro strongly endorsed American overtures to the new Sandinista junta:

> Even the United States has stated that it's ready to send food and organize other kinds of help. We're glad to hear it. They said they

were going to start an airlift and send 300 tons of food a day. We think that's a very good idea. Martí said that heaven wanted tyrants to be wise only once . . . the Government of the United States has been wise at least on this one occasion, because it's much better in every sense, more productive, and makes for better relations among the peoples and for a climate of peace all over the world to send food instead of sending bombs and marines, like they did in Vietnam and so many other places.[100]

Castro then challenged the United States to see who could do more to help the Sandinistas:

. . . we're ready to enter an emulation campaign with the United States, an emulation campaign to see who can do the most for Nicaragua. We invite the United States, we invite all the countries of Latin America, we invite all the countries of Europe, the countries of the Third World, our sister socialist nations, to take part in an emulation campaign to help Nicaragua.[101]

A year later, in his anniversary speech in Nicaragua, Castro chided the United States for not doing more to help Nicaragua, saying:

We welcome the aid that the United States has given, but our only sincere regret is that it is so little, so little for the richest country in the world, so little for a country that spends $160 billion on defense.[102]

All this was a far cry from Castro's position in the mid-1960s, when any aid from the United States was thought to corrupt and enslave the recipient.

On his return from Nicaragua, Castro actually went so far as to take credit for Washington's new tolerance and generosity toward Nicaragua:

Well, the Sandinistas triumphed and the U.S. declared itself ready to cooperate, to be friendly. We were pleased about that because a policy of cooperation seems much more sensible than a policy of hostility. . . . . Of course the imperialists have already learned something from the Cuban revolution and their plans of aggression and blockade and their hostility against Cuba. They apparently don't want to take two doses of the same medicine.[103]

Washington was obviously not the only one that did not want another dose of that medicine. Castro's bitter experience of the twenty-year U.S. embargo obviously underlay his advice to the Sandinistas of conciliation toward the United States. Although the embargo did not succeed in its original intent, which was to destabilize the Castro Government, it has placed great hardships on the Cuban economy and severely limited its development possibilities. There are, of course, many other reasons why the Cuban economy has never been especially strong. But the fact remains that after twenty years of U.S. boycott and Soviet subsidy—currently at the level of $8 million a day, excluding armaments—the Cubans are as dependent today on sugar exports as they were before the revolution. The Cuban revolution has not brought economic independence for Cuba or even the ability to survive without Soviet support.

There is also evidence that Castro has been dissatisfied with the quality of aid he has received from the Soviets, particularly capital goods and technology, which are widely recognized as inferior to those available in the West. It is rumored that in early 1980, when Cuban advisers heard that the Nicaraguans had contracted to buy some 800 East German trucks, they counseled the Sandinistas to cancel the deal. Although the terms of the East German contract were favorable, the performance of their trucks was said to be poor and spare parts almost totally unavailable. The Cuban advice was to go for the more expensive, and more reliable, Western-made trucks.[104]

There is still another reason why Castro has urged the Sandinistas to maintain good relations with the West. Castro is painfully aware that the Sandinistas cannot realistically expect to get as much aid from the Soviets as Cuba does, and certainly not as much as their devastated economy requires. The issue of Soviet aid for the Third World has long been a sore point between Moscow and Havana. During the 1960s, the Cubans advised their Third World allies to look to the socialist bloc for development aid and military protection, promising them that "any people willing to do what the Cuban people have done" could count on the complete support of the socialist bloc. As the Cubans found out, however, this was not to be. Time and again—in Peru, in Allende's Chile—Moscow made it clear that it was not willing to take on the burdens of another Cuba.

As a result, the Cubans have changed their tune. Today they advise small states to look to the West for development aid and support. In October 1979, when Castro addressed the United Nations as the head of the Nonaligned Movement, he spoke of the need for a "New International Economic Order" in which the West, and not Moscow, would be the primary source of aid:

> On more than one occasion, it has been said that we were forced into underdevelopment by colonization and imperialist neo-colonization. Therefore, the task of helping us to emerge from underdevelopment is, first of all, a historic and moral obligation of those who benefited from the plunder of our health and the exploitation of our men and women for decades and for centuries.[105]

Castro is no doubt painfully aware of how much his advice to the Sandinistas differs from his own ideology and experience. On numerous occasions over the past three years, Castro has gone before the Cuban people to justify and explain why the Nicaraguans must follow a different, less radical, course than Cuba's:

> I'm telling you this so you'll have an idea of how situations change, how different they are in each country, and therefore we cannot be thinking of a strictly Cuban formula.[106]
>
> The Sandinistas are revolutionaries. We don't deny it, nobody denies it, they don't deny it. But they are not extremists, they are realists.
>
> And it is realists who make the best revolutions, the best and most profound revolutions. I predict that they will go far because they are taking their time, because they are not extremists, because they're taking things slowly. They know what to aim for at each stage of a political and revolutionary process and the means that correspond to these aims. I am sure of that.[107]

There is more to these explanations than just the need to mobilize popular Cuban support, tolerance, and understanding for their Nicaraguan brethren. Underlying Castro's words is a plea for his own people to understand the need for similar policies of pragmatism and restraint. Not only will the old Cuban way not work for Nicaragua, it will no longer work for Cuba. As Castro told his countrymen:

> We also met with the leaders of the Sandinista front, about 100 of them. . . . And I want to tell you that in those meetings I was very critical of our Revolution, because I believe that honesty is worth more than anything else in the world and we cannot be arrogant or vain or consider ourselves servants. I do believe that we are wise; but we are wise because we know how to recognize our shortcomings, because we know how to learn from our mistakes and we are wise because we are self-critical, because we are modest. And we sincerely believe that extraordinary experience can be drawn from our Revolution.
>
> If you were to ask us what we'd do if we were to start all over again, I would tell you that we'd do exactly the same thing and we would arrive at this point where we are today, exactly the same way, except that there's no doubt that we would do it better![108]

The Cuban influence today—whether in Nicaragua, Angola, or Havana—is being used to create a very different revolution from that of the *barbudos* of the Sierra Maestra.

Debunking the Cuban Myth: First Steps Toward a New American Policy

FOR two decades, American presidents have made policy in the hemisphere (and, to some extent, around the world) based on a set of faulty assumptions about Cuba and the threat it poses to American interests. These assumptions, which have achieved almost mythic status, have led each President to commit similar, costly mistakes: Kennedy's Bay of Pigs debacle, Johnson's invasion of the Dominican Republic, Nixon's covert backing of the Chilean coup, Ford's backing of UNITA and FNLA forces in Angola and *de facto* alliance with South Africa, the Carter resurrection of the Cold War in the Caribbean. In each instance, the United States allowed its faulty perception of Cuba to take precedence over the actual situation, overestimating the significance of the Cuban threat and overreacting in an attempt to contain the alleged threat. Each time, Washington's overreaction dealt a blow to the moderate forces at hand and severely strained America's alliances. With its White Paper on El Salvador and its covert support for anti-Sandinista

266

guerrillas in Honduras, the Reagan Administration has shown that it is part of this American tradition.

THE WHITE PAPER

In February 1981, less than a month after taking office, the Administration charged that the escalating violence in El Salvador, which claimed more than 10,000 lives in the previous year, was the result of Cuban-sponsored insurgency rather than genuine popular resistance to El Salvador's military-dominated regime. According to the White Paper, the Salvadoran civil war was:

> . . . a textbook case of indirect armed aggression by Communist power through Cuba. . . . a well-coordinated, covert effort to bring about the overthrow of El Salvador's established government and to impose in its place a Communist regime with no popular support.[1]

Drawing on documents allegedly seized from guerrillas by state security forces in El Salvador, the report charged that between August 1980 and January 1981 Cuba, the Soviet Union and other Communist states, including Vietnam, Ethiopia, and the Eastern bloc, covertly shipped some 200 tons of armaments to left-wing Salvadoran guerrillas via Cuba and Nicaragua. In addition, the report claimed that over the previous two years the Castro Government had provided Salvadoran guerrillas with essential political and strategic direction, military training, and sophisticated propaganda support intended to "widen and intensify the conflict" in El Salvador, "greatly increasing the suffering of the Salvadoran people and deceiving much of the world about the true nature of the revolution." The White Paper further asserted that El Salvador was not an isolated case of Communist subversion in the Third World. It called the events in El Salvador "strikingly familiar" and part of "a pattern we have seen before, to be specific in Angola and Ethiopia."[2]

The analogy to Angola was not lightly drawn. The Reagan Administration openly blamed its predecessors in the Nixon and Carter years for "losing" Angola and Ethiopia to the Soviets, for allowing what it called the "Vietnam syndrome"—domestic opposition and congressional resistance—to hamstring U.S. efforts to contain the Communist threat in Africa. The Reagan Administration was not going to make the same mistake. It immediately announced its commitment to "drawing the line" against "Communist aggression" in El Salvador and launched a major campaign for domestic and international support. The White Paper was to be the centerpiece of that campaign.

On February 18, armed with the report and some eighteen pounds of supposedly "incontrovertible evidence" —battle plans, letters, and reports said to have been seized from Salvadoran guerrillas— Secretary of State Alexander M. Haig, Jr., was sent to Capitol Hill to brief the Senate on the Communist threat in El Salvador and request major increases in military aid to the Salvadoran junta.

U.S. military assistance to El Salvador had been completely cut off in 1977 because of human rights abuses by the repressive Humberto Romero dictatorship. The Carter Administration restored some of it—$10 million worth—during the last week of its tenure after receiving preliminary reports of Communist arms shipments to the Salvadoran guerrillas. It was clear, however, that the Carter Administration had grave doubts about restoring the aid, and cautioned the José Napoleon Duarte regime that any additional support would be contingent on the implementation of essential social reforms and the junta's ability to end security force abuses.[3]

The Reagan Administration had no such qualms. Even before the White Paper was released, Secretary Haig had announced the Administration's intention to "delink" military aid from human rights issues.[4] At the Senate briefing on El Salvador, Haig proposed that U.S. military aid be tripled, requesting an additional $25 million in arms and equipment for the Duarte regime. Haig also proposed sending thirty-five military advisers to help train the Salvadoran military in weapons use and counterinsurgency tactics, a move that was to increase the number of U.S. advisers in El Salvador to fifty-four.

At the same time, the Administration made a strong bid for international support for its new hardline policies in El Salvador, sending two top-level diplomats—Assistant Secretary of State for European Affairs–designate Lawrence Eagleburger and Lieutenant

General Vernon Walters (ret.), a veteran of the 1960s anti-Communist campaigns in Latin America, most notably Brazil during the 1964 coup—to the major capitals of Western Europe and Latin America. Armed with the same eighteen pounds of "incontrovertible" evidence of subversion in El Salvador, Eagleburger and Walters sought to drum up allied support for increased U.S. military aid for the Duarte regime and to undercut the growing sympathy for the guerrillas expressed by many social democratic parties and Roman Catholic activists. The Reagan Administration did not want to repeat the U.S. experience in Nicaragua, in which a majority of Washington's Western European and Latin American allies sided with the Sandinistas against the U.S.-backed Somoza regime.

Once the lobbying efforts on Capitol Hill and abroad were well under way, the Administration turned its full attention to gathering domestic support. On February 23, the State Department issued a briefer but equally alarmist version of the White Paper to the American press. This was preceded and followed by a series of press conferences in which President Reagan, Secretary Haig, and a number of top-level White House and State Department advisers all expressed the Administration's intention to "get tough" with the Communists in El Salvador—and elsewhere, if necessary.

On February 22, 1981, the day before the public version of the report was released to the press, the chief White House counselor, Edwin Meese III, told television reporters that the Reagan Administration did "not rule out anything" in its campaign to halt Communist arms deliveries to El Salvador. According to Meese, the Carter Administration had failed "to take the necessary effective steps to stop the expansion of Communism through the world."

When asked what steps the Administration would take to halt Cuban arms shipments, Mr. Meese replied that it was considering a wide range of responses, including direct action against Cuba:

> The President has said many times that he would like potential or real adversaries to go to bed every night wondering what we will do the next day. I don't think we would rule out anything.[5]

A week later, Secretary Haig raised the stakes even further when he said the Administration was ready "to go to the source" if arms shipments to El Salvador did not cease.[6] Except for one brief moment during the Nixon Administration when Henry Kissinger raised the possibility of U.S. military action against Cuba, fighting words like these had not been heard in the hemisphere since the resolution of the 1962 missile crisis.

A Poor Showing

Despite what was obviously considerable foresight and planning, the White Paper was not well received either at home or abroad. Italy's President Sandro Petrini told the press that he had sent President Reagan several messages urging him not to turn El Salvador into another Vietnam. French and German leaders warned that a military solution was not the way to resolve the problems in El Salvador and urged the U.S. to stay out of the conflict. In an unprecedented show of unity Mexican, Venezuelan, Brazilian, and Argentine leaders all warned against U.S. military involvement in El Salvador and called for a negotiated settlement to the civil war.[7] Mexican President José Lopez Portillo refused to meet General Walters. In a speech the day after Walters's arrival in Mexico City, Lopez Portillo underlined his opposition to the White Paper by lauding the closeness of his government's relations with the Castro regime and describing Cuba as "the Latin American state most dear to Mexico."[8]

There were three reasons for these negative responses. First, very few of the allied leaders found the report's "incontrovertible evidence" of Communist subversion in El Salvador convincing. Outside official Washington, the conflict in El Salvador looked like a genuine civil war and not a Communist conspiracy. Second, most of the allied leaders had strong doubts about the representativeness of the Duarte junta. Although Washington described the junta as "centrist" and the only remaining hope for democracy in El Salvador, other sources, including the Salvadoran Catholic church and the human-rights group Amnesty International, blamed the government security forces, and not the Communist-backed left, for most of the killings.

Finally, almost all U.S. allies in Western Europe and Latin America—the Thatcher Government of Britain was the only one to back the White Paper—seemed to agree that Washington's plan to increase its military aid and advisory presence in El Salvador would only exacerbate the problems of the entire region. As Lopez Portillo warned:

> The crisis that has its temporary epicenter in the Salvadoran conflict has become a spiral that threatens to involve all the states in the area. For this reason it is necessary to avoid the internationalization of the crisis through a combined policy that has the objective of rigorously preserving the principles of self-determination and nonintervention.[9]

Allied resistance to the White Paper was dramatically underscored the following August when the governments of Mexico and France jointly recognized El Salvador's guerrilla opposition as a "representative political force" that had a right to take part in negotiations aimed at resolving the Salvadoran conflict.[10]

The White Paper did not fare much better in Washington. After an initially positive response, both the Senate and House began to raise serious questions about U.S. commitments to El Salvador. At a March 13, 1981, closed briefing of the Senate Appropriations Committee on increased aid for El Salvador, many senators—including some prominent Republicans—expressed strong doubts about the Administration's plans. According to the committee chairman, Senator Mark Hatfield (R–Ore.), "There was a consensus at the meeting on both sides of the table. . . . The Senate is not about to retrace those steps that led us into the longest war in Southeast Asia." Senator Patrick Leahy (D–Vt.) criticized the Administration for failing to take into account the effect of its El Salvador policy on U.S. relations with the rest of the region. "It was very clear that the Administration had not thought through the implications of its policy in El Salvador for the rest of Latin America." Senator Warren Rudman (R–NH) expressed his concern that the Administration had placed no limits on the amount of aid and the level of commitment it was willing to offer El Salvador:

> What I found disturbing was the lack of a bottom line. There don't seem to be any contingency plans and none of the witnesses would

271

assure us that additional military and economic aid would not be necessary.[11]

The issue of the Duarte regime's treatment of Salvadoran citizens moved to center stage six weeks later, when the House Committee on Foreign Affairs voted twenty-six to seven that any resumption of military aid to El Salvador would require assurances from President Reagan that the "indiscriminate torture and terrorism" by Salvadoran security forces had been brought under control. The White Paper's charges of Communist subversion notwithstanding, Congress was "relinking" the issues of U.S. military aid and human rights.[12]

In expressing their doubts about the Administration's El Salvador policy, the legislators seemed to represent the genuine concerns of their constituents. Although Reagan was apparently elected because of his "get tough" image, public-opinion polls suggested that many Americans did not think El Salvador was worth getting tough about. While Reagan and his advisers warned against the debilitating effects of the so-called Vietnam syndrome—allowing public fears to sap our resolve to combat communism—many Americans seemed more afraid of the effects of another overseas involvement like that of Vietnam. According to a Gallup Poll taken in March 1981, 63 percent of the American public feared that the Administration's policies in El Salvador would lead to "another Vietnam."[13]

On the El Salvador issue, the Reagan White House showed a rare lack of sensitivity to the tenor of public opinion. The Administration seemed unaware that its hard-line statements actually seemed to be increasing public fears. At a press conference on February 24, the day after the White Paper was released, President Reagan stated that he had "no intention" of involving the United States inextricably in the Salvadoran war:

I know that this is a great concern. I think it is part of the Vietnam syndrome, but we have no intention of that kind of involvement. But there's no question but that we are in support of the government there against those who are attempting a violent overthrow of the government.[14]

272

Whatever comfort the American public may have taken in those remarks was quickly destroyed that same afternoon when, at a Pentagon ceremony honoring a Vietnam-veteran winner of the Medal of Honor, the President strongly defended U.S. involvement in Vietnam. The Americans who fought in Vietnam, Reagan said, fought "as bravely and as well as any Americans in our history." The United States withdrew, he continued, "not because they'd been defeated, but because they'd been denied permission to win."[15] These remarks on Vietnam were the lead story that evening on all three networks' evening news.

Public opposition to U.S. involvement in El Salvador was expressed in a variety of forms. Congressional leaders reported receiving hundreds of letters protesting any further U.S. commitments to El Salvador. Marches and rallies were held in cities and on campuses across the country to protest the Administration's policies. The largest demonstration, a march on Washington in the beginning of May, attracted some 25,000 demonstrators.[16]

As early as mid-March, the Administration seemed to recognize that its campaign to rally support for the new hard line on El Salvador had failed. On March 12, a senior State Department official, Acting Assistant Secretary of State for Inter-American Affairs John Bushnell, called the press into his office and, speaking off the record, urged them to tone down their coverage of the El Salvador issue. "This story has been running five times as big as it is," he said, "and we figured if we talked to you about it you might not make this thing such a big deal." Bushnell claimed that the press had exaggerated the significance of El Salvador and deflected public attention from other more important policy issues. El Salvador, said Bushnell, was actually "a subset, and a fairly minor subset" of American foreign policy.[17]

This line was clearly a far cry from the White Paper, which described the situation in El Salvador as a critical test of America's resolve to resist the expansion of international communism. No matter what Mr. Bushnell had to say about the press's allegedly exaggerated coverage of El Salvador, his suggestion that the press now play down the issue was a clear admission of defeat. The White Paper had failed to rally the necessary support on Capitol Hill, in the capitals of Western Europe and Latin America, and in the homes of American voters. Any further discussion of it, the Administration realized, would just create more embarrassment.

Debunked

The White Paper was dealt a final blow the following June, when two leading newspapers, the *Wall Street Journal* and the *Washington Post,* published front-page articles challenging the report's veracity. The *Journal*'s critique was based on a three-hour interview with White Paper author Jon D. Glassman, who "freely" acknowledged "that there were 'mistakes' and 'guessing' by the Government's intelligence analysts who had translated and explained the guerrilla documents, which were written in Spanish with code names."[18] Among the "extrapolations" Glassman admitted and that were called "questionable" by *Journal* reporter Jonathan Kwitney were the issues of the amount of Communist arms delivered to the guerrillas, the degree of Cuban political direction for the guerrillas, and the promise of PLO aid.

Kwitney questioned Glassman on "the most widely publicized statistic in the White Paper . . . 'the covert delivery to El Salvador of nearly 200 tons of . . . arms, mostly through Cuba and Nicaragua.' " Glassman admitted that nowhere in the documents was there any mention of 200 tons of arms. That figure, said Glassman, came "from intelligence based on the air traffic, based on the truck traffic. In other words it doesn't come from the documents."

Kwitney also challenged Glassman on the White Paper's claim that PLO leader Yasir Arafat met Salvadoran guerrilla leaders in Nicaragua in July 1980 and gave "promises [of] military equipment, including arms and aircraft." According to Kwitney, "Mr. Glassman acknowledge[d] that the only mention of Mr. Arafat in the documents is an aside in parentheses, which says '. . . on the 22nd there was a meeting with Arafat.' "

Glassman also admitted that the White Paper's charge that the Cubans played a central political role in the Salvadoran civil war—specifically, that the Cubans required the Salvadoran guerrillas to form a united front "as a precondition for large-scale Cuban aid"—had no actual basis in the documents. According to Glassman, this charge was extrapolated "from the Nicaraguan situation where they [the Salvadorans] saw that the Cubans wanted that [a united front]."[19]

The *Washington Post*'s critique of the White Paper was based on an analysis of the captured documents themselves—Haig's "incontrovertible evidence." Even though the sources were different, the *Post*'s conclusions were strikingly similar to the *Journal*'s. According to *Post* reporter Robert Kaiser, the White Paper contained "factual errors, misleading statements and unresolved ambiguities that raise questions about the Administration's interpretation of participation by Communist countries in the Salvadoran civil war."[20] Kaiser's specific criticisms included the charge that certain important documents that did not support the Administration's conclusions had been omitted from the White Paper, and that the translations of other documents were incorrect or incomplete.

Like Kwitney, Kaiser took issue with the report's claim of large-scale Communist arms shipments to El Salvador. According to Kaiser, the documents did not support the Administration's contention that some 200 tons of Communist arms had actually been delivered to the Salvadoran guerrillas, only that arms had been requested:

> The contention of the white paper that the Salvadoran rebels were enjoying the benefits of "nearly 200 tons" of Communist-supplied arms and materiel is not supported anywhere in these documents and is implicitly refuted by many of them. In document after document there are reports of rebels short of arms, or looking for ways to buy arms, or exhorting their comrades to produce home-made arms, or plotting to kidnap Salvadorans thought to have access to private arsenals.

Kaiser went on to point out that the White Paper's dramatic description of an arms shopping trip to Eastern Europe by Salvadoran Communist leader Shafik Handal made it "sound like an idyllic journey on which the traveler always got what he wanted." In Kaiser's view, the documents tell a very different story. "According to [the documents] Handal was repeatedly frustrated in Moscow and reported his frustration candidly." As for the report's charge that the Soviets had transported the arms to El Salvador, Kaiser stated that none of the documents "indicates that the Soviets ever did provide the requested air transport."

These glaring factual discrepancies led Kaiser to question the most basic premise of the White Paper, "the heart of the White Paper . . . the accusation that 'over the past year the insurgency in El Salvador had been progressively transformed into a textbook case of indirect armed aggression by Communist powers through Cuba.'" The documents, said Kaiser, did not support that contention.[21]

The State Department immediately issued a rebuttal that defended the conclusions of the White Paper but refused to address the specific criticisms published in both the *Journal* and the *Post.* The Department also declined to give a briefing, refusing to discuss either the rebuttal or the White Paper with reporters. According to one State Department official, the rebuttal was released late in the day to lessen the chances that it would be carried on network evening news. The official said, "We didn't want to put El Salvador back on the front pages."[22]

THE REALITY AND THE MYTH

It is difficult to determine the extent of Cuba's actual involvement in the Salvadoran civil war. The Castro Government at first denied the White Paper's charges, calling them "absolute lies," and leveled countercharges of its own that the Reagan Administration was using the White Paper as a pretext for hostile actions against Cuba.[23] Since then top Cuban officials have admitted that Cuba sent some arms to El Salvador during the January 1981 "final offensive." But Havana continues to deny the central argument of the White Paper, that Cuba is responsible for the violence in El Salvador and directing the insurgency.

There is reason to be skeptical of the Cuban denials, considering the fact that Havana denied with equal vehemence its participation in the Angolan, Ethiopian, and Nicaraguan conflicts. Yet despite the importance of the issue, the fact remains that there is little evidence to support either the report's charges or Havana's denials.

The Reagan Administration was correct to suggest there are

precedents of Cuban overseas involvement that could shed some light on Cuban policies in El Salvador. The Administration was wrong, however, when it pointed to the Cuban involvements in Angola and Ethiopia as the appropriate precedents. In neither Angola nor Ethiopia were the Cubans involved in "a well-coordinated, covert effort to bring about the overthrow of [an] . . . established government and to impose in its place a Communist regime with no popular support," as the White Paper described Cuba's effort in El Salvador.[24] In Angola, the established government, the Portuguese colonial regime, withdrew *voluntarily,* and Cuban military support was used by the MPLA to help defeat alternative guerrilla groups vying for power and their foreign backers from South Africa and Zaire. In Ethiopia, the Communist coup came three years *before* Cuban troops were ever committed and Cuban military aid used to repulse the Somali invasion. Neither experience fits the White Paper's charges or the situation in El Salvador.

A more appropriate precedent would be Cuba's participation in the Nicaraguan civil war. In Nicaragua, covert Cuban military aid as well as Cuban political, military, and strategic advice helped bring about the overthrow of an established, if illegitimate, regime and helped impose in its place a socialist, if not traditionally Communist, regime.

The similarity between the paper's charges and the Nicaraguan situation, however, ends there. The Nicaraguan revolution was not the result of Cuban or any other externally sponsored insurgency. It was a grass-roots struggle against a repressive and increasingly illegitimate regime that received military aid, advice, and political support from many political actors, both Communist and non-Communist, including Mexico, Venezuela, Panama, Costa Rica, and Cuba. Furthermore, Cuban matériel commitments to Nicaragua were apparently nowhere near the level of extensive arms shipments described in the report. Although Cuban political and strategic advice, military training, and propaganda support were apparently quite important to the Sandinistas, by no stretch of the imagination could one believe that the Cubans were "calling the shots" in Nicaragua.

According the the May 1979 CIA report, the Cubans did not

make more of a commitment to the Nicaraguan civil war because they feared that greater involvement would lead to a confrontation with Washington and jeopardize their already delicate political relations in Latin America.[25] There is little reason and very little evidence to suggest that the Cubans would significantly alter their *modus operandi* in El Salvador. If anything, there were more reasons for *restraint* in El Salvador. Under Ronald Reagan, Washington had obviously become much more hostile to the Castro Government and the Salvadoran opposition, and thus much more likely to take any suggestion of Cuban involvement in El Salvador as cause for a confrontation. Cuba's Latin American allies would also be much less tolerant of a Cuban involvement in El Salvador. Unlike the Nicaraguan civil war, in which every major liberal regime supported the Sandinistas, the Salvadoran civil war split the region's ranks, with Mexico and Panama unofficially backing the opposition and Costa Rica and Venezuela strongly backing the junta.[26]

Finally, the Salvadoran opposition was an unlikely candidate for Cuban support. In Nicaragua, Havana was very cautious about extending aid to the Sandinistas, demanding that they first overcome internal political problems, form a united front with members of the Nicaraguan business and landowning communities, and build a broad base of popular support. The Salvadoran opposition in the fall and winter of 1980—the months when Havana was alleged to have made huge arms shipments to El Salvador—was in much more political disarray and was much less assured of solid popular support than were the Sandinistas during their final offensive. If the Cubans were following the pattern established in Nicaragua, they would have counseled the Salvadoran guerrillas to hold back until they were better organized and assured of greater popular support before opening their final offensive. Cuban arms would have been withheld until Havana had determined that the time was right for the Salvadoran revolution.

In recent months, Cuban officials have admitted sending some arms to the Salvadoran guerrillas during the ill-fated 1980 "final offensive." Extraordinary circumstances apparently forced Havana to overcome its newly acquired caution. The election of Reagan was obviously a great source of concern for Castro, who saw it as the beginning of a new American backlash in the hemisphere.[27] The Cubans were likely persuaded by the Salvadoran opposition's arguments that the December final offensive really was their last chance for victory before the Reagan Administration took over and began major arms deliveries to the Salvadoran junta.[28]

Yet—even though Havana did send the Salvadoran guerrillas some military aid—logic, the available evidence, and the Nicaraguan precedent still suggest that the White Paper was wrong in its charge that the Salvadoran civil war was "a textbook case of indirect armed aggression by Communist powers through Cuba." Cuba could no more create the conditions for civil strife in El Salvador than it could guarantee the Salvadoran opposition victory in the final offensive. Havana's admissions have done nothing to restore domestic or international support for the White Paper or for Washington's policy in El Salvador.

How Could They Be So Wrong?

It was clear from the start that for the Reagan Administration the significance of El Salvador far exceeded the country's economic and strategic importance for the United States. The paper and the hard-line policies that went with it were intended to symbolize the Administration's new resolve in foreign policy—they were a test of its declared intention to "hold the line" against international Communist subversion. The White Paper was also intended to test our allies' willingness to back the new American hard line. Finally, the El Salvador policy was to be a test of the American people's will to overcome the "Vietnam syndrome" and restore America's international prestige.

The Administration staked an enormous amount of prestige on the El Salvador White Paper and lost. Obviously, they would never have wagered so much if they had expected to lose. How could the Administration have been so wrong?

In issuing the report, the Reagan Administration was evidently working under a set of faulty assumptions that severely distorted its perception of the situation in El Salvador and the attitudes of our allies and the American public. The Administration's first mistake was to believe that the Cubans were primarily responsible for the violence in El Salvador. Wedded to this assumption were the additional faulty assumptions that conditions in El Salvador were *not* in need of drastic and complete change, and that the Cubans had the ability and the desire to wreak havoc in El Salvador.

The Administration's next major mistake was to resurrect the domino theory, to suggest that if the Cuban subversion were not contained in El Salvador it would spill over into neighboring countries and ultimately threaten United States security. As candidate Reagan warned during the campaign, "We are the last domino."[29]

The Administration's final mistake was to believe that our allies and the American public shared its view of the Cuban threat.

These faulty assumptions were not new to the Reagan Administration. At their base lie a series of time-honored myths about Cuba and the threat it poses to the United States. What are the myths that have played such an important and destructive role in American policy making over the last two decades?

Myth #1: The Cubans Are Soviet Pawns

Of all the myths about Cuba, this one is the most prevalent. It is also the most difficult to explode because it is so basic to our perception of Cuba and because it is difficult to disprove methodologically. Without access to diplomatic cables and meetings between Moscow and Havana, it is hard to say where critical decisions are made and by whom. Furthermore, the logic of the "Cubans as pawns" argument is compelling. The Cubans depend economically and militarily on the Soviets for their survival, and the Cubans are staunch Soviet supporters in the international arena.

However, it must also be recognized that on numerous occasions in the past the Castro Government has acted independently of its Soviet backers, even in opposition to them: Cuba's public split with the Soviets in 1967 over the issue of armed struggle in Latin America is only the most dramatic example of numerous Cuban–Soviet disagreements over the past two decades of alliance.

An analogous relationship that should be instructive is the U.S.–Israeli alliance. Without American military support, Israel would not survive—its geopolitical position is even more precarious than Cuba's. Israel also has traditionally been a strong American supporter in the international arena. Yet when the Communist bloc accuses Israel—as it does regularly—of being a pawn of Western or specifically U.S. imperialism, the argument is rejected out of hand in the United States. The U.S. knows it has influence over the Israelis, but recent events in the Middle East have shown vividly that it is by no means total. The charge that Cuba is a pawn of the Soviet Union should be treated with similar skepticism.

Myth #2: The Cubans Are Everywhere

According to this myth, Cuban agents are fomenting revolution all over the world. Anywhere the interests of the United States or its allies are in trouble, the Cubans are there. During the 1960s, there were almost daily reports of Cuba's subversive activities in Latin America. Havana was blamed for labor unrest in Argentina, student strikes in Colombia, nationalist riots in Panama, drug trafficking in Puerto Rico, and a civil war in the Dominican Republic. The Cubans were even said to have trained the Black Panthers.[30]

With time, each of these charges has been proved either vastly exaggerated or completely untrue. Although Castro's revolution did inspire many Latin American radicals of the 1960s, Cuba's actual matériel and personnel commitments to the region were comparatively small. Throughout the 1960s, there were never more than a few hundred Cubans fighting in all of Latin America.

Yet the myth of Cuba's omnipresence still prevails. The Reagan Administration blames Havana for the current civil strife in El Salvador as well as for the developing crises in Guatemala and Honduras. Since 1981 Cubans have allegedly been sighted trying to land on Salvadoran beaches in boats from Nicaragua, and a contingent of 500 to 600 Cuban commandos was said to be responsible for the destruction of the strategic Punta del Oro bridge in eastern El Salvador.[31] Cubans are also said to have been sighted fighting alongside Ethiopian troops in Eritrea, marching alongside Libyan troops in Chad, invading Kampuchea with the Vietnamese, and even keeping the Moscow-imposed peace in Afghanistan. With time, most of these reports have proved groundless. Even so, each new report of a Cuban presence in another of the world's hot spots is believed. But then, why not? If the Cubans could be anywhere from the Dominican Republic to Bogotá to the Canal Zone in the 1960s, then why not everywhere from El Salvador to Eritrea to Afghanistan today?

There are several reasons why this myth has been allowed to persist. First, it is a logical extension of another American myth: that of the success of the "international Communist conspiracy" in Cuba. While it is a matter of record that the Communist International was in no way responsible for the Castro revolution (the PSP, the Comintern party in Cuba, actually opposed Castro for most of the revolution), most Americans still believe the Cuban revolution to be the result of some sophisticated international Communist plot. It is just one logical step from there to the next allegation: With Soviet blessings and material support, Havana is continuing Moscow's work and subverting other Third World states.

A second reason for the myth's persistence is that it serves the interests of many right-wing governments in the hemisphere and around the world. Identifying the opposition as Cuban-led, armed, or even inspired is a solid justification for brutally repressive measures. It is also a proved method to receive more military aid from the United States. What makes Chile's authoritarian Pinochet regime "friendly" *other* than its hostility to "international Communism"? The current Magaña regime in El Salvador, like many others before it, is following that route.

Washington is also in part directly responsible for the myth's persistence. As we have seen, throughout the 1960s, misinformation about Cuba's activities in the hemisphere was regularly disseminated by U.S. intelligence agencies and other official organs of the U.S. Government. This tradition continues today, as evidenced by the White Paper. Whether the government has deliberately lied about Cuba's activities or has been simply misinformed is hard to determine. To be fair, it must be recognized that intelligence-gathering is always a difficult business. Even under the best conditions, such as a peaceful demonstration in Washington, official estimates of the number of participants often vary by as much as 50 percent. It should not be too surprising when, in one year, the State Department's figures for the number of Cuban troops in Ethiopia fluctuate between 12,000 and 18,000. Although such errors are understandable, they are also dangerous, particularly when allegations of a Cuban presence become the justification for Washington's commitment of military aid, as in El Salvador.

Sensationalism is also well rewarded when the subject is the Cubans. Most Third World leaders know that they are assured of wide press coverage and Washington's attention if they claim their opposition is somehow involved with the Cubans. Some reporters say they are willing to listen to these claims, even when evidence is scarce, because they know that their editors are more likely to run a story with a Cuban-threat angle. CIA and State Department officials know they are much more likely to extract aid from Congress if they can produce reports of Cuban subversion. Consequently, it is not surprising that charges of Cuban subversion are common and frequently poorly documented.

Havana must also take a good deal of responsibility for the myth. Cuban propaganda claims like Che Guevara's late-1960s symbolic pledge to create "many Vietnams" certainly reinforced the impression that the Cubans were committed to fomenting revolution wherever they could. The reality of Cuba's globe-spanning diplomacy is also the stuff of which myths are easily spun. Even during the 1960s, when Havana had neither the arms nor the troops to pursue an international foreign policy, Cuban internationalists turned up regularly in remarkably far-flung places. The fact that there were rarely more than a few hundred Cubans in any of these places (and usually many fewer) did not diminish the impression of a worldwide Cuban presence. Today, with some 35,000 Cuban troops stationed in Africa and another 15,000 Cuban advisers around the world, there is more objective evidence for the myth than ever before.

Myth #3: The Cubans Are Always Subversive

According to this myth, a Cuban presence in any state leads inevitably to civil strife, the overthrow of legitimate regimes, and their replacement by Communist puppets. Even the most humane Cuban advisory mission is believed to be underlain with nefarious and subversive intentions. Cuban literacy teachers in Nicaragua are really indoctrinating Nicaraguan children in Communist propaganda. Cuban construction workers in Grenada are building an airport not, as they claim, to enhance tourism, but to give Moscow a new stage on the Latin American mainland.

The reality is usually much more mundane. Even during the 1960s, when Havana talked a great game of international revolution, preaching the gospel of guerrilla warfare according to Guevara and Debray, most of Havana's overseas missions were committed to normal diplomatic activities. Cuban military missions in Congo-Brazzaville and Guinea devoted most of their energies to training presidential guards and people's militias for the Massemba-Debat and Sékou Touré regimes. These African leaders were neither traditional Marxist–Leninists nor Moscow's puppets. Havana's presence in these states was intended not to radicalize or subvert these regimes but to stabilize their positions.

Today, it continues to be true that most of Havana's overseas missions are committed to traditional diplomatic and foreign aid programs. Even in Ethiopia and Angola, which together have over 30,000 Cuban troops, the role of these troops is to protect governments, not subvert them. Although Washington may not like these regimes, it must acknowledge that the regimes Havana is supporting are recognized as legitimate by the United Nations, the Organization of African Unity, and most U.S. allies. When the Reagan Administration lobbies Congress to reinstate military aid to Jonas Savimbi's UNITA guerrillas in Angola, it is Washington that is committed to subverting a legitimate regime, not Havana.

Today at least, a Cuban presence seems to be a stabilizing rather than a radicalizing force. In Nicaragua and Angola, the two states in which Havana apparently has the most influence, Cuban advisers have counseled moderation and caution both at home and abroad. Once again, when Washington gives aid to Nicaraguan exiles seeking to overthrow the Sandinista Government, it is Washington that is taking subversive actions against a legitimate government—primarily because of its alleged relationship with Cuba.[32] Havana learned a long time ago that revolutions cannot be exported. It is time that Washington learned that lesson, too.

Myth #4: The Cubans Always Win

According to this myth, Cuba is a formidable enemy, able to use subversion as well as more traditional military means to impose its will and its chosen regimes on the countries of the Third World. The revolutions in Angola, Ethiopia, and Nicaragua are thought to be prime examples of Cuba's near invincibility. A natural corrollary is the belief that Cuba's invincibility can be contained only through the use of the most extreme, hard-line military policies.

The reality could not be farther from the myth. Throughout the 1960s, Havana's attempts to export revolution met one crushing defeat after the next. Cuba did not have much more success in the 1970s. The only successful revolutions that Havana thus far has managed to support were in Angola and Nicaragua. Two revolutions in twenty-two years is not a very impressive record.

What, then, is the source of the myth of Cuba's invincibility? One source is Cuba's remarkable ability to resist U.S. invasion, economic embargo, and twenty-two years of diplomatic isolation. The Castro Government's continued survival in the face of Washington's unremitting hostility is a feat that has yet to be matched in the hemisphere. Arbenz in Guatemala, Goulart in Brazil, Allende in Chile all failed, while Castro managed not only to survive but actually endure.

The primary source for the myth is the United States's inability to see the true causes of the revolutions in Angola, Nicaragua, and El Salvador. Because we believe the Cubans to be responsible for the upheavals in these countries, we also give them credit for the victories. The reality, however, is that the force behind these three rebellions was domestic circumstances: long histories of poverty, inequality, and government repression. Although Havana did help to speed the process by sending arms or troops or advisers, Havana did not create the revolutions or win them. The Angolan and Nicaraguan people staged and won their own revolutions.

Even in Angola, where Cuban troops played an essential role in turning back invading forces from South Africa, the MPLA victory did not result solely from Cuba's absolute military might. The South Africans were turned back only after their invasion had been condemned internationally, and Washington had withdrawn its covert support. The MPLA victory was forged as much in the arenas of the United Nations, the OAU, and the United States Senate as on the battlefields of southern Angola. Much the same can be said about the Sandinista victory in Nicaragua, which came after Somoza had lost all popular support and had completely discredited himself in most major capitals of Latin American and Western Europe.

If the Cubans give the impression of invincibility, it is due in large part to their newly acquired ability to choose the right side in Third World conflicts. This invincibility can be contained only through the use of the most brutal and repressive military tactics and at the cost of America's international reputation as a defender of democracy and human rights.

Myth #5: The Cubans Are International Outlaws

Those who believe this myth hold Cuba as beyond the diplomatic pale, much like Qadaffi's Libya or Uganda under Idi Amin. It is a country that is unresponsive to diplomatic convention or international law, one that can be dealt with only by force, not reason. This sort of insularity may have seemed true of Cuba during the mid to late 1960s, when U.S. hostilities forced the Castro Government into almost complete isolation in the hemisphere. Under repeated attack from the United States, forcibly excluded from the OAS, and unsure of its alliance with the Soviet Union (particularly after Khrushchev's betrayal during the missile crisis), it is not surprising that Havana was given to desperate words and defiant acts.

Yet even during the worst days of the 1960s, Havana tried to create its own international constituency and its own diplomatic channels. Cuban leaders made regular diplomatic tours of Africa and the socialist bloc, concentrating on organizing other Third World and Communist states that shared Havana's distrust of the superpowers. Cuban leaders faithfully attended the few international conferences to which they were welcome—meetings of the Afro Asian Peoples' Solidarity Organization and the Movement of Nonaligned Nations. When Havana felt its interests to be out of step with existing organizations, the Cubans tried to create their own international organizations, such as the Tricontinental Congress.

As Cuba's diplomatic standing has improved over the past decade, the Castro Government has grown increasingly sensitive to international opinion and respectful of traditional international organizations. Havana has been passionately committed to its recent role as leader of the Nonaligned Movement. At the 1979 Havana Conference, Castro struggled valiantly to smooth over Cuba's differences with its colleagues, diplomatically avoiding inevitable areas of conflict like Cuba's thesis of "natural alliance." The Cubans are regular and vocal participants in the United Nations. In addition, the Cubans are painfully sensitive to the opinions of their hemispheric neighbors and conscious of the fragility of their newly acquired diplomatic acceptance. According to U.S. intelligence experts, a major reason for Havana's restraint in Nicaragua was its fear of jeopardizing diplomatic relations in the hemisphere. Cuba's restraint in the Salvadoran conflict can be explained similarly.

Washington fails to see this sensitivity for two reasons. First, Washington's mythical perception of Cuba as international terrorist and outlaw precludes such an understanding. Moreover, Washington, particularly under Reagan, does not think that Havana exercised any restraint in Nicaragua or El Salvador, and blames the Cubans for both revolutions. Thus it has no need to acknowledge the diplomatic sensibilities that are the source of that restraint. At the same time, Washington's own experience with Havana regularly confirms the impression of Cuba as a country beyond rational persuasion. The legacy of hostility and distrust is so strong in both Washington and Havana that it has been impossible to maintain even the most basic lines of communication. Whenever Cuba and the United States talk, the conversation falls on deaf ears.

Over the past seven years—once during the Ford Administration and then again in the early Carter years—Washington and Havana did make some tentative overtures toward rapprochement. These were abandoned when Cuba sent troops to Angola and Ethiopia. Both times Washington charged the Cubans with betraying the United States's trust by sending troops overseas. Both times the Cubans denied that such trust existed. Havana had never agreed not to send troops to Africa. There was so much distrust that neither side was willing to discuss this area of conflict, preferring to abandon the talks and returning immediately to their previous stance of mutual hostility.

This shared misperception and mutual hostility escalated significantly under the Reagan Administration. Even before his election, Ronald Reagan set the stage when he spoke of the possible strategy of blockading Cuba to get the Soviets out of Afghanistan. Since taking office, Reagan and his advisers regularly have threatened Cuba with blockade, and even possible military retaliation. The Cubans have reacted to these threats in much the same way as they reacted during the 1960s—with defiance and desperation. In a September 1981 speech, Castro described Reagan as a "fascist. . . . smeared with the blood of . . . thousands of murdered Salvadorans."[33] A few weeks later, Havana announced that it had placed its militia on a war alert in anticipation of an American attack.

Myth #6: The Cubans Are Inevitably Anti-United States

According to this myth, Cuba's hostility toward the United States is believed to be Havana's driving force. Whether Havana is shipping troops to Angola, arms to El Salvador, or advisers to Nicaragua, Havana can be counted on also to transfer its hostility to the United States.

Cuba's hostility to the United States should not be minimized; it is real and strong. It is based on history dating back at least to José Martí and the 1898 revolution against Spain. The Castro Government has ample reasons to fear and hate the United States: the embargo, the Bay of Pigs invasion, two decades of dirty tricks, and innumerable attempts to assassinate Castro. Havana also blames the United States for its role in Vietnam and its support for Somoza and Pinochet. Much like the Reagan Administration, the Castro Government sees "patterns" in American foreign policy.

There is little doubt that Havana allows this hostility to influence its choice of allies and policies. It was Cuba's desire to contain the American threat that underlay its strong showings in Angola and Nicaragua: Undoubtedly it contributes to its hostility to the Magaña Government in El Salvador. To Havana, being a "puppet of American imperialism" is as grievous a sin as being a "Soviet pawn" is to Washington.

Yet despite their hostility to the United States, the Cubans have not advised their Third World allies to follow that route. The Cubans have urged the Sandinistas to maintain their economic and political ties with the West in general and the United States in particular. This is not to say that Havana has suddenly become pro-Washington. It has not. Rather, Cuba's repeated economic failures and heavy dependence on the Soviet Union have made Havana realistic about the alternatives open to small states. These states, Havana is saying, cannot afford the luxury of opposing the United States.

Myth #7: Anyone Who Is Cuba's Enemy Is Our Friend

This is a myth that, over the years, has matched Washington with the strangest and most morally repugnant political bedfellows: the Somozas of Nicaragua, Trujillo of the Dominican Republic, Pinochet of Chile, and South Africa's apartheid regime. Alliances with the despots, simply because they too abhor the Cubans, contradict America's moral commitment to democracy and human rights and endanger our world standing.

Even the *de facto* alliance with the South Africans in Angola did immeasurable damage to Washington's relations with the rest of black Africa, which considered South Africa's racism much more dangerous than Moscow's or Havana's territorial ambitions. As it turned out, despite our worst fears, an MPLA victory in Angola has not been that costly to the United States. Gulf Oil rigs produce even more millions of barrels per day now than they did under the Portuguese, and Angola has not become a military base for Moscow. The high cost of saving diplomatic face in Washington is continued opposition to Luanda and *de facto* alliance with Pretoria, an alliance no African state can accept.

Myth #8: Anyone Who Is Cuba's Friend Is Our Enemy

This myth, the converse of the previous one, makes about as much sense. Why should Washington allow Havana to define who should be its friends or enemies and thus severely limit potential areas of influence? Change is a reality and a necessity in Central America today. The United States has a choice: It can either back change and progress or once again dig in its heels and resist for fear that change will lead to the creation of another Cuba. If the United States supports change and hopes to influence it in a positive, democratic, and pro-West direction, then ties to states like Nicaragua or Grenada, or even a left-wing El Salvador, must be maintained. In a head-to-head competition for influence with any of these states, there is little doubt that America's wealth and freedom can give the Cubans at least a run for their money. If Washington does not want Nicaragua, El Salvador, Honduras, or Guatemala to become other Cubas, then those lines of communication must be safeguarded, even if these states insist on communicating with Cuba as well.

Myth #9: The Cubans Never Change

This is the myth of the bad seed, the belief that ever since Cuba went Communist and embraced the Soviet bloc, it was irrevocably lost to all Western values, diplomatic influence, and positive change. There is much in this myth that recalls the old myth of Communist totalitarianism: Soviet Russia or Red China would never become less hostile or more responsible because any change would inevitably lead to the immediate collapse of their regimes.

Washington has jettisoned that myth about Russia and China, seeking rapprochement with both and recognizing over the years the increasing number of areas for negotiation and accommodation. But it has not abandoned the myth when it comes to Cuba. It refuses to see that the years have mellowed the Cuban *barbudos,* made them more sophisticated politically, and more sensitive to diplomatic and political realities. These changes are clearest when the Cubans are giving their advice to the Nicaraguans and Angolans, warning them not to repeat Cuba's mistakes.

The United States must realize that these changes have taken place. Cuba today does not resemble the Cuba of the missile crisis or the Tricontinental Congress any more than the United States is the same country that brought us the Bay of Pigs or the Vietnam

War—one hopes. Each side must recognize the growth, maturity, and change of the other.

Myth #10: Everyone Agrees with Our View of the Cubans

This grand myth holds that all our allies share the same myths about Cuba. All see Cuba as a terrorist and an international pariah coldly subverting Third World regimes wherever it can, and refusing to discuss anything except in the language of force. There has never been such unanimity about Cuba, not even in the heyday of the OAS sanctions during the mid-1960s. It took the United States four years to get those sanctions passed by the OAS, with untold political pressures, and millions of dollars funneled into the Alliance for Progress and security assistance programs. Even then, Mexico, one of Washington's closest allies, still refused to break relations with Cuba.

Today, there is much less agreement about Cuba. Over the past decade, Cuba has steadily improved its diplomatic position and today has correct, if not cordial, relations, with most Latin American and Western European nations. No better example of how much the allies diverge from Washington's mythical perception of the Cuban threat is the skepticism with which the Reagan Administration's White Paper on El Salvador was greeted in the major capitals of Latin America and Europe.[34]

This is not to suggest that Cuba's diplomatic relations are anywhere near perfect. Particularly since the 1980 exodus of over 100,000 refugees, Havana has been on increasingly shaky ground in the hemisphere. The Reagan Administration's repeated charges of Cuban subversion in El Salvador and throughout Central and South America have strained Cuba's hemispheric relations even further. In March 1981, Colombia suspended relations over Havana's alleged training of M-19 guerrillas, the same ones who held fifteen diplomats hostage in Bogotá the previous year. Two months later, Costa Rica cut consular ties with Havana and expelled several Cubans from San José on charges of arms smuggling.[35]

Yet Washington's failure to provide conclusive proof of Cuban subversion, coupled with Latin America's natural resentment of

U.S. strong-arm tactics, has kept most Latin American leaders from verbalizing their fears. None of our allies is pleased by the resurrection of Cuban internationalism in Africa or the allegations of a deeper Cuban involvement in Central America. But most have been willing to give Havana the benefit of the doubt. Cuba is seen as a normal diplomatic actor who makes mistakes, offends its allies, and at times even betrays them, but ultimately as a political actor who must be dealt with carefully and judiciously.

WHITE PAPER REDUX

In October, the Reagan Administration issued a second, more extensive report on alleged Cuban subversion in the hemisphere. This classified report charged Havana with promoting terrorism and subversion in almost every country in Central and Latin America. According to the report:

> Cuba's immediate goals are to exploit and control the revolution in Nicaragua and to induce the violent overthrow of the governments of El Salvador and Guatemala. At the same time, Cuba is working to sustain terrorism in other countries and to fan political instability in the hemisphere.

The report specifically charged the Castro Government with:

> Bringing prospective insurgents secretly to Cuba for training in urban and rural guerrilla operations. . . .
>
> Supplying weapons, principally of non-Soviet manufacture, infiltrated by clandestine surface and air routes through third countries. . . .
>
> Promoting political and military contacts with terrorist organizations and sympathetic states, including Vietnam, Libya and Palestinian groups. . . .
>
> Fabricating and disseminating propaganda to discredit targeted governments, non-Communist groups and the United States.[36]

Like the earlier White Paper on El Salvador, the report on Cuban subversion in the hemisphere was sent to members of the Senate Foreign Relations Committee and to American ambassadors in Latin America, Europe, and Japan with instructions to brief "appropriate political and governmental officials" about the growing Cuban threat. This time, however, the Administration issued no documentary evidence to support the new charges of Cuban subversion. And the State Department specifically told its ambassadors not to circulate copies of the report and to use it only for briefing purposes. Such precautions may have saved the Administration the embarrassment of being discredited in public, but they did little to enhance the report's credibility.

There is no doubt that the Castro regime strongly opposes the right-wing regimes currently ruling in El Salvador, Guatemala, Chile, and Argentina. And it is true that over the past two and a half years Havana has shown renewed interest in the strategy of armed struggle. On July 26, 1980, in his annual speech commemorating the attack on the Moncada Barracks, Castro declared that:

> The experiences of Guatemala, El Salvador, Chile and Bolivia teach us that there is no other way than revolutionary armed struggle.[37]

Nevertheless, Cuba is still severely constrained—both materially and diplomatically—in terms of the material support it can give to any of these revolutionary struggles. Cuba still has no arms industry; it still suffers from a severe balance of payments problems, is still seeking to improve its diplomatic and economic relations both in the hemisphere and out, and still fears the possibility of a direct confrontation with the United States. All the reasons that kept the Castro Government from getting seriously involved in the Nicaraguan civil war still seem to hold today.

If, however, the Reagan Administration is right when it asserts that these constraints never applied, that:

> since 1978 Cuba has markedly intensified covert efforts to stimulate armed violence and destabilize its neighbors, abandoning its earlier policy of fostering state-to-state relations. . . .[38]

then the burden is on the Administration to prove that fact with solid evidence that can stand up to public scrutiny. Like last March's disastrous press conference with an alleged Nicaraguan guerrilla, every attempt thus far by the Administration to produce conclusive evidence of Cuban subversion in Central America has backfired.

The Administration must also be careful not to let the fact of renewed Cuban interest and involvement in the hemisphere obscure the real, internal causes for the current instability in the hemisphere and the pressing need for change.

An Olive Branch and a Gaffe

In late March 1982, senior Cuban officials began to express publicly a strong interest in improving relations with the Reagan Administration and to finding a solution to the conflict in El Salvador based on negotiations and the exercise of "mutual restraint."[39]

Cuban diplomats—usually difficult to reach for comment—suddenly became available for candid interviews on several previously sensitive subjects, including the nature of Cuba's involvement in El Salvador. After more than a year of repeated and, at times, vehement denials, the Castro Government now admitted sending arms to the Salvadoran guerrillas. Their officials insisted, however, that direct Cuban aid to the guerrillas had stopped almost fourteen months before, soon after the failure of the January 1981 final offensive, and that in recent months Cuba had ceased to transport arms from third countries. Cuba, they said, was now exercising self-restraint in Central America and was ready to play a "positive role" in resolving disputes and reaching a negotiated settlement of the problems in El Salvador.

Cuban diplomats also disclosed that for the last several months top Cuban and American officials had been meeting in secret to work out some compromise agreement. But after a March meeting in Havana with U.S. Ambassador-at-Large Vernon A. Walters, the talks were at a standstill. Havana's decision to go public was clearly an attempt by the Castro regime to drum up popular support in the United States for a revival of the negotiation process.

There were several signs that the Cubans sincerely wanted negotiations. The very fact that they were willing to admit to sending arms to El Salvador—a dangerous move in terms of their diplomatic standing in the hemisphere—was obviously designed to give the Cubans bargaining chips for the negotiations. This was also the first time in twenty years that Cuba had publicly expressed its will-

ingness to negotiate with the United States without any preconditions, such as first normalizing relations or lifting the economic
embargo.

To sweeten the pot, Cuban officials tried to distance themselves
from their Soviet allies, expressing public disapproval for a variety
of Soviet policies considered important to the United States. In
an early April interview in Havana, with a group of visiting American foreign policy experts, one highly placed Cuban official said
that his government was "worried" about the situation in Afghanistan and was using its position as chairman of the Nonaligned Movement to negotiate a settlement that would lead to a Soviet withdrawal. The same official also described the situation in Poland
as a "socialist tragedy," but added that the current state of martial
law was far preferable to either civil war or Soviet intervention.

Inevitably, there was the question of why the Cubans, after such
a long period of intransigence and hostility, were so interested in
an accommodation with the United States. The explanation appears
to be an interesting mixture of fear that the Salvadoran conflict
could escalate into an open confrontation between Cuba and the
United States and optimism that the concurrent political situation
in El Salvador had become increasingly problematic for the Reagan
Administration, particularly since the right-wing came out ahead
in the March elections.

Cuba made no bones about the fact that it was seriously concerned
about the Reagan Administration's repeated threats to "go to the
source" of the subversion. When one Cuban diplomat in New York
was asked how he could possibly think that the United States would
attack Cuba, he replied, "Did most Americans expect their government to launch the Bay of Pigs invasion? We have not forgotten
that episode. Why have you?" When reminded that the United
States was restrained from attacking Cuba by the accord that grew
out of the 1962 missile crisis, the diplomat then expressed concern
that even if the agreement continued to be upheld, the Reagan
Administration might vent its frustration against Nicaragua or El
Salvador. Recent reports in the U.S. press of a multi-million CIA
covert training program for anti-Sandinista guerrillas in Honduras

have been taken seriously in Havana as well as Managua—particularly since fighting has escalated along the Nicaraguan–Honduran border.[40]

The Cubans also expressed fears that they were being drawn into a widening conflict in Central America that might even lead to a direct confrontation between the United States and the Soviet Union. Although they insisted that their Soviet allies had no designs on Central America, Cuban officials also warned that sometimes such events were difficult to control. A confrontation, they said, had to be avoided.

The Cubans also admitted that they have strong doubts about the prospects for socialism in the region, and, indeed, in all of Latin America. Conditions, the Cubans now insist, are not ideal for socialist revolution. The Cubans do, however, expect that left-leaning and strongly nationalist governments will come to power in the region—preferably through political means, but, if necessary, through armed struggle. But these new governments, much like the Sandinistas, will have to maintain strong economic and political ties with the West if they wish to resolve their development problems. Cuban officials say that they do not expect the United States to be happy with any of these regimes, but they insist that such change is a reality to which the United States will have to adapt at some point soon.

Not all of Havana's reasoning has been pessimistic or accommodating. Castro has not become an agrarian reformist or a social democrat. Although the Cubans admit that the time is not right for the Central American revolution, they are not predicting the triumph of capitalism or abandoning their commitment to revolution. Cuban officials say they believe that time is on their side, but for now and for a good many years to come, negotiation and limited progress is the best they can hope for in Central America.

The final reason the Castro Government expressed a willingness to negotiate in 1982 was that it believed that the Reagan Administration was in a weakened position. The Salvadoran elections, the Cubans insisted, resulted in more than a symbolic defeat for the guerrillas in terms of the large voter turnout. The outcome was also a

296

grave setback for the Reagan Administration. The Cubans expected that the White House would soon find that an alliance with El Salvador's new right-wing ruling coalition was too great a political liability, both with the Congress and with the American public, to maintain. The Administration would soon find that it needed a way out of El Salvador and would even be willing to sit down and negotiate with the Cubans to get it.

Washington did not, however, see it that way. Administration officials refused to discuss the Cuban overtures. The only official response was a tightening of travel and currency restrictions on Cuba in the third week in April 1982.[41] The State Department said it was again considering extending the trade embargo to include goods produced by foreign subsidiaries of American companies.

Two days after the restrictions were announced, Secretary of State Haig told a group of Massachusetts businessmen that Castro was "anguishing" over an offer by the United States to cut its links with the Soviet Union and ally Cuba with the West. The Cuban economy, according to Haig, was a "shambles." Castro, Haig said, is a "man in his declining years of his leadership who's done nothing for his people but make them subservient to Soviet influence and largesse." Haig continued:

> Isn't it time for him to step back and ask whether or not the aspirations of his own talented people would be better satisfied if he were a legitimate member of the Western Hemisphere community of nations? And we've let him know that option is open to him. We know that he's anguishing with it himself.[42]

A State Department spokesman later qualified Mr. Haig's comments, saying that there was no "specific offer on the table that Castro now is anguishing about. What we have said consistently is that if Cuba were to change its policies in certain areas, then we would be willing to change our relationship with Cuba."[43]

Initially, Havana reacted with confusion. Members of the Foreign Ministry complained of "double signals" from Washington but said that even after the new restrictions were imposed they still were willing to keep the negotiation process going. According to one official, "We were willing to believe that the administration needed the restrictions. It was a get tough move more for domestic consumption. Still we were confused."

After Haig's comments, that confusion immediately changed to incredulity and then anger. Foreign Ministry officials called the Secretary of State's statement "insulting" and "stupid." On May 17, speaking before a congress of Cuban farmers, Castro formally rejected Haig's claim that he was anguishing over an American offer. "The government of the United States must know," Castro said, "that our people, our party, our leaders will never rent ourselves, will never sell ourselves, will never surrender ourselves."[44]

Privately, Cuban officials expressed pessimism about any possible Cuban–American rapprochement during the Reagan Administration. Earlier overtures from Washington were dismissed as "a propaganda trick" designed for domestic consumption and to placate the Mexicans. Cuban officials continued to insist that multilateral negotiations were the best possible solution for the current crisis in Central America and for the administration's growing problems in El Salvador. "What is unfortunate," one official said, "is that Washington doesn't understand what it is facing in Central America. It has never understood what caused the upheavals there and now it doesn't understand how to solve them. The Reagan Administration apparently doesn't even realize that it is in trouble in El Salvador."

A NEW POLICY

For twenty years, the United States has made policy in the hemisphere based on a distorted and highly exaggerated image of Cuba and the threat it poses to American interests. To contain the Cuban threat, Washington landed marines in the Dominican Republic, gave covert and illegal backing to right-wing coups in Brazil and Chile, and consistently allied itself with right-wing regimes whose disregard for democratic practices and abuse of human rights is as inimical to American values as any of the abuses of Cuba's Castro Government.

These policies have not served American interests well. It is true that until the Sandinistas took power in Nicaragua in July 1979, the United States succeeded in its primary goal of preventing any further left-wing revolutions in the hemisphere. But that success has been won at great cost to both American prestige and American power. The reason that the American public, as well as many of our democratic allies in Europe, may not have recovered from the so-called Vietnam syndrome may be that Vietnam, to many observers, was just one symptom of a much larger syndrome of foolhardy and dangerous overextensions of American power. U.S. involvements in Guatemala, Cuba, the Dominican Republic, Chile and, more recently, El Salvador only reinforce the lessons of Vietnam and the distrust of American motives abroad.

The loss of prestige might be justified in realpolitik terms had it been accompanied by an increase in U.S. influence in the region. And in the past this is exactly what happened: When the United States "bought" a right-wing dictator like Nicaragua's Luís Somoza, he generally stayed bought. Today this is no longer true. Over the past decade, Washington has had to face increasing opposition from right-wing governments in the hemisphere not only on "soft" issues such as human rights but also on strategically significant issues such as nuclear technology and weapons sales.

When Washington refused to sell Brazil a nuclear reactor, Brazil's military-dominated regime signed a deal with a West German company, over Washington's public protests. Argentina's avowedly anti-Communist military regime has not only turned to Moscow as its number one client for grain exports—taking advantage of markets vacated by Washington's post-Afghanistan grain embargo—in recent months the Argentines have signed an agreement with the Russians for enriched uranium for a nuclear research reactor and extended their new Soviet ally's fishing rights in the rich waters between the Falkland Islands and Argentina. During the Falklands crisis Buenos Aires let it be known that it was receiving technical support from the Soviets. During the prewar negotiations the Reagan Administration was apparently unable to exercise more influence over this supposedly "friendly authoritarian" regime for fear that such pressure would further estrange Buenos Aires and undercut Washington's plan to use Argentine soldiers as a proxy military force in Central America.

The Reagan Administration has been unable to influence the new right-wing regime in El Salvador to continue the reforms begun under the Duarte Government. Immediately after its election, the new government suspended the U.S.-backed land reform program, despite Washington's threat to suspend military aid. This is another symptom of the "Vietnam syndrome": Washington locking itself into anti-Communist alliances with regimes that it can neither respect nor control.

The First Steps

It is time that the United States adopt a new policy for the hemisphere that is more consistent with U.S. ideals and interests. As a first step, the United States must stop overestimating the Cuban threat. American policy makers must recognize that except for the Cuban missile crisis, Cuba does not now and has never posed an objective threat to American power or security in the hemisphere. The few hundred guerrillas the Castro regime was able to muster and send to Latin America during the 1960s were not the cause of the region's instability. Nor has the limited amount of Cuban military aid sent to El Salvador, Honduras, and Guatemala been the cause of the instability in those countries. The escalating violence in Central America has indigenous causes: poverty, inequality, and repression, too little land and too many people.

Strong anti-Communist containment policies by the United States will not resolve these problems or end the conflicts in the region. Indeed, much of the current instability is the result of Washington's decision, two decades ago, to side with the Latin American right. These regimes used the Cuban threat as an excuse to avoid the economic and social reforms that would have guaranteed human rights and stability based on governmental legitimacy rather than military force. The United States must not continue to make the same mistakes.

As a second step toward a more effective hemispheric policy, the United States must clearly define its interests in the region.

Haig, while Secretary of State, said that El Salvador differs from Vietnam in that the interests we are defending in El Salvador are "vital" while those in Vietnam were not. If we are to avoid repeating the errors of Vietnam, we must have a clear definition of U.S. interests and regularly subject it to critical public scrutiny lest we waste more lives on a conflict we later discover was not really vital.

The vital interest in Central America that the administration most often cites is hemispheric security: specifically, the danger of Central American sea lanes coming under the control of pro-Soviet powers, and the even more alarming possibility of hostile Central American regimes giving the Soviet Union strategic basing rights in the hemisphere.

The sea lanes argument did not originate with the Reagan Administration, or with this conflict. Nor is it particularly convincing. Secretary of State Kissinger lobbied for a commitment of American troops to Angola by raising the specter of a pro-Soviet regime in Luanda gaining control of strategic sea lanes in the southern Atlantic and cutting off American supply lines for Middle Eastern oil. As it turned out, the U.S. Senate did not accept Kissinger's arguments, Angola did fall into the hands of a pro-Soviet regime, but in the seven years the MPLA has ruled in Luanda, the sea lanes of the southern Atlantic have yet to be menaced.

Even more important is the fact that the sea lanes argument does not make much sense. The view of sea lanes as a strategic threat to the United States presupposes a scenario in which the United States was involved in a protracted, worldwide conflict with the Soviet Union, using only conventional weapons. This seems highly unlikely. It must also be kept in mind that the Soviets already have access to these sea lanes through naval bases in Cuba. And even without Cuba, the Soviets would have free access to the Caribbean, Central America, and the Panama Canal by means of its long-range submarines, which have regularly used the Caribbean for the last decade. The strategic value of getting involved in a military conflict in El Salvador basically to prevent greater access to sea lanes is debatable.

By contrast, the possibility of a pro-Soviet regime in Central America giving the Soviet Union basing rights for the placement of offensive strategic weapons in the hemisphere is alarming. It was to prevent just such an action that President Kennedy brought the United States to the brink of nuclear war with the Soviet Union two decades ago. But it must be remembered that this issue was resolved at that time by mutual agreement of Washington and Moscow. It is doubtful that the Soviets would be willing to go back to the brink for the sake of missiles in Grenada or Nicaragua when it has not done so for Cuba, its more important ally.

Rather than lessening the possibility of Moscow defaulting on that agreement, the Reagan Administration's hard-line rhetoric—particularly its threats to "go to the source" of regional subversion in Cuba and Nicaragua—actually increases it. It must be remembered that while the 1962 missile crisis accord was heralded as a victory for the United States, the agreement was really a compromise in which the Soviets promised to keep offensive weaponry out of Cuba in exchange for a U.S. pledge not to attack Cuba. When it threatens to attack Cuba, the Administration is sending messages to Moscow—perhaps unintentionally—that *it* considers defaulting on the 1962 accord.

There is also the important question of whether a pro-Soviet regime in Central America would be willing to give the Soviets basing rights. In spite of its debt to both Havana and Moscow for military support during its revolution, the MPLA regime in Angola has not allowed Moscow to establish military bases on Angolan territory. But if the Administration continues to threaten Nicaragua by training and funding anti-Sandinista exiles, it might actually induce the Nicaraguans to seek Moscow's military protection. Certainly Nicaragua will continue the rapid and extensive military build-up that has so concerned Washington in recent months. This is exactly the scenario that led to Cuba's rapid militarization and the placement of Soviet missiles on the island in the early 1960s.

Another vital interest in the region that is repeatedly cited by the Administration is the danger of the United States being inundated by refugees fleeing the instability in Central America. In 1979, when Castro forced hundreds of criminals and mental patients to join the Cubans in the so-called Mariel boat lift to the U.S., traditional xenophobia intensified. Even liberal Americans who usually

302

would be sympathetic to the refugees' plight, feared that the already severely strapped American economy could not absorb so many more people looking for work.

The Reagan Administration's current containment policies will not solve the refugee problem. There is little evidence that fewer refugees flee right-wing regimes of the sort that Washington currently backs in Haiti, Guatemala, and El Salvador than leave countries with left-wing governments. Of course, the refugees who flee left-wing regimes are different from those fleeing right-wing regimes. The U.S. takes those who leave Cuba because it considers them political refugees and it is America's moral and political duty to grant them asylum. Refugees from Haiti and El Salvador are, in the eyes of American law, merely economic refugees. The U.S. has fewer qualms about sending them back to a life of extreme poverty and government repression. As long as there continues to be poverty and repression, whether from the left or the right, there will continue to be refugees seeking entry to the United States. If Washington wishes to address the refugee problem, it must address its causes. Containment policies will inevitably lead to explosions.

American prestige is a vital interest in Central America. Administration officials argue that failure to hold the line in El Salvador will damage American prestige and power worldwide. It is important to remember, however, that this damage would be completely self-inflicted. The Reagan Administration originally chose to draw the line in El Salvador as a way of recovering the prestige that we lost in the Vietnam debacle. Now that the Administration has found that this "splendid little war" could not be won so easily, it must find a way out as quickly and honorably as possible. This can be done only through negotiations.

If negotiations are successful and the turmoil in El Salvador can be brought to a relatively peaceful and equitable resolution, America will gain more prestige as a peacemaker and champion of human rights than it would from a military victory. The only way to overcome the "Vietnam syndrome" is not to recreate another Vietnam and win this time, but to demonstrate that the United States does not always have to fight, that it can assert its influence and power constructively and toward equitable ends.

As a third step toward a more effective foreign policy, Washington must adopt a set of goals for the region based on a realistic analysis of current conditions rather than our own idealistic images or invidious fears. As one observer has noted, what the Reagan Administration would like to see in Central America is "a cluster of friendly stable nations which hold honest elections and respect human rights, welcome U.S. private investment and support Washington internationally."[45]

These goals, although laudable, are also utterly unrealistic. The problems in Central America run too deep and have been present far too long for any easy or amicable solutions. In almost every country the economy is shattered, government repression and violent reaction are a way of life, and the much-yearned-for "center" of the political arena is almost completely depopulated. No matter what policies Washington adopts, political instability, crushing underdevelopment, and vulnerability to extremist influences will continue in Central America for a long time to come. And when order is finally imposed, by either the left or the right, it is likely that American influence will not be welcome immediately. The legacy of anticolonial sentiment in Central America is real and lasting, if only as a propaganda tool to divert popular attention from domestic failings.

Washington has come to accept instability and anti-American sentiment in Africa as an unpleasant but inevitable part of their development. We must now accept it as an unpleasant and unavoidable part of the development process in Third World nations closer to home.

Although the best-case scenario is not possible in Central America, the worst-case scenario that is envisioned by the Administration is equally unlikely. What it fears most in Central America is the domino effect: a series of left-wing takeovers starting in Nicaragua, then moving to El Salvador, Honduras, Guatemala, and finally Mexico; a plethora of Cubas menacing our sea lanes, harboring Soviet missiles, exporting thousands of refugees, and controlling Mexican oil.

There are several reasons why this is unlikely, the most important being that these countries, despite their proximity and shared problems, are not the same. Their governments are not the same: The Salvadoran junta is not so universally reviled as was Somoza's dictatorship. Their peoples are also not the same. This fact was strikingly clear in the Salvadoran elections last March. The Salvadoran voters were no more willing to choose a Nicaraguan solution and follow the guerrillas' lead and boycott the election than they were to choose an American-style solution and follow the Duarte regime's route of controlled reforms. Although Americans may disagree with the election's outcome, few will dispute that it was genuinely and uniquely Salvadoran.

It is important to recognize that the Mexicans, who are closer to Central America than we are and have much more to lose, reject the domino scenario. Some observers have suggested that the Mexicans' revolutionary tradition has blinded them to the danger in Central America. Others suggest that the Mexican commitment to the Central American left is merely rhetorical and that the Mexicans parrot revolutionary rhetoric in order to coopt and divert their internal resistance to what are basically conservative domestic policies. Whatever the rationale for the Mexican position, we must recognize that the Mexican Government has a long and demonstrated tradition of coopting and controlling domestic dissent. The Mexicans apparently believe that with similar mechanisms of negotiation and cooptation the problems in the region can effectively be resolved. As for how things will turn out in Mexico, experts generally predict that the more left-wing Central America becomes, the more conservative Mexico will become. And the one way to guarantee the ascendancy of the left in Mexico is for the United States to intervene in Central America on the side of the right.

What then is the likely outcome in Central America? To say that "Nicaragua will become another Cuba" or that "Mexico is the next Iran" would be to indulge in gross oversimplification. Before Reagan was elected and Washington was keeping the lines of communication open to Managua, the Sandinistas seemed sincerely interested in some accommodation with the United States. Since then, the Nicaraguans have moved further and further left as the talk from Washington has grown more hostile. Even centrist opponents of the Sandinistas—like businessman and former junta member Alphonse Robelo—endorsed the imposition of martial law last March as necessary to defend the country against U.S.-trained and funded exiles. One could argue that hostile actions like these from the United States could turn Nicaragua into another Cuba.

As a fourth step toward a new foreign policy in the region, the United States must sit down and begin realistic negotiations with Cuba. Recent overtures from Havana seem sincere. But before the United States sits down at the bargaining table, it must be clear about what negotiations can and cannot accomplish. In the past, negotiations with Havana failed because the United States overestimated its bargaining strength and asked for too much: specifically, that the Cubans forswear any and all future overseas involvements. Each time the Cubans refused. Beyond the issue of national sovereignty, the Cubans are not going to let *anyone,* not even the Soviets, tell them what they can and cannot do in their foreign policy. They have gotten too many benefits from their overseas involvements: international prestige, Soviet assistance, domestic pride.

The Reagan Administration has little to offer the Cubans to offset those benefits. Certainly the Cubans want the embargo lifted, they want access to American technology, to diversify their trading partners, and to lessen their dependence on the Soviet Union. But at the same time, the Castro Government is realistic about what it can and cannot expect from the United States. So long as Cuba remains socialist, the Soviet Union will be its mentor, protector, and major trading partner. And so long as the Soviet Union remains its major trading partner, Cuba's foreign exchange will be severely limited. Its ability to take advantage of American markets will be no less limited. For limited access to American markets the Cubans are not going to give up their presence in Angola and Ethiopia or cede all discretionary control over future international forays into Central America or elsewhere.

But the Cubans *have* offered to exercise restraint in El Salvador in return for similar U.S. promises. This offer, although not as spectacular as a promise of a full Cuban démarche, should not be minimized. If the United States really wants the Salvadorans to have the freedom to resolve their own problems without outside interference, having the Cubans withdraw from that conflict is a major victory.

Such a *quid pro quo* agreement with Havana would get the United States out of what is becoming an increasingly difficult situation. The Reagan Administration claims that it must stay in El Salvador to offset Cuban subversion. However, the recently elected right-wing coalition that it is protecting embodies few of our principles. It has already proved itself to be difficult to control. If the Cubans withdrew from the conflict, the Reagan Administration would gain a much-needed opening to get out of El Salvador as well.

Havana's recent willingness to negotiate on El Salvador should be a hopeful sign for the rest of Central America. If the Cubans really thought they could win in El Salvador, they undoubtedly would continue to ship arms, train insurgents, and do whatever else they could to ensure a socialist victory. They evidently believe that such a victory is now impossible.

There are several reasons for the Castro Government's willingness to negotiate. In addition to their doubts about socialism in El Salvador, the Cubans fear that any further commitment to the conflict will bring them into a direct confrontation with the United States. Havana is also conscious that its own international prestige and diplomatic contacts have begun to suffer as a result of its role in El Salvador. The specter of renewed Cuban subversion in the hemisphere is not taken lightly by Cuba's neighbors. For all these reasons, Cuba can be expected to exercise only a very limited role in future Central American conflicts.

Recognizing these constraints on Havana's behavior should not, however, invite even more hard-line pressures from the United States. Now is *not* the time to step up the pressure on Havana and solve the Cuban problem once and for all. The Cubans, although constrained, are not cowed. In the past, hostile actions against Cuba or its allies led the Castro regime to adopt even more militant and hostile postures of its own, regardless of the material constraints. This was the reason for Havana's embrace of armed struggle after the 1965 Dominican invasion. This was also the reason for Havana's decision to arm the Salvadoran guerrillas after the Reagan election.

The Castro Government apparently believes that it has good reason to exercise restraint in the region. The U.S. can either reinforce that belief through negotiations, by exercising restraint of its own, or it can seek direct confrontation with the Castro Government in Cuba and in Central America. The latter course will certainly be costly in terms of American lives and matériel; it could also run the risk of a direct confrontation with the Soviets. Like Cuba, the U.S. too has much to fear from a deeper involvement in Central America.

As a fifth step toward peace in the region, the Reagan Administration must be willing to sit down and negotiate with the Sandinistas. Once again, Washington must be careful not to overestimate its strength in such negotiations. Washington will not be able to turn Nicaragua into a stable, prosperous, capitalist, pro-American state, either by negotiation or military confrontation. No matter what policies Washington adopts, the Sandinistas will continue to pursue a predominantly socialist line at home. And no matter what policies Washington adopts, the Sandinistas will continue to flaunt their independence of the United States abroad: voting with the socialist bloc at the UN; denouncing U.S. "imperialism" in Nicaragua; holding public fêtes with Cuban and Soviet visitors; and generally rubbing U.S. faces in their independence and opposition for a long time to come. That is the legacy of past interventions and the cost of current policies.

At the same time, the United States, by promising to exercise similar restraint, may be able to persuade the Nicaraguans to stop sending arms to the Salvadorans and other guerrillas in the region. The U.S. also may be able to get the Nicaraguans to disarm partially and send some of their Cuban advisers home in return for promises to stop aiding and abetting anti-Sandinista guerrillas.

In the long run, the United States may have even more influence and leverage with the Nicaraguans because it has more to offer. Unlike Cuba, Nicaragua needs Western trade and assistance to survive. Havana has warned its Sandinista allies all along that it must moderate its domestic and international positions in order to guarantee the internal support of its professional and middle classes and maintain access to Western markets and lending sources. The Cubans have told Nicaragua that it cannot become another Cuba because the Soviets will not foot the bill. The sort of influence that can be achieved through trade and aid will not lead to instant solutions. But the long-range influence the United States could gain could be considerable.

To make negotiations work with Cuba and Nicaragua, the United States must be willing to give up something as well. This is the sixth step toward a new American foreign policy: The United States must forswear the use of military force against Cuba and Nicaragua and in El Salvador. The Reagan Administration says that it will not rule out any option, but if it wishes to resolve the conflicts in Central America, it must abandon the option of military force.

If the United States stopped threatening military intervention, Cuba would not need to send so many arms to the Nicaraguans or the Salvadoran guerrillas. Nicaragua would not need to request so much Cuban and Soviet aid or maintain such a large military force or send so many arms to the Salvadorans. The United States must forswear the use of force to put an end to what has become a dangerous cycle of escalation and counterescalation, a latter-day arms race in Central America.

The seventh step toward peace in the region is for the United States to back a negotiated settlement in El Salvador. With the Cubans and Nicaraguans out of the picture and the United States committed to restraint, the left may be more willing to lay down its arms and negotiate. Once the United States stops backing the right, it may find that there are many on the left who wish to compromise and have no desire for their country to become a second Nicaragua or another Cuba. When the Salvadoran right finds that the United States is no longer willing to underwrite its campaign of decimation, it too will have to negotiate.

Will negotiations bring peace to El Salvador? The divisions in the country run deep and the prospects are not bright. Yet the settlement in Zimbabwe is a testament to the possibilities of negotiation, even in the most polarized circumstances. With no foreign intervention to drive the protagonists further apart, there is hope for a settlement of the Salvadoran conflict.

The eighth step toward a more effective policy in the hemisphere is for the United States to stop underestimating its strength. This step is the converse of the first step. For twenty years, the United States not only has overestimated the Cuban threat, it has consistently underestimated its own strength. That is why the United States consistently has sought military solutions to the problems of the hemisphere. In fact, there are many more effective ways to influence and direct development in the region that rely on even greater American strengths.

In addition to military strength, the United States has a strong economy, technological sophistication, international respect, and a strong moral imperative. If it concentrates its efforts on helping to develop the economies, improving the quality of life, and resolving regional disputes in Central America through compromise rather than confrontation, the U.S. will find that it has power and influence that far outdistances that of the Cubans—who are financially strapped—and the Soviets, who share neither culture nor proximity and are perceived as a foreign power.

It takes a strong country to lay down its arms and find other solutions. The United States not only can, but must. Any President who tries to do so will face strong domestic opposition, as a result of the irrational fear of "the Cuban threat" of the last twenty years. Along the way there will also be setbacks and defeats for which the leader who chooses this route will be blamed. There are no easy solutions, and it will take a strong leader to keep to this course in the face of such opposition. A strong country may choose the strength of reason over atavistic fears. The United States has such strength.

The final step is to redefine the Cuban threat. For twenty years, the United States has been obsessed with the Cuban threat without really understanding it. The threat has never been military. The Cubans, despite their wishes and their rhetorical claims, have never had the means to foment revolution throughout the hemisphere.

The real threat from the Castro Government has been symbolic. It is a threat to our hegemony, to our ability to impose complete agreement in "our" hemisphere. It is not clear whether we ever really had such complete agreement, the pretensions of the Monroe Doctrine notwithstanding. Even before the Castro revolution, the United States faced opposition from left-leaning leaders like Guatemala's Arbenz and right-leaning leaders like Argentina's Juan Perón. Briefly during the 1960s the U.S. was able to command complete agreement, in reaction to the Cuban threat. But such agreement was costly in terms of progress and human rights in the hemisphere; and, inevitably, it was temporary. As Washington found out, it could no more agree with the right-wing reactionaries to the Cuban threat than it could agree with Cuba's followers.

The end of hegemony is a reality of the modern world and one the United States and the ex-colonial powers have had to learn to accept. More than any moral imperative, the U.S. must learn to accept opposition in the hemisphere because the costs of overreaction are so high. The Pinochets and the D'Aubuissons are no better allies and no more easily controlled than their left-wing opponents.

The real Cuban threat may be the reaction that forces the United States into untenable alliances with right-wing regimes, involves the United States in unpopular and often illegal overseas entanglements, alienates many of its citizens, and undercuts its prestige and influence abroad. The real Cuban threat may well come from within the United States.

Notes

CHAPTER 1

1. Several fine books have been written on the Dominican intervention, see particularly: Abraham F. Lowenthal, *The Dominican Intervention* (Harvard University Press, 1972); Tad Szulc, *Dominican Diary* (Delacourt, 1965); Jerome Slater, *Intervention and Negotiation* (Harper & Row, 1970).

2. Lyndon B. Johnson, "Radio and Television Report to the American People on the Situation in the Dominican Republic," *Public Papers of the Presidents: Lyndon B. Johnson, 1965*, p. 471.

3. Lowenthal, *Dominican Intervention*, pp. 215–27, fn. 42.

4. One particularly scathing critique of the list of alleged Communists was written by James Nelson Goodsell, "Are Dominican Rebels Reds?", *Christian Science Monitor*, May 19, 1965.

5. Lowenthal writes, "every specific report of actual foreign Communist involvement on the rebel side turned out to be unsubstantiated except for information about the prior training of a score of Dominican Communists and about the public encouragement given to rebels by Radio Havana broadcasts." See *The Dominican Intervention*, pp. 215–26.

6. "The Tricontinental Conference of African, Asian and Latin American Peoples," A staff study prepared for Internal Security Subcommittee, U.S. Senate Judiciary Committee, September 20, 1966.

7. State Department White Paper, "Communist Interference in El Salvador," Special Report Number 80, February 23, 1981. "Cuba's Renewed Support for Violence in the Hemisphere," paper presented to Subcommittee on Western Hemisphere Affairs, U.S. Senate Foreign Relations Committee, December 14, 1981.

8. *Miami Herald,* January 27, 1982.

9. "Soviet Naval Activities in the Caribbean," Hearings before the Subcommittee on Inter-American Affairs, U.S. House of Representatives Committee on Foreign Affairs, 1971, Part 2, p. 16.

10. Jonathan Kwitney, "Apparent Errors Cloud U.S. 'White Paper' On Reds in El Salvador," *Wall Street Journal,* June 8, 1981; Robert Kaiser, "White Paper on El Salvador Is Faulty," *Washington Post,* June 9, 1981.

11. *New York Times,* March 6, 1982.

12. Ibid., March 13, 1982.

13. CIA estimates in "Communist Aid Activities in Non-Communist, Less Developed Countries, 1979 and 1954–1979," National Foreign Assessment Center Research Paper #ER 80–10218U (Washington, 1980), pp. 15, 21.

CHAPTER 2

1. For the complete story of the *Granma,* which has been told many times, see: Hugh Thomas, *Cuba: The Pursuit of Freedom* (Harper & Row, 1971), pp. 894–902; Carlos Franqui, *Los Doce* (Lyle Stuart, 1968); Ernesto Guevara, *Remembrances of the Cuban Revolutionary War* (Monthly Review Press, 1968).

2. Richard Gott, *Guerrilla Movements in Latin America* (Anchor Books, 1972), p. 13.

3. Andrés Suárez, *Cuba: Castroism and Communism, 1959–66* (MIT Press, 1967), p. 94.

4. Fidel Castro, *Declaración de La Habana* (Havana: Oficina del Primierato, 1960).

5. Tad Szulc, "Exporting the Cuban Revolution" in John Plank, ed., *Cuba and the United States* (Brookings Institution, 1967), p. 79.

6. Gott, *Guerrilla Movements,* p. 14.

7. Geoffrey Warner, "Latin America" in Geoffrey Barraclough, ed., *Survey of International Affairs 1959–1960* (Oxford University Press, 1964), p. 471.

8. Charles D. Ameringer, *The Democratic Left in Exile* (University of Miami Press, 1974), pp. 273–275; *New York Times,* April 20, 1959.

9. There are several, sometimes conflicting, accounts of the Cayo Confites expedition against Trujillo, including: Thomas, *Cuba,* pp. 755–756; Ameringer, *The Democratic Left,* pp. 64–72; Robert Crassweller, *Trujillo: The Life and Times of a Caribbean Dictator* (Macmillan, 1966), pp. 231–250.

10. Szulc, "Exporting the Cuban Revolution," p. 79.

11. Suárez, *Cuba,* p. 68.

12. Warner, "Latin America," pp. 478–479.

13. For a full account of the exploits of the Caribbean Legion, see Ameringer, *The Democratic Left,* Chapter 2.

14. Thomas, *Cuba,* p. 1089.

15. Ibid., p. 1090.

16. Castro's visit to the United States is described in the *New York Times,* April 18, 19, 20, 21, 22, 23, 24, 25, 26, 1959.

17. *New York Times,* April 21, 1959.

18. Javier Pazos, "Cuba—Was a Deal Possible in '59?," *The New Republic,* January 12, 1963, pp. 10–11.

19. Fidel Castro, "Discursos pronunciados por cmdte Fidel Castro Ruz en tres Capitales de América Latina: Buenos Aires, Montevideo, Rio de Janeiro" (Havana: MINFAR, 1959).

20. *New York Times,* May 3, 1959.

21. Pazos, "Cuba."

22. For early Cuban views of the OAS see: *Cuba en la OEA* (Havana: Imprenta Nacional, 1960); Ernesto Guevara, *Cuba en Punta del Este* (Havana: Editorial en Marcha, 1961); Ernesto Guevara, *Interpreta Che Guevara la conferencia de Uruguay* (Havana: Imprenta Nacional, 1961).

23. Thomas, *Cuba,* p. 453.

24. The breakdown of U.S.–Cuban relations will be discussed in detail in Chapter 3.

25. The development of the Cuban–Soviet alliance will be discussed in detail in Chapter 4.

26. Suárez, *Cuba,* p. 138.

27. Thomas, *Cuba,* p. 1293.

28. "Resolution of OAS Condemnation in OAS Official Record," *Current History,* January 1965, pp. 40–44. On the Cuban reaction see: *Declaraciones de la Habana y de Santiago* (Havana: Editora Politica, 1965).

29. *Report to Inter-American Peace Commission of OAS,* OEA/SerL/III (1p/1/62), p. 2; for an exile's view of Cuba's alleged subversive activities see: Manuel Braña, *La diplomacia de Fidel Castro en la América ·Latina* (Miami: Distribuidor, Feramín Peraza, 1964.)

30. Suárez, *Cuba,* p. 105; "Dos asambleas y dos declaraciones," *INRA* (October 1960).

31. "Resolution of OAS Condemnation."

32. Fidel Castro, *El más grande acto celebrado en América: II Declaración de La Habana* (Havana: MINREX, 1962).

33. Szulc, "Exporting the Cuban Revolution," p. 78.

34. David Collier, "The Bureaucratic Authoritarian Model: Synthesis and Priorities for Future Research" in David Collier, ed., *The New Authoritarianism in Latin America* (Princeton University Press, 1979), pp. 363–397.

35. For a full account of the Cuban–PCV split, see D. Bruce Jackson, *Castro, The Kremlin and Communism in Latin America* (Johns Hopkins Press, 1969).

36. Szulc, "Exporting the Cuban Revolution."

37. "Communist Activities in Latin America," Report of the Subcommittee on Inter-American Affairs, U.S. House of Representatives Committee on Foreign Affairs, July 1967, p. 7.

38. Maurice Halperin, *The Rise and Decline of Fidel Castro* (University of California Press, 1972), p. 30.

39. Fidel Castro, "On Setting Accounts with some Latin American Communists," speech to the Twelfth Congress of the Central Organization of Trade Unions, August 29, 1966, reprinted in *Granma Weekly Review,* Sept. 4, 1966.

40. M. Michael Kline, "Castro's Challenge to Latin American Communism" in Jaime Suchlicki, ed. *Cuba, Castro and Revolution* (University of Miami Press, 1972).

41. For more on the 1964 Havana Compromise, see Jacques Levesque, *The USSR and the Cuban Revolution* (Praeger, 1978), pp. 103–106; "Comunicado de la conferencia de los Partidos Comunistas de América Latina," *Cuba Socialista* (February 1965).

42. Ibid.

43. Ibid., p. 106.

44. Ibid.

45. Jackson, *Castro, the Kremlin,* p. 29.

46. Fidel Castro, "Speech Commemorating the Tenth Anniversary of the Attack on the Presidential Palace, March 13, 1967," text reproduced in *Granma Weekly Review,* March 19, 1967.

47. "The Tricontinental Conference of African, Asian and Latin American Peoples," Staff Study prepared for Internal Security Subcommittee, Senate Judiciary Committee, September 20, 1966, pp. 23–24; Council of the OAS, *Report on the First Afro–Asian–Latin American Peoples Solidarity Conference and Its Projections* (Pan American Union, November 28, 1966).

48. Levesque, *The USSR,* p. 121.

49. Ibid., pp. 119–124.

50. Jackson, *Castro, the Kremlin,* p. 75.

51. Ibid., p. 77.

52. For conference documents and more on the Cuban view see: Fernando Tabío Alvarez, "Primera Conferencia de Solidaridad de los Pueblos de Africa, Asia y América Latina," *Política Internacional 1* (1966); Fidel Castro, "Discurso en la clausura de la Conferencia Tricontinental," *Cuba Socialista* (February 1966); "Declaración general de la Primera Conferencia," *Tricontinental* (November–December 1966); "La Primera Conferencia de Solidaridad de los Pueblos de Africa, Asia y America Latina," *Cuba Socialista* (February 1966).

53. Jackson, *Castro, the Kremlin,* pp. 84–85.

54. Suárez, *Cuba,* pp. 234–235.

55. *Granma Weekly Review,* March 20, 1966.

56. Jacques Levesque makes this point very persuasively in *The USSR,* pp. 115–119.

57. M. M. Drachkovitch and L. H. Gann, eds., *The Yearbook of International Communist Affairs, 1969* (Hoover Institution, 1970), pp. 203–205; William R. Garner, "The Sino-Soviet Ideological Struggle in Latin America," *Journal of Inter-American Studies* (April 1968).

58. Levesque, *The USSR,* p. 122.

59. Régis Debray, *Revolution in the Revolution?* (Monthly Review Press, 1967). For an analysis of Debray's work see Leo Huberman and Paul M. Sweezy, eds., *Régis Debray and the Latin American Revolution* (Monthly Review Press, 1968).

60. *Granma Weekly Review,* March 19, 1967.

61. Ibid.

62. Ibid.

63. Criteria for membership in OLAS spelled out in the pamphlet, "What is OLAS?" (Havana, 1967). For move on OLAS see: Fidel Castro, *Revolución, revolución, OLAS, solidaridad* (Havana: Instituto del Libro, 1967); OLAS, *Documentos aprobados* (Havana, 1967); OLAS, *Informe de la delegación cubana a la primera conferencia de la OLAS* (Havana, 1967).

64. Levesque, *The USSR,* p. 131.

65. Raúl Roa, Cuban Foreign Minister, speaking to the UN in May 1968, stated: "At the level of international relations, the fundamental antagonism of our epoch is expressed in the struggle between imperialism and the peoples of the underdeveloped world." *Granma Weekly Review,* May 19, 1968.

66. Suárez, *Cuba,* p. 144.

67. *Granma Weekly Review,* May 21, 1967.

68. *Verde Olivo,* October 10, 1968.

69. *Granma Weekly Review,* December 22, 1963.

70. Suárez, *Cuba,* p. 194.

71. Che Guevara, "Vietnam and the World Struggle against Imperialism," translated in Rolando E. Bonachea and Nelson P. Valdés, eds., *Che: Selected Works of Ernesto Guevara* (MIT Press, 1969), p. 147.

72. Ibid.

73. *Granma Weekly Review,* March 19, 1967.

74. Ibid.

75. Levesque, *The USSR,* p. 131.

76. "Communist Activities in Latin America," p. 7.

77. Gott, *Guerrilla Movements,* p. 399.

78. Ibid., p. 484.

79. "Survey of the Alliance for Progress: Insurgency in Latin America," Study prepared for the Subcommittee on American Republics Affairs, U.S. Senate Committee on Foreign Relations, January 1968, pp. 5–6.

80. "Castro Communist Subversion in the Western Hemisphere," Report to U.S. House of Representatives Committee on Foreign Affairs, April 4, 1963.

81. Lynn Darrell Bender, *The Politics of Hostility* (Inter American University Press, 1975), p. 39; "Soviet Naval Activities in the Caribbean," Hearings before the Subcommittee on Inter-American Affairs, U.S. House of Representatives Committee on Foreign Affairs, 1971, Part 2, p. 16.

82. Ibid.

83. Gott, *Guerrilla Movements,* p. 29.

84. Jaime Suchlicki, *Cuba, Castro and Revolution,* p. 5.

85. Che Guevara's Bolivian adventures are described in Gott, *Guerrilla Movements,* pp. 397–481.

86. Daniel James, ed., *The Complete Bolivian Diaries of "Che" Guevara and Other Captured Documents* (Stein and Day, 1968); Ernesto Guevara, *El diario del Che en Bolivia: noviembre 7, 1966 a octobre 7, 1967* (Havana: Instituto del Libro, 1968).

87. Fidel Castro, "Eulogy for Che," in James Kenner and Martin Petras, eds., *Fidel Castro Speaks,* pp. 246–247.

88. The argument of Cuba as pawn of the Soviet Union has been made many, many times in different forums. My favorite is "Castro: Russia's Cat's Paw," *U.S. News and World Report* (June 12, 1978).

89. A good overview of Soviet policy in Africa can be found in David Albright, "The USSR and Africa: Soviet Policy," *Problems of Communism* (January–February 1978), pp. 20–39.

90. The first thorough overview of Cuban involvement in Africa was William J. Durch's "The Cuban Military in Africa and the Middle East: From Algeria to Angola," Center for Naval Analyses Professional Paper No. 201 (Alexandria, Virginia: CNA, 1977).

91. For a good analysis of Cuba's ongoing African involvements, see William M. LeoGrande, "Cuba's Policy in Africa, 1959–1980" IIS Monograph #13 (Berkeley: Institute of International Studies, 1980).

92. Ted Roberts, "Cuba and the Nonaligned Movement," *Cuba's Foreign Policy: Proletarian Internationalism*, Center for Cuban Studies Newsletter, Vol. 3 (Winter 1976) 4–5:15

93. *Granma Weekly Review*, January 1966.

94. Durch, "The Cuban Military," p. 18.

95. *Hoy*, January 23, 1965.

96. Ted Roberts, *Cuba's Foreign Policy*, p. 14.

97. Ernesto Guevara, "Revolution and Underdevelopment," in Rolando E. Bonachea and Nelson P. Valdés, eds., *Che: Selected Works of Ernesto Guevara* (MIT Press, 1969), p. 350.

98. Ibid., p. 351.

99. Ibid.

100. Ibid.

101. Ibid., p. 357.

102. Ibid., p. 352.

103. Ibid., p. 356.

CHAPTER 3

1. Fulgencio Batista, *Cuba Betrayed* (Vantage Press, 1962); James Moushan and Kenneth O. Gilmore, *The Great Deception* (Farrar, Straus, 1963); Nathaniel Weyl, *Red Star Over Cuba* (Devin-Adair, 1962); Mario Lato, *Dagger in the Heart* (Funk and Wagnalls, 1968).

2. Maurice Zeitlin and Robert Scheer, *Cuba: Tragedy in Our Hemisphere* (Grove Press, 1963).

3. Karl Meyer and Tad Szulc, *The Cuban Invasion: Chronicle of a Disaster* (Praeger, 1962), p. 7.

4. For a history of U.S.–Cuban relations in the 19th century see Lester D. Langley, *The Cuban Policy of the United States* (Wiley, 1968).

5. For an informative review of U.S. interventions in Latin America see Cole Blasier, *The Hovering Giant* (University of Pittsburgh Press, 1976).

6. *New York Times*, February 24, 1957.

7. Hugh Thomas describes this scene in *Cuba: The Pursuit of Freedom* (Harper & Row, 1971), pp. 919–920.

8. Pawley's trip to Cuba was described by Earl E. T. Smith in *The Fourth Floor* (Random House, 1962), pp. 166–168.

9. William Appleman Williams, *The U.S., Cuba, and Castro: An Essay in the Dynamics of Revolution and the Dissolution of Empire* (Monthly Review Press, 1962), p. 157.

10. Ibid., pp. 157–159.

11. Thomas, *Cuba*, p. 1075.

12. Ibid., p. 1074.

13. Thomas makes this point very convincingly in *Cuba*, p. 1074.

14. Meyer and Szulc, *The Cuban Invasion*, p. 32.

15. Thomas, *Cuba*, p. 1076.

16. Accounts of the trials were carried in *New York Times*, January 20, 21, 23, 24, 1959.

17. *New York Times*, April 18, 1959.

18. Ibid., April 19, 1959.

19. Ibid., April 21, 1959.

20. Ibid., April 19, 1959.

21. Ibid.

22. Ibid., April 25, 1959.

23. Meyer and Szulc, *The Cuban Invasion*, p. 35.

24. Richard M. Nixon, *Six Crises* (Doubleday, 1962), pp. 351–352.

25. Ibid.

26. Thomas, *Cuba*, p. 1077.

27. *New York Times*, October 29, 1959.

28. Meyer and Szulc, *The Cuban Invasion*, p. 59.

29. Zeitlin and Scheer, *Cuba*, p. 106.

30. Hugh Thomas describes the Agrarian Reform Law in *Cuba*, pp. 1215–1233.

31. *Wall Street Journal*, June 24, 1959.

32. *New York Times*, June 12, 1959.

33. "Testimony of Maj. Pedro Díaz Lanz," Hearings before the Subcommittee to Investigate the Administration of the Internal Security Act, U.S. Senate Committee on the Judiciary, July 14, 1959, pp. 7–8.

34. Ibid., p. 9.

35. Dwight D. Eisenhower, "Statement by the President Restating U.S. Policy Toward Cuba," January 26, 1960, *Public Papers of the Presidents of the United States: Dwight D. Eisenhower, 1960–61*, p. 136.

36. Facts on File, "Cuba, The Soviet Union and The United States,

1960–63," p. 6; Fidel Castro, "Los Estados Unidos dejan venir las avionetas o están muy mal preparados militarmente," *Revolución*, May 14, 1960.
37. *New York Times,* January 22, 1960.
38. Zeitlin and Scheer, *Cuba,* p. 134.
39. Ibid., p. 136.
40. Ernesto Guevara, "The Most Dangerous Enemies and Other Stupidities," translated in Rolando E. Bonachea and Nelson P. Valdés, eds., *Che: Selected Works of Ernesto Guevara* (MIT Press, 1970), p. 46.
41. This fact was disclosed eighteen months later by former President Eisenhower in a news conference, *New York Times,* June 13, 1961.
42. *New York Times,* June 12, 1960.
43. Zeitlin and Scheer, *Cuba,* p. 175.
44. Fidel Castro, "Cambiaremos cuota por inversiones," *Revolución*, June 25, 1960. See also: Fidel Castro, *Discursos memoraldes en una hora decisiva* (Havana: Imprenta Nacional, 1960).
45. Zeitlin and Scheer make this argument in *Cuba,* pp. 174–182.
46. Arthur W. Schlesinger, Jr., *A Thousand Days* (Houghton Mifflin, 1965), p. 224.
47. "Testimony of Earl E. T. Smith and Arthur Gardner," Hearings Before the Subcommittee to Investigate the Administration of the Internal Security Act, U.S. Senate Commitee on the Judiciary, August 27 and 30, 1960.
48. Meyer and Szulc, *The Cuban Invasion,* p. 67.
49. *New York Times,* October 19, 1960.
50. Ibid., October 20, 1960.
51. Ibid., October 22, 1961.
52. Ibid., October 23, 1961.
53. Ibid., October 22, 1961.
54. Zeitlin and Scheer, *Cuba,* p. 195.
55. *New York Times,* January 5, 1961.
56. *New York Times,* January 8, 1961; Fidel Castro, "Sobre el rompimiento de relaciones entra los Estados Unidos y Cuba," *Revolución,* January 3, 1961.
57. Dwight D. Eisenhower, *Public Papers of the Presidents of the United States: Dwight D. Eisenhower, 1960–61,* p. 891.
58. *New York Times,* January 22, 1961.
59. On the Bay of Pigs see Meyer and Szulc, *The Cuban Invasion;* Peter Wyden, *Bay of Pigs* (Simon and Schuster, 1979); Hugh Thomas,

Cuba, pp. 1355–1371; Lisandro Otero, *Historia de una agresión* (Havana: Ediciones Venceremos, 1962).

60. John F. Kennedy, *Public Papers of the Presidents of the United States: John F. Kennedy, 1961*, p. 304.

61. Ibid.

62. Ibid., pp. 305–306.

63. Ibid.

64. On the Cuban missile crisis see: Herbert S. Dinerstein, *The Making of a Missile Crisis* (The Johns Hopkins University Press, 1976); Graham Allison, *Essence of Decision* (Little, Brown, 1971); Robert F. Kennedy, *Thirteen Days* (Norton, 1969); Elie Abel, *The Missile Crisis* (J. P. Lippincott, 1965).

65. Schlesinger, *A Thousand Days*, p. 802.

66. Robert F. Kennedy's memoir of the Cuban missile crisis, *Thirteen Days*, recounts the Ex-Com discussions in great detail.

67. John F. Kennedy, "Radio and Television Report to the American People on the Soviet Arms Buildup in Cuba," October 22, 1962, *Public Papers of the Presidents of the United States: John F. Kennedy, 1962*, pp. 806–809.

68. Ibid.

69. Schlesinger, *A Thousand Days*, p. 816; Adlai E. Stevenson, "UN Security Council Hears U.S. Charges of Soviet Military Buildup in Cuba," *Dept. of State Bulletin*, November 12, 1962.

70. Schlesinger, *A Thousand Days*, p. 816.

71. John F. Kennedy, "Message in Reply to a Broadcast by Chairman Khrushchev on the Cuban Crisis," October 28, 1962, *Public Papers of the Presidents*, pp. 814–815.

72. Andrés Suárez, *Cuba: Castroism and Communism, 1959–66* (MIT Press, 1967), p. 169.

73. Foreign Policy Association, *The Cuban Crisis: A Documentary Record* (Headline Series, 1963).

74. Fidel Castro, "Fija Fidel las 5 garantías contra la agresión a Cuba," *Revolución*, October 29, 1962.

75. Fidel Castro, "Se Evitó la guerra pero no se ganó la paz," *Revolución*, January 16, 1963; "La respuesta de Cuba a Kennedy," *Revolución*, November 26, 1962.

76. Halperin, *The Rise and Decline*, p. 72.

77. Levesque, *Cuba and the USSR*, p. 82.

78. Carla Anne Robbins, "To Russia Cuba Is Worth (Its) SALT," *Baltimore Sun*, October 4, 1979.

79. Meyer and Szulc, *The Cuban Invasion,* p. 70.

80. Lynn Darrell Bender, *The Politics of Hostility* (Inter American University Press, 1975), p. 28.

81. Reports from the Senate Select Intelligence Committee were leaked to the press throughout the spring of 1976. See *New York Times,* April 13, April 22, May 21, June 25, 1976. Warren Hinkle and William Turner, *The Fish Is Red: The Story of the Secret War Against Castro* (Harper & Row, 1981).

82. Bender, *The Politics of Hostility,* p. 30.

83. Jerome Levinson and Juan de Onis, *The Alliance That Lost Its Way* (Quadrangle Books, 1970), pp. 5–6.

84. Ibid., p. 6.

85. Schlesinger, *A Thousand Days,* pp. 193–94.

86. Ibid., p. 8.

87. Ibid., p. 17.

88. Schlesinger, *A Thousand Days,* p. 191.

89. Ibid., p. 195.

90. Ibid.

91. John F. Kennedy, "Address Before the American Society of Newspaper Editors," April 20, 1961, *Public Papers of the Presidents,* pp. 304–306.

92. For a comprehensive study of U.S. counterinsurgency training in Latin America see: Willard F. Barner and C. Neale Ronning, *Internal Security and Military Power* (Ohio State University Press, 1966).

93. Richard Gott, *Guerrilla Movements in Latin America* (Anchor Books, 1972), p. 488.

94. Levinson and de Onis, *The Alliance,* pp. 8–16.

95. Ibid., p. 9.

96. On the failings of the Alliance see: Victor Alba, *Alliance Without Allies* (Praeger, 1965); Herbert K. May, *Problems and Prospects of the Alliance for Progress* (Praeger, 1968).

97. Levinson and de Onis make this argument in *The Alliance,* Chapter 1.

98. David Collier, ed., *The New Authoritarianism in Latin America* (Princeton: Princeton University Press, 1979).

99. Ibid., chaps. 1 and 9.

100. Alfred Stepan, *The Military in Politics* (Princeton University Press, 1971), pp. 123–133; 172–187.

101. Ibid., pp. 127–128.

102. The positive evaluation of the military's nation-building role is expressed in Lucian Pye, "Armies in the Process of Modernization," in John J. Johnson, ed. *The Role of the Military in Underdeveloped Countries* (Princeton University press, 1962); Morris Janowitz, *The Military in the Political Development of New Nations* (University of Chicago Press, 1964).

103. Samuel P. Huntington, *Political Order in Changing Societies* (Yale University Press, 1968), pp. 7–8.

104. On the role of the United States in the Chilean coup, see: James Petras and Morris Morley, *The United States and Chile* (Monthly Review Press, 1975); Elizabeth Farnsworth, "More Than Admitted," *Foreign Policy,* 16 (Fall 1974), pp. 127–141. For a denial of U.S. involvement see: Paul E. Sigmund, *The Overthrow of Allende and the Politics of Chile* (Pittsburgh University Press, 1977).

105. Stepan, *The Military in Politics.*

106. On the U.S. role in Brazil's coup see: Phyllis R. Parker, *Brazil and the Quiet Intervention* (University of Texas Press, 1979).

107. "The Tricontinental Conference of African, Asian and Latin American People," A staff study prepared for the Internal Security Subcommittee, U.S. Senate Judiciary Committee, September 20, 1966.

108. Ibid., pp. 27–28.

109. Ibid., p. 32.

110. Ibid.

111. Gott, *Guerrilla Movements,* p. 31.

112. *Report to the Inter-American Peace Committee of the Organization of American States,* OEA/SerL/III (1p/1/62).

CHAPTER 4

1. Roger E. Kanet, "The Soviet Union and the Colonial Question," in Roger E. Kanet, ed., *The Soviet Union and the Developing Nations* (Johns Hopkins University Press, 1974), pp. 1–26.

2. David Albright, "Soviet Policy," *Problems of Communism* (January–February 1978), p. 21.

3. Roger E. Kanet, "Soviet Attitudes toward Developing Nations since Stalin," in Roger E. Kanet, *The Soviet Union,* pp. 27–50.

4. Ibid., p. 31.

5. Several books on Soviet attitudes toward Latin America are of interest, including: J. Gregory Oswald and Anthony J. Strover, eds., *The Soviet Union and Latin America* (Praeger, 1968); F. Parkinson, *Latin America,*

the Cold War and the World Powers, 1945–1973 (Sage, 1974); Rollie E. Poppino, *International Communism in Latin America* (Free Press, 1964).

6. There is some disagreement in the literature about which came first, the theory of National Democracy or the Cuban revolution. Jacques Levesque argues that Castro's revolution was the inspiration for this new theory. Roger Kanet, however, suggests that although the theory was not named until after the Cuban revolution, it was nevertheless the fulfillment of ideas expressed at the Twentieth Congress of the Communist Party of the Soviet Union in 1956, three years before Castro came to power.

7. Edward Crankshaw, *Khrushchev Remembers* (Little, Brown, 1970), pp. 489–490.

8. Jacques Levesque follows the intricacies of Soviet theoretical thinking on Cuba and the Latin American revolutions in *The USSR and the Cuban Revolution* (Praeger, 1980).

9. Ibid., p. 10.

10. Ibid., p. 15.

11. *Pravda,* July 10, 1960.

12. Levesque, *The USSR,* p. 15.

13. *New York Times,* July 6, 1960.

14. Levesque, *The USSR,* p. 19; Nikita S. Khrushchev, "Rockets Over Cuba a 'Symbolic' Declaration," *Current Digest of the Soviet Press* (Ann Arbor, Michigan, November 30, 1960).

15. This debate has been well documented in D. Bruce Jackson, *Castro, the Kremlin and Communism in Latin America* (Johns Hopkins University Press, 1969).

16. *Obra Revolucionaria,* April 16, 1961.

17. Crankshaw, *Khrushchev Remembers,* p. 491.

18. Ibid., p. 494.

19. Arthur M. Schlesinger, Jr., *A Thousand Days* (Houghton Mifflin, 1965), pp. 95–96.

20. Robert F. Kennedy, *Thirteen Days* (Norton, 1969).

21. Kanet, "Soviet Attitudes," p. 36.

22. Levesque, *The USSR,* p. 36.

23. Arthur Jay Klinghoffer, "The Soviet Union and Africa," in Kanet, *The Soviet Union,* pp. 51–78.

24. Georgi Mirski, "The Proletariat and National Liberation," *New Times,* May 1, 1964.

25. Herbert S. Dinerstein, "Soviet Policies in Latin America," *American Political Science Review,* Vol. 61 (March 1967), 1:80–90.

26. Brian Crozier, "Soviet Pressures in the Caribbean: The Satellisation of Cuba," *Conflict Studies* (May 1973), 35:12.

27. "The Tricontinental Conference of African, Asian and Latin American People," A staff study prepared for the Internal Security Subcommittee, U.S. Senate Judiciary Committee, September 20, 1966, pp. 81–87.

28. *New York Times,* February 17, 1966.

29. Levesque, *The USSR,* p. 110.

30. Albright, "Soviet Policy."

31. Ibid., p. 24.

32. Wolfgang W. Berner, "The Place of Cuba in Soviet Latin American Strategy," in Oswald and Strover, *The Soviet Union,* p. 94.

33. Klinghoffer, "The Soviet Union and Africa," p. 59.

34. Richard Lowenthal, "Soviet Counter-Imperialism," *Problems of Communism* (November–December 1976), pp. 52–63.

35. Elizabeth Kridl Valkenier, "New Trends in Soviet Economic Relations with the Third World," in Erik P. Hoffman and Frederic J. Fleron, eds., *The Conduct of Soviet Foreign Policy* (Aldine, 1971), pp. 409–425.

36. Parkinson, *Latin America, the Cold War;* J. Gregory Oswald, "Postscript" in Oswald and Strover, *The Soviet Union,* pp. 185–188.

37. Levesque, *The USSR,* p. 138.

38. *Pravda,* July 14, 1963.

39. Kevin Devlin, "The Castroist Challenge to Communism" in Oswald and Strover, *The Soviet Union,* p. 169.

40. Levesque, *The USSR,* p. 135.

41. M. M. Drachkovitch and L. H. Gann, *Yearbook of International Communist Affairs* (Hoover Institution, 1970), p. 206.

42. Ibid., p. 205.

43. Ibid., p. 206.

44. Jackson, *Castro, the Kremlin,* p. 138.

45. Ibid., p. 141.

46. Drachkovitch and Gann, *Yearbook,* p. 206.

47. Levesque, *The USSR,* p. 132.

48. Raúl Castro, "Aníbal Escalante and Other Traitors," *Granma Weekly Review,* February 4, 1968.

49. Hugh Thomas, *Cuba: The Pursuit of Freedom* (Harper & Row, 1971), p. 1468.

50. *Granma Weekly Review,* April 4, 1968.

51. *Granma Weekly Review,* January 20, 1968.

52. Brian Crozier, "Soviet Pressures in the Caribbean: The Satellisation of Cuba," *Conflict Studies* (May 1973), 35:5–18.

53. "Communist Threat to the United States through the Caribbean, Testimony of Orlando Castro Hidalgo," Hearings before Internal Security Subcommittee, Senate Committee on the Judiciary, October 16, 1969.
54. Ibid., p. 1425.
55. Ibid., p. 1426.
56. Parkinson, *Latin America, the Cold War*, p. 225; Devlin, "The Castroist Challenge," p. 172.
57. "Communist Threat through the Caribbean, Testimony of Orlando Castro Hidalgo."
58. M. Michael Kline, "Castro's Challenge to Latin American Communism" in Jaime Suchlicki, ed., *Cuba, Castro and Revolution* (University of Miami Press, 1972), p. 212.
59. Jorge Domínguez, *Cuba* (Harvard University Press, 1978), p. 162.
60. Kenneth Jowitt, "The Romanian Communist Party and the World Socialist System," *World Politics,* XXIII (October 1970), 1:38–60.
61. William J. Durch, "The Cuban Military in Africa and the Middle East: From Algeria to Angola" Professional Paper No. 201 (Center for Naval Analyses, 1977), p. 10.
62. Albert Hirschman, "Beyond Asymmetry: Critical Notes on Myself as a Young Man and on Some Other Old Friends," *International Organization,* Vol. 32 (Winter 1978), 1:45–50.
63. David Ronfeldt, "Superclients and Superpowers," P-5945 (Rand Corporation, 1978).
64. Parkinson, *Latin America, the Cold War*, p. 225.

CHAPTER 5

1. *Granma Weekly Review,* August 25, 1968.
2. In *Cuba in the 1970s* Carmelo Mesa-Lago writes, "Most specialists on Cuban affairs believe, regardless of their ideological coloration, that since Prime Minister Fidel Castro endorsed the Soviet invasion of Czechoslovakia, the USSR has played an increasing role in Cuban affairs, particularly since 1970." He then cites K. S. Karol, *Guerrillas in Power* (Hill and Wang, 1970); Edward González, "Relationship with the Soviet Union" in Mesa-Lago, ed., *Revolutionary Change in Cuba* (University of Pittsburgh Press, 1970); Charles Bettelheim, "La revolution cubaine sur la voie sovietique," *Le Monde,* May 12, 1971; Leon Goure and Julian Weinkle, "Cuba's New Dependency," *Problems of Communism* (March–April 1972). In addition, see Edward González, *Cuba Under Castro: The Limits of Charisma*

(Houghton Mifflin, 1974); Irving Louis Horowitz, ed. *Cuban Communism* (Trans-Action Press, 1977); Jaime Suchlicki, ed. *Cuba, Castro and Revolution* (University of Miami Press, 1972).

3. "Communist Threat Through the Caribbean, Testimony of Orlando Castro Hidalgo," Internal Security Subcommittee, U.S. Senate Judiciary Committee, October 16, 1969; Brian Crozier, "Soviet Pressures in the Caribbean: The Satellisation of Cuba," *Conflict Studies* (May 1973) 35:5–18.

4. Mesa-Lago, *Cuba in the 1970s,* pp. 9–10.

5. *Granma Weekly Review,* August 25, 1968.

6. Ibid.

7. For a full discussion of Cuba's radical economic development policies, their failure, and the effect on the Cuban–Soviet alliance, see Edward González, *Cuba Under Castro.*

8. Since the mid-1970s, and particularly since Cuba's return to internationalism, there has been some attempt to revise the earlier analyses, adding a variety of other causes for the change in Cuban policy, other than Soviet pressures. For discussion of elite changes in Cuba, see Edward González, "Castro and Cuba's New Orthodoxy," *Problems of Communism* (January–February 1976). On the institutional needs of the military and their effects on Cuban policy, see Jorge Domínguez, "Institutionalization and Civil-Military Relations in Cuba," *Cuban Studies* (January 1976), 6.

9. For discussion of the failure of the "ten million tons" campaign, see Edward González, *Cuba Under Castro,* chapter 9.

10. Personal conversation in Havana, Cuba, July 1982.

11. *Granma Weekly Review,* August 2, 1970.

12. Ibid., December 20, 1970.

13. Ibid., May 3, 1970.

14. Ibid., July 20, 1969.

15. Ibid., May 3, 1970.

16. Ibid.

17. Coverage of Castro's trip to Chile begins in *Granma Weekly Review,* November 21, 1971.

18. Ibid., December 19, 1971.

19. Ibid.

20. For Cuban reaction to the Chilean coup see *Granma Weekly Review,* September 23, 30, and October 7, 1973.

21. Ibid., April 20, 1976.

22. González, *Cuba under Castro,* p. 230.

23. The course of Cuban–U.S. relations in the late 1960s and early

1970s is examined in Lynn Darrell Bender, *Cuba and the U.S.: The Politics of Hostility* (Inter American University Press, 1975).

24. "Communist Activities in Latin America," Report of the Subcommittee on Inter-American Affairs, U.S. House of Representatives Committee on Foreign Affairs, July 1967, p. 7.

25. "United States Policy toward Cuba," Hearing before the U.S. Senate Committee on Foreign Relations, May 1971, p. 4.

26. Douglas Bravo's attack on Castro is cited in K. S. Karol, *Guerrillas in Power,* p. 536.

27. Description of Cuba's recent humanitarian foreign policies is found in Jorge Domínguez, "The Armed Forces and Foreign Relations" in Carmelo Mesa-Lago and Cole Blasier, eds., *Cuba in the World* (University of Pittsburgh Press, 1979).

28. For discussion of the very limited aid the Soviet Union provided Chile under the Allende regime, see Joseph L. Nogee and John W. Sloan, "Allende's Chile and the Soviet Union," *Journal of Interamerican Studies and World Affairs* (August 1979).

29. One of the most dramatic demonstrations of Castro's new attitude toward the Soviet Union is his April 22, 1970 speech commemorating the centennial of V. I. Lenin's birth, reprinted in *Granma Weekly Review,* May 3, 1970.

30. World reaction to the Soviet invasion of Czechoslovakia is detailed in *New York Times,* August 22, 1968.

31. Goure and Weinkle, "Soviet-Cuban Relations," p. 153.

32. Ibid., p. 155.

33. A description and analysis of these events is offered in Mesa-Lago, *Cuba in the 1970s,* chapter 1.

34. *Granma Weekly Review,* November 7, 1971.

35. For an analysis of the costs and benefits of Cuba's admission to Comecon see Cole Blasier, "COMECON in Cuban Development" in Mesa-Lago and Blasier, *Cuba in the World,* pp. 225–255.

36. Edward A. Hewett, "Cuba's Membership in the CMEA," in Martin Weinstein, ed. *Revolutionary Cuba in the World Arena* (Institute for the Study of Human Issues, 1978).

37. Fidel Castro's report on the new Cuban-Soviet economic agreement is reprinted in *Granma Weekly Review,* January 14, 1973.

38. The Cuban debt is estimated by Carmelo Mesa-Lago in *Cuba in the 1970s,* p. 18.

39. "Impact of Cuban-Soviet Ties in the Western Hemisphere, Spring 1980," Hearings Before the Subcommittee on Inter-American Affairs, U.S.

House of Representatives Committee on Foreign Affairs, March 26, 1980, p. 7.

40. Henry Kissinger, *The White House Years* (Little, Brown, 1979), pp. 635–651.

41. *New York Times,* September 26, 1970.

42. Ibid., October 14, 1970.

43. Private Conversation, Havana, Cuba, July 1982.

44. *Granma Weekly Review,* May 3, 1970.

45. Fidel Castro, *Report to the First Party Congress, December, 1975* (Moscow: Progress Publishers, 1976).

46. Defense Intelligence Agency, *Handbook on the Cuban Armed Forces,* DDB-2680-62-79, April 1979.

47. *Granma Weekly Review,* May 3, 1970.

48. Ibid., October 31, 1971.

49. On Cuba's relations with its Caribbean neighbors, see Ronald E. Jones, "Cuba and the English Speaking Caribbean" in Mesa-Lago and Blasier, *Cuba in the World,* pp. 131–45.

50. *New York Times,* April 14, 1974; *Granma Weekly Review,* March 10, 1974.

51. On Cuban attempts to diversify trade see Lawrence Theriot and Linda Droker, "Cuban Trade with the Industrialized West, 1974–79" East West Trade Policy Staff Paper, Project D-76 (Department of Commerce, 1981).

52. Carmelo Mesa-Lago, "The Economy and International Relations" in Mesa-Lago and Blasier, eds., *Cuba in the World,* pp. 169–198.

53. Pamela S. Falk, "Cuba's Foreign and Domestic Policies, 1968–78: The Effect of International Commitments on Internal Development" Ph.D. Dissertation, New York University, 1980, pp. 187–188.

54. For a thorough overview of the Cuban economy see Carmelo Mesa-Lago, *The Economy of Socialist Cuba: A Two Decade Appraisal* (University of New Mexico Press, 1981).

55. On CIA "dirty tricks" in Cuba including attempts to assasinate Castro see *New York Times,* November 21, 1975. See also Warren Hinckle and William Turner, *The Fish Is Red* (Harper & Row, 1981).

56. *Granma Weekly Review,* December 1, 1974.

57. Cole Blasier, "The Soviet Union in the Cuban-American Conflict" in Mesa-Lago and Blasier, *Cuba in the World,* p. 41.

58. An analysis of the comparative pricing of sugar and oil can be found in Jorge F. Perez-Lopez, "Sugar and Petroleum in Cuban-Soviet Terms of Trade" in Mesa-Lago and Blasier, *Cuba in the World,* p. 282.

59. These costs are tentative, see Blasier, "The Soviet Union in the Cuban–American Conflict," pp. 45–46.

60. This term was coined by Castro and is analyzed in González, *Cuba Under Castro,* pp. 233–235.

61. *Granma Weekly Review,* December 19, 1971.

62. For the development of U.S. attitudes toward rapprochement see: Edward González, "The United States and Castro: Breaking the Deadlock," *Foreign Affairs* (July 1972); Jorge Dominguez, "Taming the Cuban Shrew," *Foreign Policy* (Spring 1973).

63. "Hijacking Accord between the United States and Cuba," Subcommittee on Inter-American Affairs, U.S. House of Representatives, Committee on Foreign Affairs, (Government Printing Office, 1973).

64. A plethora of statements favoring rapprochement were issued by major political figures during this period including: Jacob K. Javits, "The United States and Cuba, A Propitious Moment" (Government Printing Office, 1974); George S. McGovern, "Cuban Realities, May 1975" (Government Printing Office, 1975); Stephen J. Solarz, "United States Relations with Cuba" (Government Printing Office, 1975).

65. *New York Times,* March 29, 1977.

66. Ibid., December 21, 23, 1975.

67. Hugo Blanco's and Hector Béjar's critiques of Castro are outlined in Mesa-Lago, *Cuba in the 1970s,* pp. 117–118. See also Hugo Blanco, *Land or Death: The Peasant Struggle in Peru* (Pathfinder Press, 1972).

68. Ibid.

69. Karol, *Guerrillas in Power,* p. 536.

70. Private conversation in Havana, Cuba, May 1982.

71. William M. LeoGrande, "Evolution of the Nonaligned Movement," *Problems of Communism* (January–February 1980).

72. Mesa-Lago, *Cuba in the 1970s,* p. 156.

73. *Granma Weekly Review,* October 24, 1971.

74. Castro's 1972 visit to Eastern Europe and Africa was elaborately documented in photographs and reprinted speeches in *El futuro es el internationalismo* (Havana: Instituto Cubano del libro, 1972).

75. William J. Durch, "The Cuban Military in Africa and the Middle East: From Algeria to Angola" Professional Paper #201, (Center for Naval Analyses, September 1977), pp. 25–31.

76. Ibid., pp. 26–28.

77. Ibid., pp. 28–30.

78. On Cuba's alleged involvement in Syria see Yoram Shapira, "Cuba

and the Arab-Israeli Conflict" in Mesa-Lago and Blasier, *Cuba in the World,* pp. 152–66.

79. William M. LeoGrande, "Cuba's Policy in Africa, 1959–1980," Institute for International Studies Monograph #13 (Institute of International Studies, 1980), p. 12.

80. Jorge Domínguez is the author of numerous very fine articles on the predominantly domestic roots of Cuban policy in Africa including, "Cuban Foreign Policy," *Foreign Affairs,* Vol. 57 (Summer 1978), 1:83–108. Yet when he writes about other domestic and foreign policy choices, Domínguez uses terms like "capitulation" and "Soviet hegemony." In his monumental work *Cuba,* Domínguez describes the critical 1968 Cuban–Soviet trade agreement and oil cutback in these terms:

> As when facing the United States in 1960, Cuba had two choices: either to turn to other sources or to capitulate. Turning to the United States was impractical, if not unthinkable. . . . Cuba capitulated. The endorsement of the Soviet invasion of Czechoslovakia in August 1968 was the first evidence that a capitulation was coming. . . . The Soviet government acted as a successful hegemonic power should." *Cuba,* p. 163.

81. "Castro: Russia's Cat's Paw," *U.S. News and World Report* (June 12, 1978), pp. 20–33; Michael A. Samuels, Chester A. Crocker, et al., "Implications of Soviet and Cuban Activities in Africa for U.S. Policy," *Significant Issues Series,* Vol. I, No. 5 (Center for Strategic and International Studies, 1979).

82. Jiri Valenta, "The Soviet-Cuban Intervention in Angola, 1975," *Studies in Comparative Communism,* Vol. XI (Spring/Summer 1978), 1,2:8.

CHAPTER 6

1. The story of *Heroic Vietnam* is part of Gabriel García Márquez's semiofficial account of the Cuban involvement in Angola, "Operation Carlotta: Cuba's Role in Angolan Victory," *Cuba Update* (April 1977), no. 1.

2. Western estimates range from 15,000–18,000. A table of Cuban troop commitments based on Western intelligence estimates and Cuban/MPLA estimates was compiled by William M. LeoGrande in "Cuba's Policy in

Africa, 1959–1980," Institute for International Studies Monograph #13 (Institute of International Studies, 1980), p. 20.

3. CIA estimates are from "Communist Aid Activities in Non-Communist Less Developed Countries, 1979 and 1954–1979," National Foreign Assessment Center Research Paper #ER 80-10318U, 1980, pp. 15, 21.

4. For an analysis of Cuba's on-going problems with its Third World allies, see Carla Anne Robbins, "Looking for Another Angola: Cuban Policy Dilemmas in Africa," The Wilson Center Latin American Program Working Papers #38 (Woodrow Wilson International Center for Scholars, 1979).

5. William J. Durch, "The Cuban Military in Africa and the Middle East: From Algeria to Angola, Professional Paper No. 201 (Center for Naval Analysis, 1977), p. 42.

6. Ibid., pp. 25–35.

7. The best history of Angola is John A. Marcum's *The Angolan Revolution: Exile Politics and Guerrilla Warfare, 1962–1976* (MIT Press, 1978). For a fascinating view of Washington's motivations in Angola during the Nixon years, see John Stockwell, *In Search of Enemies* (Norton, 1978).

8. John A. Marcum, "Lessons of Angola," *Foreign Affairs,* Vol. 54 (April 1976), 3:409.

9. Colin Legum, "The Soviet Union, China and the West in Southern Africa," *Foreign Affairs,* Vol. 54 (July 1976), 4:745–762.

10. Marcum, "Lessons of Angola," p. 412.

11. George Yu, "The USSR and Africa: China's Impact," *Problems of Communism,* Vol. 27 (January–February 1978), 1:40–50.

12. Durch, "The Cuban Military," pp. 19–22.

13. Marcum, "Lessons of Angola," p. 408.

14. Stockwell, *In Search of Enemies,* p. 52.

15. Jiri Valenta, "The Soviet–Cuban Intervention in Angola, 1975," *Studies in Comparative Communism,* Vol. XI (Spring–Summer 1978), 1–2:10.

16. Stockwell, *In Search of Enemies,* pp. 67–68.

17. Marcum, "Lessons of Angola," p. 407.

18. Durch, "The Cuban Military," p. 42.

19. LeoGrande, "Cuba's Policy in Africa," p. 17.

20. Valenta, "The Soviet–Cuban Intervention," pp. 10–11.

21. Marcum, *The Angolan Revolution,* p. 183.

22. Durch, "The Cuban Military," p. 43.

23. Nelson P. Valdés, "Revolutionary Solidarity in Angola," in Cole

Blasier and Carmelo Mesa-Lago, eds., *Cuba in the World* (University of Pittsburgh Press, 1979), p. 99.

24. LeoGrande, "Cuba's Policy in Africa," p. 18.

25. Ibid., p. 20.

26. There is considerable confusion about the size of the invading South African forces. Valdés, working with estimates from the government of Mozambique, puts the number at 10,000. LeoGrande, working with Western data, says half that number, 5,000, invaded.

27. *Granma Weekly Review,* March 28, 1976.

28. There is confusion about the size of the Cuban commitment in Angola. Western estimates range from 15,000 to 18,000, whereas Castro has claimed that, at its peak, the number of Cuban troops reached 36,000. See LeoGrande, "Cuba's Policy in Africa," p. 20.

29. *New York Times,* February 2, 1976.

30. Ibid., January 18, 28; February 19, 1976.

31. Ibid., January 14, 1976.

32. Fidel Castro's speech, "Angola: Africa Giron," is printed in full in *Granma Weekly Review,* April 18, 1976.

33. Durch, "The Cuban Military," p. 45.

34. William Green and Gordon Swanborough, *The Observer's Soviet Aircraft Directory* (Frederick Warne, 1975).

35. Marcum notes this increased Soviet–Cuban coordination in *The Angolan Revolution,* p. 273.

36. *Granma Weekly Review,* April 18, 1976.

37. *New York Times,* November 28, 1978.

38. "Documents of the Fifth Conference of Heads of State or Government of Nonaligned Countries held at Colombo, Sri Lanka, August 16–19, 1976," A/31/197 (United Nations General Assembly, 1976), p. 24.

39. *New York Times,* December 21, 1975.

40. Personal discussions with officials of Cuban foreign ministry, May and July 1982.

41. Barry A. Sklar, "Cuba: Normalization of Relations," Congressional Research Service Issue Brief N IB75030 (Library of Congress, 1977), p. 33.

42. LeoGrande, "Cuba's Policies in Africa," p. 20.

43. Gerald J. Bender, "Angola, the Cubans, and American Anxieties," *Foreign Policy* 31 (Summer 1978).

44. *New York Times,* April 6, 27, June 8, 1980.

45. *Granma Weekly Review,* January 4, 1976.

46. Ibid.

47. Jorge Domínguez, "Institutionalization and Civil-Military Relations in Cuba," *Cuban Studies* 6 (January 1976), no. 1.

48. Durch, "The Cuban Military," p. 14.

49. *New York Times,* November 15, 1977.

50. *Granma Weekly Review,* March 26, 1978.

51. *New York Times,* February 19, 1978.

52. *Granma Weekly Review,* March 26, 1978.

53. *Washington Post,* September 27, 1977.

54. *New York Times,* August 19, 1977.

55. *Washington Post,* February 27, 1978.

56. *New York Times,* April 27, 1978.

57. *Granma Weekly Review,* April 30, 1978.

58. *Granma Weekly Review,* July 23, 1978.

59. *Le Monde,* August 15, 1978.

60. *Baltimore Sun,* April 24, 1978.

61. *New York Times,* June 22, 1978.

62. Ibid., July 18, 1978.

63. Ibid., July 20, 1978.

64. *Washington Post,* July 26, 1978; *New York Times,* July 30, 1978.

65. Foreign Broadcast Information Service II, #145, July 27, 1978, p. I1.

66. Ibid., #138, July 18, 1978, p. I8.

67. Ibid., #142, July 24, 1978, pp. I6–I8.

68. Ibid., January 19, 1981.

69. *Latin American Weekly Report,* Nov. 16, 1979.

70. Roland E. Jones, "Cuba and the English-Speaking Caribbean," in Cole Blasier and Carmelo Mesa-Lago, eds., *Cuba in the World* (University of Pittsburgh Press, 1979), pp. 131–145.

71. Ibid., p. 140.

72. Anthony P. Maingot, "Cuba and the Commonwealth Caribbean: Playing the Cuban Card," *Caribbean Review,* Vol. IX (Winter 1980), no. 1.

73. *Time,* October 22, 1979, p. 45.

74. Tad Szulc, "Storm Winds in the Caribbean," *New York Times Magazine,* May 25, 1980.

75. Ibid.

76. "Impact of Cuban–Soviet Ties in the Western Hemisphere, Spring 1980," Hearings before the Subcommittee on Inter-American Affairs, U.S.

House of Representatives Committee on Foreign Affairs, March 26, 1980, p. 12.

77. Ibid., p. 13.

78. A variety of sensationalist articles on the alleged Cuban threat in the Caribbean have been published, including, "Powder Keg at our Doorstep," *U.S. News and World Report*, 88, May 19, 1980; "Caribbean Rot," *National Review*, September 5, 1980.

79. "Impact of Cuban–Soviet Ties," p. 25.

80. *New York Times*, October 17, 1979.

81. Ibid., October 2, 1979.

82. Hugh Thomas, *Cuba: The Pursuit of Freedom* (Harper & Row, 1971), p. 1311.

83. *New York Times*, July 4, 1979.

84. *Granma Weekly Review*, August 3, 1979.

85. Ibid.

86. Ibid., September 9, 1979.

87. For an excellent analysis of Cuba's conduct at the 1979 Nonaligned Conference, see William M. LeoGrande, "Evolution of the Nonaligned Movement," *Problems of Communism* 1 (January–February 1980).

88. *New York Times*, January 15, 1980.

89. Ibid., January 7 and 8, 1980.

90. *Granma Weekly Review*, January 27, 1980.

91. "Communist Aid Activities," p. 15; 21.

92. Ibid.

93. Bender, "Angola, the Cubans," pp. 14–15.

94. Ibid.

95. *Washington Post*, July 20, 1980.

96. Marlise Simons, "Castro Advises Nicaraguans to Avoid His Errors," *Washington Post*, November 9, 1980.

97. *Granma Weekly Review*, August 4, 1980.

98. Ibid.

99. Ibid.

100. *Granma Weekly Review*, August 3, 1979.

101. Ibid.

102. *New York Times*, July 20, 1980.

103. *Granma Weekly Review*, August 4, 1980.

104. *Washington Post*, November 9, 1980.

105. Fidel Castro's Address to the United Nations, October 12, 1979. Reproduced by the Cuban Permanent Mission to the United Nations, pp. 37–38.

106. *Granma Weekly Review,* August 4, 1980.

107. Ibid., August 3, 1979.

108. Ibid., August 4, 1980.

CHAPTER 7

1. State Department's White Paper entitled "Communist Interference in El Salvador," Special Report Number 80, February 23, 1981. Reported in *New York Times,* February 20, 24, 1981.

2. Ibid.

3. In his first news conference, Secretary of State-designate Haig announced that the Reagan Administration was shifting Washington's foreign policy focus from human rights and toward the containment of international terrorism. At that time, he indicated that this shift would include a change in U.S. military and economic aid policies. (Reported in *New York Times,* January 29, 1981). For a discussion of the theory behind this, see Jeane J. Kirkpatrick, "Dictatorships and Double Standards," *Commentary* (November 1979).

4. Further discussion of the Carter Administration's attitude toward the civil war in El Salvador is found in William M. LeoGrande and Carla Anne Robbins, "Oligarchs and Officers: The Crisis in El Salvador," *Foreign Affairs,* Vol. 58 (Summer 1980), 5:1084–1103. On the decision to send military aid to the Duarte regime, see the *New York Times,* January 19, 1981.

5. *New York Times,* February 23, 1981.

6. *Washington Post,* February 28, 1981.

7. *New York Times,* February 14, 18, March 10, 1981.

8. Ibid., February 21, 1981.

9. Ibid., February 24, 1981.

10. Ibid., August 29, 1981.

11. Ibid., March 14, 1981.

12. Ibid., April 30, 1981.

13. Ibid., March 26, 1981.

14. Ibid., February 25, 1981.

15. Ibid.

16. *Washington Post,* May 4, 1981.

17. *New York Times,* March 13, 1981.

18. Jonathan Kwitney, "Apparent Errors Cloud U.S. 'White Paper' On Reds in El Salvador," *Wall Street Journal,* June 8, 1981.

19. Ibid.

20. Robert Kaiser, "White Paper on El Salvador is Faulty," *Washington Post,* June 9, 1981.

21. Ibid.

22. Robert Kaiser, "State Department Issues Rebuttal to Salvador White Paper Critics," *Washington Post,* June 9, 1981.

23. Castro's most recent reply to Washington's charges of subversion came in personal letters to the *New York Times* and the *Washington Post,* November 12, 1981.

24. "Communist Interference in El Salvador."

25. *New York Times,* July 4, 1979.

26. On the events in Nicaragua see William M. LeoGrande, "The Revolution in Nicaragua: Another Cuba?" *Foreign Affairs,* Vol. 58 (Fall 1979), 1:28–50.

27. As early as July 1980, Castro began to express his concern about the effect of a Reagan election on Cuba's security and the future of Central America. In his annual July 26 speech, Castro denounced the foreign policy platform of the Republican party as "extremely reactionary and extremely dangerous," *Granma Weekly Review,* August 7, 1980. See also *New York Times,* December 18, 1980.

28. This argument was suggested to me in personal conversations with Cuban officials.

29. NBC News White Paper: The Castro Connection, aired October 1980.

30. Claire Sterling, *The Terror Network* (Holt, Rinehart and Winston, 1981), pp. 247–257.

31. *Washington Post,* October 19, 1981.

32. *New York Times,* November 18, 1981; "The Secret War for Nicaragua," *Newsweek,* November 8, 1982.

33. Foreign Broadcast Information Service VI, #182, September 17, 1981, pp. Q9, Q14.

34. *New York Times,* February 24, 1981.

35. Ibid., May 21, 1981.

36. This classified report was originally sent as a telegram entitled "Cuban Covert Activities in Latin America" from the State Department to diplomatic posts around the world sometime in October 1981. A very similar research paper entitled "Cuba's Renewed Support for Violence in the Hemisphere" was presented to the Subcommittee on Western Hemisphere Affairs, U.S. Senate Foreign Relations Committee on December 14, 1981.

37. *Granma Weekly Review,* August 7, 1980.

38. "Cuban Covert Activities in Latin America."

39. *New York Times,* April 6, 1982; Leslie H. Gelb, "Those Nice Noises From Cuba Could Be a Signal or Just Static," *New York Times,* April 18, 1982; private talks with Cuban diplomats.

40. *Washington Post,* March 10, 1982; *Newsweek,* November 8, 1982.

41. *New York Times,* April 20, 1982.

42. Ibid., April 23, 1982.

43. Ibid., April 24, 1982.

44. *Granma,* May 18, 1982.

45. Abraham F. Lowenthal, "Let the Latins Have Their Turmoil in Peace," *Washington Post,* March 28, 1982.

Index

Afghanistan invasion, 167, 251–253, 295
  U.N. condemnation, 251–253
Africa, 57–64
  Communist parties, 60
  Cuban arms and advisers, 53, 57–64, 207–209, 234–237, 283
    training programs, 61, 64, 203
  Cuban involvement, 53, 62–64, 202–204
  Cuban-Soviet cooperation, 58–59, 235–237
  guerrilla movements, 59–61
  liberation movements, 59, 204–206
  Portuguese and French interests, 61
  Soviet policy, 58–60, 150, 153, 204–206, 235–237
  U.S. interests, 58, 60–61
Afro-Asian People's Solidarity Organization (AAPSO), 33–36, 60, 286
  Che Guevara's address, 66–70
Agrarian reform, 86–88, 90, 119, 144
Agricultural productivity, 124
Alarcón, Ricardo, 202
Alessandri, Jorge, 23
Algeria, 150, 203
  Cuban involvement, 61–62, 204
  FLN (National Liberation Front), 59, 61–62
  military coups, 59, 64
  Moroccan border dispute, 61–62
  Soviet aid, 62
Allende, Salvador, 15, 23, 177–178
  overthrow of, 23, 127–129
  (See also Chile)

Alliance for Progress, 3, 15, 19, 99–100, 117–127, 245
  American advisers, 122–123
  Castro and, 70
  containing the threat, 117–127
  counterinsurgency training, 120–123
  development goals, 123–124
  establishment of, 15, 118–119
  evolution not revolution, 25
  objectives, 119–124
  security goals, 120–123
Alves, Nito, 255–256
American Society of Newspaper Editors, 13, 82–83, 102–103
Angola, 5, 202
  Alvor Agreement, 212–214
  Chinese interest in, 210–212
  civil war, 214–219
  Cuban advisers, 65, 211, 290
  Cuban involvement, 222–227, 254–257, 276–277
    negative reactions, 225–227
  Cuban troops in, 59, 114, 198–199, 204, 225, 284
    air lift, 217, 221
  FNLA (National Front for the Liberation of Angola), 209–212
  guerrilla movements, 209–219
    power struggle between, 214–219
  MPLA (Popular Movement for the Liberation of Angola), 61, 207–212, 214–219
    victory, 222–227, 285–286, 289
  Portuguese colonial policy, 209, 212–214
  South African intervention, 216–219

339

Angola (*cont.*):
  Soviet involvement, 206, 210–214, 219–221, 255–257, 302
  UNITA (National Union for the Total Independence of Angola), 209–212
  UN aid, 213
  U.S. interests in, 210–214, 266–267
Arafat, Yasir, 274
Arbenz, Jacobo, 12, 15, 16, 134, 311
  (*See also* Guatemala)
Arévalo, Juan, 12
Argentina, 52, 55, 191, 281
  Communist Party, 158
  Cuban guerrilla operations, 3
  grain exports, 299
  military coups, 15, 23, 125–126
  Montoneros, 4
  opposition to U.S., 311
  Soviet aid, 299
Armed struggle, 40–41
  abandoned by Venezuelan Communist Party, 44
  Castro's commitment to, 27–29, 39–44
  Castro's retreat from, 169–171
  Cuban-Soviet differences, 30, 47, 151
  new Cuban attitudes, 176–182
  Sino-Soviet split, 37–39
  Tricontinental Conference and, 36–37
  (*See also* Export of revolution)
Arms limitation talks, 5, 223
Auténtico party, 78

Bandung Conference (1955), 33
Barbados, 191, 238–239
Barbudos, 12, 20
Barrientos, René, 56
Bartholomew, Frank, 14
Batista, Fulgencio, 11, 26, 74
  atrocities, 80–81
  overthrow of, 7–8, 41, 76–78, 80–81
  U.S. support for, 77–78
Bay of Pigs invasion, 16, 48, 73, 247, 266, 288, 295
  CIA trained Cuban exiles, 101–102
  effects of, 105
Béjar, Héctor, 199–200
Ben Bella, Ahmed, 59, 61–62
Berle, Adolph, 120
Betancourt, Ernesto, 118
Betancourt, Romulo, 12, 22–25
"Big Stick" policies, 3, 5, 104, 244
Bishop, Maurice, 240–241
Blanco, Hugo, 199–200

Blockade of Cuba, 107–109
Boat lift (1980), 226, 302–303
Bolívar, Simón, 75
Bolivia, 20, 54–57, 155
  Communist Party, 38–39, 54–56
  Guevara's mission, 55–57
  military coups, 23
  U.S. aid, 56–57
Bonsal, Philip, 82
Bosch, Juan, 12
Branco, Gen. Castello, 128
Bravo, Douglas, 42, 54, 62, 155, 179, 230
  criticism of Castro, 200
Bravo, Flavio, 214
Brazil, 127–129
  Castro's influence, 99
  military coups, 15, 23, 125–129
  nuclear reactor purchase, 299
  overthrow of Goulart, 127–129
  Soviet aid, 155
  U.S. involvement, 127–129
Brizola, Leonel, 55
Bundy, McGeorge, 106
Burnham, Forbes, 239–240, 246
Bushnell, John, 273–274
Byrd, Sen. Robert, 198

Caldera, Rafael, 190
Cámpora, Héctor, 191
Cape Verde, 202
Cárdenas, Lázaro, 15
Caribbean area, 237–247
  American policies, 75, 300–311
  Communist subversion, 131
  Cuban policies, 237–247
  diplomatic relations, 237–241
  export of revolution to, 90–91
  left-leaning regimes, 239–240
  ripe for revolution, 245–246
  Soviet basing rights, 301–302
Caribbean Contingency Joint Task Force, 244
Caribbean Legion, 12–13, 25
Carter Administration, 114, 224–225, 238, 244, 266
Castro, Fidel:
  assassination attempts, 116, 288
  barbudo, or bearded guerrilla leader, 12
  bargaining ability, 168, 175–176
  commitment to liberation, 9
  communism embraced by, 12, 43–44, 72–74, 83, 89, 139–140

conflict between Communist Parties and, 27–30
Cuban revolution, 7–8, 76–81
(*See also* Cuban revolution)
Czech speech, 169–171
"Declaration of Havana," 9, 20
defiance of, 75
diplomatic relations, 12–18, 20–22
effect on American policy, 2–6, 72–75
eulogy of Che Guevara, 57
export of revolution, 8, 12, 27–30, 39–44, 53, 90–91
abandonment of, 171–176, 179
Latin America, influence in, 14–15, 98–99
Marxism-Leninism, 28, 261
Mexican exile, 12
on peaceful coexistence, 46
political skills, 20, 35, 168, 175–176
popularity, 22–23, 240
"Second Declaration of Havana," 21
on Soviet military ties, 190
speeches, 9, 12, 20–21
suspicious of American intervention, 79–80
"ten million tons" speech, 174–175, 179, 184
visit to Africa, 202–203, 228, 256
visit to Canada, 14
visit to U.S., 10, 13–14, 82–85
visit to Venezuela, 24–25
Castro, Raúl, 18, 47, 76–77, 81, 89, 134, 161–162
visit to Soviet Union, 18, 189
Castro Hidalgo, Orlando, 163–164
Catholic Church, role in Nicaragua, 260–261
Celler, Rep. Emanuel, 81
Central America, 290
American prestige, 303–304
Cuban involvement in, 292, 296
(*See also* Latin America)
Chile, 155, 282
Castro's warnings, 177–178
Cuban aid, 23, 177–178
election of Allende, 173
MIR, 4
military coups, 15, 125, 127–129
overthrow of Allende, 23, 89, 127–129, 266
U.S. intervention, 6, 74, 127–129, 298
Chinese People's Republic, 2–3, 20, 29
Angolan involvement, 210–212
Cuba's split with, 37–38
sugar purchases, 100
trade relations with Cuba, 17, 100

Tricontinental Conference and, 33–39
(*See also* Sino-Soviet conflict)
Chipenda, Daniel, 211, 214
Christianity and religion, 260–261
Church, Sen. Frank, 116, 128
Cienfuegos Bay, Soviet submarine base, 113–114, 187–189
Clark Amendment, 218
Cold War, 195
Colombia, 3–4, 18, 281
communists, 29–30, 50
drug smuggling, 4
guerrilla movements, 4, 29, 291
Soviet relations, 155
Colonialism and neocolonialism, 66–67, 69, 70
Comecon membership, 185–186, 253
Communism, 97
international, 27–30, 132
(*See also* International Communist movement)
Communist bloc countries, 5, 18
(*See also* Socialist bloc countries)
Communist Parties in Latin America, 27–30
conflict between Castro and, 8, 27–30, 39–44, 49–57
"defeatist" elements, 39
political control of, 40–41
revolutionary strategies, 31
Sino-Soviet split, 33–39
Soviet support, 39–44
united front strategy, 31, 144
Communist Party, "Old" Cuban (Partido Socialista Popular (PSP), 27–28, 74
Communist subversion:
in Caribbean area, 90–91
Dominican Republic, 1–3
Reagan's hard-line rhetoric, 295, 302
(*See also* Cuban threat)
Communists in Castro regime, 89
Compensation for expropriated property, 87–91
Congo Brazzaville, 63, 211
Cuban aid, 63–65, 284
Containing the threat:
Alliance for Progress, 117–127
Brazil, 127–129
Chile, 127–129
Cuban obsession, 129–132
Corválan, Luís, 158
Costa Rica, 10, 12, 278, 291

Council for Mutual Economic Assistance (Comecon), 185–186, 253
Counterinsurgency, 120–126
  training schools, 56, 122
Cuba:
  American military occupation (1898), 16, 75
  Communist Party, 27–28, 74, 89, 282
  fear of U.S. intervention, 16, 74, 100
  intelligence service, 162
  military training and arms, 9, 281–283
Cuban-American relations, 75–96
  accommodation with U.S., 85
  American intervention, 74
  arms shipments to Cuba suspended, 78
  breakdown in, 75–96, 100
  Castro's visit to U.S., 82–85
  disagreements, 95–96
  exile attacks on Cuba, 85
  export of revolution, 90–91
  expropriation of American-owned property, 85
  fear of American aggression, 16, 48, 74, 100
  history of, 75–96
  hostility and distrust, 72, 74–75, 100–101
  human rights campaign, 238
  independence from U.S., 240–241
  rapprochement problems, 192–204
  role of American business interests, 74–75
  sanctions against Cuba, 92–93
  trade embargo, 97
  U.S. election campaign (1960), 96–101
  U.S. investments, 90
Cuban Communist Party, 27–28, 74, 89, 282
Cuban exiles, 17
  Bay of Pigs invasion, 17, 94–95, 101–105
  CIA training, 85, 98
Cuban refugees, 226
  boat lift, 226, 302–306
Cuban revolution, 9, 22, 282
  American attitude toward, 78–79
  Batista's defeat, 40–41
  Castro's victory, 7–8, 40–41
  effect on Moscow, 139–141
  Eisenhower Administration and, 78–79
  political trials, 80–82
  Rebel Army, 8
  shift to socialism, 135, 144–146
  Soviet doubts about, 135–136
  strategy, 26
  success of, 28, 40

Cuban-Soviet alliance, 8, 17–18, 51, 67, 91–94, 135–168, 306
  African liberation movements, 204–206
  Angolan civil war, 219–221
  Bay of Pigs invasion and, 105
  benefits of cooperation, 221
  Castro's retreat from, 169–206
  collision course, 156–165
  covert political pressure, 161–165
  change in Cuban policy, 180–183
  criticism of Cubans, 156–160
  criticism of Soviets, 44–47
  Cuban-transferred Soviet arms, 151
  Cuba's power, 166–168
  debt repayment, 186
  definition of true Communist, 43–44
  dependence on Soviets, 24, 27, 70, 97, 170–176, 195, 205–206, 263
  diplomatic relations, 17
  disagreements, 44–47, 156–165, 280–281, 295
  economic necessity for Cuba, 17, 92
  export of revolution and, 129–132
  fear of American attack, 16, 30, 48, 100, 194
  fear of Soviet abandonment, 48
  ideological diversity, 44–47, 156–165
  military aid to Cuba, 114, 222–223
  missile crisis, 47, 106–112, 141–149
  new Cuban attitudes, 176–183
  poor quality Soviet goods, 263
  Sino-Soviet conflict and, 157
  Soviet direction of Cuba's foreign policy, 163–164
  Soviet economic aid, 162–165, 174–175, 194–196
  Soviet military commitments, 18, 186–190
  strategy of linkage, 113–114
  subsidy, amount of, 263
  threats to, 27, 71
  threats to American security, 98
  trade agreements, 92–94, 100, 140, 164, 185–186, 222–223
Cuban studies, 132–133
Cuban threat, 1–6, 283
  containing, 3, 72–134
  Dominican Republic, 1–3
  myths and misperceptions, 4–5, 129–134, 281–283
  origins of U.S.-Cuban hostilities, 72–134
  overestimation of, 266, 300
  Reagan Administration report, 292–294

re-definition of, 310–311
revolution for export, 7–71
Cuban War of Independence (1898), 16
Czechoslovakia, invasion of, 165, 167
 endorsed by Castro, 169–172, 183–184,
 205, 252
 world opposition, 183–184

Debray, Régis, 39–41, 54, 57, 158, 160
Debt repayments, 186
"Declaration of Havana," 9, 20
"Declaration of San José," 20
Defoliants, 122
Déjoie, Louis, 12
Democratic left, 124
 plotting overthrow of dictators, 9–12
Dependence, Cuban, 24, 27, 70, 170–176,
 263
 on socialist bloc, 200–201
 on Soviets, 97, 170–176, 195, 205–206
 on U.S., 92
Détente, 17, 61, 181, 201
Development assistance, 117–127, 173
 Third World, 71, 126–127
Díaz Lanz, Pedro, 86, 90–91
Diplomatic relations, 12–18, 286–287, 291–
 292
 with Africa, 57–66, 207–209
 with Caribbean area, 237–241
 end to isolation, 190–192
 with Latin America, 18–23, 178–180, 190–
 192, 199–200
 nonaligned nations and, 233–237
 shifts in Cuban aid policies, 178–180
 with Soviet Union, 17–18
Dobrynin, Anatoly, 148, 188
Domestic policy, 170–176
 failure of development programs, 173
 failure of sugar drive, 174–175
 Soviet pressure and, 173–176
Dominican Republic, 281
 Cuban exiles in, 11
 Cuban threat, 1–3
 dictatorships, 11–12
 U.S. invasion, 1–3, 30, 74, 266, 298
Domínguez, Jorge, 226
Domino theory, 280, 304
Dorticós, Osvaldo, 63, 185
Drug-smuggling, 3–4, 131
Duarte, José Napoleon, 268
Dubček, Alexander, 171
Duvalier, François "Papa Doc," 11–12

Eagleburger, Lawrence, 268–269
Earthquake aid to Latin America, 179–180
Economic conditions, 53
 Angolan involvement and, 225–227
 failures, 80, 183–184, 259
Ecuador, 155
Education, improvements in, 22, 124
Egypt, Soviet loan to, 138
Eisenhower Administration, 14, 16, 74, 84–
 86
 Bay of Pigs planning, 94–95, 102
 cut in sugar quota, 94–95
 nonintervention policy in Cuban affairs,
 85, 96–101
 opposition to land reform, 85–91
 reaction to Castro, 78–96
 severing of ties with Cuba, 100–101
 social development programs for Latin
 America, 117–118
 Soviet oil sale to Cuba, 94–95
El Salvador, 276–296
 arms shipped via Cuba and Nicaragua,
 267–268, 275–276, 294
 break with Cuba, 20
 Catholic activists, 269–270
 Cuban involvement, 133, 267, 276–279,
 281, 287, 294
 Duarte regime, 268
 elections, 305
 guerrillas, 278
 human rights abuses, 268–270, 272
 negotiated settlement proposals, 294–298,
 302, 306–310
 Cuban offer to exercise restraint, 306–
 308
 Reagan Administration policy, 267–276,
 296–297, 307–308
 faulty assumptions, 279–280
 resistance to military regime, 4, 268
 right-wing coalition, 300, 307
 U.S. policy, 4–5, 268, 271–272
 White Paper, 4, 267–276
 allied opposition, 270–274, 291
 Congressional opposition, 271–272
 Cuba's denial of charges, 276–278
 distorted perceptions, 279–280
 documents, 267–268, 276
 public opposition, 273–276
 Wall Street Journal critique 274–276
 Washington Post critique, 274–276
Embargo on Cuban trade, 97, 115–117, 192–
 193, 263, 288, 297, 306
Eritrean problem, 231–233

Escalante, Aníbal, 161–162
Escalante microfaction, 161–162
Ethiopia, 227–233
  Cuban involvement, 207–208, 224, 227–
    233, 254–258, 276–277, 281, 284
  criticism of Cuba, 236–237
  Cuban troops, 227–228, 232, 284
  Eritrean problem, 231–233
  Somali invasion, 228–231
  Soviet involvement, 230–231, 258
Exiles (see Cuban exiles)
Exodus of 1980, 259, 291
  boat lift, 226, 302–303
Export of revolution, 4, 7–71, 129–132
  African involvements, 57–66
  Castro's commitment to, 8, 12, 27–30, 39–
    44, 53
    abandonment of, 171–176, 179
  creation of revolutionary conditions, 24–
    25, 80, 245
  Cuban ideology, 8
  Cuban mutiny, 49–57
  Cuban self-interest and, 199–202
  Cuban–Soviet tensions, 44–49
  diplomatic imperative, 12–18
  early years, 7–12
  fomenting revolutions, 24–25
  guerrilla warfare, 23–27
  Havana's split with Venezuelan
    Communist Party, 42–44
  isolation of Cuba, 18–23
  retreat from, 54–57, 171–176, 179
  Third World liberation and, 66–71
  Tricontinental Conference and, 31–39
Expropriation of American-owned property,
    85, 95
  compensation for, 87–88
  oil refineries and sugar mills, 95

Falkland Islands, 299
Figueres, José, 12
Financial problems, 192, 237
Foco, small armed guerrilla bands, 11, 41
Fomin, Alexander, 109–110
Food shortages, 259
Ford, Gerald, 224, 266
Foreign exchange, 53, 68, 193, 306
Foreign policy, Cuban, 53, 132–134, 173, 233
  in Africa, 202–206
  Soviet direction of, 163–164
  Soviet invasion of Czechoslovakia, 169–
    170

Third World, 209
  trade relations and, 192–196
Foreign Relations, Council on, 83
Foreign Service Institute, 122
Fort Bragg, Special Warfare Center, 121–122
Franqui, Carlos, 142
Frei, Eduardo, 23
Frondízi, Arturo, 15, 22
Fundamental contradictions, 44–47

Gairy, Eric, 240
Gardner, Arthur, 97
Gasoline rationing, 164–165
Ghana, 63, 150
  military coups, 60, 64
Ghioldi, Rodolpho, 158–159
Glassman, Jon D., 274
Gobeze, Negedde, 258
Goodwin, Richard, 118, 120
Gott, Richard, 51–52
Goulart, João, 23, 127–129
Granma invaders, 7–8, 11, 24, 77
Grau San Martín, Ramón, 76
Grechko, Andrei A., 189
Green Berets, 56, 121
Grenada, 180, 240–244, 246
  Cuban-built airport, 243–244
Group of 77, 59, 191
Guantánamo, U.S. naval base, 108, 112, 244
Guatemala, 180, 281
  Arbenz regime overthrown, 16–17, 86,
    102, 311
  break with Cuba, 20
  CIA base for training Cuban exiles, 98
  Cuban subversion, 30, 51, 133–134
  guerrilla movements, 29
  Rebel Armed Forces, 31, 54
  U.S. intervention, 16–17, 74
Guerrilla movements:
  Africa, 59–61, 64
  Communist support for, 29
  Cuban support for, 51–52, 54, 177–179
  failure of, 54–57
Guerrilla training programs, 3–4, 52–53
  in Africa, 61, 64
Guerrilla warfare, 121–122, 284
  Cuba's commitment to, 23–27, 130
  handbook on, 39–41
Guevara, Che, 15, 89, 93, 121, 283
  address in Algiers, 66–70
  African tour, 63–64, 220
  architect of Castro's victory, 2
  Bolivian diaries, 57, 160

Bolivian mission, 52, 55–57
Castro's eulogy, 57
death of, 39, 56–57, 65–66, 170, 173
on export of revolution, 22
Haitian invasion, 12
infiltration in Dominican Republic, 2
invincibility of strategy, 8
on Panama expedition, 10
on Soviet commitments, 47–48
Guinea, 150, 203
Cuban involvement, 64–65, 284
guerrilla training base, 65
military coups, 59
Guinea-Bissau, 202
Guyana, 180, 191, 242–244, 246
relations with Cuba, 239–240

Haig, Alexander M., 268–270, 275, 297–298, 301
Haiti, 303
guerrilla movements, 29
invasion from Cuba, 11–12
Handal, Shafik, 275
Hart, Armando, 89
Hatfield, Sen. Mark, 271
Havana Compromise (1964), 64, 150–151, 156
Havana Conference (1964), 29, 32, 34–35
Havana Conference (1979), 250–254, 287
Cuba's deteriorating position, 250–251
Health care, 22, 124
Helicopters, 122
sale to Cuba, 90–91
Heroic Vietnam (Cuban ship), 48, 207, 217
Herter, Christian A., 14, 19, 84
Hijacking agreement, 197
Hilsman, Roger, 110
Hirschman, Albert, 166
Honduras, 20, 180
anti-Sandinista guerrillas, 267
CIA training programs, 295–296
guerrilla movements, 29
Horn of Africa, Communist influence, 230–232
Hostility and distrust of U.S., 100–101, 113, 287–289, 299
Eisenhower Administration, 129–130
origins of, 72–75
Reagan Administration, 276–278
Human rights, 238, 298–299
Humanitarian aid, 179–180, 242–243
Hungary, 167

Ideology, Cuban, 8, 71
changes in, 176–183
internationalism vs. state interest, 230, 233
Income distribution, 123–124
India, 234
Industrial development, 70, 124
InterAmerican Conference of Foreign Ministers, 197
Inter-American Development Bank, 117–118
International Communist movement, 27–30, 43–44, 57–66, 132, 230, 233, 282
Castro seceded from, 8
Cuban leadership, 8, 50–51
Moscow's domination, 49
Moscow's right to lead, 136
Proletarian Internationalism, 66, 68, 201–202
International Monetary Fund, 241
International Telephone and Telegraph Corporation, 127
Iran, 166–167, 203
Isolation of Cuba, in Latin America, 18–24, 116
end to, 190–192
Israel-U.S. alliance, 280–281

Jagan, Cheddi, 15, 239–240
Jamaica, 180, 191, 241–243, 246
relations with Cuba, 239
Japan-Cuban trade relations, 193
Jingoism, 38
Johnson Administration Cuban policy, 1–3
Brazil policy, 128–129

Kaiser, Robert, 275–276
Keating, Sen. Kenneth, 106
Kennedy, Sen. Edward M., 198
Kennedy, President John F., 14
Cuba as campaign issue, 96–101
on Cuban threat, 2
hostility toward Cuba, 102
missile crisis, 105–113, 148–149
Kennedy, Robert F., 110
Kennedy Administration, 74
Alliance for Progress, 15, 118–127
Angolan involvement, 211–212
containing the threat, 101–105
missile crisis, 105–113, 148–149
nonintervention policy, 103–105
Khrushchev, Nikita S., 18, 20–21, 33, 95, 168
on Cuban revolution, 140–148
missile commitments to Cuba, 141–144

Khrushchev, Nikita S. (*cont.*):
  missile crisis, 106–113, 147–149
  ouster of, 153–154
Kissinger, Henry, 187–188, 197–198, 213,
    224, 270, 301
  Angolan policy, 218–219
Kosygin, Alexei, 185
Kwitney, Jonathan, 274–276

Land reform, 22, 72, 86–89, 124
  compensation for American land, 87–88
Latin America:
  Castro's influence, 98–99, 116
  causes of instability, 99, 300
  common market proposal, 13
  Cuban aid, 179–180, 300
  Cuban commitment to, 9–12
  Cuban military presence in, 51–54
  Cuban relations with, 20, 58, 98–99, 116,
      129–134, 242–243
    breakdown in, 18–23
  diplomatic relations with Cuba, 237–241,
      291–292
  effect of Dominican intervention, 3
  export of revolution to, 129–132
  international communism, 98
  isolation of Cuba, 116
  limitations on Cuban policy, 51–54
  military coups, 23
  military officers trained by U.S., 122–123
  myth of Cuban threat, 133
  new American policy, 298–311
  political condition, 22–23
  private American investment, 118
  revolutionary movements, 199–200
  social change, need for, 5–6, 13, 15, 25,
      79, 99
  Soviet policy, 52, 143–144, 150–155
  trade agreements with Cuba, 190–193
  U.S. aid, 117–127
  U.S. attitudes toward, 245–246
  U.S. influence, 19, 238
  U.S. military intervention, 1, 122–123
  U.S. policy, 2–6, 22, 76, 300–311
Latin American Communist parties, 27–30,
    150–151, 160–161, 199–200, 248
  Soviet support, 156–157
Latin American Solidarity Organization
    (OLAS), 36, 44, 158, 160–161, 200
  new International, 50–51
Leahy, Sen. Patrick, 271
Left-wing takeovers, 124
  fear of, 304–306

myth of Cuban threat, 133
plotting overthrow of dictators, 9–12
Nicaragua, 305–306
LeoGrande, William, 215
Leoni, Raúl, 155
Liberation movements, 37
  in Africa, 59
  Cuban support of, 63–64
  National Liberation Movements, 37, 136
"Linkage," strategy of, 113–114
Lopez Portillo, José, 270–271
Los doce (twelve survivors), 8
Luce, Henry R., 14

McGovern, Sen. George S., 198
Machado, Gerardo, 76
Mali, 63, 150
Manley, Michael, 241, 246
Mao's ideology, 37–38
Mariel boat lift, 226, 302–303
Marshall Plan, 117, 119
Martí, José, 22, 288
Martinez-Boucher, Col. Ralph, 243–244
Marxist-Leninist ideology, 18, 21, 24–25, 43,
    72–73, 149
Masetti, Jorge, 52
Masetti expedition, 55
Massemba-Debat, Alphonse, 65, 211
Matthews, Herbert, 77–78
Meese, Edwin, 269
Mengistu Haile-Mariam, Col., 228, 231–232,
    257–258
Mesa-Lago, Carmelo, 170–171
Mexico, 23, 252, 278, 298, 304
  Cuban relations, 291
  opposition to White Paper, 270–271
Meyer, Karl, 118
Middle East, Cuban military presence, 203–
    204
Mikoyan, Anastas, 17, 92, 94, 140
Military coups, 125–126
  (*See also under* name of country)
Military elite, seizure of power by, 125–126
Military involvement:
  in Africa, 64–65, 105–117, 209
  in Angola, 209–214
Military officers, training by U.S., 122
Military service, resentment of, 226–227
Missile crisis (1962), 18, 30, 96
  accords, 295, 302
    Castro's rejection of, 111–112, 195–206
  blockade of Cuba, 107–109
  Castro's five conditions, 111–112

Cuban–Soviet tensions, 111–112, 114
diplomatic negotiations, 107–113
effect on world balance of power, 112–117
exclusion of Castro from negotiations, 111–112
Executive Committee, 107–110
Kennedy's speech, 108–109
no-invasion pledge, 110–111, 115
nuclear confrontation and, 148–149
nuclear missile sites, 106–107
precedents set by, 113–117
Soviet placement of missiles, 106–107, 141–149
Soviet removal of missiles, 109–110
world reaction, 108–109, 112–117
Mobuto, Joseph, 64
Moncada Barracks, attack on, 29, 74, 76
Monroe Doctrine, 16, 72, 75, 98, 142, 311
missile crisis and, 147
Movement of Nonaligned Nations (see Nonaligned Nations, Movement of)
Moynihan, Sen. Daniel Patrick, 205
Mozambique, 202
Cuban advisers, 66
FRELIMO guerrillas, 59, 64
Music and musicians, 59
Myths about Cuba, 279–282
allies share U.S. views, 291–292
Cuban threat, 132–134
Cubans always subversive, 283–284
Cubans are everywhere, 281–283
Cubans are international outlaws, 286–288
Cubans are Soviet pawns, 280–281
Cubans never change, 290–291
Cuba's enemy becomes U.S. friend, 289
Cuba's friend becomes U.S. enemy, 289–290
Cuba's invincibility, 285–286

Namibia, 202, 216, 224
Napalm, 122
National Democratic states, 137–140, 145–146
National Liberation Movements, 37, 136
(See also Liberation movements)
National Press Club, 83
Nationalization of foreign enterprises, 72, 88–90, 142, 144
Neto, Agostinho, 207, 211, 220, 255–257
New York Post, 83
New York Times, 77, 83

Nicaragua, 180, 247–250
anti-Sandinistas, 29, 267
CIA training, 295–296
arms sent to Salvadorans, 308
attack against Somoza, 10–11
break with Cuba, 20
Castro's advice, 254, 290
Cuban involvement, 52, 254, 258–260, 276–277, 281, 283–290, 308–309
matériel commitments, 208, 247–250, 277
economic problems, 259
left-wing takeovers, 305–306
multiclass alliance, 260
negotiations with Cuba, 306–308
negotiations with U.S., 208–209
Reagan Administration threats, 5, 302
press conference with alleged guerrilla, 293
revolution in, 247–250
role of Catholic Church, 260–261
Sandinista Government, 4
Sandinista guerrillas, 52, 258–260, 286
Cuban military aid, 208, 247–250
formation of united front, 248–250
relations with West, 263–264
support for, 208
U.S. policy, 4–5, 261–262, 302
Nigeria, 234
Nixon, Richard M., 14, 16
Cuba as campaign issue, 96–101
meeting with Castro, 84–85
Nixon Administration:
Chile policy, 127–129
Cuban-American talks, 197–199
Nkrumah, Kwame, 60, 65
No-invasion pledge by U.S., 110–111, 115, 149, 302
Nonaligned Nations, Movement of, 31, 33, 62–63, 181, 286–287
criticism of Cuba, 235–237
Cuban influence, 201–202
Cuba's involvement in Angola, 233–237
Cuba's involvement in Eritrea, 232–233
Cuba's involvement in Ethiopia, 233–237
Cuba's leadership, 6, 208, 223, 250–251
Nuclear Nonproliferation Treaty, 45, 165
Nuclear technology, 299
Nugouabi, Marien, 65
Núñez Jiménez, Antonio, 89

OAS (see Organization of American States)
Ochoa, Gen. Arnaldo, 228

Odlum, George, 240–241
Oil:
    expropriation of American refineries, 95,
        141–142
    Soviet sale to Cuba, 94–95
OLAS (*see* Latin American Solidarity
    Organization)
Organization of African Unity (OAU), 31,
    59–60, 208, 233, 284
    Angola admitted to, 218
Organization of American States (OAS), 10,
    13–15
    "Declaration of San José," 20
    development aid, 88
    missile crisis, 108
    Punta del Este meetings, 15, 119
    San José meeting, 19–20
    sanctions against Cuba, 18–21, 23, 26, 116,
        291
        abolished, 191–192
Organization of Petroleum Exporting
    Countries (OPEC), 58, 201, 250
Overseas commitments, 203–204, 284, 306
    in Africa, 53
    troops and influence, 254–265

Palestine Liberation Organization (PLO), 31,
    274
Panama, 20, 278, 281
    invasion from Cuba, 9–10
Panama Canal, 10, 301
Paraguay, guerrilla movements, 29
Parker, Phyllis, 128–129
Partido Socialista Popular (PSP), Cuban
    Communist Party, 27–28, 74
Pawley, William, 78
Pazos, Felipe, 15
Pazos, Javier, 15
Peaceful coexistence, 45–47, 112, 143
    Cuban opposition, 46–47, 181–182
People's Republic of China (*see* Chinese
    People's Republic)
Perón, Juan, 311
Peru, 18, 20, 55, 173
    Cuban aid, 179–180
    Cuban involvement in insurgency, 51–52
    military coups, 23
    Velasco Government, 89
Platt Amendment, 16, 85
Poland, 17, 167, 295
    trade agreement with, 93–94
Political instability, 304
Political trials in Cuba, 80–82

Portugal, 61
    Angolan civil war and, 209, 212–214
Poverty and underdevelopment, 80, 99, 245
    (*See also* Third World)
Power, 104
    small states, 166–168
    techniques for seizing, 53
Pravda, 30, 157–158, 160, 184
Press censorship, 226
Pride in military successes, 222, 225
Propaganda, Cuban, 20, 52, 91
Proletarian Internationalism, 66, 68, 201–
    202
Puerto Rico, Cuban threat, 3, 281

Qadaffi, Muammar, 202
Quadros, Jânio, 15, 22, 99

Radio Havana, 52
Rapprochement, 193–199
    benefits of, 193–196
    conditions for, 196–199
    effect of Angolan involvement, 224–225
    negotiated settlement of Salvadoran
        problem, 294–298
    new negotiations with Cuba, 306–308
    overtures toward, 14–15, 287–288, 298
Reagan Administration:
    blockade threat, 288
    El Salvador involvement, 4, 267–279, 291
    hostility toward Cuba, 276–278
    misperception of Cuba, 287–288
    obsession with Cuban subversion, 3–6
    report on Cuban subversion, 292–294
        lacked documentary evidence, 293
    right-wing regimes, 299–300
    threats of unilateral action, 5, 269, 288,
        295
    White Paper on El Salvador, 4, 267–276,
        291
        charges of Cuban involvement, 276–
            278
Red Sea, Communist influence, 229–231
Refugee problem, 302–303
Revolución (newspaper), 27
Revolution, 245, 285–286
    change in Castro's policy, 199–202
    Cuban-style, 3
    for export (*see* Export of revolution)
    myths of Cuba's invincibility, 285–286
    (*See also* Cuban revolution)
Revolution in the Revolution? (Debray), 39–
    41, 57

Revolutionary Democracy theory, 149–151, 153
Rice plantations, 86
Right-wing regimes, 125–127, 133, 298
alliances with, 311
U.S. influences, 299–300
Roa, Raúl, 100, 252
Robelo, Alphonse, 306
Roberto, Holden, 211–212
Rodríguez, Carlos Rafael, 178–179, 184–186, 231
Ronfeldt, David, 166
Roosevelt, Franklin Delano, Good Neighbor Policy, 16, 118, 120–121
Rostow, Walt W., 122
Rudenko, B. T., 152
Rudman, Sen. Warren, 271–272
Rusk, Dean, 110

St. Lucia, 180, 240–241, 244, 246
Salazar, Antonio, 209, 212
SALT talks, 5, 61, 114, 223
Salvador, David, 89
Salvador (see El Salvador)
Sanctions against Cuba, 19, 21, 23, 92, 115–116, 291
lifting of, 191–192
Sandinistas (see under Nicaragua)
Santamaria, Mongo, 59
Savimbi, Jonas, 284
Scali, John, 109–110
Scheina, Martin, 243–244
Schlesinger, Arthur M., Jr., 96–97, 106, 118
Sea lanes, control of, 301–302
Seaga, Edward, 246
Seko, Mobutu Sesse, 64
Selassie, Haile, 229, 231
Sierra Maestra, 9, 22, 41, 77
guerrilla base, 7–11, 22, 41
Sihanouk, Norodom, 202
Sino-Soviet conflict, 141–142, 151, 157
Afro Asian People's Solidarity Organization, 33–37
Cuban missile crisis, 147–148
Tricontinental Conference, 33–39
Small states, 264, 289
dependency, 257
power, 166–168
Smathers, Sen. George, 84
Smith, Earl E. T., 77, 97
Social change in Latin America, 5–6, 13, 15, 25
revolutionary change, 79

Social democracy, 15
Social welfare, 22
Socialism, 69–70
Cuba's transition to, 144–146, 149
irreversibility of, 167–168
Socialist bloc, 30–31, 50
Castro's commitment to, 252
Cuban mutiny, 49–57
Cuban trade with, 93
Cuba's admission to, 139
nonaligned countries and, 235
Soviet defense of, 143
Third World responsibilities, 66–71
Solodovnikov, V., 206
Somalia, 203
Cuban involvement, 229–231
invasion of Ethiopia, 228–231
Somoza, Anastasio, 180, 247
Somoza, Luis, 10, 24, 52, 247, 299
Sosa Blanco, Maj. Jesús, 82
Sourwine, J. G., 90
South Africa, 289
Angolan intervention, 216–219
South West Africa People's Organization (SWAPO), 216
Soviet "combat brigade" in Cuba, 114
Soviet Communist Party, 45
Soviet Institute of African Affairs, 206
Soviet Union, 17
aid for Latin America, 52, 151–156
Angolan involvement, 210–221
arms limitation talks, 5
basing rights, 301–302
China and (see Sino-Soviet conflict)
doubts about Cuban Revolution, 91–94
economic and military aid, 24
foreign aid responsibilities, 153–154
missile aid, 20–21
naval visits to Cuba, 186–189, 301
strategy of social revolution, 25
Third World and, 67–71, 136–146, 223
trade relations, 67–68, 70
Vietnam policy, 47–49
(See also Cuban-Soviet alliance)
Soviet Union–United States relations:
confrontation issue, 186–189, 195
detente, 17, 61, 181, 201
missile crisis, 105–117
Nuclear Nonproliferation Treaty, 45
overestimating Soviet influence, 95–96
peaceful coexistence, 44–47
Spanish American War, 16, 75
Sparkman, Sen. John, 84

Stalin, Josef, 136, 168
Stepan, Alfred, 125, 128
Stevenson, Adlai, 109
Strategic Arms Limitation Treaty (SALT), 5, 61, 114, 223
Sugar, 70, 86, 100, 263
  seizure of mills, 94–95
  Soviet purchases, 17–18, 194
  "ten million tons" campaign, 174–175, 179, 184
  trade agreements, 192
  U.S. cut in import quotas, 17–18, 94–95
Sulzberger, Arthur Ochs, 14
Syria, Cuban military aid, 203–204

Tanzania, 203
Taylor, Gen. Maxwell, 121–122
Technical assistance, 68, 70, 118–119
Terrorism, urban, 11, 26
Third World countries, 5
  Castro's leadership role, 250
  communism, 30–31
  containing threat, 103–105
  Cuban commitment to, 57–59, 66–71, 250–254, 286
  development process, 126–127
  economic development, 63, 66–71
  National Democratic states, 137–139
  national liberation struggles, 37, 45, 136
  responsibilities, 69–70
  revolution for export, 12
  Revolutionary Democracy theory, 149–150
  socialist bloc responsibilities, 66–71
  Soviet responsibilities, 33, 67–71, 136–155, 160, 171, 223, 263–264
Time magazine, 83
Totalitarianism, 19–20
Touré, Sékou, 59, 65
Trade relations, 68–71
  diversification and new markets, 192–193
Tricontinental Conference (1966), 31–39, 48–49, 71, 130–132, 286
  Castro's leadership, 31–39
  history of, 32–39
  Sino-Cuban split, 37–39
  Sino-Soviet split, 33–39
  Soviet-bloc allies, 32–39
Trinidad and Tobago, 191
Trujillo, Rafael, 11, 24
Tshombe, Moise, 64
26th of July Movement, 27, 74, 77, 89

U-2 overflights, 112, 141, 187
Unemployment, 80, 124
United Arab Republic, 150
United fronts, 31, 248
  formation of, 144
United Nations, 31, 111, 284
  Afghanistan condemnation, 251–254, 257
  Castro's address (1979), 241, 264
  Cuban participation, 241, 264, 287
  bid for seat on Security Council, 252, 254
  "Group of 77," 59, 191
  missile crisis, 108–109, 111–112
United Press International, 83
United States:
  Angolan involvement, 210–219
  attitude toward communism, 4, 30–31, 91
  "Big Stick" policies, 3, 5, 104, 244
  business interests, 73–74, 80
    land reform and, 88–89
  containment policies, 6, 101–105, 244–245, 300
  Defense Intelligence Agency, 53, 243
  "Forty Committee," 213, 216, 218
  House Foreign Affairs Committee, 51, 174, 243
  Latin American policy, 2–6, 13–14, 98–99, 117–127
    (See also Alliance for Progress)
  national security, 80
  new hemispheric policy, 300–311
    acceptance of opposition, 311
    definition of vital interests, 300–301
    development of region, 310
    fear of left-wing takeovers, 304–306
    negotiations with Cuba, 306–308
    Nicaraguan negotiations, 308
    realistic goals, 304–306
    redefining Cuban threat, 300, 310–311
    Salvadoran negotiations, 309–310
    sea lane argument, 300
    Soviet basing rights, 301–302
    U.S. power and influence, 310
  overestimation of Cuba and Soviets, 132, 300
  paternalism, 22, 25
  policy mistakes, 96
  presidential campaign (1960), 96–101
  prestige and power, 299, 303, 310–311
  security policy, 8
  Senate Foreign Relations Committee, 14, 52, 84, 179

Senate Internal Security Subcommittee, 86, 90–91, 97, 130–132, 163
Senate Select Intelligence Committee, 116, 194
strategy of democratic reform, 25
subversive actions, 284
trade embargo, 24
(*See also* Embargo on Cuban trade)
United States–Cuban relations, 2–6, 72–75
access to American markets, 306
attempt to overthrow Castro, 9
attitudes toward Cuba, 4, 78–79, 245–246
Bay of Pigs invasion, 3, 16–17, 48, 73, 247, 266, 288, 295–296
breakdown in, 15–17, 25, 100
CIA report (1979), 277–278
CIA training programs, 3, 16, 85, 98, 101–102, 295–296
Communist threat, 16–17
confrontation with U.S., 293, 307–308
Cuban overtures to, 14–15
Cuban responsibility for El Salvador, 276–278
Cuba's refusal to negotiate, 71
destabilization of Cuba, 116
effort to isolate Cuba, 18–23
fear of U.S. intervention, 16, 30, 48, 100, 194, 295–296
hijacking agreement, 197
hostility and distrust, 16, 276–278, 286–289, 307
missile crisis (*see* Missile crisis)
myths and assumptions about Cuba, 4–6, 129–132, 266–267, 279–292
new American policy, 298–311
no-invasion pledge, 110–111, 115, 149, 302
rapprochement, 287–288
(*See also* Rapprochement)
reaction to Cuba's involvement in Africa, 205–206, 210–219
revival of negotiation process, 294–298
Soviet Union and, 17–18
sugar import quotas, 17–18
trade embargo, 24, 115–117, 297
travel and currency restrictions, 297–298
(*See also* Cuban-American relations)
U.S. News and World Report, 205
Urban uprisings, 11, 26

Uruguay, 4, 20, 152, 155
military coups, 15, 125–126

Valenta, Jiri, 215
Venezuela, 23–27
break with Cuba, 18, 20, 24–25
Castro's visit to, 13, 22–25
communists, 30
Cuban arms shipped to, 3, 26, 51–52
FALN, 54, 62, 200
guerrilla movements, 29, 42
National Liberation Front, 32
resources, 25–26
Soviet relations, 155
U.S. aid, 25–26
Venezuelan Communist Party (PCV), 30, 44, 54, 151, 200
Castro's split with, 31, 42–44, 49–57
FALN, 54, 62, 200
Verde Olivo magazine, 93, 226
Vietnam Heróico—Heroic Vietnam, 48, 207, 217
"Vietnam Syndrome," 3, 267, 272, 299–300, 303
Vietnam War, 30–32, 149, 167, 197
Cuba and, 47–49
Soviet policy, 44–49

Wall Street Journal, 87, 92–93, 274–276
Walters, Gen. Vernon A., 269, 294
Warsaw Pact, 148, 165, 183
Cuban membership, 189–190
Czech invasion, 169–172
Washington Post, 118, 274–276
Wheelock, Jaime, 248–249
White Paper on El Salvador, 267–276
Williams, William Appleman, 78–79

Yemen, 203
Young, Andrew, 224
Yugoslavia, 17, 168, 234–235

Zaire, 64, 256–257
Angolan war, 214
Zaldivar, Lieutenant, 81
Zambia, Angolan involvement, 211
Zedong, Mao, 121–122
Zimbabwe, 202, 309

DATE DUE

DATE DUE			
MAR 5 '85			
MAR 18 '86			
JAN 20 '87			
MAR 25 '87			
GAYLORD			PRINTED IN U.S.A.